Slavery and the University

HISTORIES AND LEGACIES

EDITED BY
Leslie M. Harris,
James T. Campbell &
Alfred L. Brophy

The University of Georgia Press
Athens

*Published with generous support from Emory University
and the University of North Carolina–Chapel Hill*

© 2019 by the University of Georgia Press
Athens, Georgia 30602
www.ugapress.org
All rights reserved
Designed by Melissa Bugbee Buchanan
Set in 11/14 Garamond Premier Pro

Most University of Georgia Press titles are
available from popular e-book vendors.

Printed digitally

Library of Congress Control Number: 2018957953
ISBN: 9780820354439 (hardcover: alk. paper)
ISBN: 9780820354422 (paperback: alk. paper)
ISBN: 9780820354446 (ebook)

CONTENTS

Acknowledgments vii

Introduction 1
   James T. Campbell, Leslie M. Harris & Alfred L. Brophy

PART I. PROSLAVERY AND ANTISLAVERY
THOUGHT AND ACTION

Chapter 1. "Sons from the Southward & Some from the West Indies":
The Academy and Slavery in Revolutionary America 21
   Craig Steven Wilder

Chapter 2. Princeton and Slavery: Holding the Center 46
   Craig B. Hollander & Martha A. Sandweiss

Chapter 3. Proslavery Political Theory in the Southern
Academy, 1832–1861 65
   Alfred L. Brophy

Chapter 4. Negotiating the Honor Culture: Students and Slaves
at Three Virginia Colleges 84
   Jennifer Bridges Oast

Chapter 5. Making Their Case: Religion, Pedagogy, and the Slavery
Question at Antebellum Emory College 99
   Patrick C. Jamieson

Chapter 6. "I Whipped Him a Second Time, Very Severely": Basil Manly,
Honor, and Slavery at the University of Alabama 114
   A. James Fuller

Chapter 7. "Two Youths (Slaves) of Great Promise": The Education of David
and Washington McDonogh at Lafayette College, 1838–1844 131
   Diane Windham Shaw

Chapter 8. "I Am a Man": Martin Henry Freeman (Middlebury College, 1849) and the Problems of Race, Manhood, and Colonization   148
   William B. Hart

Chapter 9. Towers of Intellect: The Struggle for African American Higher Education in Antebellum New England   179
   Kabria Baumgartner

Chapter 10. "I Have At Last Found My 'Sphere'": The Unintentional Development of a Female Abolitionist Stronghold at Oberlin College   197
   J. Brent Morris

PART 2. REMEMBERING AND FORGETTING SLAVERY AT UNIVERSITIES

Chapter 11. Slavery and Justice at Brown: A Personal Reflection   215
   Ruth J. Simmons

Chapter 12. Harvard and Slavery: A Short History   224
   Sven Beckert, Balraj Gill, Jim Henle & Katherine May Stevens

Chapter 13. Scholars, Lawyers, and Their Slaves: St. George and Nathaniel Beverley Tucker in the College Town of Williamsburg   251
   Ywone D. Edwards-Ingram

Chapter 14. The "Family Business": Slavery, Double Consciousness, and Objects of Memory at Emory University   277
   Mark Auslander

Chapter 15. Engaging the Racial Landscape at the University of Alabama   298
   Ellen Griffith Spears & James C. Hall

Chapter 16. Forgetting Slavery at Yale and Transylvania   315
   R. Owen Williams

Afterword   338
   Evelyn Brooks Higginbotham

Contributors   343

Index   347

ACKNOWLEDGMENTS

It has been a distinct privilege to work on this project. The essays herein represent only the beginning of a project that promises to help us all live more fully into the potential of higher education to change lives and communities. We are grateful for all who have participated in the work of creating a more honest history of slavery and higher education in the United States and beyond over the last few decades.

The 2011 "Slavery and the University" conference from which most of these essays are drawn brought together for the first time many people who had been laboring alone within their institutions as researchers, teachers, and administrators. The three days over which we were able to share our joys, triumphs, and disappointments in doing this work were critical to the histories told in this volume. For helping to bring that conference to fruition, we'd like to thank Emory University, especially former president James Wagner and former provost Earl Lewis; Brown University, especially the Brown University Steering Committee on Slavery and Justice and former president Ruth Simmons; and the Ford Foundation, especially the late Alison Bernstein, who as program officer of the Education, Creativity, and Free Expression Program provided critical financial and intellectual support through the Difficult Dialogues Initiative.

The staff of the Transforming Community Project of Emory University attended to details large and small in the creation of the conference and in particular provided Leslie Harris with the support necessary to launch the first stage of this volume. We thank JoNell Usher, codirector; Melissa Sexton and Andrew Urban, TCP postdoctoral research fellows; Jyotsna Vanapalli, associate program administrator; and Arlene Robie, administrative assistant, for their commitment to this work. Our program committee, including the editors of this volume, the staff of the Transforming Community Project, and Susan Ashmore and Mark Auslander, were critical in setting a strong intellectual path for the conference. We thank all conference participants and audience members for their respectful and constructive work throughout the weekend.

As we came to the final months of the volume, Alex Trapps-Chabala and

Sarah McCabe provided critical research support on the introduction. We are most grateful that Utz McKnight stepped in to assist Al Brophy in completing the final edits on his essay as Al recovered from a traumatic illness.

At the University of Georgia Press, Lisa Bayer, Walter Biggins, Melissa Bugbee Buchanan, Mary M. Hill, and Christina Cotter patiently and persistently nudged us to conclusion. We thank all of our essayists for their patience in a process that took much longer than we originally imagined.

Finally, we dedicate this volume to all who helped to create, willingly and unwillingly, a higher education system unmatched in its variety and in its openness to not only the U.S. but the global population. Even as we discuss and debate its merits and faults in the past and present, colleges and universities in the twenty-first century continue to press forward in providing pathways to greater equity for individuals and communities. May acknowledging the full truth of our complex past strengthen us further for the tasks ahead.

Slavery and the University

INTRODUCTION

James T. Campbell, Leslie M. Harris & Alfred L. Brophy

For more than a century now, students walking across McCorkle Place, the main quadrangle at the University of North Carolina, have passed in the shadow of Silent Sam, standing sentinel atop a tall granite pedestal. The statue, erected in 1913 with funding from the United Daughters of the Confederacy, honors soldiers who fought for southern independence, a group that included some 40 percent of UNC's 1860 student body. As several historians have shown, Silent Sam and the countless other "common soldier" monuments erected on campuses and courthouse lawns in the first decades of the twentieth century marked the climax of a long struggle over how the American Civil War would be remembered and represented, a struggle waged not on the battlefield but in school pageants and political campaigns, history textbooks and Hollywood films. In the version that prevailed—the version that still prevails in some quarters today—disunion became a defense of constitutional principle and southern independence a romantic "Lost Cause," while the war itself became a kind of unifying trial, the crucible of a truly united United States. Slavery, if it featured at all in such accounts, appeared only as an incident, an unfortunate but essentially benign institution for governing relations between two differently endowed races; while the years of Reconstruction, during which African Americans briefly exercised civil and political rights, became "the Tragic Era," a baleful age of corruption and racial fanaticism mercifully cut short by southern "Redemption."[1]

Sam recently acquired new company on the quad. In 2005 the University of North Carolina unveiled the Unsung Founders Memorial in honor of the "people of color, bound and free, who helped build the Carolina that we cherish today." Funded by a gift from the graduating class of 2002, the new memorial features a polished black granite tabletop upheld by the outstretched arms of hundreds of bronze figurines. "What we do today will not rectify what our ancestors did in the past," declared James Moeser, UNC chancellor, in his speech at the dedication ceremony, "but this memorial, I believe, attests to our commitment to shed light on the darker corners of our history." In keeping with that sentiment, the university library used the occasion to unveil a major exhibition, *Slavery and the Making of the University*, sharing documents and photographs from its collections to illuminate the university's relationship to slavery.[2]

Though just a stone's throw from one another, the two memorials conjure radically different pasts, a fact vividly expressed at their respective dedications. The tone of contrition and sober self-reflection at the 2005 ceremony was conspicuously absent at Sam's dedication in 1913. The keynote speech on that occasion, delivered by Julian Shakespeare Carr, a local tobacco magnate, Confederate veteran, and UNC alumnus, was a paean to the Lost Cause—to the honor and devotion of southern soldiers and the "grand principle of local self government and State sovereignty" for which they fought. Carr paid particular homage to UNC's student legions, whose "courage and steadfastness," first in the war and later in the violent struggle against Reconstruction, had "saved the very life of the Anglo-Saxon race in the South." He illustrated the point with a personal anecdote, recounting how, on his return to campus after Appomattox, he had "horse-whipped a negro wench until her skirts hung in shreds" after she "publicly insulted and maligned a southern lady."[3]

The change in official memory at the University of North Carolina offers just one example of a process playing out in recent years at American universities, a growing number of which have chosen (or in a few cases been compelled) to confront their historical ties to slavery. In early 2002 a group of graduate students at Yale, responding to a recent university history portraying Yale as a citadel of abolitionism, published an independent report exposing some of the seamier aspects of the institution's racial history. Later that same year, Ruth Simmons, president of Brown University and the first African American to head an Ivy League institution, appointed an official university committee to investigate and publicly disclose Brown's historical entanglement with slavery and the transatlantic slave trade. In 2004 faculty members at the University of Alabama adopted a formal resolution of apology for their forebears' role in perpetuating and promoting slavery; the apology was accompanied by a commitment to raise markers on the previously unmarked graves of slaves buried on the campus. In 2005 Emory University launched the Transforming Community Project, a five-year "process of discovery and dialogue about Emory's racial history." The Emory initiative was doubly significant, since it was a dispute over the ownership of an enslaved woman by the president of the university's board of trustees that cleaved the Methodist

Church into northern and southern wings, a watershed moment in the nation's descent into disunion and war.[4]

Other institutions have followed suit. In 2009 William and Mary, the nation's second-oldest college, launched The Lemon Project: A Journey of Reconciliation, named for an enslaved man once owned by the school. Among the outcomes of the project was a formal institutional apology, issued by the university's board of visitors in 2018. The University of Virginia appointed the President's Commission on Slavery and the University in 2013 and a second commission, the University in the Age of Segregation, in 2018. In 2017 Princeton University hosted an international conference to share the fruits of its five-year Princeton and Slavery Project, a conference that included a keynote address by Nobel laureate Toni Morrison. While stopping short of official inquiries, several other prominent universities, including Harvard, Columbia, Georgetown, and the University of Maryland, have sponsored exhibitions, seminars, conferences, and research projects illuminating their ties to slavery.[5]

The recent raft of campus investigations and disclosures has attracted considerable public interest. It has also spawned fresh historical research. Scholars, some working under the auspices of university committees and others independently, have documented the ways in which campuses became seedbeds for racial thought. They have traced the shifting attitudes of students and faculty toward slavery and assessed the contribution of slave-generated wealth in establishing and endowing some of the nation's most revered institutions. Sources long gathering dust in university archives—commencement addresses, records of student debating societies, old textbooks, and curricula—have been unearthed and examined.[6] Inevitably, excavations of the racial past have invited reflection about the racial present—about the current state of campus race relations, as well as the responsibilities of elite universities to the communities of color around them, communities that in many cases continue to serve as reservoirs of manual labor, just as they did in the era of slavery. Several universities, following the lead of the University of North Carolina, have erected memorials and historical markers to recognize their previously unacknowledged debts to the enslaved. Others have engaged the question in reverse, debating whether to remove existing monuments or to rename buildings named in honor of slaveholders and secessionists.

Though seemingly local and specific, the debates have spilled beyond the campus gates, provoking broad public interest and, in some cases, igniting fierce controversy. Historians have long been aware that Georgetown University staved off financial ruin in the 1830s by selling 272 enslaved men, women, and children to sugar plantations in southern Louisiana, but when an alumnus and amateur genealogist managed to track down some of their descendants, still living in Louisiana, the sale became front-page national news. The episode touched off a roiling debate not only about appropriate forms of commemoration but also about whether and how the university should compensate the descendants, a debate that continues to this day.[7] In Charlottesville, Virginia, the removal of a statue of Robert E. Lee in 2017 prompted an incursion onto the campus of the University of Virginia by the Ku Klux Klan and other white supremacist and neo-Nazi groups. The ensuing melee left one woman dead.

What are we to make of all this? What have recent revelations about universities and slavery taught us about our nation's history and about the history of American higher education in particular? Equally important, what do they tell us about our own time? Why has the relationship between slavery and universities—a relationship hiding in plain sight for the better part of two centuries—become such a pressing concern today? Why are some seemingly so threatened by such investigations? What do these forays into difficult pasts actually accomplish? Do they portend a new, more inclusive era in our nation, or are they (as some critics have alleged) just the latest manifestation of "political correctness" on American campuses—"contrition chic," as some have called it? The essays in this book, which examine some of the recent university explorations of slavery and its legacies, suggest a few answers to these questions.[8]

Americans learning today of the relationship between universities and slavery respond in different ways, but the most common response is simply surprise. This response bespeaks many things, not least the nation's continuing failure to come to grips with slavery's scope, scale, and historical significance. But it also reflects a kind of cognitive dissonance, the difficulty many of us have reconciling slavery, an institution now universally reviled as unnatural and abhorrent, with the ideals and values that we associate with universities—with progress, enlightenment, the unfettered pursuit of knowledge. Just as generations of Americans have struggled to comprehend the presence of slavery in a nation formally dedicated to freedom and human equality, so are we perplexed to discover evidence of slavery on college campuses.

Yet why should we be surprised? Slavery was not a marginal institution in American history, nor was its presence or political influence confined to a particular period or region. The cornerstone of New World colonization, slavery existed in the Americas for nearly four hundred years, from the late fifteenth century—at least one enslaved African accompanied Columbus on his second voyage to Hispaniola in 1493—to the final abolition of slavery in Brazil in 1888. Because British North America was settled relatively late, slavery's history in what is today the United States is shorter, but the institution still endured for 246 years, from the arrival of John Smith's "twenty Negars" at Jamestown in 1619 to the ratification of the Thirteenth Amendment to the U.S. Constitution in December 1865. Contrary to common belief, slavery existed in all thirteen British North American colonies and, for a time, in all thirteen original states. The population of New York City, for example, was about 20 percent enslaved at the time of the American Revolution, and it would take another half century, until 1827, for New York to abolish the institution outright. Neighboring New Jersey, which adopted a gradual emancipation bill in 1804, never got around to final abolition: the last few slaves there were freed by the Thirteenth Amendment.[9]

By the eve of the Civil War, the nation's enslaved population exceeded four million, making the United States one of the two largest slave societies in human history. (The far-flung Roman Empire at its height included an estimated five million slaves.) The capital embodied by those four million men, women, and children in 1860 exceeded the value of all of the nation's banks, factories, and railroads combined. While centered in the plantation South, slavery's economic and political reach extended to every corner of American society: from the mill towns of Massachusetts, where slave-produced cotton was woven into textiles, to the account books of the nation's burgeoning insurance industry, which did a bustling business in slave insurance; from Wall Street, where enslaved people were routinely accepted as collateral for mortgages and loans, to the Capitol in Washington, D.C., whose soaring rotunda, crested by a bronze statue of Freedom, was raised by enslaved workers. Ten of the first twelve American presidents owned slaves, as did hundreds of U.S. congressmen and senators and at least two-thirds of the justices serving on the Supreme Court before 1865. Today we extoll the heroism of abolitionists, but in their own time they were a small, often beleaguered minority.[10]

In light of all this, why should we be surprised to find slavery's shadow on campus? And yet some of the revelations from recent university investigations remain frankly jarring: that thirty members of the governing board of the College of Rhode Island, what is today Brown University, owned or captained slave ships; that enslaved people were sold at auction on the steps of the Princeton president's house; that the first endowed professorship of law in American history, the Royall Chair at Harvard, was established with wealth wrought from an Antiguan plantation; that the Jesuits who oversaw Georgetown sold 272 human beings in 1838; that students at Maryland's Washington College resolved an 1856 debate—"Is the institution of slavery necessary for the most perfect development of Society?"—in the affirmative by a three-to-one margin; that the president of the University of Alabama personally whipped a man in his office; or that students at the Medical College of Virginia, what is today Virginia Commonwealth University, trained on the cadavers of enslaved men and women, whose bodies were then unceremoniously dumped in a nearby well. One could multiply such examples almost indefinitely. Yet even that would not do full justice to slavery's presence on American campuses, to the routine reality of enslaved men, women, and children constructing the classrooms, cooking the food, tending the grounds, scouring the latrines, and even staffing the brothels of the nation's most venerable institutions.[11]

To be sure, not everyone on American campuses supported slavery. Universities were and are quarrelsome places, home to a diversity of political opinion. The essays that follow offer examples of university presidents and professors resigning their posts rather than compromise their values, of student commencement orators decrying slavery as a moral and political evil, of universities nurturing emergent antislavery thought. Not surprisingly, such sentiments sprouted more readily on northern than southern campuses, but there was no tidy sectional divide. Oberlin College, celebrated as a citadel of abolitionism, was established precisely because of the hostility that its antislavery founders encountered at other northern schools. Harvard graduated many of the abolitionist movement's most outspoken leaders, including Ralph Waldo Emerson, Wendell Phillips, Henry David Thoreau, William Ellery Channing, Theodore Parker, and Charles Sumner, but it also explicitly prohibited faculty members from discussing abolition. At least two faculty members were dismissed in the 1840s for violating the ban.[12]

The picture at southern campuses was also complex. At the level of both formal ideology and shared "common sense," southern universities provided critical support to the slave regime. As the sectional crisis escalated in the

1850s, many also became hotbeds of southern nationalism. To take one notorious example: members of the University of Virginia's Jefferson Literary and Debating Society responded to the brutal caning of Charles Sumner on the floor of the U.S. Senate by sending his assailant, Preston Brooks, a new gold-headed cane. Yet even in these fevered circumstances, some southern students continued to question the morality and efficacy of slavery right up until the Civil War, keeping open a small, narrowing space for debate in a region rushing headlong to secession and war. If there is a single generalization to be drawn from the essays that follow, it is that the relationship between slavery and universities defies easy generalization. One of the primary objects of this book is to tease out these historical particularities, to reconstruct the struggles of students, faculty, and administrators on different campuses to come to terms with an institution that many came to recognize as the central political, intellectual, and moral question of their age.[13]

Before getting down to cases, let us briefly consider one other question. Why now? How did an institution abolished in 1865 become such a compelling concern on college campuses in the early 2000s? Here again, there is no single answer: as the essays in this book show, different institutions came to the slavery question in different, sometimes quite idiosyncratic, ways. Yet it is also possible to identify broad changes in historical context, some international in scope and others distinctively American, that have helped to create a receptive climate for the kind of retrospective confrontations described here.

Probably the first point to make is that American universities are not the only institutions in the world today that find themselves exploring the "darker corners" of their pasts. On the contrary, recent decades have seen a veritable explosion of such historical reckonings, as well as a multiplication of vehicles for pursuing them, including truth commissions, monetary reparations programs, collective apologies, days of remembrance, and the erection (or removal) of public memorials. Given the dizzying variety of ventures, it is difficult to generalize about them, but the sheer number of initiatives suggests a sea change in international political culture, a growing consensus on the importance of confronting and, as much as possible, redressing gross historical injustice.[14]

Where does this consensus come from? Clearly, the answer has something to do with the crumbling of the Cold War order, which propelled more than a score of violent, authoritarian societies awkwardly down the road toward liberal democracy. The first truth commissions, for example, were established to determine the fate of the so-called disappeared, men and women abducted and killed during the decades of military rule in Latin America. But the impulse to confront painful pasts reflects more than circumstance. It also reflects a convergence of important, if little remarked, changes in Western political and intellectual life: the growing influence of nongovernmental organizations (including several dedicated explicitly to promoting historical redress and reconciliation); increased emphasis on victims' rights within both international humanitarian law and the American criminal justice system; the emergence of what philosopher Charles Taylor has called "the politics of recognition," a politics keyed not to individual rights but to the collective rights of groups to have the identities and histories they value acknowledged in the public sphere. Perhaps most important, the commitment to confronting painful pasts reflects the influence of therapeutic culture, particularly of the "trauma" paradigm. Extending an insight only recently embraced in the field of psychology, advocates of historical redress insist that, for societies as for individuals, traumatic experiences must be unearthed and addressed in order for the afflicted to heal and move forward.[15]

The growing popularity of historical redress has attracted sharp criticism, especially in the United States, where such ventures run up against widely held beliefs about progress, self-reliance, and personal (as opposed to collective) responsibility. Perhaps not surprisingly, the loudest criticism has come from commentators on the political Right, for whom the endless rehashing of group grievances offers just one more index of the "fraying of America," of the nation's descent into balkanization and the culture of victimhood. But criticism has also come from the Left. For historian John Torpey, for example, the current vogue for "reparations politics" bespeaks not historical progress but progressive collapse, a paralysis brought about by the failure of socialist and social democratic governments and the rise of neoliberal hegemony. When human beings lose the capacity to imagine better futures, Torpey writes, the past "rushes to fill the vacuum."[16]

Notwithstanding such skepticism, the United States has been the site of important retrospective justice ventures. The most obvious example—and still the most successful historical redress exercise in U.S. history—is the campaign on behalf of Japanese American citizens interned during the Second

World War. So familiar are the facts of the internment today that it is easy to forget how thoroughly memories of the episode were repressed in the decades after the war, including by internees themselves, for whom the experience remained a source of shame and embarrassment. This culture of silence was finally broken in the late 1970s by a grassroots popular movement spearheaded by internees' children and grandchildren. The movement succeeded in pressuring the U.S. Congress to appoint a formal commission of inquiry, which led in turn to the 1988 Civil Liberties Act, a bipartisan bill that was signed by President Ronald Reagan and that extended a formal apology and individual monetary reparations in the amount of $20,000 to each surviving victim of the internment.[17]

Though little noted at the time, the Civil Liberties Act included an amendment introduced by North Carolina senator Jesse Helms "to preclude . . . this legislation from being used as a precedent in the courts or elsewhere to give precedent or standing to any future claims on the part of . . . any other citizen or group claiming to have been dealt an injustice by the American Government at some point in the past." If Helms's goal was to prevent a run on the U.S. Treasury by the historically aggrieved, his efforts succeeded: Japanese American internees remain virtually alone in having received individual monetary reparations from the federal government. But if his goal was to forestall future exercises in historical redress, he succeeded less well. The years since 1988 have seen a proliferation of such ventures, several of which culminated in formal government apologies, including presidential apologies to indigenous Hawaiians and survivors of the Tuskegee syphilis experiment, a U.S. Bureau of Indian Affairs apology to Native Americans for the BIA's role in "ethnic cleansing" and the deliberate destruction of Native cultures, and a U.S. Senate resolution apologizing for that body's decades-long obstruction of federal anti-lynching legislation. While Congress has not authorized additional inquiries along the lines of the internment commission, the model has been used at the state level to examine previously neglected historical crimes, including the Wilmington, North Carolina, race riot of 1898, the Tulsa riot of 1921, and the Rosewood, Florida, massacre of 1923.[18]

All these factors provide important context for understanding the recent wave of university investigations and disclosures. Ultimately, however, the most important factor in forcing slavery onto campus dockets was the emergence in the late 1990s and early 2000s of a vocal slavery reparations movement. No other historical redress claim posed such profound questions about the structure and essential character of American society; none spawned such bitter controversy or racially polarized opinion. College campuses would be one of the terrains on which the reparations controversy played out.

The question of whether or not enslaved African Americans or their descendants are entitled to some compensation for their centuries of unrequited toil has a long history in the United States, from Reconstruction-era claims to "forty acres and a mule" to the 1969 Black Manifesto, which demanded $500 million "as the beginning of the reparations due us as people who have been exploited and degraded, brutalized, killed, and persecuted." After a period of relative quiescence, reparations demands surged anew in the 1990s, inspired by the success of other historical redress claims, particularly of the movement on behalf of Japanese American internees. In early 1989 Congressman John Conyers introduced a bill to create a nonpartisan commission "to examine the institution of slavery, subsequent de jure and de facto racial and economic discrimination against African Americans, and the impact of those forces on living African Americans" and to recommend to Congress appropriate remedies. Conyers designated the bill H.R. 40, symbolically linking it with freedpeople's historical claim to forty acres after the Civil War, but the language of the bill was taken almost verbatim from the legislation establishing a commission of inquiry about Japanese American internment.[19]

While Conyers proposed legislation, others pursued litigation, filing a brace of lawsuits against the federal government in the mid-1990s. When these cases were dismissed on procedural grounds (including the federal government's sovereign immunity from suit), reparations litigators tried a different tack, preparing class-action lawsuits against private corporations alleged to have profited from slavery and related industries—a tactic that had been used with some success in cases involving corporations implicated in Nazi-era forced labor policies. The first such case, directed against Boston Fleet Bank, CSX Railroad, Aetna Insurance, and up to one thousand "Corporate (John) Does" to be named later, was filed in federal court in early 2002. While no university ever became a named party in reparations litigation, universities figured prominently in discussions of the issue, including Yale, Harvard, and Brown, all of which were publicly identified as "probable targets of future lawsuits" by reparations advocates.[20]

The rise of the slavery reparations movement produced fierce reaction, which cleaved along starkly racial lines. Indeed, public opinion polls revealed a wider racial gulf on reparations than on any issue ever surveyed.

While roughly half of African Americans expressed some support for the idea (numbers varied depending on how the question was worded), upward of 95 percent of white respondents expressed opposition, often vehemently. What the movement did not produce was actual reparations. Resubmitted annually, H.R. 40 has yet to secure the votes necessary to move it out of committee and onto the floor of the House. Litigation has fared no better. The various suits filed against corporations were consolidated into a single case in 2004 and heard by the U.S. Court for the Northern District of Illinois, which promptly dismissed them on a variety of procedural grounds, including plaintiffs' failure to establish standing and the expiration of relevant statutes of limitations.[21]

Yet if the reparations movement of the 1990s and early 2000s failed to achieve its stated objective, it did not prove entirely fruitless. In 2002 Chicago became the first of a dozen major American cities to adopt a municipal slavery disclosure ordinance, requiring all firms doing business with the city to investigate their historical records and disclose any ties to slavery. Perhaps more important, the ferment over reparations prompted a cascade of voluntary disclosures by private actors, including not only universities but also churches, corporations, and newspapers, acknowledging and in some cases offering amends for their complicity in slavery. Perhaps the most thoroughgoing self-examination came from the *Hartford Courant*, the nation's oldest continually published newspaper. Exploring the paper's archives for background material about Aetna Insurance, a Hartford company named as a defendant in an early reparations lawsuit, reporters were startled to discover evidence of the *Courant*'s own ties to slavery, including the publishing of runaway notices and advertisements for slave auctions. Editors responded to the discovery with a front-page editorial, "Courant Complicity in an Old Wrong," formally apologizing for the paper's involvement "in the terrible practice of buying and selling human beings." They also produced a special issue, subsequently expanded into a book, detailing their city's and state's previously unacknowledged debts to slavery and the transatlantic slave trade.[22]

It was against this backdrop of rising interest in historical redress and roiling controversy over reparations that universities confronted the slavery question. The range of institutional responses can be gauged by the experiences of Yale and Brown, the campuses where the issue first broke. In 2002 a group of Yale graduate students published "Yale, Slavery, and Abolition," an online report exposing previously unacknowledged aspects of the university's relationship to slavery.²³ Cast as a response to a celebratory official history published by Yale on the occasion of its 2001 tricentennial, the report was also a salvo in a bitter labor dispute between the university and graduate students attempting to form a union, a circumstance that doubtless contributed to the report's distinctly adversarial tone. While attracting some media attention, the Yale report prompted neither sustained campus dialogue nor any substantive response from the school's administration.²⁴

At Brown too the slavery issue came to campus amid controversy, but with very different results. In early 2001 David Horowitz, a conservative columnist, submitted a paid advertisement to several college newspapers, including the *Brown Daily Herald*, deriding the idea of slavery reparations. Entitled "Ten Reasons Why Reparations for Slavery Is a Bad Idea—and Racist Too," the ad offered a litany of arguments, at least some of which appear to have been calculated to provoke a reaction from students: that African Americans had benefited from slavery; that they lacked gratitude to "the nation that gave them freedom"; that they had already received reparations in the form of welfare checks and affirmative action; that whatever racial disparities existed in the United States were a product not of history but of black people's own "failures of individual character." If Horowitz's object was indeed to incite controversy, he got his wish at Brown, where a group of students demanded that the *Daily Herald* retract the ad. When editors refused, the students stationed themselves at the paper's distribution points and made off with an entire day's press run.²⁵

The theft of the newspapers at Brown ignited a media firestorm. Stories appeared in papers like the *New York Times*, the *Washington Post*, and the *Christian Science Monitor* and on news networks like Fox, MSNBC, and even the BBC, typically accompanied by editorial comment condemning Brown for its betrayal of fundamental principles of free speech. The fact that the controversy revolved around the racially charged issue of slavery added fuel to the fire. Not only had Brown already been identified as a "probable target" of a reparations lawsuit; it had also, just weeks before, announced the appointment of a new president, Ruth Simmons, who on her accession that fall would become the first African American to lead an Ivy League institution.

Given the circumstances Simmons faced—the rancorous atmosphere left by the advertisement and the theft of the papers, the threat of future litigation, the special scrutiny she faced not only as a new president but also as a black woman—one might have expected her to give the slavery issue a wide berth.

She chose the opposite course. She dedicated her first speech as president, delivered at that fall's Convocation, to the recent campus controversy, reminding new freshmen that the university was a "quarrelsome enterprise" whose survival depended on preserving the widest possible scope for the expression and exchange of ideas, even ideas that they found erroneous or gratuitously hurtful. "If you come to this place for comfort," she said, pointing to the university gates through which the entering class had just ceremonially processed, "I would urge you to walk to yon iron gate, pass through the portal and never look back."[26]

But Simmons's response went beyond mere rhetoric. Determined to show students the possibility and value of reasoned, academically rigorous dialogue on even the most controversial issues, she appointed the University Steering Committee on Slavery and Justice. Composed of faculty, students, and administrators, the committee was asked not only to investigate and publicly disclose Brown's historical relationship to slavery and the transatlantic slave trade but also to reflect on the meaning and significance of that history in the present. In particular, Simmons charged the committee "to organize events and activities that might help the nation and the Brown community think deeply, seriously and rigorously about the questions" posed by the raging national debate over slavery reparations. Reparations, she acknowledged, was a highly fraught topic "about which men and women of good will may ultimately disagree," but it was also a topic on which Brown, by virtue of its own history, "had a special obligation and a special opportunity" to provide intellectual leadership.[27]

The Brown committee released its final report, with recommendations, in 2006. By that time, several other prominent American universities had launched ventures of their own. Doubtless they were encouraged by the example of Brown, but equally critical was the comprehensive defeat of slavery reparations litigation in federal court in 2004, which alleviated fears that whatever information institutions uncovered would promptly be used against them in court. Today, more than fifteen years after the first ventures were launched, more than forty universities have formally addressed the slavery question, and others seem poised to follow. We may be entering an era in which publicly disclosing historical ties to slavery and the slave trade will not seem outlandish at all but rather a basic institutional responsibility. At such a time as this, it seems worthwhile to survey the field, to consider what we have learned and what it means.

Coda

On August 20, 2018, as this book went to press, protesters at the University of North Carolina toppled Silent Sam from his perch atop the Confederate monument on McCorkle Place, deliberately defying a 2015 state law prohibiting the removal, relocation, or alteration of any historical monument or marker on public land.

What will come of this remains unclear. At this writing, more than a dozen people have been arrested for their role in the toppling or in the protests and counterprotests that followed. Sam remains in university custody, held at an undisclosed location while state officials debate his fate. By the letter of the 2015 law, the statue must be restored to its original location—or to a site of "similar prominence, honor, visibility . . . and access"—within ninety days. Pundits and politicians have weighed in, some decrying the triumph of "mob rule" at UNC, others asking why a monument explicitly dedicated to white supremacy had been allowed to shadow a campus for so long.

If monuments are assertions, statements by one generation to those that follow, the bare pedestal on which Sam once stood has become a question, a symbol of so much that remains unresolved in the history of the American nation, and of American universities in particular. What better introduction to the essays that follow.

NOTES

1. David Blight, *Race and Reunion: The Civil War in American Memory* (Cambridge, Mass.: Belknap Press, 2001); Kirk Savage, *Standing Soldiers, Kneeling Slaves: Race, War, and Monument in Nineteenth-Century America* (Princeton, N.J.: Princeton University Press, 1997). See also Alice Fahs and Joan Waugh, eds., *The Memory of the Civil War in American Culture* (Chapel Hill: University of North Carolina Press, 2004), especially James McPherson, "Long-Legged Yankee Lies: The Southern Textbook Crusade." On neo-Confederate renderings of the Reconstruction era, see Claude G. Bowers, *The Tragic Era: The Revolution after Lincoln* (Cambridge: Houghton Mifflin, 1929).

2. Moeser's speech is quoted in Renee Ater, "The Challenge of Memorializing Slavery in North Carolina: The Unsung Founders Memorial and the North Carolina Freedom Monument Project," in *Politics of Memory: Making Slavery Visible in the Public Space*, ed. Ana Lucia Araujo (New York: Routledge, 2012). A virtual version of the *Slavery and the Making of the University* exhibition can be found at https://exhibits.lib.unc.edu/exhibits/show/slavery.

3. The text of Carr's speech is available at http://hgreen.people.ua.edu/transcription-carr-speech.html.

4. The "Yale, Slavery and Abolition" report is available at http://www.yaleslavery.org/YSA.pdf. For information on Brown, see http://www.brown.edu/Research/Slavery_Justice. On Emory, see http://emoryhistory.emory.edu/issues/discrimination/transforming-community-project.html. The circumstances that led to the apology at Alabama are recounted in Alfred L. Brophy, "The University and Its Slaves: Apology and Its Meaning," in *The Age of Apology: Facing Up to the Past*, ed. Mark Gibney et al. (Philadelphia: University of Pennsylvania Press, 2009).

5. All of the cited initiatives have websites. See https://www.wm.edu/sites/lemonproject; http://slavery.virginia.edu; https://slavery.princeton.edu; https://www.harvard.edu/slavery; https://columbiaandslavery.columbia.edu; http://slavery.georgetown.edu; and http://dcicblog.umd.edu/legacyofslaveryinmaryland/. At several institutions, student researchers played a leading role. See, for example, Sven Beckert, Katherine Stevens, and students of the Harvard and Slavery Research Seminar, "Harvard and Slavery: Seeking a Forgotten History" (Cambridge, Mass., 2011) and Students of History 429, "Knowing Our History: African American Slavery and the University of Maryland" (University of Maryland, College Park, 2009).

6. For introductions to the burgeoning literature on slavery and universities, see Craig Steven Wilder, *Ebony and Ivy: Race, Slavery, and the Troubled History of America's Universities* (New York: Bloomsbury Press, 2013); and Alfred L. Brophy, *University, Court, and Slave: Pro-slavery Thought in Southern Courts and Colleges and the Coming of the Civil War* (New York: Oxford University Press, 2016).

7. Rachel Swarns, "272 Slaves Were Sold to Save Georgetown: What Does It Owe Their Descendants?," *New York Times*, April 16, 2016.

8. See Renee Jeffrey, "When Is an Apology Not an Apology? Contrition Chic and Japan's (Un)apologetic Politics," *Australian Journal of International Affairs* 65, no. 5 (2011): 607–17.

9. For overviews, see David B. Davis, *Inhuman Bondage: The Rise and Fall of Slavery in the New World* (New York: Oxford University Press, 2006); and Ira Berlin, *Many Thousands Gone: The First Two Centuries of Slavery in North America* (Cambridge, Mass.: Harvard University Press, 1998). On slavery in New York, see Ira Berlin and Leslie M. Harris, eds., *Slavery in New York* (New York: New Press, 2005); Harris, *In the Shadow of Slavery: African Americans in New York City, 1626–1863* (Chicago: University of Chicago Press, 2003); and David Gellman, *Emancipating New York: The Politics of Slavery and Freedom, 1777–1827* (Baton Rouge: Louisiana State University Press, 2006).

10. Sven Beckert and Seth Rockman, eds., *Slavery's Capitalism: A New History of American Economic Development* (Philadelphia: University of Pennsylvania Press, 2016). On slave-owning presidents, see http://hauensteincenter.org/slaveholding. On slavery in the Roman Empire, see Walter Scheidel, "The Roman Slave Supply," in *Cambridge World History of Slavery*, ed. Keith Bradley and Paul Cartledge (New York: Cambridge University Press, 2011).

11. On slave traders in the Brown Corporation, see Brenda Allen et al., *Slavery and Justice: Report of the Brown University Steering Committee on Slavery and Justice* (Providence, R.I.: Brown University, 2006), 12. On the auction at Princeton, see https://slavery.princeton.edu/sources/two-women-a-man-and-three-children. For a reflection on the Royall Chair at Harvard, see Janet Halley, "My Isaac Royall Legacy," *Harvard Black-Letter Law Journal* 24, no. 117 (2008): 117–31. The Georgetown case has become a major national news story; see, for example, Swarns, "272 Slaves." On the Washington College debate, see Alfred L. Brophy, "Debating Slavery and Empire in the Washington College Literary Societies," *Washington and Lee Journal of Civil Rights and Social Justice* 22, no. 2 (2016): 273–86. On the Well Project at Virginia Commonwealth, see https://emsw.vcu.edu.

12. The Oberlin and Harvard cases are discussed in the essays that follow.

13. On southern universities and slavery, see Brophy, *University, Court, and Slave*. For the Preston Brooks episode, see "Another Cane for Mr. Brooks," *Richmond Enquirer*, May 30, 1856.

14. Recent decades have produced a burgeoning scholarly literature on problems of historical redress. For a sampling, see Elazar Barkan, *The Guilt of Nations: Restitution and Negotiating Historical Injustices* (New York: Norton, 2000); Martha Minow, *Between Vengeance and Forgiveness: Facing History after Genocide and Mass Violence* (Boston: Beacon Press, 1998); Erin Daly and Jeremy Sarkin, *Reconciliation in Divided Societies: Finding Common Ground* (Philadelphia: University of Pennsylvania Press, 2007); Mark Gibney et al., eds., *The Age of Apology: Facing Up to the Past* (Philadelphia: University of Pennsylvania Press, 2008); Pablo de Greiff, ed., *The Handbook of Reparations* (New York: Oxford University Press, 2006); Priscilla B. Hayner, *Unspeakable Truths: Facing the Challenge of Truth Commissions* (New York: Routledge, 2001); Robert Rotberg and Dennis Thompson, eds., *Truth v. Justice: The Making of Truth Commissions* (Princeton, N.J.: Princeton University Press, 2000); Tristan Anne Borer, ed., *Telling the Truths: Truth Telling and Peace Building in Post-conflict Societies* (Notre Dame: Notre Dame University Press, 2006); Ruth Rubio-Marin, *What Happened to the Women: Gender and Reparations for Human Rights Violations* (New York: Social Sciences Research Council, 2006); and James Young, *The Texture of Memory: Holocaust Memorials and Meaning* (New Haven, Conn.: Yale University Press, 1994).

15. See Charles Taylor et al., *Multiculturalism: Examining the Politics of Recognition* (Princeton, N.J.: Princeton University Press, 1994). On the historical origins of the trauma paradigm, see Judith Herman, *Trauma and Recovery: The Aftermath of Violence—from Domestic Abuse to Political Terror* (New York: Basic Books, 1992).

16. John Torpey, *Making Whole What Has Been Smashed: On Reparations Politics* (Cambridge, Mass.: Harvard University Press, 2006), 24. See also Charles Maier, "A Surfeit of Memory? Reflections on History, Melancholy, and Denial," *History and Memory* 5, no. 2 (1993): 13–51. For critiques from the Right, see Robert Hughes, *The Culture of Complaint: The Fraying of America* (New York: Oxford University Press, 1993); and Da-

vid Horowitz, *Uncivil Wars: The Controversy over Reparations for Slavery* (San Francisco: Encounter Books, 2002).

17. *Personal Justice Denied: Report of the Commission on Wartime Relocation and Internment of Civilians* (Washington, D.C.: Government Printing Office, 1982). On the history of the redress movement, see Peter Irons, *Justice at War: The Story of the Japanese American Internment Cases* (New York, 1983); Leslie T. Hatamiya, *Righting a Wrong: Japanese Americans and the Passage of the Civil Liberties Act of 1988* (Stanford, Calif.: Stanford University Press, 1993); and Alice Yang Murray, *Historical Memories of the Japanese American Internment and the Struggle for Redress* (Stanford, Calif.: Stanford University Press, 2007).

18. Brian Weiner, *Sins of the Parents: The Politics of National Apologies in the United States* (Philadelphia: Temple University Press, 2005), 68, 72, 82, 165–66, 190n13. See also Roy L. Brooks, ed., *When Sorry Isn't Enough: The Controversy over Apologies and Reparations for Human Injustice* (New York: New York University Press, 1999); and Melissa Nobles, *The Politics of Official Apologies* (New York: Cambridge University Press, 2008). On the Bureau of Indian Affairs apology, see Rebecca Tsosie, "The BIA's Apology to Native Americans: An Essay on Collective Memory and Collective Conscience," in *Taking Wrongs Seriously: Apologies and Reconciliation*, ed. Elazar Barkan and Alexander Karn (Stanford, Calif.: Stanford University Press, 2006), 185–212. On state-level truth commissions, see David S. Cecelski and Timothy Tyson, eds., *Democracy Betrayed: The Wilmington Race Riot and Its Legacy* (Chapel Hill: University of North Carolina Press, 1998); Alfred L. Brophy, *Reconstructing the Dreamland: The Tulsa Riot of 1921—Race, Reparations and Reconciliation* (New York: Oxford University Press, 2002); and Brophy, "The Tulsa Race Riot Commission, Apology, and Reparation: Understanding the Functions and Limitations of a Historical Truth Commission," in Barkan and Karn, *Taking Wrongs Seriously*, 234–258. On Rosewood, see Florida Board of Regents, *A Documented History of the Incident Which Occurred at Rosewood, Florida, in January, 1923* (Tallahassee: Florida Board of Regents, 1993).

19. On the early 2000s slavery reparations debate, see Alfred Brophy, *Reparations: Pro and Con* (New York: Oxford University Press, 2006); Raymond A. Winbush, *Should America Pay: Slavery and the Raging Debate on Reparations* (New York: Amistad, 2003); Michael T. Martin and Marilyn Yaquinto, eds., *Redress for Historical Injustices in the United States: On Reparations for Slavery, Jim Crow, and Their Legacies* (Durham, N.C.: Duke University Press, 2007); and Randall Robinson, *The Debt: What America Owes to Blacks* (New York: Dutton, 2000). For earlier episodes, see LaWanda Cox, "The Promise of Land for the Freedmen," *Mississippi Valley Historical Review* 45, no. 2 (1958): 413–40; Mary Frances Berry, *My Face Is Black Is True: Callie House and the Struggle for Ex-slave Reparations* (New York: Knopf, 2005); and Boris I. Bittker, *The Case for Black Reparations* (New York: Random House, 1973). The quotation comes from the "Black Manifesto," adopted by the Black National Economic Conference in 1969; see James Forman et al., *Black Manifesto: Religion, Race, and Reparations* (New York: Sheed and Ward, 1969).

20. In re: African American Slave Descendants Litigation, 2004 U.S. Dist. Lexis 872 (N.D. Ill. 2004). For the suits against the federal government, see Cato v. United States, 70 F.3d 1103 (9th Cir. 1995) and Berry v. United States, 1994 U.S. Dist. Lexis 9665 (N.D. Cal. 1994). On the Nazi forced labor litigation, see Michael J. Bazyler, *Holocaust Justice: The Battle for Restitution in America's Courts* (New York: New York University Press, 2003). On threats of litigation against universities, see Charles Ogletree, "Litigating the Legacy of Slavery," *New York Times*, March 31, 2002.

21. Contemporary polls on popular attitudes toward slavery reparations include Michael C. Dawson and Rovana Popoff, "Reparations: Justice and Greed in Black and White," *Du Bois Review* 1, no. 1 (2004): 47–91; and *U.S.A. Today*, February 22, 2002. For a more recent poll, see https://ropercenter.cornell.edu/12810-2/. On the dismissal of reparations litigation by the federal court, see *In re: African American Slave Descendants Litigation*. The case was reheard in 2005, with the same result; see 375 F.Supp. 2d 721 (N.D. Ill. 2005).

22. Chicago, Illinois, Municipal Code § 2-92-585. One of the first significant disclosures prompted by the new ordinance came from J. P. Morgan Bank, which acknowledged having accepted, through two predecessor banks in Louisiana, some thirteen thousand enslaved African Americans as collateral for loans, some 10 percent of whom became the bank's property when borrowers defaulted. See "J. P. Morgan Discloses Past Links to Slavery," *Washington Post*, January 21, 2005. On the *Hartford Courant*, see Anne Farrow, Joel Lang, and Jenifer Frank, *Complicity: How the North Promoted, Prolonged, and Profited from Slavery* (New York: Ballantine Books, 2005). For the original apology, see the *Courant*, July 4, 2000. For the special issue, see the *Courant*, September 29, 2002.

23. The *New York Times* published an article on the report on August 13, 2001; see http://www.nytimes.com/2001/08/13/nyregion/slave-traders-in-yale-s-past-fuel-debate-on-restitution.html.

24. Antony Dugdale, J. J. Fueser, and J. Celso de Castro Alves, "Yale, Slavery and Abolition» (Amistad Committee, 2001), http://www.yaleslavery.org.

25. David Horowitz, "Ten Reasons Why Reparations for Slavery Is a Bad Idea—and Racist Too," *Brown Daily Herald*, March 13, 2001, https://repository.library.brown.edu/studio/item/bdr:40830/.

26. Simmons's convocation address is at http://www.brown.edu/Administration/News_Bureau/2001-02/01-014t.html.

27. Simmons's charge to the committee is available at http://brown.edu/Research/Slavery_Justice/about/charge.html.

PART ONE

Proslavery and Antislavery Thought and Action

CHAPTER ONE

"Sons from the Southward & Some from the West Indies"

The Academy and Slavery in Revolutionary America

Craig Steven Wilder

> I learn from Messrs [James] Madison & [Caleb] Wallace how much
> I am indebted to you for your favourable Opinions & Friendship[,]
> the Continuance of which I will do [my] best to deserve.
>
> PRESIDENT JOHN WITHERSPOON, PRINCETON,
> TO COLONEL HENRY LEE, VIRGINIA, 1770

"Give us a *merchant acquainted with trade!*" workingmen in Bristol, England, shouted in support of Henry Cruger Jr. during a special election to fill a vacant seat in Parliament. Five years into a costly war between Britain and its North American colonies, many Bristol citizens were tying their political and economic futures to a colonial slave trader. Slavers and planters had become symbols of prosperity in Britain and America. Henry Cruger Jr. lost that 1781 election but won the Bristol mayoralty later that year. He reclaimed a seat in the House of Commons shortly after the war when the kingdom's economy was even more flaccid. The Cruger commercial network extended throughout the Atlantic world: from New York to Britain, Jamaica, Saint Croix, Curaçao, and the West African coast. Cruger ships brought enslaved Africans to the Caribbean and the North American mainland, supplied the West Indian and southern plantations, carried the products of enslaved labor to Europe, and transported European goods to the colonies. Cruger had studied in New York City at King's College, where his father and uncle were founding trustees. In 1739 his grandfather became mayor of New York, and his uncle claimed the mayoralty in 1757. Slave traders, planters, and land barons underwrote the institutional development of the colonies. The elite established schools, libraries, churches, and hospitals and combined to govern these new institutions.

Colonial academies were born in the slave economy, and that same economy funded the expansion of the educational infrastructure in the early years of the United States.[1]

Although established, sponsored, and, to differing degrees, governed by Christian denominations—Congregational, Anglican, Presbyterian, Baptist, Dutch Reformed, German Reformed, Methodist, Catholic, and Lutheran—early colleges and academies were poorly supported. The governors of Harvard (founded 1636) exploited the dense commercial networks that linked New England, the South, and the British Caribbean. Boston was second only to London as a destination for Barbadians. New England ships circled in and out of the West Indies, where successive Harvard administrations campaigned for donations and solicited students. While in port at Bridgetown, Barbados, in 1709, the Harvard graduate Thomas Prince logged the continual arrival of ships from the northern colonies, particularly Newport, Boston, New York, and Philadelphia.[2]

Colonial North America was a hostile environment for schools. In 1718 the trustees of the Collegiate School (founded 1701) in New Haven, Connecticut, received a donation from the Welsh merchant Elihu Yale: four hundred books, some cash, and a painting of George I. The board recognized the gift by renaming the college for Yale. In 1722 the governors built a house for the rector—the more ministerial term used before the trustees established a presidency—by taking subscriptions, selling lands, and getting the General Assembly of Connecticut to tax rum imported from the West Indies. A year later, the Yale board bestowed a medical degree upon Daniel Turner, a respectable guild-licensed surgeon in London who lacked the academic credentials to join the Royal College of Physicians. It was the first medical degree ever granted in North America. Turner sent twenty-five books and a brief letter outlining his qualifications to New Haven, and at the September commencement the trustees awarded him in absentia an honorary doctorate in medicine. Yale had no medical school and no science faculty. The Royal College declined to recognize Turner's colonial credentials.[3]

The actions of Yale's trustees were not unusual. From the establishment of Jamestown through the Civil War, Americans began several hundred academies, but 80 percent of them failed. "Small and unknown as we are in respects of the great and famous universities w[hi]ch adorn the Kingdomes of Great Britain," the trustees of Harvard wrote to the embattled King George I before describing their institution as "yo[u]r Maj[es]ty[']s Loyal and Humble College in America." Governors had little choice but to forge or affirm such ties. For most of its first hundred years, Harvard did not have a single professor but instead relied upon tutors for instruction. The presidents of colonial colleges lived like itinerants, spending much of the year journeying from town to town and province to province, by horseback and in rough coaches, hats in hands. They delivered sermons and academic addresses in churches and local associations, frequently publishing these lectures to raise a bit more money for their schools.[4]

Historian Frederick Rudolph neatly captured the hand-to-mouth realities of the early academy: "Often when a college had a building, it had no students. If it had students, frequently it had no building. If it had either, then perhaps it had no money, perhaps no professors; if professors, then no president[;] if a president, then no professors." In 1724 the Reverend Hugh Jones complained that William and Mary (founded 1691) had a seminary without a chapel, a college without scholarships, a library without books, all under a "President without a fix'd Salary till of late." Seeking to solve his financial woes, President James Blair unsuccessfully promoted Virginia as a site for servicing and building ships for slave traders in Bristol, England.[5]

Higher education in the colonies ascended as the Atlantic slave trade peaked. In the decades before the Revolution, slaving families like the Crugers transformed British North America. In the quarter century between 1745 and 1769, ministers, merchants, and land speculators organized seven new colleges in the British colonies: Codrington College in Barbados in 1745; the College of New Jersey, now known as Princeton, in 1746; King's College (Columbia) in 1754; the College of Philadelphia (University of Pennsylvania) in 1755; the College of Rhode Island (Brown) in 1764; Queen's College (Rutgers) in 1766; and Dartmouth College in 1769. More schools also meant greater competition for money, including money linked, directly and indirectly, to the slave economy.

A coincidence of religious and economic developments excited this academic revolution. The First Great Awakening, the spiritual revival in the first half of the eighteenth century, brought attempts to institutionalize new theologies and religious practices. The wave of college building responded to these denominational rivalries: Presbyterians in New Jersey and Pennsylvania; Anglicans in Barbados, New York, and Pennsylvania; Baptists in Rhode Island; Reformed Dutch in New Jersey and New York; and Congregationalists in New Hampshire.[6] Families like the Crugers of New York, the Livingstons in New Jersey and New York, the Allens of Philadelphia, the Browns in Rhode Island, and the Lees of Virginia became the new patrons of colonial education. This generosity facilitated their political rise and allowed them simultaneously to meet the expectations of their faiths and their economic positions.

Colonists also established preparatory schools, formal and informal, to feed the new colleges. College-bound boys frequently studied privately with ministers and tutors. Elisha Williams, a 1711 Harvard graduate who "attained the dignity of land and slaves" through his marriage to Eunice Chester, writes his biographer, kept a school at Wethersfield, Connecticut. In September 1725 Williams became the rector of Yale, where he and a single tutor constituted the faculty. In 1743 the Reverend Francis Alison began New-Ark Academy (now the University of Delaware) in his home to counter New Light theology in the Mid-Atlantic. The evangelicals countered with "log colleges," ephemeral frontier schools, to train young men for the college in Princeton. The Jesuits (the Society of Jesus) had a preparatory school at their secluded slave plantation at Bohemia Manor, Maryland, where they educated Catholic boys away from the hostile gaze of the Protestant majority. Wealthier Catholic families then sent their sons to finish their educations in Europe. The cousins Charles Carroll of Carrollton, an affluent slaveholder and a signer of the Declaration of Independence, and John Carroll, a slave owner and the first Catholic bishop in the United States, had both studied at Bohemia. In 1774, on the eve of the American Revolution, the Reverend Alexander MacWhorter—who trained at New-Ark Academy in Delaware, graduated from the College of New Jersey, and received a doctorate from Yale—helped found Newark Academy.[7]

In the upper Mid-Atlantic and New England, families whose incomes came from the slave trade and from provisioning the southern and Caribbean plantations financed the new schools, while in the lower Mid-Atlantic, the South, and the British West Indies, plantation families largely sponsored education. However, the integration of these slave economies increased intercolonial social contacts and philanthropy.

The officers and trustees of northern schools knew that wealthy clients sat at the other end of the trade routes that brought fish, meat, produce, horses, wood, candles, rope, cloth, and human beings to the southern and Caribbean plantations. "Whereas the Drafts of several Letters have been prepared to be Transmitted to the several West India Islands by a committee," began the minutes of the October 1759 meeting of the trustees of King's College, where the board, which largely comprised merchants, launched its first Caribbean fund-raising campaign before the college had a building. Hezekiah Smith, a College of Rhode Island trustee, headed south to solicit money from the Baptist communions in the plantations, particularly South Carolina. Shortly after the Scottish minister John Witherspoon took the helm of the floundering College of New Jersey, he went to New York and New England to meet the most prominent families and then left for a tour of the South. Upon his return, Reverend Witherspoon used his new connections to bring Colonel Henry Lee's son, Harry Jr., from Virginia to Princeton. In 1770 the Reverend James Caldwell raised £700 in South Carolina for the Princeton college. Two years later, President Witherspoon authored a communiqué to the British West Indies, welcoming donations and cataloging the benefits of educating sons in New Jersey. That same year, Dr. Hugh Williamson traveled to the West Indies on behalf of New-Ark Academy.[8]

The wealth of traders, planters, and landowners raised the prospects of American academies and colleges. New York's merchants designed a grand campus for King's College to display their status and their city's growing prestige. Their vision for the college differed significantly from that of the founding president, Samuel Johnson, who called his board a gang of dullards who elevated the aesthetic over the academic. "Our Building (now finished) has cost so much, that I see not how we shall have stock enough to provide sufficient salaries," Reverend Johnson complained to the archbishop of Canterbury only four years after the college received its charter. Faced with escalating costs, President Johnson protested that he had done "all that I can do to save it" and begged Providence to protect his college from its trustees.[9]

The wealth generated in Atlantic slavery swelled the confidence of many boards and officers. When it opened, Nassau Hall, the nucleus of the College of New Jersey in Princeton, was the largest building in British America, a monument to its merchant benefactors. It stood three stories, could house nearly 150 students, and included a library, chapel, dining halls, and meeting rooms. The Reverend Eleazar Wheelock planned Dartmouth Hall as the focal point of his campus, located on a small hill and topped by cupola and weathervane to balance the surrounding terrain. Sometimes college governors referenced British tradition for campus designs, but they as frequently seized the opportunity to make statements about the economic and social importance of the colonies. The trustees of the College of Philadelphia drew upon an emerging vernacular architecture. They even cut a new path with the most significant early decision that trustees could make—how to house their school—by choosing to purchase and renovate a preexisting building.[10]

The economic networks of the Atlantic also brought flows of students and money that routinely crossed denominational and national boundaries. In 1764 an eighteen-year-old William Churchill Houston set out from his father's South Carolina slave plantation on horseback to enroll at the College of New Jersey. Recent alumni were tutoring and running preparatory academies throughout the Carolinas and sending a stream of southern boys like Houston—who carried a pocket full of cash and letters of recommendation—to Princeton. Thomas Martin, a graduate of New Jersey, tutored the white children at the Madison family's Montpelier plantation in Virginia. In the summer of 1769 the young James Madison, the future president of the United States, arrived in Princeton on horseback and attended by his slave, Sawney. Sawney returned to Montpelier once Madison was settled on campus.

In 1771 Nicholas Cruger and a small group of traders and planters in Saint Croix sent the sixteen-year-old orphan Alexander Hamilton to study at Elizabethtown Academy—one of a few early colonial preparatory schools to survive into the revolutionary era—under Francis Barber, a recent graduate of the College of New Jersey. In May 1773 John "Jacky" Custis moved into a suite in King's College with his slave, Joe. General George Washington had escorted his stepson to New York City, and King's president, Myles Cooper, and the faculty bent over backward to cater to the demands of the wealthy young Virginian, earn the general's favor, and make new connections to the southern planter class.[11]

School officers traded indulgences to solve real problems. Despite the enthusiasm of the trustees, eighteenth-century campuses remained rude, libraries were mean, and study areas lacked basic teaching materials. Most early colleges had a single main building that housed study halls, libraries, kitchens, residences for students and sometimes faculty, and chapels. Challenged by the proliferation of schools and the aggressive recruiting of the northern colleges, William and Mary had trouble attracting Virginia students, and the governors relied upon donations from local planters as well as British friends to stay solvent. (The latter source of funds quickly dried up as the American Revolution approached.) "The college makes a very agreeable appearance," Josiah Quincy Jr. wrote upon entering Williamsburg on the eve of the American Revolution, but once he got past the lovely gardens and into the buildings, he was troubled to discover that William and Mary "is in a very declining state."[12]

The American Revolution brought greater stress. While the British electorate suffered the economic dislocations caused by the North American revolt, people in the colonies endured shortages of goods, military occupations, confiscations of property, an unraveling economy, and armed warfare. The U.S. government also sought alliances that brought foreign Catholic soldiers onto American soil, no small concession for a historically anti-Catholic people. In 1778 France recognized the United States, and American ambassadors and their French allies were soon pressuring King Louis XVI to send troops. Spain secretly supplied the rebellion through the Mississippi corridor and in 1779 declared war on England. "We have lived to see perilous times in our once happy & peaceful Country;—Times which, more or less, affect us all in a very uncommon Manner," lamented James Manning, the first president of the College of Rhode Island and a graduate of New Jersey. Manning spent much of the war worrying about the future of his college and recording the destruction of its facilities. The British navy and army disrupted the economies of the ports and plantations: "This Town has been a Garrison ever since the Troops came to Newport; and the College, which is converted into Barracks, and the adjoining Land, have severely felt the Effects" of the war.[13]

The benefits of campuses were apparent to commanders on all sides of the conflict. "It is not possible to have our troops winter in North America," a French intelligence report cautioned. "There is not a military barrack on the continent or an edifice where the troops could be placed and kept under military discipline." Complete with furnished living quarters, servants' facilities, additional rooms and offices, large kitchens, supplies of water, and, often, farms, colleges were of obvious value to generals looking to quarter troops and organize military operations. Colleges' strategic locations in port cities and along accessible roads in the interior made them even more attractive. Weeks before Christmas 1776, American forces seized the College of Rhode Island and remained for more than three years. When they finally departed in April 1780, allied French soldiers took the campus and converted it into a military hospital and barrack.[14]

Several colleges ceased operations during the war; others survived by moving away from the coast. "By the present War into which the American Colonies have been driven to save themselves from Oppression & Despotism," Harvard's governors defiantly declared, "the College has been several Months in an interrupted & dispersed State." The faculty and students migrated inland to Concord, where local officials swiftly ordered renovations to the meetinghouse, the grammar school, and the courthouse to accommodate classes. About a hundred professors and students arrived in the first weeks. "By the good Providence of God, the Society is at length collected in the Town of Concord, & restored to order," the faculty celebrated at their October 1775 meeting.[15]

Enslaved people helped usher Concord and Harvard through the crisis. Slavery was ordinary in Concord, where the townspeople maintained a lively commerce in human beings. In the preceding years, Sarah Melvin had given Captain William Wilson thirty pounds for a two-year-old girl named Nancy. Peter Hubbard had bought Cato, a six-year-old boy, from Henry Spring for thirty-seven pounds and some change. Both children were sold without any reference to their parents. Dr. Joseph Lee, a slave owner whose son Samuel was in the senior class, boarded Harvard students. An undergraduate during the Revolution, the Reverend William Bentley even returned after the war to visit his former landlord, Samuel Potter, and Potter's slave, Boston.[16]

In late December 1776 President Naphtali Daggett and the fellows of Yale dismissed the students for winter break and began searching for alternative sites for the college. The governors begged New Haven officials to protect their buildings from troops and vandals, authorized the president and treasurer to move the library and any valuable papers and equipment "some distance from the sea," and began praying for the moment when "God in his kind Providence shall open a door for their return to this fixed and ancient seat of learning." The college relocated north to Hartford County, which was a distance from the coast and had the second largest enslaved population in Connecticut. The following spring, sophomores and juniors were studying in Glastonbury, just east of the town of Hartford, where the governors were also hiding the college bell, while freshmen had gathered in Farmington, to the west. Meanwhile, President Daggett was searching for a place to reconvene the senior class. Given the growing dangers brought by war, the Reverend Ezra Stiles of Newport, Rhode Island, asked Yale's officers to send his son home. The officers read that letter at the same meeting in which they voted to offer Reverend Stiles the presidency.[17]

Few officers were in as untenable a position as Eleazar Wheelock, who found himself on the opposite side of a war from his primary benefactors, Governor John Wentworth and William Legge, Earl of Dartmouth. At Whitehall, Lord Dartmouth was maneuvering to contain the colonial uprising. He instructed the British generals to treat with the northern Native nations to create a cordon of Canadian and Native American soldiers to harass New England. Wheelock embraced the colonial cause. He promoted his college as an instrument for solidifying alliances between Indian nations and the colonists, gathering intelligence, and planting missionaries to hold the Indians neutral or bind them to the rebellion. Samuel Kirkland, Wheelock's most prominent white student, was acting as General George Washington's ambassador to the powerful Iroquois Confederacy, serving as a chaplain to the troops, and spying on friendly and hostile Native nations. Dartmouth's location protected it from direct invasions, and Wheelock was thus spared the problems of damage to his campus or loss of his slaves. The president still aggressively sought arms and ammunition from the Continental Congress and the regional government "for defence against the savages." He also encouraged New Hampshire men to enlist with the New England forces and authorized numerous reconnaissance missions.[18]

Matters were worse in the Mid-Atlantic. King's new president, Myles Cooper, an Anglican and a royalist, had fled to England, and the trustees put the Reverend Benjamin Moore, only seven years after his graduation, in charge of the historically Tory college. Continental troops seized the campus in May 1776. The British invasion and occupation of New York, which began in the late summer of 1776, did nothing to improve the prospects of the Anglican college. Black militias, allied with the English, were waging their own revolution, attacking and raiding colonial strongholds throughout New York and New Jersey, and black people were pouring into the city under the British proclamation of freedom for the enslaved. Several of King's trustees were cowering, the students were scattered, and the campus was inaccessible. The governors moved operations to a Wall Street house owned by the merchant and trustee Leonard Lispenard but had difficulty gathering a quorum. In May 1777 the remaining trustees described their predicament: "Many of the Gov[erno]rs. being in England," General Oliver DeLancey and Colonel John Cruger were in the field leading regiments loyal to George III, and several Tories were "in the power of the Rebels and not able to Come to Town." Three years into the war, the board was meeting in a Manhattan tavern, and they had lost another prominent trustee: Governor William Tyron, who had been commissioned a major general in the British army and was busy sacking New Haven. (The college effectively stopped operations until the state reorganized it in 1784 under a new patriotic name: Columbia.)[19]

Philadelphia and Princeton were also in chaos. "New Jersey College, long the peaceful seat of science and haunt of the Muses, was visited with the melancholy tidings of the approach of the enemy," an undergraduate wrote. "Our worthy President [Witherspoon] deeply affected at this solemn scene, entered the hall where the students were collected, and ... very affectionately bade us farewell." Numerous students were stranded, with no way to get home. This undergraduate retreated from campus to join the American forces. British troops captured the college as they hunted General Washington. They destroyed and burned buildings, pillaged livestock and supplies, and terrorized the public. Soldiers occupied and wrecked Witherspoon's estate, Tusculum. The trustee Richard Stockton left his homestead, Morven, in the hands of his slaves. It was destroyed. Farther south, President William Smith, an Anglican, fled the shuttered College of Philadelphia, in part because of his royalist politics. He headed to Maryland, where, with the support of prominent planters, he later founded Washington College (1784) in honor of the victorious general.[20]

As the war came to campus, colleges went to war. Alexander Hamilton left King's and took a commission in the colonial army. Simeon DeWitt—the only graduate in the class of 1776 at Queen's—was promoted to chief geographer in the Continental forces. Queen's was closed for the next two years. Lewis Vincent, one of Eleazar Wheelock's Native students, served as a scout and interpreter. John Wheelock, who succeeded to the Dartmouth presidency after his father's death in April 1779, secured an appointment as an army major and, despite mixed results in the field, rose to lieutenant colonel. William Churchill Houston left his chair as professor of mathematics and natural philosophy at the College of New Jersey to accept a captaincy. Francis Barber of Elizabethtown Academy took a commission as a lieutenant colonel. Shortly after he offered his resignation, President Daggett of Yale joined several students and townsfolk in an unsuccessful attempt to stop the British invasion of New Haven. On July 5, 1779, two British ships landed with troops under the command of General William Tyron and General George Garth. They captured Daggett and chased off the students. An undergraduate at Yale, James Kent—later the founder of the law course at Columbia and a slaveholder—went home to his family farm, where he plowed fields, sat by the kitchen fire in the evenings reading from his father's limited library, and waited for the military situation to change.[21]

Higher education in the United States began a remarkable era of expansion in the decades after the American Revolution. The war left almost all of the campuses damaged or in ruins and facing uncertain futures, but Americans rebuilt and broadened the educational infrastructure of the new nation by attaching their schools to the resurgent slave economies. Americans founded eighteen new colleges between the end of the Revolution and the beginning of the new century, two-thirds of them in the plantations of the South and lower Mid-Atlantic, where there had been only one college, William and Mary, before the Revolution. Colleges promised to unify the American people, protect young republicans from the corrupting influences of European schools, and level the regional inequities in the nation. The Presbyterians broke ground on seven new schools, only two of them in the North. The Episcopalians raised three colleges in the South. North Carolina, Georgia, and Tennessee chartered public universities. Shortly after the war ended, Father John Carroll called his fellow priests to the White Marsh slave plantation in Maryland, where they organized a governing body, eventually the Corporation of Roman Catholic Clergy, for the newly decriminalized Catholic Church. The corporation administered the former Jesuit slave plantations and funded the church's missions, which included the founding of Georgetown, the first Catholic college in the nation.[22]

College governors' initial challenge was rebuilding. On November 8, 1783, before the defeated British army had finished evacuating from New York City, James Manning sat down at his desk in the reclaimed College of Rhode Island and wrote several pleas to wealthy Baptists in England. In a tone more desperate than brazen, the president stressed the unity of the communion above the obvious barrier of "our independence." The trustee Morgan Edwards had personally called upon these donors during his earlier fund-raising trip to England. Manning now prayed that the two nations would become firm allies in the future and suggested that the progress of religious education was a greater concern than any immediate political wounds and insults. He sweetened the appeal by promising to name the college after a major benefactor, preferably but not necessarily a Baptist. "Can you find no gentleman of fortune among you who wished to rear a lasting monument to his honor in America?" he wrote to the Reverend John Ryland. The college already had "an elegant edifice . . . which waits for a name from some distinguished benefactor." In his letter to the Welsh classicist Thomas Llewelyn, Manning listed the British sponsors who had endowed colleges in the colonies and added how pleased he would be to see, hear, and speak the name "Llewelyn College" throughout New England.[23]

College leaders found few benefactors, foreign or domestic. "Among the numerous consequences of the late war, the destruction of the college buildings, the funds & revenues of the institution under the care of your memorialists have been almost annihilated," Reverend Witherspoon pleaded to the New Brunswick presbytery, which authorized a fund-raising campaign in the mid-Atlantic churches. The trustees had called upon "friends of literature in Europe," he continued, either naively or disingenuously, but they "have, from sundry unexpected causes, failed in their foreign solicitations." President John Wheelock sailed for England to reconnect Dartmouth to its British benefactors. He returned with little money and few commitments. To make matters worse, the ship carrying him home wrecked at Cape Cod, where he nearly died and where he lost his strongbox.[24]

The Americans had few friends in Britain, and their allies in France were sinking into financial crisis after rapidly growing their debt in support of the American rebellion. President Manning begged his Rhode Island board to send him abroad to find money. The trustees chose a cheaper option by naming a European representative to appeal to Louis XVI and then hedged their bets by also appointing a delegate in the South. Both agents declined. The board then asked Thomas Jefferson, the U.S. minister in Paris, to deliver their petition to the king. Louis chose not to assist. Reverend Witherspoon also sought to capitalize on the French king's obvious interest in assuring the success of the United States. John Jay, who had decades of experience lobbying for King's College, advised the New Jersey president that aristocratic support would determine the success of any European effort: "If indeed the Court should set the Example, and really wish to promote it, the Thing would then become fashionable."[25]

Not every republican was canvassing the European courts for money. College officers did not have to wait for King Louis to be dragged to the guillotine to know that American institutions had to fend for themselves. President Jacob Hardenbergh concluded the 1787 Queen's College commencement with an unusual if honest call to self-reliance and self-interest. A native Dutch speaker, Hardenbergh began by apologizing for his difficulties with English but showed great rhetorical skill in hammering his audience on the importance of generosity. Thanking the families who had donated, he cautioned those who had yet to give. "Has kind heaven blest any of your Sons with a more than ordinary Genius," the minister bluntly asked, concluding that the liberal support of academies remained parents' best insurance against the stinginess of nature. Despite, or perhaps because of, such efforts, the New Brunswick college ceased operations from 1795 to 1807.[26]

Atlantic slavery allowed American college educators to rediscover their capacity for self-reliance. In 1787 a group of men in Flatbush, Kings County (today's Brooklyn), organized a preparatory school. Named for the Dutch Catholic philosopher Desiderius Erasmus, the new academy was located along a Dutch slaveholding belt that reached from Nassau County on Long Island to Morris and Somerset Counties in New Jersey. Virtually all the free families in Flatbush owned someone. Brooklyn, then a separate village, and nearby Newtown, Queens, and Hempstead, Long Island, had larger populations of enslaved people, but none of these towns approached the density of slaveholding in Flatbush. By 1790 a third of the 4,495 residents of Kings County were enslaved, and in Flatbush enslaved black people were 40 percent of a total population of 941 people. In fact, black slaves outnumbered white adults in the village. The charter trustees of Erasmus Hall Academy collectively held more than a hundred human beings in bondage, including more than a quarter of all the black people in Flatbush. The Reverend John H. Livingston, the founding principal and later the president of Queen's College in New Brunswick, and his successor Peter Wilson, a classics professor at Columbia, were both slaveholders.[27]

Slavery empowered Catholics to institutionalize their claims to equality in the new nation. In 1789 Pope Pius VI appointed John Carroll as the first Catholic bishop of the United States. That same year, Carroll presided over the founding of Georgetown College. The Catholic clergy had taken control of the old Jesuit slave plantations at Bohemia, White Marsh, St. Inigoes (Ignatius), Newtown, and Saint Thomas, as well as the lesser properties in Maryland and Pennsylvania, and subsidized Georgetown with proceeds from the farms. The regulations of the college gave the vice president the responsibility for overseeing the college servants. The officers and faculty regularly used slaves on campus, and the Catholic clergy even sold slaves off the plantations to fund the college.[28]

The postwar recovery and expansion of higher education in the United States were the consequences of the restoration and escalation of Atlantic slavery. James Manning leaned upon the merchant families of Rhode Island to help his college recover from the war. His trustees committed several hundred pounds of their own money to repair and improve the campus. In 1784 John Brown alone gave a gift of £200, while Governor Stephen Hopkins arranged to get fourteen hundred volumes for the library.[29]

College leaders also turned their attention back to the plantations. The fate of the College of New Jersey, Reverend Witherspoon confessed, rested on maintaining "the great Concourse of Gentlemen[']s sons from the Southward & some from the West Indies." The president included that phrase in a letter to St. George Tucker, whose son had just matriculated—a letter that included a mild apology for the cost of boarding, which the president explained had been rising with the population of wealthy southern students. Witherspoon housed the young Virginian with Witherspoon's own relatives and provided the young man's father with a survey of the positive experiences of other southerners at Nassau Hall. "I have the pleasure to inform you that your son gave complete satisfaction in his examination and is admitted into the Sophomore Class," Witherspoon wrote to Governor Nicolas Van Dyke of Delaware. "I am happy to find that you judge so well as to his education." The flow of students went both ways. Like Witherspoon, James Manning strengthened his school's ties to the plantations by recruiting southern students and sending ministers, teachers, and other graduates to the South and West Indies. In a letter to his friend Samuel Jones, the president worried that a South Carolina benefactor had twice requested a minister and had yet to get a satisfactory response. Manning had a student in mind for the post, "if he could think of going Southward."[30]

Boys from the South and the West Indies were also traveling to northern schools, and the diversity of these students is telling. The governors of Erasmus Hall in Flatbush asked New York State to exempt their students from militia service because so many of the boys were from the South and the West Indies. The son of a once prominent family from Antigua and Dominica, William Alexander Duer, later the president of Columbia College in New York City, studied at Erasmus Hall in its first decade. William Livingston, the grandson of Philip Livingston, a slave trader and a signer of the Declaration of Independence, also attended Erasmus during that era. William's mother was from Jamaica, where his father had managed one arm of the family's business. Henry Cruger Jr. returned to New York City after his final term in the House of Commons and purchased slaves for his house. Cruger's mother was born in Jamaica. Three of his nephews enrolled at Erasmus in its first years. By early 1790, just three years after it opened, more than a fifth of Erasmus's ninety-seven students were from the West Indies, Europe, and the South. Those classes included three students from Saint Croix, two from Saint Thomas, a Jamaican, two Portuguese boys, two French scholars, and the brothers John and William Lambert, who simply listed their home as the West Indies.[31]

At Georgetown, émigrés could be found in the presidency, professoriate, and undergraduate classes. Fathers Robert Plunkett and Robert Moyneux, the first two presidents, were both born in England and trained in Europe. Bishop John Carroll deployed the French, Belgian, and Creole expatriate priests—who fled to Maryland from the revolutions in France and Haiti—to build the Catholic Church in the United States. The Reverend Louis-Guillaume-Valentin Dubourg, a refugee of the revolution in Saint-Domingue (Haiti), served as Georgetown's third president. Dubourg was the first of two early Georgetown presidents from Saint-Domingue. The college's first classes included students from Hispaniola, Cuba, Guadeloupe, Martinique, and Saint Lucia. It was likely the most diverse college campus in the early nation, and its primary rival was St. Mary's College in Maryland, which was founded by Father John Dubois and other French Sulpicians (the Society of Saint Sulpice) in 1805.[32]

The labor and the bodies of unfree black people paid for this educational revolution. "Agreed that the Rev. Mr. [Uzal] Ogden be empowered to sell the negro Man James, given by Mr. Watts, for as much money as he will sell for," the trustees of Newark Academy resolved during their March 9, 1795, meeting. A New Jersey alumnus and slave owner, Uzal Ogden ministered at Trinity Church in Newark. Other Newark trustees had similar ties to the mid-Atlantic colleges, including Uzal Johnson, who graduated from the medical school at King's College. British soldiers had burned Newark Academy during the Revolution, and in 1792 Alexander MacWhorter, a trustee of the College of New Jersey, organized a small local committee to reopen the school. "The intention of this lottery being to compleat and finish an Academy, in the Town of Newark," read a broadside published the following year, "there is little doubt but that every person, desirous to promote Science and encourage Literature, will become an adventurer." The lottery did not provide all the funds that the trustees needed. In May 1795 the board voted to "sell [the]

Negro James, a Donation to the Academy, to Moses Ogden," a trustee and the brother of Uzal Ogden who promised to pay forty pounds within two months.³³ It appears that the money was used to finish the roof.

Slaveholding patrons such as Stephen Van Rensselaer and Henry Rutgers saved Queen's College. In 1810 the Reverend John H. Livingston, pastor of the Dutch Reformed Church in New York and the former principal of Erasmus Hall, accepted the presidency. He reminded the New Jersey legislature that the Revolution came during his school's infancy. He then explained the college's plight during the war: "A revolution which however destructive for the moment to establishments of this kind, is ever to be held in grateful remembrance by the lovers of learning & science, as well as by the lovers of liberty and the rights of man." Father Livingston reported that his campus was "wasted & destroyed," the professors were now "devoted to other pursuits," the students were "dispersed," the donors were "worn out with fatigue," and his treasury was "depreciated and sunk," leaving his college with only "a naked charter and little else." The first solution—a lottery—had failed. The War of 1812 and the death of President Livingston forced another decade-long closure that ended in 1825, when a gift of $6,000 from Henry Rutgers allowed a reopening. President Philip Milledoler, who had arranged the Rutgers donation, then had the trustees rename the college in Rutgers's honor.³⁴

Rhode Island's governors were also able to name their campus for a prominent donor: not a Bristol or Welsh philanthropist but Nicholas Brown Jr., who gave his alma mater $5,000 in memory of his deceased brother, also a graduate. The postwar Rhode Island campus became a retreat for the sons of the merchant elite, including the sons of the DeWolfs, who launched more slaving ventures than any other family in U.S. history. The DeWolfs would continue slaving long after the state of Rhode Island had barred the trade and even after the congressional prohibition of 1808. The family also owned a slave plantation in Cuba through the 1820s.³⁵

As slaveholding receded from the northern states and the United States approached an end to its involvement in the slave trade, college trustees and presidents forged new ties to Atlantic slavery. They seized the economic rewards of human slavery, followed the westward push of cotton agriculture to and across the Mississippi River, fought to rebuild their connections to the Caribbean plantations, and courted the emerging industrialists of the Northeast to sustain their schools. In 1818 the Reverend Charles Van Quickenborne and a group of Belgian Jesuits—and their slaves—established St. Louis University, the first college west of the Mississippi River. It was about the same time that sugar refiners and textile manufacturers began funding engineering and technical colleges in the Northeast to service the mills and plants that were using the products of slavery to launch an industrial revolution. Legislative and judicial actions to end slavery in the North lived with continual reminders of the importance of Atlantic slavery to the nation. American colleges embraced that contradiction in order to find funds, to recruit students, and to protect the flows of money and scholars by dispatching their graduates to staff the slave regimes of the Atlantic world.[36]

NOTES

1. One opponent highlighted Cruger's divided sympathies and demanded the election of "a *real* friend to OLD ENGLAND" rather than a political interloper. Another enemy accused Cruger of intrigue and disloyalty, rhetorically tying him to the blood and treasure that Britain had lost because of the American rebellion. "I shall (with unshaken integrity) persevere to the last moments of my life, in every effort to promote the cause of Liberty," Cruger had promised when he was first elected to Parliament in October 1774. He had then countered concerns about his colonial origins by arguing that the mutual rewards of commerce between England and its North American possessions created a bilateral investment in union and peace. The second promise of his acceptance speech flowed from his profession: "to render essential benefits to the Trade and Commerce of this opulent and flourishing City." *The Whole Proceedings of the Late Contested Election, of the City of Bristol; Between Messrs. Cruger, Burke, Clarke, & Brickdale: Which Began on Monday, October 9th, 1774; and Was Carried on for Twenty-Three Days, with Unremitting Ardour on All Sides* (London: J. Browne, ca. 1774), 8–9, 41; Henry C. Van Schaack, *The Life of Peter Van Schaack, LL.D., Embracing Selections from His Correspondence and Other Writings, During the American Revolution, and His Exile in England* (New York: D. Appleton, 1842), 30; *The Bristol Contest; Containing a Particular Account of the Proceedings of Both Parties, from the Death of Sir Henry Lippincott, Bart. To the Close of the Poll. Together with the Various Papers, Letters, Advertisements, Squibs, Songs, & c. which were printed at the contested Election, between Henry Cruger, Esqr. And George Daubeny, Esqr., In 1781* (Bristol: W. Pine, ca. 1781), 42–44, 57–58.

2. Donald G. Tewksbury, *The Founding of American Colleges and Universities before the Civil War with Particular Reference to the Religious Influences Bearing upon the College Movement* (New York: Teachers College, 1932), 16–33, 55–60; Richard S. Dunn, *Sugar and Slaves: The Rise of the Planter Class in the English West Indies, 1624–1713* (1972; New York: Norton, 1973), 111; Samuel Eliot Morison, *The Maritime History of Massachusetts, 1783–*

1860 (Boston: Houghton Mifflin, 1921), 11–12; entries for April–June, 1709, in Thomas Prince, "A Journal of a Voiage from New-England to Berbados," Journal of Voyages to Barbados, 1709–1711, Massachusetts Historical Society, Boston.

3. The college was founded in Killingsworth in 1701, moved to Saybrook in 1707, and then moved to New Haven in 1716. Entry for September 10, 1718, "Yale University Corporation and Prudential Committee Minutes," Manuscripts and Archives, Yale University Library, New Haven, Conn.; Gerard N. Burrow, *A History of Yale's School of Medicine: Passing Torches to Others* (New Haven, Conn.: Yale University Press, 2002), 13–15; Thomas Clap, *The Annals or History of Yale-College, in New-Haven, in the Colony of Connecticut, from the First Founding Thereof, in the Year 1700, to the Year 1766: With an Appendix, Containing the Present State of the College, the Method of Instruction and Government, with the Officers, Benefactors and Graduates* (New Haven, Conn.: John Hotchkiss and B. Mecom, 1766), 94–96.

4. Frederick Rudolph, *The American College and University: A History* (New York: Knopf, 1962), 47; Tewksbury, *Founding of American Colleges*, 27–40; "Address of the President, & Fellows of Harvard College in Cambr. In the county of Middlsx with in ye Majtys Province of Massachusetts Bay in New England in America," February 5, 1723, Records of the Harvard Corporation, 1650–1992, 1:150, Harvard University Archives, Cambridge, Mass.; Richard Hofstadter, *Academic Freedom in the Age of the College* (1955; New York: Columbia University Press, 1961), 85.

5. Rudolph, *American College and University*, 47; Hugh Jones, *The Present State of Virginia. Giving a Particular and Short Account of the Indian, English, and Negroe Inhabitants of that Colony. Shewing Their Religion, Manners, Government, Trade, Way of Living, &c. With a Description of the Country. From Whence is Inferred a Short View of Maryland and North Carolina. To Which are Added, Schemes and Propositions for the Better Promotion of Learning, Religion, Inventions, Manufactures, and Trade in Virginia, and the Other Plantations. For the Information of the Curious, and for the Service of Such as are Engaged in the Propagation of the Gospel and Advancement of Learning, and for the Use of All Persons Concerned in the Virginia Trade and Plantation* (London: J. Clarke, 1724), 83; Henry Harwell, James Blair, and Edward Chilton, *The Present State of Virginia, and the College* (London: John Wyat, 1727), 4.

6. Tewksbury, *Founding of American Colleges*, 16–33, 55–60.

7. Alison's school was first opened in New London, Pennsylvania. John Langdon Sibley, *Biographical Sketches of Graduates of Harvard University, in Cambridge, Massachusetts* (Cambridge, Mass.: Charles William Sever, 1873–), 5:588–97; John A. Munroe, *The University of Delaware: A History* (Newark: University of Delaware Press, 1986), 9–25; John A. Munroe, *History of Delaware* (1979; Cranbury, N.J.: Associated University Presses, 2006), 111; Douglas Sloan, *The Scottish Enlightenment and the American College Ideal* (New York: Teachers College Press, 1971), esp. 28–59; John D. Krugler, *English and Catholic: The Lords Baltimore in the Seventeenth Century* (Baltimore, Md.: Johns Hopkins University Press,

2004), 242–43; Annabelle M. Melville, *John Carroll of Baltimore: Founder of the American Catholic Hierarchy* (New York: Charles Scribner's Sons, 1955), 1–12; Thomas Meagher Field, ed., *Unpublished Letters of Charles Carroll of Carrollton; and His Father, Charles Carroll of Doughoregan* (New York: United States Catholic Historical Society, 1902), 20; James McLachlan, *Princetonians, 1748–1768: A Biographical Dictionary* (Princeton, N.J.: Princeton University Press, 1976), 194–99; *Catalogue of All Who Have Held Office in or Have Received Degrees from the College of New Jersey at Princeton in the State of New Jersey* (Princeton, N.J.: Princeton University Press, 1896), 7; "Brief Sketch of McWhorter Family of New Jersey," *Proceedings of the New Jersey Historical Society* (Newark: Daily Advertiser, 1867), 10:52–54; William H. Shaw, comp., *History of Essex and Hudson Counties, New Jersey* (Philadelphia: Everts & Peck, 1884), 1:652–53.

8. Entry for October 2, 1759, "Minutes of the Governors of King's College," vol. 1, Rare Book and Manuscript Library, Columbia University, New York; Scott Bryant, *The Awakening of the Freewill Baptists: Benjamin Randall and the Founding of an American Religious Tradition* (Macon, Ga.: Mercer University Press, 2011), 57–58; Samuel Miller, *Memoirs of the Rev. John Rodgers, D.D.: Late Pastor of the Wall-Street and Brick Churches in the City of New-York* (New York: Whiting and Watson, 1813), 197–98; John Witherspoon to Colonel Henry Lee, December 20, 1770, folder 11, box 1, John Witherspoon Collection, Manuscript Division, Firestone Library, Princeton University, Princeton, N.J.; William Nelson, ed., *Documents Relating to the Colonial History of the State of New Jersey* (Paterson, N.J.: Press Printing and Publishing, 1905), 27:112; John Witherspoon, *Address to the Inhabitants of Jamaica, and other West-India Islands, in Behalf of the College of New-Jersey* (Philadelphia: William and Thomas Bradford, 1772); Hugh Williamson, "To the Human and Liberal, Friends of Learning, Religion and Public Virtue, in the island of Jamaica. The Memorial and Humble Address of Hugh Williamson, M.D. One of the Trustees of the Academy of New-Ark, in Behalf of That Institution," *Philadelphia Packet*, June 15, 1772.

9. Set back from the Hudson River near St. John Chapel and a short walk from Trinity Church, the campus offered views of the harbor, Staten Island, and East Jersey. There was a large courtyard and garden. The main building was planned as a long, three-story, stone structure divided into four sections, each with stone stairs leading to a dozen student residences and halls. A windowed cupola offered panoramic views. Inside there was a lecture hall, a library, a chapel, a museum, and an anatomical theater. The labor that kept the college running was done in the main hall and a series of informal outbuildings. Samuel Johnson to Dr. [Thomas] Secker, the archbishop of Canterbury, November 20, 1760, and Samuel Johnson to William Samuel Johnson, February 1, 1762, Samuel Johnson Letter Books, vol. 2, Samuel Johnson Papers, Rare Book and Manuscript Library, Columbia University, New York; "Description of Columbia College, in the City of New-York," *New York Magazine, or Literary Repository*, May 1790.

10. Frederick Rudolph, *Curriculum: A History of the American Undergraduate Course of Study since 1636* (San Francisco: Jossey-Bass, 1977), 26; John Frelinghuysen Hageman,

History of Princeton and Its Institutions . . . (Philadelphia: J. B. Lippincott, 1879), 2:246; George E. Thomas and David B. Brownlee, *Building America's First University: An Historical and Architectural Guide to the University of Pennsylvania* (Philadelphia: University of Pennsylvania Press, 2000), 27–34.

11. Thomas Allen Glenn, *William Churchill Houston, 1746–1788* (Norristown, Pa.: Privately printed, 1903), 7–12; Varnum Lansing Collins, *President Witherspoon: A Biography* (Princeton, N.J.: Princeton University Press, 1925), 2:216–17; James Madison to the Reverend Thomas Martin, August 10, 1769, in *The Papers of James Madison*, ed. William T. Hutchinson and William M. E. Rachal (Chicago: University of Chicago Press, 1962), 1:42–44; Ron Chernow, *Alexander Hamilton* (New York: Penguin, 2004), 29–38; Willard Sterne Randall, *Alexander Hamilton: A Life* (New York: Harper Collins, 2003), 45–50; James L. O'Neill, "Col. Francis Barber, A Soldier of the Revolution," *Journal of the American-Irish Historical Society* 7 (1907): 42; Ron Chernow, *Washington: A Life* (New York: Penguin, 2010), 155–64; Helen Bryan, *Martha Washington: First Lady of Liberty* (New York: John Wiley and Sons, 2002), 162–66.

12. Josiah Quincy, *Memoir of the Life of Josiah Quincy Jun. of Massachusetts, by His Son, Josiah Quincy* (Boston: Cummings, Hilliard, 1825), 124–25.

13. Thomas E. Chávez, *Spain and the Independence of the United States: An Intrinsic Gift* (Albuquerque: University of New Mexico Press, 2002), 8–12; Lee Kennett, *The French Forces in America, 1780–1783* (Westport, Conn.: Greenwood, 1977), 7–36; James Manning to Samuel Jones, March 9, 1777, A26, box A, Samuel Jones Papers, John Hay Library, Brown University, Providence, N.J.

14. Stephen Bonsal, *When the French Were Here: A Narrative of the Sojourn of the French Forces in America, and Their Contribution to the Yorktown Campaign Drawn from Unpublished Reports and Letters of Participants in the National Archives of France and the MS. Division of the Library Congress* (Garden City, N.Y.: Doubleday, Doran, 1945), 4; *Report of the Committee of Claims, to Whom Was Referred on the 21st Ultimo, the Petition of the Corporation of Rhode-Island College. Together with Former Reports Thereon. 17th February, 1800* (By Order of the House of Representatives, 1800).

15. Entry for October 10, 1775, Harvard University, Faculty Minutes, 1725–1890, 4:14–16, Harvard University Archives, Cambridge, Mass.; Robert A. Gross, *The Minutemen and Their World* (New York: Hill and Wang, 1976), 134–35; Pauline Maier, *From Resistance to Revolution: Colonial Radicals and the Development of American Opposition to Britain, 1765–1776* (1972; New York: Norton, 1991), 308.

16. Gross, *Minutemen and Their World*, 94–97, 134–38; Lemuel Shattuck, *A History of the Town of Concord; Middlesex County, Massachusetts, from Its Earliest Settlement to 1832; and of the Adjoining Towns; Bedford, Acton, Lincoln, and Carlisle; Containing Varios Notices of County and State History Not Before Published* (Boston: Russell, Odiorne, 1835), 120–21; Bills of Sale for Slaves, by or to Concord, Mass., Residents, 1740–1755, Special Collections, Concord Free Public Library, Concord, Mass.; *Concord, Massachusetts:*

Births, Marriages, and Deaths, 1635–1850 (Concord, Mass.: Printed by the Town, 1891), passim; Elise Lemire, *Black Walden: Slavery and Its Aftermath in Concord, Massachusetts* (Philadelphia: University of Pennsylvania Press, 2009), 101–11.

17. Entries from December 10, 1776, to September 10, 1777, "Yale University Corporation and Prudential Committee Minutes"; *An Account of the Number of Inhabitants, in the Colony of Connecticut, January 1, 1774; Together with an Account of the Number of Inhabitants, Taken January 1, 1756* (Hartford, Conn.: Ebenezer Watson, 1774).

18. Frederick Chase, *A History of Dartmouth College and the Town of Hanover, New Hampshire* (Cambridge, Mass.: John Wilson and Son, 1891), 1:324–40, 380; Robert S. Allen, *His Majesty's Indian Allies: British Indian Policy in the Defence of Canada, 1774–1815* (Toronto: Dundurn, 1992), 44–46; Eleazar Wheelock to Governor Jonathan Trumbull (775369.2), Rauner Library, Dartmouth College, Hanover, N.H.; Collin G. Calloway, *The American Revolution in Indian Country: Crisis and Diversity in Native American Communities* (Cambridge: Cambridge University Press, 1995), 1–64.

19. In 1775 Virginia's last royal governor, Lord Dunmore, granted freedom to any enslaved people who joined the British forces. In 1779 General Henry Clinton published a proclamation from Philipsburg, New York, freeing any enslaved people who reached British lines. Entries for May 14, 1776, May 13, 1777, June 11, 1779, "Minutes of the Governors of King's College," vol. 2; Graham Russell Hodges, "Black Revolt in New York and the Neutral Zone: 1775–83," in *New York in the Age of the Constitution, 1775–1800*, ed. Paul A. Gilje and William Pencak (Rutherford, N.J.: Fairleigh Dickinson University Press, 1992), 20–40.

20. "A Campaign Journal from November 29, 1776, to May 6, 1777," in Glenn, *William Churchill Houston*, 22–35 (originally published in the *Princeton Standard*, May 1863); John Frelinghuysen Hageman, *History of Princeton and Its Institutions . . .* (Philadelphia: J. B. Lippincott, 1879), 1:121–26; William Smith, *An Account of Washington College, in the State of Maryland* (Philadelphia: Joseph Crukshank, 1784).

21. John Howard Raven, comp., *Catalogue of the Officers and Alumni of Rutgers College (Originally Queen's College) in New Brunswick, N.J., 1766–1909* (Trenton, N.J.: State Gazette Publishing, 1909), 41; Chase, *History of Dartmouth College*, 1:372–73, 390; Glenn, *William Churchill Houston*, 19; William Nelson, *New Jersey Biographical and Genealogical Notes from the Volumes of the New Jersey Archives with Additions and Supplements* (Newark, N.J., 1916), 135–36; Ebenezer Elmer, *An Elogy on Francis Barber, Esq., Lieutenant-Colonel Commandant of the Second New Jersey Regiment* (Chatham, N.J., 1783), 7; Charles Hervey Townshend, *The British Invasion of New Haven, Connecticut, Together with Some Account of Their Landing and Burning the Towns of Fairfield and Norwalk, July 1779* (New Haven, Conn., 1879), 30–72; M. Louise Greene, "New Haven Defenses in the Revolution and in the War of 1812," *Connecticut Quarterly* 4 (January–December 1898): 272–80; entry for April 1, 1777, "Yale University Corporation and Prudential Committee Minutes"; Benjamin Franklin Miller, "Notebook from Chancellor Kent's Lectures," Lecture Notes and

Memorabilia, 1817–1915, box 1, Rare Book and Manuscript Library, Columbia University, New York; William Kent, *Memoirs and Letters of James Kent, LL.D.: Late Chancellor of the State of New York, Author of "Commentaries on American Law," etc.* (Boston: Little, Brown, 1898), 99–100.

22. I have included Kentucky in this grouping since it was the western migrations and speculations of the Virginians that led to the founding of Transylvania College (1783). Tewksbury, *Founding of American Colleges*, 34–35; Robert Emmett Curran, *Shaping of American Catholicism: Maryland and New York, 1805–1915* (Washington, D.C.: Catholic University of America Press, 2012), 15–16.

23. James Manning to Henry Kane, John Ryland, Samuel Sennett, and Thomas Llewelyn, November 8, 1783, in *Life, Times, and Correspondence of James Manning, and the Early History of Brown University*, by Reuben Aldridge Guild (Boston: Gould and Lincoln, 1864), 307–20; Hywel M. Davies, *Transatlantic Brethren: Rev. Samuel Jones (1735–1814) and His Friends, Baptists in Wales, Pennsylvania, and Beyond* (Cranbury, N.J.: Associated University Presses, 1995), 109–11.

24. The Memorial of the Trustees of the College of New Jersey to the Rev'd Presbytery of New Brunswick, September 30, 1784, folder 12A, box 1, Witherspoon Collection; John Wheelock to T. Russell, Esq., January 4, 1784 (784104), and John Wheelock to Theodore Atkinson, February 28, 1784 (784178), Rauner Library, Dartmouth College, Hanover, N.H.

25. James Manning to David Howell, January 9, 1784, James Manning to William Rogers, January 9, 1784, and reports of meetings of the corporation, September 3, 1783–March 19, 1784, folder 2, box 2, Rhode Island College Miscellaneous Papers, 1763–1804, Brown University, Providence, R.I.; Guild, *Life, Times, and Correspondence*, 301–4; John Jay to John Witherspoon, April 6, 1784, folder 21C, box 1, Witherspoon Collection.

26. Jacob R. Hardenbergh, Commencement Address of 1787, MC 089, folder 17, box 2, Elizabeth R. Boyd Historical Collection, Special Collections and University Archives, Alexander Library, Rutgers University, New Brunswick, N.J.

27. *Heads of Families at the First Census of the United States Taken in the Year 1790: New York* (Washington, D.C.: Government Printing Office, 1908), esp. 97–98; *Return of the Whole Number of Persons within the Several Districts of the United States, According to "An Act Providing for the Enumeration of the Inhabitants of the United States," Passed March the First, One Thousand Seven Hundred and Ninety-One* (Philadelphia: Childs and Swaine, 1791), 36–41; Regents of the University of the State of New York, Charter of Erasmus Hall Academy in Kings County, November 12, 1787, Erasmus Hall Academy Records, 1787–1896, folder 3, box A0068, Brooklyn Historical Society, Brooklyn, N.Y.; Craig Steven Wilder, *Ebony & Ivy: Race, Slavery, and the Troubled History of America's Universities* (New York: Bloomsbury, 2013), 245.

28. Thomas W. Spalding, *The Premier See: A History of the Archdiocese of Baltimore, 1789–1989* (Baltimore, Md.: Johns Hopkins University Press, 1989), 21–27; Thomas Murphy, S.J., *Jesuit Slaveholding in Maryland, 1717–1838* (New York: Routledge, 2001);

Georgetown College, "Minutes of the Board of Directors of Georgetown College from 1797–1815," entries for December 20, 1797, and March 29–31, 1808, in Minutes of the Board of Directors, September 1, 1797, through July 11, 1815, box 1, Special Collections Research Center, Georgetown University Library, Washington, D.C.

29. Guild, *Life, Times, and Correspondence*, 301–4; William E. Foster, *Stephen Hopkins: A Rhode Island Statesman: A Study in the Political History of the Eighteenth Century* (Providence, R.I.: Sidney S. Rider, 1884), 105–7.

30. John Witherspoon to St. George Tucker, May 1, 1787, and John Witherspoon to Nicolas Van Dyke, 1786, folders 16A and 17, box 1, Witherspoon Collection; James Manning to Samuel Jones, March 23, 1791, A29, box A, Jones Papers.

31. "Biographical Account of Col. William Duer by William Alexander Duer," undated, folder 29, box 1, Duer Family Papers, Rare Books and Manuscripts Library, Columbia University Library, New York; United States Bureau of the Census, *Heads of Families at the First Census of the United States Taken in the Year 1790—New York* (Washington, D.C.: Government Printing Office, 1908), 116; Erasmus Hall Academy Account Book, 1787–1875, esp. folios 2–9, 43, Erasmus Hall Academy Records, 1787–1896, folder 2, box A0068, Brooklyn Historical Society; Wilder, *Ebony & Ivy*, 52–53; entry for November 1, 1788, and the student rolls at the end of the book, Minute Book of the Corporation of Trustees of Erasmus Hall, 1787–1896, vol. 1, Erasmus Hall School Archives, New-York Historical Society, New York.

32. "College Catalogues, 1791–1850," vol. 1, box 1, Special Collections Research Center, Georgetown University Library; *Georgetown University Alumni Directory* (Washington, D.C.: Georgetown University Alumni Association, 1957); James Hennesey, S.J., "Neither the Bourbons nor the Revolution: Georgetown's Jesuit Founders," in *Images of America in Revolutionary France*, ed. Michèle R. Morris (Washington, D.C.: Georgetown University Press, 1990), 1–11; *Maryland Gazette*, January 3–24, 1805.

33. "Minutes of the Board of Trustees Newark Academy, February 3rd, 1792, to December 9th, 1811," 9–19, 43–44, MG 1303, Collection of the New Jersey Historical Society, Newark; Jonathan F. Stearns, *Historical Discourses, Relating to the First Presbyterian Church in Newark; Originally Delivered to the Congregation of that Church during the Month of January, 1851* (Newark: Daily Advertiser Office, 1853), 216–18; Milton Halsey Thomas, *Columbia University Officers and Alumni, 1754–1857* (New York: Columbia University Press, 1936), 106; William Ogden Wheeler, comp., *The Ogden Family in America: Elizabethtown Branch and Their Ancestry: John Ogden, the Pilgrim and His Descendants, 1640–1906, Their History, Biography & Genealogy* (Philadelphia: J. B. Lippincott, 1907), 64, 85–86; "Scheme of the Newark Academy Lottery . . ." (Newark, July 3, 1793). Lotteries were an old source of funds for schools. They required no layout from the governments and could be carried out by paid agents. Before the College of New Jersey opened, its founders held a lottery in Connecticut that was followed by a Philadelphia game. In 1754 the trustees of the College of Philadelphia announced a lottery in anticipation of their

charter. In 1772, twenty years after his graduation, Jeremiah Halsey oversaw a Delaware lottery for the College of New Jersey. A slaveholder and Presbyterian minister, Halsey had served as a tutor at the college. Harvard was beneficiary of a 1773 Massachusetts lottery. The priests at Georgetown College wagered a small sum on a local lottery ticket. They also used lotteries to help fund St. Mary's Seminary in Baltimore. Samuel Jones, a classmate of James Manning who helped secure the charter for the College of Rhode Island, suggested a lottery to replenish the endowment after the Revolution. "We need funds exceedingly," conceded a frustrated Jonathan Maxcy, who had succeeded to the presidency, adding that a recent lottery had failed. McLachlan, *Princetonians*, 53–55; "Pettie's Island Cash Lottery, For Raising the Sum of Fourteen Hundred and Fifty Pounds . . ." (Philadelphia, 1772); *Pennsylvania Gazette*, March 12, 1745, December 12, 1749, October 3, 1754; "The Managers of the Delaware Lottery for the College of New-Jersey, &c." (Philadelphia, March 24, 1774); entry for March 6, 1797, Georgetown College, "Ledger A, Financial Ledgers," 1789–1799, vol. 1, Special Collections Research Center, Georgetown University Library; John Gilmary Shea, *The Life and Times of the Most Rev. John Carroll, Bishop and First Archbishop of Baltimore, Embracing the History of the Catholic Church in the United States, 1763–1815* (New York: John G. Shea, 1888), 607; "List of the Numbers That Came Up Prizes in the Delaware Lottery, for the Use of New-Jersey College, the Presbyterian Church at Princetown, and the United Congregations of Newcastle and Christiana Bridge . . ." (Philadelphia, 1774); William B. Weeden, *Economic and Social History of New England, 1620–1789* (New York: Hillary House, 1963), 2:737; Thomas Harrison Montgomery, *A History of the University of Pennsylvania from Its Founding to A.D. 1770* (Philadelphia: George W. Jacobs, 1900), 378–79; Jonathan Maxcy to Samuel Jones, May 3, 1794, A31, box A, Jones Papers.

34. Milledoler began tutoring at the college in 1793 after his graduation from Columbia. He later pastored churches in Philadelphia, Albany, and New York and guided Dutch Reformed missions to the Indians. When he arrived at New Brunswick on April 20, 1825, he had found "the West Wing . . . was in a very unfinished state—other parts of the College[,] excepting [the] chapel, also unfinished or very much needing repair." Funds from Van Rensselaer allowed the main hall to be completed, but the academic program was in ruins. The new president hired a mathematician and a language professor and had the theology professors offer courses in the literary departments. By stretching the faculty, he was able to reopen the seminary and the college at little cost. J. H. Livingston, president of Queen's College, "To the Honourable the Legislative Council & General Assembly of the State of New Jersey," also see petitions dated October 28, 1809, and November 6, 1822, all in folder 12, box 1, Boyd Historical Collection, and record of Henry Rutgers's gift, folder 5, box 2, Boyd Historical Collection; "Private Memoirs, 1825–1832: Private Memoirs relating to my call and events connected with the revival of Queens, now Rutgers College," box 5, Philip Milledoler Papers, New-York Historical Society.

35. Nicholas Brown Jr. to the Honorable Corporation of Rhode Island College, September 6, 1804, folder 2, box 2, Rhode Island College Miscellaneous Papers; *Historical Catalogue of Brown University, 1764–1919* (Providence, R.I.: Published by the University, 1914), passim; the records for the Cuba plantations and operations are in folders 1 and 2, box 8, DeWolf Papers, Papers of the American Slave Trade, Series A, Part 2, Reel 11, Rhode Island Historical Society; James Coughtry, *The Notorious Triangle: Rhode Island and the African Slave Trade* (Philadelphia: Temple University Press, 1981), 31–49, 94, 236, passim; James A. McMillin, *The Final Victims: Foreign Slave Trade to North America, 1783–1810* (Columbia: University of South Carolina Press, 2004), 37, 88–89; Benjamin Franklin Grady, *The Case of the South against the North: or, Historical Evidence Justifying the Southern States of the American Union in Their Long Controversy with the Northern States* (Raleigh, N.C.: Edwards & Broughton, 1899), 151.

36. Gilbert J. Garraghan, "The Beginnings of St. Louis University," *St. Louis Catholic Historical Review*, October 1918, 85–101; *Catholic Telegraph*, August 31, 1837. See also Joseph Aloysius Griffin, *The Contribution of Belgium to the Catholic Church in America, 1523–1857* (Washington, D.C.: Catholic University of America, 1932); Wilder, *Ebony & Ivy*, 285–87.

CHAPTER TWO

Princeton and Slavery

Holding the Center

Craig B. Hollander & Martha A. Sandweiss

In the spring of 1766 Samuel Finley, fifth president of the College of New Jersey (now Princeton University), planted two sycamore trees in front of the President's House, a stone's throw from Nassau Hall, the only other building on campus. Campus lore claims the trees celebrated the repeal of the Stamp Act, and more than two and a half centuries later, those aged trees still frame the old clapboard house, now home to the university's alumni association. Tour guides point to the towering sycamores as living reminders of the college's devotion to the revolutionary cause.[1] But the guides do not mention what happened at the house just a few months later, after Finley died in July 1766. His executors announced they would sell his possessions: furniture, cattle, books, and "two Negro women, a negro man, and three negro children." "The Negro Women," the executors explained, "understand all Kinds of House Work, and the Negro Man is well fitted for the Business of Farming in all its Branches." The slaves not sold beforehand would be auctioned off on August 19 at the President's House beside those two young liberty trees.[2]

Princeton University, founded in 1746, exemplifies the central paradox at the heart of American history. From the very start, liberty and slavery were intertwined. The university boasts of being the site of an American victory during the Revolutionary War and of hosting the Continental Congress in Nassau Hall in 1783. The campus literature fails to note, however, that the first nine presidents of the university, serving until 1854, held slaves at some point in their lives.[3] Early college regulations required prospective students to present themselves to the president for examination before enrolling in the school. For generations of Princeton students, then, the first person they met

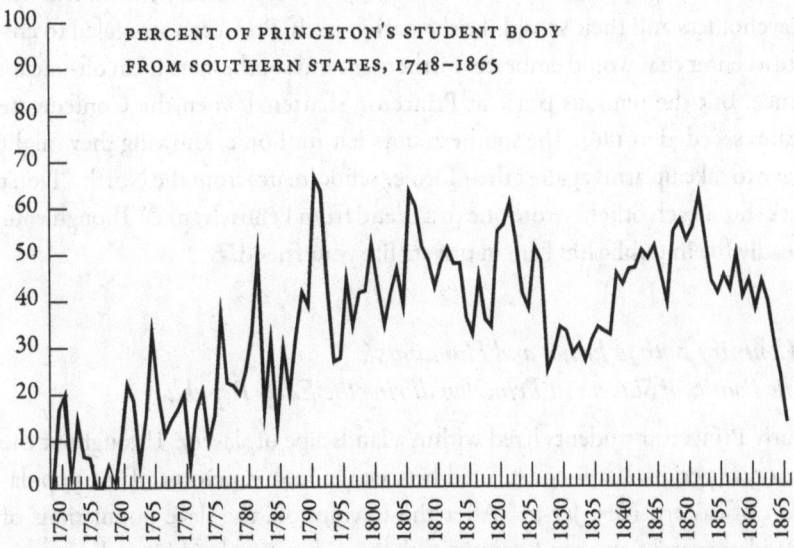

PERCENT OF PRINCETON'S STUDENT BODY FROM SOUTHERN STATES, 1748–1865

on campus may have been the enslaved man or woman who answered their knock on the president's front door. If Nassau Hall provided the storied backdrop of Princeton University, slavery was literally the face of the school.

More than any other early American college, Princeton was a truly national institution, drawing its students not just from the surrounding mid-Atlantic region but also from the South. Presbyterian ministers who trained at Princeton during the colonial period spread word of the college to the cotton frontier of the early Republic. From there, money and boys flowed to the college in New Jersey. Throughout the antebellum period, even as North and South developed increasingly different views about slavery, on average, nearly 40 percent of Princeton's student body came from the slave states, providing crucial financial support for the college's operations.[4] As one mother in Georgia wrote in 1850, "Princeton of all colleges ... has long had the preference for our dear boys."[5] Indeed, in the class of 1851, 63 percent of Princeton's students were from slave states.[6]

If Princeton embodied the paradoxical connections of liberty and slavery during the revolutionary era, the institution also exemplified the central tensions of antebellum American life, seeking—in a northern state only mildly antipathetic toward slavery—to maintain a comfortable environment for slaveholders and their sons. Like the nation itself, Princeton struggled to create a center that would embrace northerners and southerners in an oft-uneasy truce. But the tenuous peace at Princeton shattered when the Confederate states seceded in 1861. The southern boys left for home, knowing they might have to take up arms against their former schoolmates from the North. "Don't let's shoot each other," wrote one to a friend from Pennsylvania. "Though your deadly foe in public life I am in private life your friend."[7]

"Contrary Both to Justice and Humanity": The Politics of Slavery at Princeton during the Early Republic

Early Princeton students lived within a landscape of slavery. Throughout the colonial period, slaves constituted between 12 and 15 percent of the population of eastern New Jersey.[8] After the Revolution, the slave populations of Middlesex and Somerset Counties—the two counties that bisected the town of Princeton—increased.[9] In 1794 the college formally prohibited students from bringing their own servants to campus.[10] Nevertheless, students did not have to wander far from Nassau Hall to encounter slaves.[11] Although New Jersey passed in 1804 an act for the gradual abolition of slavery, the state was painfully slow to relinquish the institution. There were 7,557 slaves in New Jersey in 1820 and still 236 slaves remaining in 1850.[12] In 1865 New Jersey became the only state in the North to vote against the ratification of the Thirteenth Amendment, which abolished slavery.

Although no evidence yet suggests that Princeton students brought their own slaves to campus during the colonial and early national periods, the students regularly encountered enslaved people delivering wood to their rooms, working in town, or laboring in the fields of the privately owned farm adjacent to the campus.[13] They also crossed paths with the slaves who resided at the President's House, even after New Jersey passed the 1804 act for the gradual abolition of slavery. For example, shortly after moving to Princeton in 1813, Ashbel Green, the college's eighth president, purchased a twelve-year-old named John and an eighteen-year-old named Phoebe to work as servants in the house. Although Phoebe's and John's birth years (approximately 1794 and 1801) denied them a right to freedom under the state's 1804 gradual emancipation act, they may have made an informal arrangement with their new master. Ashbel Green wrote in his diary that he would free them each at the age of twenty-five, or twenty-four "if they served me to my entire satisfaction."[14] In the meantime, in 1817 he manumitted another one of his slaves, Betsey Stockton, who went on to a remarkable career as a missionary in Hawaii and as a teacher in a school for black children in Princeton.[15]

Yet within this landscape of slavery, Princeton during its first seventy-five years produced a staggering number of leaders of the American clergy, military, and government, many of whom were "antislavery" in the sense that they disapproved of slavery and sought to abolish the institution.[16] The venerated Dr. Benjamin Rush (class of 1760) and the theologian Jonathan Edwards Jr. (class of 1765) provided crucial moral leadership during the North's transition into the "free states." As Edwards wrote in 1791, "You... to whom the present blaze of light as to this subject has reached, cannot sin at so cheap a rate as our fathers."[17] Edwards meant "our fathers" literally. His own father, Jonathan Edwards Sr., had been a slaveholder and Princeton's third president.

Antislavery members of the Princeton community proved particularly active during the so-called First Emancipation, the period from the Revolution through the early nineteenth century when northern states passed laws for the gradual abolition of slavery, the United States abolished the foreign slave trade, and many slaveholders emancipated their slaves. John Witherspoon provided the intellectual underpinnings for this antislavery sentiment at Princeton. Witherspoon emigrated from Scotland in 1768 to become the college's sixth president. During his twenty-six-year tenure, Princeton became a primary conduit for the diffusion of Scottish moral-philosophical thought, which, in the words of Margaret Abruzzo, emphasized "both human benevolence and sympathy as the foundations of all morality." Although Witherspoon owned slaves, his teachings gave a generation of students "a language for challenging slavery."[18]

Witherspoon became a political role model for his students. Almost from the start, he criticized the British for encroaching upon American rights, and he later signed the Declaration of Independence and served in the Continental Congress. The Princeton community followed the president's lead. "No other college in North America," writes the historian John Murrin, "was so nearly unanimous in support of the Patriot cause. Trustees, faculty, and nearly all alumni and students rallied to the Revolution in a colony fiercely divided by these issues."[19] As the site of a battle in 1777 and temporary home for the

Congress of the United States in 1783, Princeton emerged from the Revolution distinctly aligned with national concerns, and the institution consciously and proudly linked its own success to that of the American Republic.[20]

The college's close identification with the Republic came with added responsibility. "With such a stake in the new government," writes historian Mark Noll, "the spirits of Princeton officials rose and fell with the perceived health of the nation."[21] Witherspoon's successor, Samuel Stanhope Smith (class of 1769), taught his students that slavery posed a particularly dire threat to the nation's spiritual, moral, and political well-being. Like his six predecessors, Smith was—or had been—a slaveholder. In 1784 he advertised to sell or trade a young slave, "well acquainted with the business of a plantation, and used to taking care of horses."[22] Smith nonetheless became an important, if sometimes eccentric, critic of racism and slavery in the early United States. In his 1787 treatise titled an "Essay on the Causes of the Variety of Complexion and Figure in the Human Species," he posited that racial differences stemmed from nothing more than climate. Later, in 1812, he argued against the ancient Aristotelian notion that civilized nations had a natural right to wage war on barbarians to enslave prisoners and contended instead that such forms of enslavement constituted "the most unjust title of all to the servile subjection of the human species." He asserted that "to reduce [prisoners of war] to slavery is contrary both to justice and humanity." He also noted that "men deceive themselves continually by false pretenses, in order to justify the slavery which is convenient for them."[23]

However, Smith stopped well short of calling for the immediate abolition of American slavery. "No event," he exclaimed, "can be more dangerous to a community than the sudden introduction into it of vast multitudes of persons, free in their condition, but without property, and possessing only habits and vices of slavery." Smith also doubted that the state had the right to compel slaveholders to give up their property. "Neither justice nor humanity," he wrote, "requires that [a] master, who has become the innocent possessor of that property, should impoverish himself for the benefit of the slave." As an alternative, Smith floated a few ideas to both encourage voluntary manumission and diminish racial prejudice, including one plan to assign a "district out of the unappropriated lands of the United States, in which each black freedman, or freedwoman, shall receive a certain portion." He then proposed that "every white man who should marry a black woman, and every white woman who should marry a black man, and reside within the territory, might be entitled to a double portion of the land." Smith hoped that such interracial marriages would "bring the two races nearer together, and, in a course of time... obliterate those wide distinctions which are now created by diversity of complexion."[24]

Smith's views on race and slavery helped shape those of his students. According to William Birney, the son of James G. Birney (class of 1810), Smith had "great influence over his pupil, an influence perceptible for many years." The elder Birney eventually manumitted his slaves and became an important champion of the abolitionist movement. William Birney wrote that Smith had "a deep interest in all questions touching slavery and the African race" and "taught his pupils that men are of one blood, and that slavery is wrong morally and an evil politically." Indeed, his father kept Smith's works on his bookshelf—alongside those of the famed British abolitionists James Ramsay and Thomas Clarkson—even though Smith himself believed there could be "no remedy [to slavery] except in voluntary manumissions by masters."[25]

During Smith's administration (1795–1812), Princeton produced many graduates who sought a solution to the moral and political problems associated with slavery. Unlike Birney, most dismissed the thought of immediate abolition and refused to question the property rights of slaveholders. Nevertheless, they contributed to the pro-reform discourse during the early Republic, which, in turn, set the stage for the rise of the abolitionist movement. For example, in 1816 Smith's pupil Charles Fenton Mercer (class of 1797), a slaveholder from Virginia, helped to organize the American movement to colonize free blacks. Mercer did not invent the idea of colonization. He latched onto it because, like Smith, he worried that emancipated slaves were a drain on public resources and a threat to social order.[26] Mercer echoed Smith's fear that racism would prevent blacks from assimilating into white society, but while Smith proposed sending blacks to the western frontier, Mercer wanted to send them to Africa.[27]

Mercer considered his time at Princeton to be his personal golden age.[28] He remained active in the college community throughout his life and enlisted Princeton associates in his endeavor to colonize free blacks. In 1816 he asked Elias B. Caldwell (class of 1796) to pitch the colonization idea to his brother-in-law, the Reverend Robert Finley (class of 1787), director of the Princeton Theological Seminary. Finley supported colonization because he believed that slaveholders would be more willing to manumit their slaves if they could then send them far away. With that in mind, Mercer, Caldwell, Finley, and their friend John Randolph—a statesman from Virginia who had briefly attended

Princeton—organized the American Society for Colonizing the Free People of Colour of the United States (also known as the American Colonization Society [ACS]). Attorney General Richard Rush (class of 1797) attended the first meeting. Like his father, Benjamin Rush, he, too, sought a solution to the slavery problem.

In effect, Princeton was ground zero for the colonization movement in the United States. The college's support for the movement drew other Princeton affiliates into the ACS's effort to colonize free blacks and suppress the African slave trade. Members of the Princeton community helped arrange for Lieutenant Robert F. Stockton—the scion of Princeton's most illustrious family—to receive command of a new cruiser that the navy planned to use in its campaign against the African slave trade. Stockton conducted two tours of the African coast. In addition to suppressing the African slave trade, he personally negotiated on behalf of the ACS the purchase of a 130-mile-long and 40-mile-wide swath of coastline. This land would form the basis of Liberia, the American colony for free blacks.[29]

Ultimately, Stockton became the president of New Jersey's chapter of the ACS, unsurprisingly based in Princeton. However, the real steward of the ACS in New Jersey was a young professor at Princeton named John Maclean Jr., who had graduated from the college in 1816. Maclean took a deep and abiding interest in colonization. As a northern clergyman, he sought a vehicle to encourage voluntary manumissions, protect society from an influx of newly freed blacks, spread Christianity to Africa, and suppress the African slave trade. But Maclean could also empathize with the reluctance of slaveholders to part with their property. His own father, Princeton's first chemistry professor, had died in 1814 while in possession of two slaves: a girl named Sal and a boy named Charles.[30] Maclean's interest in the colonization movement dovetailed with his attachment to Princeton. He dedicated his life to the college, rising through the ranks to become its tenth president in 1854, and throughout his long career he sought to promote harmony between the northern and southern members of his beloved community. Princeton's close affiliation with the ACS seemed useful and beneficial. After all, the ACS allowed members of the college community to demonstrate their distaste for slavery without having to call for its abolition. "Humanity and justice," exclaimed Samuel Southard of New Jersey (class of 1804), "exult in the belief, that the gradual emancipation of the slave, and the restoration of the free to the land of their fathers, may yet afford a remedy [to the evil of slavery]."[31]

In the long run, though, Princeton could not depend on the colonization movement to mediate the conflicting desires of slaveholders and nonslaveholders. During the 1830s a new generation of abolitionists began to call for the immediate abolition of slavery. Consequently, the colonization movement came under pressure both from those who called for the slaves to be freed and from the increasingly defensive slaveholders who responded that slavery was actually a positive good for society, rather than a necessary evil. Abolitionists abandoned the ACS, and slaveholders became suspicious of the colonization movement, which had tacitly encouraged voluntary manumissions. This polarization sapped the popularity of the ACS, especially in conservative areas like Princeton. "The New Jersey Col. Society is at a low ebb," wrote one ACS member to Maclean in 1842. "The gentlemen from Princeton," he added, "appear wholly to have neglected it."[32] Instead, the Princeton gentlemen were becoming more concerned with abolitionism, which, in their view, now constituted a greater threat than slavery to the survival of their beloved republic. Maclean, vice president of the college during the 1830s and 1840s, found himself presiding over an increasingly conservative institution.

"The College of the Union": The Politics of Slavery at Princeton during the Late Antebellum Period

On May 9, 1848, Henry Craft sat down to write in his diary. The twenty-five-year-old from Holly Springs, Mississippi, had come to the college just a few months earlier to study law.[33] He spent some time that day with Daniel Baker, an undergraduate from his hometown. Baker was an aspiring minister who sought a post in New England, but he was anxious about working in a region that held "erroneous opinions & prejudices" regarding slavery.[34] As Craft confided in his diary: "We think almost all slaveholders look upon the institution as an evil, a curse to the country & would gladly blot it out could any feasible plan be devised, but in complete destitution of any such plan think that the evil is a necessary one & should be made as tolerable as possible."[35] As southerners, Baker argued, they ought to defend slavery and "give any *information* in [their] power."[36]

The increasing sectional conflict during the late antebellum period presented a special dilemma for Princeton, where a significant number of students still came from the slaveholding states. In essence, the college faced the same persistent challenge as the United States itself: the challenge of preserving a community of both slaveholders and nonslaveholders. The university's location in New Jersey magnified the problem. Some southern parents worried about exposing their sons to abolitionism. "I am anxious to know all about Princeton before I consent to give you up to the Institution for the formation of your character," wrote one father in Louisiana to his son in 1856. "If there be . . . [a] strong . . . abolition feeling there," he clarified, "I should not desire you to remain in it."[37] And for many students, from both North and South, the town of Princeton's sizeable free black community challenged their preconceived views. In 1850 Charles C. Jones Jr. of Georgia wrote to his parents that the Negro Sons of Temperance had paraded through town. "It was a strange sight to those of us who were from the slave states," he noted.[38] Similarly, a student from Pennsylvania reported to his mother in 1851 that "there are more niggers here than ever I saw in one town before. They have more impudence, too."[39]

College administrators sought to make their southern students and slaveholding patrons feel welcome. In 1835 the trustees turned down an offer of $1,000—a tremendous sum at the time—if the college would admit students "irrespective of color."[40] Members of the faculty, including the acclaimed theologian Charles Hodge, reassured their southern students that the Bible sanctioned slavery. Others made no secret of their sympathies for the South. Jones raved about the "truly southern" chemistry professor Richard Sears McCulloch (class of 1836), who would later attempt to build a chemical weapon for the Confederacy.[41] And he praised John Maclean Jr., then the college's vice president, for being "more of one of our regular hospitable Southern gentlemen than almost any other person with whom I have met."[42]

During the 1830s, 1840s, and 1850s Princeton became increasingly conservative on the subject of slavery. "Whilst I was a student at Nassau Hall," recalled Edward W. Smith of Alabama (class of 1848), "the political elements that existed there seemed to be entirely conservative, and friendly to the South, and no prejudice to all external appearances, existed in the minds of educated and thoughtful men, in that locality, against our institutions."[43] In 1851 Jones also conveyed to his parents that Princeton was "*very good* for the *Empire State of the South*." He noted that he and his friends had "established a Georgia table in the refectory, and enjoy a sociable meal among ourselves, served à la mode Jersey but eaten Georgia fashion, spiced with Georgia interchange of feeling."[44] To maintain this intersectional harmony, most of the students—northerners and southerners alike—avoided discussion of slavery.

"There is also one subject in particular on which your letters would be read with pleasure by parents at the South generally, and that is the subject of slavery and non-slavery being alike excluded from Princeton," said one father in Louisiana to his son in 1856.[45]

Indeed, students focused less on the nation's peculiar institution than on threats to the status quo. As Henry Craft wrote, "Our experience is that the most fanatical on both sides are the most ignorant."[46] Abolitionists in particular raised the students' ire. In 1835 John Witherspoon Woods (class of 1837), the grandson of President Witherspoon, wrote to his mother that sixty of his fellow students nearly lynched an abolitionist. The students "went down to a negro man's house, where they heard this Abolitionist was holding a meeting . . . & taking the fellow by the arms asked him to come along with them." The abolitionist "refused & told them to stand off, for he had the law on his side & that he would make use of it." The students retorted that "they had Lynch law which was sufficient for them." They proceeded to burn the abolitionist's subscription paper and force him "to run for his life" out of town.[47] Southern students also attempted to impose their own notions of racial superiority on Princeton's relatively sizable free black community. In 1846 two southern students, Grenville Peirce and Jerry Taylor, instigated a brawl between southern and northern students when they sought retribution against a local black man who had scuffled with them on the street two days earlier. One student recorded in his diary that the black man was ultimately "recaptured—taken out & whipped within an inch of his Life." And such violence, he added, elicited "the silent Satisfaction of all the arrayed Collegians from the South!"[48]

On that occasion, John Maclean Jr., a longtime professor and administrator of the college, tried to keep the southern students from disturbing the peace in Princeton. In general, though, Princeton's administrators encouraged the notion that abolitionism—not slavery—posed the most pressing threat to the preservation of peace at both the local and the national levels. In 1850 they invited U.S. Representative David Kaufman of Texas (class of 1833) to give a commencement speech. Kaufman spent much of his hour-and-a-half-long address warning the students to "beware of demagogues in the guise of Abolitionists." He called them "murderers and dis-unionists" who threatened the very existence of American life. "Abolish slavery," he exclaimed, "and after that the same men would abolish the Bible."[49]

To keep the peace during a period of mounting sectional tensions over slavery, the Princeton community agreed to disagree. As one proslavery student wrote to an antislavery friend in 1860: "Though politically we differ, and each has tried to convince the other that the Constitution does not & does recognize 'property in men,' yet in the broad platform of the Union I think we meet."[50] Some students even boasted of their tolerance for political pluralism. In 1856 Henry Kirk White Muse of Louisiana informed his father that "politics is the engrossing topic here now, and we have every class: Southern Fire-eaters, ultra-Democrats, Black Republicans, Abolitionists, old line Whigs, etc." This type of tolerance had its limits, though. "The Black Republicans and abolitionists," Muse assured, "are very few, and have sense enough to keep their principles to themselves."[51]

Princetonians promoted their community as an example for the broader American public. In one letter to his father, Muse reported that Yale—an institution of "abolition higher lawism"—had allowed the abolitionist Henry Ward Beecher to encourage students to take up arms against slaveholders.[52] "Be sure," Muse wrote, "that such a thing could never take place at Nassau Hall." He then added: "Let the Southerners come here. I believe that old Princeton College is THE College, not the college of the South, nor of the North, but the college of the *Union*."[53]

Muse may have been right about Princeton. As the Union began to rupture in November 1860, Maclean—now the president—sent a letter to the editors of the *Central Presbyterian* in Virginia, scolding them for contributing irresponsibly to the "unhappy excitement existing in some of the Southern states" by reprinting inflammatory excerpts from northern newspapers. Maclean assured the editors that the people of the North were not clamoring for conflict. "I say this the more freely," he wrote, "as I took no part in the late election for a president of the U.S." Despite his sectional impartiality, Maclean then added: "My preference was for a Southern man: but I know many influential men among the Republicans who would give no countenance to any persons or party engaged in assailing the people of the South either by word or deed."[54]

But "the college of the *Union*" could not remain intact without the Union itself. When the Union crumbled in 1861, the college community divided, too. Having endeavored for so long to make southerners feel at home in Princeton, President Maclean could only advise his students to follow their hearts in picking sides. "Remember Dr. McLean's [*sic*] advice to us when he spoke of the present agitation in our country," wrote one member of the class of 1861 to another. "He bid us [to] decide for ourselves which was right &

then go in calmly yet manfully & support our opinion at all cost."⁵⁵ With such advice in mind, southern students in 1861 began writing after their signatures "CSA"—the new abbreviation for the Confederate States of America.

The Politics of Memory

Princeton's antebellum distinctiveness as a northern institution seeking a middle ground on slavery that would placate both southern and northern students did not end with the peace at Appomattox. The Civil War monument in the entry foyer of Nassau Hall preserves in marble the school's middle path, testifying to a distinctive strain of reconciliationist memory that celebrated brotherly sacrifice over politics or moral causes and denied the very real differences over the institution of slavery that once divided North and South, not to mention the college community.⁵⁶

The northern universities honored their Civil War dead in different ways. In 1866 Brown University dedicated a tablet honoring its twenty-one Union dead. Harvard dedicated its monumental Memorial Hall, inscribed with the names of the school's 176 Union dead, in 1874. Both memorials excluded the Confederate dead in a postwar effort to honor the political and moral meaning of the Union cause. But Civil War memory shifted over time. Yale dedicated its Civil War memorial in 1915, a half-century after the war's end. It included the names of both the Union and Confederate dead, with each student's name appearing with his military affiliation and rank, as well as his place of death. The sacrifice of Confederate soldiers became the moral equivalent to the sacrifice by the men who died for the Union cause.

At Princeton University, which saw some seven hundred of her sons enlist for military duty during the Civil War, the erasure of history would be even more complete. The original plans for the university's Civil War memorial carved in 1921–22 called for the students to be grouped by their Union or Confederate affiliation. But university president John Grier Hibben rejected this plan: "No, the names shall be placed alphabetically, and no one shall know on which side these young men fought."⁵⁷ The resulting memorial is one of only a few in the nation to list the dead from both sides without indicating the cause for which they died. Well into the twentieth century, then, Princeton sought to remain a congenial home for northerners and southerners alike, emphasizing the sacrifice that drew its students together rather than the politics that pushed them apart.

Meanwhile, far away from campus, Princeton employed the politics of memory in order to regain its reputation as a welcoming oasis in the North for white southerners. In 1924 the university held its biennial convention of the Princeton Alumni Association in Atlanta, where the members promoted the university's long-standing connections with the South. They donated $1,000 toward the construction of the Confederate monument on Stone Mountain and enjoyed a tour of the site. The *Trenton Sunday Times* noted that Gutzon Borglum, the famous sculptor of the monument, had received an honorary degree from the university. The newspaper also remarked that the Alumni Association's generous "tribute" to the new Confederate monument could be considered "a memorial to the association of Princeton, from its beginning, with the South, for in antebellum days the sons of Southern families were numerously represented at the old college of New Jersey." Many of Princeton's southern students "gave their lives for the lost cause." Robert E. Lee himself, the primary subject of the Stone Mountain monument, was closely connected with Princeton, too, through his father, Henry Lee III (class of 1773).[58]

Not surprisingly, the representatives from Princeton who attended the meeting also took the opportunity to assure southerners of the university's commitment to sectional reconciliation. In a radio address broadcast from Atlanta, President Hibben stated proudly: "It might be of interest to draw attention to the fact that on the memorial tablet in Nassau Hall, our oldest college building, in memory of Princeton men who died in the Civil War, we have placed the names of men of the North and of the South in alphabetical order, indicating that they are all united without distinction in our memory."[59] In failing, at that particular moment, to grapple as an institution with the larger meanings of the Civil War, Princeton University once again proved itself a mirror to a nation that even now has not fully reckoned with the legacy of slavery.

NOTES

This essay grew out of research done for the Princeton and Slavery Project, a research effort based in an undergraduate research seminar and begun in 2013. The authors are grateful to the Princeton University Humanities Council for its generous support of the project. A fuller account of the project's findings is available at www.slavery.princeton.edu.

1. John Maclean Jr., *History of the College of New Jersey, from Its Origin in 1746 to the Commencement of 1854, Vol. I* (Philadelphia: J. B. Lippincott & Co., 1877), 263. The orig-

inal President's House is now known as Maclean House. Close examination of college records suggests that although the tree planting roughly coincided with the repeal of the Stamp Act, the project had been planned earlier.

2. "To Be Sold," *Pennsylvania Journal*, July 31, 1766, 3.

3. Jonathan Dickinson (president in 1747) purchased an enslaved girl named Genny in Elizabethtown in 1733. The bill of sale is reproduced in *Familiar Letters to a Gentleman, upon a Variety of Seasonable and Important Subjects in Religion* (Edinburgh: William Gray, 1757), 443.

Aaron Burr Sr. (1748–57) purchased an enslaved man named Caesar in 1756 shortly before moving into the President's House in Princeton. The bill of sale is reproduced in Milton Meltzer, *Slavery: A World History* (Boston: Da Capo, 1993).

Jonathan Edwards (1758) owned several slaves from the 1730s through the 1750s, including Venus (purchased in 1731), Leah (who lived in his household in 1736), Rose (who lived in the household in 1751), and Titus (listed in Edwards's 1753 will). The full text of "Receipt for Slave Venus" is reprinted in *A Jonathan Edwards Reader*, ed. John E. Smith, Harry S. Stout, and Kenneth P. Minkema (New Haven, Conn.: Yale University Press, 2003), 296–97; Kenneth P. Minkema, "Jonathan Edwards's Defense of Slavery," *Massachusetts Historical Review* 4 (2002).

Samuel Davies (1759–61) owned at least two slaves while living and working as a minister in Hanover, Virginia. The only extant evidence for his slaveholding comes from a 1755 sermon in which Davies addressed the enslaved members of his congregation and said: "You may ask my own negroes whether I treat them kindly or no." Samuel Davies, *Sermons on Important Subjects, by the Late Reverend and Pious Samuel Davies, A.M. Some Time President of the College in New Jersey* (Boston: Lincoln & Edmands, 1810), 126.

Samuel Finley (1761–66) owned several slaves while living in Princeton. After Finley's death in 1766, his executors advertised the sale of six of his slaves (two women, one man, and three children) along with other property; the sale took place at the President's House. *New York Mercury*, August 4, 1766, 3.

John Witherspoon (1768–94) owned slaves at his country home, Tusculum, near Princeton, including a "body servant" whose duties included driving Witherspoon into town. After Witherspoon's death in 1794, an inventory of his estate listed two slaves. *The Princeton Book: A Series of Sketches Pertaining to the History, Organization, and Present Condition of the College of New Jersey* (Boston: Houghton, Osgood and Company, 1879), accessed March 28, 2017, https://archive.org; John Witherspoon Records, 1772–1996, Biographical Information, box 2, Office of the President Records: Jonathan Dickinson to Harold W. Dodds Subgroup, Princeton University Archives, Department of Rare Books and Special Collections, Princeton University Library.

Samuel Stanhope Smith (1795–1812) owned at least one slave while living in Princeton, a farmhand Smith wished to sell or exchange in 1784 for "a servant accustomed to cooking and waiting in a genteel family." "To Be Sold," *New Jersey Gazette*, March 30, 1784.

Ashbel Green (1812–22) owned or hired at least three enslaved people who can be identified by name. Betsey Stockton, whom Green manumitted in 1817, had been given to his wife, Elizabeth Stockton, as a gift. In 1813 Green recorded in his diary that he "purchased the time" of a twelve-year-old boy named John and an eighteen-year-old girl named Phoebe. Diary, 1790 June 14–1800 February 21, folder 1, box 1, Princeton University Library Collection of Ashbel Green Materials, Princeton University Archives, Department of Rare Books and Special Collections, Princeton University Library.

James Carnahan (1823–54) owned two slaves under the age of fourteen in 1820 while living in Georgetown; in each federal census from 1830 to 1850, Carnahan's household included various "free colored persons" working as servants. See 1820, 1830, and 1840 federal census, accessed March 21, 2017, www.ancestry.com.

Philip Lindsley, acting president between Ashbel Green's and James Carnahan's terms as president, also owned slaves; in 1830, after moving to Tennessee, the federal census recorded three enslaved people (one man and two women) in his household. See 1830 federal census, accessed March 28, 2017, www.ancestry.com.

4. By comparison, Harvard averaged 8 percent and Yale averaged 11 percent. For more information, see Margaret Abruzzo, "A Humane Master—an Obliging Neighbor—a True Philanthropist: Slavery, Cruelty, and Moral Philosophy," *Princeton University Library Chronicle* 66 (Spring 2009): 493–512.

5. Mary Jones to Charles Colcock Jones, June 5, 1850, in Robert Manson Myers, *A Georgian at Princeton* (New York: Harcourt Brace Jovanovich, 1976), 24.

6. Researchers for the Princeton and Slavery Project cross-referenced three different sources—the university's alumni files, the nongraduate card index, and the printed editions of the annual catalogs—in order to determine the number of southern students. Each of these sources contains significant gaps, as well as contradicting and otherwise incorrect information. We therefore estimate our margin of error to be about 8 percent. For more information about our methodology, see the "Student Origins Exhibit" on the Princeton and Slavery website.

7. Henry A. Stinnecke to Winfield S. Purviance, Purviance, Winfield, 1861, box 20, Autograph Book Collection, Princeton University Archives, Department of Rare Books and Special Collections, Princeton University Library.

8. James J. Gigantino II, *The Ragged Road to Abolition: Slavery and Freedom in New Jersey, 1775–1865* (Philadelphia: University of Pennsylvania Press, 2014), 17.

9. Ibid., 68. Mercer County, where Princeton is located, was not founded until 1838.

10. *Laws of the College of New Jersey; Revised, Amended and Adopted by the Board of Trustees* (Princeton, N.J.: Printed by John T. Robinson, 1851), 24.

11. William Birney, the son of James G. Birney (class of 1810), wrote that his father could not, as a college student, avoid the subject of slavery because "it was ... daily suggested by the presence of slaves who swept the corridors of the dormitories." William Birney, *James G. Birney and His Times: The Genesis of the Republican Party with Some Account of Aboli-*

tion Movements in the South Before 1828 (New York: D. Appleton and Company, 1890), 28. But there is actually no evidence that the college itself ever owned slaves or even rented enslaved workers. It is possible, though, that the college occasionally hired contractors who used slave labor. For instance, during the late 1780s, George Morgan, the owner of the Prospect Farm, next to campus, hired a free black man named Cezar Trent to cut wood for the students at the college. Trent was a slaveholder, and he might have used his enslaved workers to complete this job. And there is no doubt that the college employed former slaves. In his autobiography, Samuel I. Prime recalled that his father, Nathaniel Scudder Prime (class of 1804), had befriended a young servant named Peter Scudder "who had been a slave in the Scudder family of Princeton." Samuel Prime then met Peter Scudder in Princeton years later. Samuel Irenaeus Prime, *Autobiography and Memorials*, ed. Wendell Prime (New York: Anson D. F. Randolph & Company, 1888), 9–11.

12. *Census for 1820* (Washington, D.C.: Printed by Gales & Seaton, 1821), 71; *The Seventh Census of the United States: 1850* . . . (Washington, D.C.: Robert Armstrong, Public Printer, 1853), 136.

13. Donated to the college in 1878, this farmland became the site of Prospect House, which served as the residence of the university president between 1879 and 1968.

14. Diary, 1790 June 14–1800 February 21, Green Materials.

15. There are several secondary sources about Betsey Stockton, including John A. Andrew III, "Betsey Stockton: Stranger in a Strange Land," *Journal of Presbyterian History* 52, no. 2 (Summer 1974): 157–66; Karen A. Johnson, "Undaunted Courage and Faith: The Lives of Three Black Women in the West and Hawaii in the Early 19th Century," *Journal of African American History* 19, no. 1 (Winter 2006): 4–22; and Eileen F. Moffett, "Betsey Stockton: Pioneer American Missionary," *International Bulletin of Missionary Research* 19, no. 2 (April 1995): 71–76.

16. After Princeton published the *Triennial Catalogue* in 1863, a newspaper reported that a total of 3,980 students had graduated from the college since its founding. Among those alumni, 748 had entered the ministry, 379 had earned a doctorate in medicine, 100 had served in the U.S. House of Representatives, 48 had served in the U.S. Senate, 31 had been state governors, 6 had been appointed to the U.S. Supreme Court, 2 had been elected vice president, and 1 had been elected president (James Madison). For more of these figures, see "College of New Jersey," *Daily Age* (Philadelphia, Pa.), November 28, 1863, 1.

17. Jonathan Edwards Jr., *The Injustice and Impolicy of the Slave-Trade, and the Slavery of the Africans* (New Haven, Conn.: Printed by John Carter, 1791), 27.

18. Abruzzo, "A Humane Master," 500–501.

19. John Murrin, preface to *Princeton, 1746–1896*, by Thomas Jefferson Wertenbaker (1946; Princeton, N.J.: Princeton University Press, 1996), xxi.

20. Mark A. Noll, *Princeton and the Republic, 1768–1822: The Search for a Christian Enlightenment in the Era of Samuel Stanhope Smith* (Vancouver: Regent College Publishing, 1989), 81.

21. Ibid., 91.

22. "To Be Sold," *New Jersey Gazette* (Trenton, N.J.), April 13, 1784, 1.

23. Samuel Stanhope Smith, *The Lectures, Corrected and Improved, Which Have Been Delivered for a Series of Years; in the College of New Jersey; on the Subjects of Moral and Political Philosophy* (Trenton, N.J.: Daniel Fenton, 1812), 2:165, 168.

24. Ibid., 2:172, 171, 176–77. For more information about Samuel Stanhope Smith's views on race, see Nicholas Guyatt, "Samuel Stanhope Smith: Was Princeton's Seventh President a Bigot, a Progressive, or Both?," *Princeton Alumni Weekly*, May 11, 2016.

25. Birney, *James G. Birney*, 26, 27.

26. Several American leaders—including Samuel Hopkins, Ezra Stiles, Thomas Jefferson, and James Monroe—had already toyed with the idea of colonizing blacks. Jefferson had even inquired whether the United States could send blacks to the British colony of Sierra Leone. For more information, see Allan Yarema, *The American Colonization Society: An Avenue to Freedom?* (Lanham, Md.: University Press of America, 2006), 5.

27. For a thorough examination into Mercer's reasoning, see Douglas R. Egerton, "'Its Origin Is Not a Little Curious': A New Look at the American Colonization Society," *Journal of the Early Republic* 5, no. 4 (Winter 1985): 463–80.

28. Douglas R. Egerton, *Charles Fenton Mercer and the Trial of National Conservatism* (Jackson: University Press of Mississippi, 1989), 31.

29. R. John Brockmann, *Commodore Robert F. Stockton, 1795–1866: Protean Man for a Protean Nation* (Amherst, N.Y.: Cambria Press, 2009), 58.

30. Inventory, John Maclean Sr., 1814, folder 11, box 4, John Maclean Jr. Papers, Princeton University Archives, Department of Rare Books and Special Collections, Princeton University Library.

31. Samuel Southard, *Address Delivered Before the Newark Mechanics' Association, July 5, 1830* (Newark, N.J.: Printed by W. Tuttle & Co., 1830), 25.

32. William Halsey to John Maclean Jr., October 24, 1842, p. 1, Papers 3: American Colonization Society, 1820–1849, folder 6, box 23, Office of the President Records: Jonathan Dickinson to Harold W. Dodds Subgroup.

33. Princeton had a Department of Law between 1847 and 1852.

34. Stephen Berry, ed., "The Diary of Henry Craft," May 9, 1848, in *Princes of Cotton: Four Diaries of Young Men in the South, 1848–1860* (Athens: University of Georgia Press, 2007), 445.

35. Ibid.

36. Ibid.

37. J. H. Muse to Henry Kirk White Muse, July 1856, in *Correspondence with My Son, Henry Kirk White Muse: Embracing Some Brief Memorials of His Character, and Essays from His Pen, Whilst a Student at Princeton College, New-Jersey*, ed. J. H. Muse (New York: John A. Gray, Printer, 1858), 160.

38. Charles C. Jones Jr. to Mrs. and Rev. C. C. Jones, September 16, 1850, in Myers, *A Georgian at Princeton*, 88.

39. John Beatty Kyle to Mary Kyle, February 12, 1851, p. 1, folder 2, box 5, John Beatty Kyle Letters, 1850–1851, Student Correspondence and Writings Collection, Princeton University Archives, Department of Rare Books and Special Collections, Princeton University Library.

40. Papers 2: Alumni Association of Nassau Hall, 1820–1879, folder 5, box 23, Office of the President Records: Jonathan Dickinson to Harold W. Dodds Subgroup.

41. Charles C. Jones Jr. to Mary Jones, June 17, 1851, in Myers, *A Georgian at Princeton*, 191.

42. Charles C. Jones Jr. to Mary Jones and Charles Colcock Jones, October 9, 1851, in Myers, *A Georgian at Princeton*, 232. Similarly, Edward Wall (class of 1848) remembered that Maclean's "character was so well known and he was so popular in the South, that it was said of him during the Civil War, that he could have gone any where in the Confederacy unchallenged." Edward Wall, *Reminiscences of Princeton College, 1845–1848* (Princeton, N.J.: Princeton University Press, 1914), 7.

43. Edward W. Smith to John Maclean Jr., April 28, 1861, 1, Series 1: Correspondence, 1794–1892, Maclean Jr. Papers.

44. Charles C. Jones Jr. to Mrs. and Rev. C. C. Jones, August 9, 1851, in Myers, *A Georgian at Princeton*, 215.

45. J. H. Muse to Henry Kirk White Muse, March 13, 1856, in Muse, *Correspondence with My Son*, 94–95.

46. Berry, "Diary of Henry Craft," May 9, 1848, 445–46.

47. John Witherspoon Woods to Mrs. Marianne Woods, September 14, 1835, 2, folder 10, box 7, John Witherspoon Woods Letters, 1835–1838, Student Correspondence and Writings Collection.

48. John Robert Buhler, "My Microscope," entry dated February 1, 1846, manuscript, Manuscripts Collection, Department of Rare Books and Special Collections, Princeton University Library.

49. "Correspondence for the State Gazette Commencement of the College of New Jersey Princeton, June 25," *State Gazette* (Trenton, N.J.), June 26, 1850, 2.

50. James J. Coale to James M. Ludlow, Ludlow, James M., 1861, box 20, Autograph Book Collection.

51. Henry Kirk White Muse to J. H. Muse, March 13, 1856, in Muse, *Correspondence with My Son*.

52. During the 1850s abolitionists often referred to their obedience to "the higher law" to justify their opposition to legal protections for the institution of slavery. The phrase itself stemmed from William H. Seward's 1850 speech "Freedom in the New Territories," in which the U.S. senator from New York famously proclaimed that "there is a higher

law than the Constitution." Seward, "Freedom in the New Territories," U.S. Congress, Senate, *Congressional Record*, 31st Cong., 1st sess., appendix, 260–69, available at "Classic Senate Speeches," United States Senate, https://www.senate.gov/artandhistory/history/resources/pdf/SewardNewTerritories.pdf, quote on 308.

53. Henry Kirk White Muse to J. H. Muse, April 5, 1856, in Muse, *Correspondence with My Son*, 113–14.

54. John Maclean Jr. to the editors of the *Central Presbyterian*, November 20, 1860, Letters, folder 3, box 17, Office of the President Records: Jonathan Dickinson to Harold W. Dodds Subgroup.

55. Thomas McGowan to Edward S. Wilde, Wilde, Edward S., 1861, box 21, Autograph Book Collection.

56. Orange Key tour guides often claim that Princeton's Civil War memorial displays an equal number of Union and Confederate dead—a testament to the genuinely "national" character of the college during the antebellum period. We now know, however, that there are as many as forty-five Princetonians who died in the war but whose names are not listed on the monument. Of the 115 known dead, at least 62 fought for the Confederacy (a total of 54 percent).

57. W. Barksdale Maynard, "Princeton in the Confederacy's Service," *Princeton Alumni Weekly*, March 23, 2011.

58. "Offer Tribute to Southern Heroes," *Trenton (N.J.) Sunday Times*, April 13, 1924, 28.

59. Ibid.

CHAPTER THREE

Proslavery Political Theory in the Southern Academy, 1832–1861

Alfred L. Brophy

> Slavery is a material element of southern power and southern polity. There is no labor so profitable, none so free from pernicious influences to society, as slave labor.... [T]o rightly defend and direct it, constitutes an important duty on the part of those who form the mind and habits of our southern youth.
>
> SUPERINTENDENT FRANCIS HENNEY SMITH,
> VIRGINIA MILITARY INSTITUTE, 1856

Given all the important findings on the presence of enslaved people at southern universities—that schools and faculty owned human beings, that they worked on campus, that students casually and viciously attacked enslaved people on campus, and that students' educations were financed by profits made from slavery—it is easy to overlook the intellectual connections of southern schools to slavery. Yet southern academics generated a lengthy set of justifications of slavery. They wrote about the history of slavery, its economic benefits, its place in constitutional and political theory, and its basis in religion and "science." They told the children of the wealthy that what the children were doing was right; and they helped propagate the belief that slavery was so central to the South that threats to it undermined the Constitution and their society. Then, as civil war threatened, some academics went to the public stage, such as pulpits and legislative halls, to urge secession. Slavery did not just sustain the southern academy; the southern academy sustained slavery.

The Academy and Slavery in the 1830s

It was a long journey to the justification of slavery. At times the academy had defended slavery in publications going back to the eighteenth century—such

WASHINGTON COLLEGE, LEXINGTON, (VA.)

This detailed image of Washington College, which appeared on Washington College stationery, gives a sense of the college's appearance shortly before the Civil War. The building in the center, Washington Hall, is where the literary societies met. Courtesy of Leyburn Library, Washington and Lee University Special Collections, Misc. Trustee Papers, box 1, folder 5.

as William Graham's defense at Washington College.[1] Sometimes the academy attacked slavery, to be sure. In the spring of 1832, not even a year after the Nat Turner rebellion, William Gaston spoke at the University of North Carolina's graduation and charged the graduates with dealing with slavery and ending it.[2] That was not much, but it reflects the sentiments of many that something needed to be done about slavery. At Washington College in Lexington, Virginia, President Henry Ruffner spoke openly against slavery in 1847. That opposition to slavery seems to have had something to do with his departure from the school the next year.[3]

Yet for many people in the South, doing something about slavery meant supporting it and making sure that it was protected against slave rebellion and attacks by abolitionists. Ralph Waldo Emerson captured the close connections of the academy and other institutions—northern and southern—to slavery in an 1851 address. "The learning of the Universities, the culture of the eloquent society, the acumen of lawyers, the majesty of the Bench, the eloquence of the Christian pulpit, the stoutness of Democracy, the respectability of the Whig party are all combined" in the proslavery mission of kidnapping a fugitive slave, Emerson told an audience in Concord, Massachusetts.[4]

The vigorous and comprehensive defense of slavery in the southern academy began when William and Mary professor Thomas Roderick Dew published an article in the September 1832 issue of the *American Quarterly Review*. Dew was writing ostensibly a review of the debates over the future of slavery in the Virginia legislature in the spring of 1832. Inspired by the Nat Turner rebellion, the legislature debated slavery's necessity, its role in the southern economy and southern society, and its evils. Some in the legislature spoke of gradual abolition. Their plans were not successful or even well developed, but the debates covered many arguments against slavery, and they drew forth proslavery arguments too. Defenders of slavery said property could not be taken away, that abolition would upend Virginia society, and that the state's economy depended on slavery. Dew synthesized the debates and added his own arguments about the economic necessity of slave labor and the profits from the sale of slaves, as well as the impracticality of the termination of slavery and colonization of formerly enslaved people. Soon the article appeared in expanded form under the title *Review of the Debate in the Virginia Legislature*.

The longest section of the *Review* was on the origins of slavery and its effects on civilization. Dew portrayed slavery as a humane alternative to killing humans captured in war and, thus, a step forward in civilization. Later, the labor that slaves provided led to agriculture and to yet higher states of civilization as enslaved people supported others. The protection of property (and particularly property in humans) was central to Dew's world, for its protection allowed markets to flourish and property owners to stabilize society. It was property—particularly property in humans—more than anything else that shaped a government's character. Slavery was, quite simply, "the principal means for impelling forward the civilization of mankind."[5]

Dew's defense of slavery was an empirically based argument. He cautioned against abstract theories of right such as "all men are born equal," "slavery in the abstract is wrong," and "the slave has a natural right to regain his liberty." "No set of legislators ever have," he thought, "or ever can, legislate upon purely abstract principles, entirely independent of circumstances, without the ruin of the body politic."[6] That focus on the particular circumstances of slavery appeared in just about all the other defenses of slavery; it set up a debate between what was practical and the world reformers dreamed about. In the process, it tried to make reforms look laughable.

Dew included a catalog of other proslavery arguments, though he did not develop them as fully as the economic argument and the argument about the impracticality of abolition and colonization. For instance, he argued that slavery supported freedom for the white community. It gave all white people a common interest and a class to labor for them. And he argued that slaves in the United States were the happiest people on earth.[7] That seems to be a subtle rebuttal of David Walker's *Appeal to the Coloured Citizens of the World*. Walker wrote that there is not a more miserable person than a slave in the United States: "We Coloured People of these United States, are, the most wretched, degraded, and abject set of beings that ever lived since the world began."[8]

Dew then turned to the impracticality of abolition. The value of humans as property simply would not allow it. Some had proposed elaborate colonization schemes, but they were doomed to failure. Virginia's 470,000 enslaved people were worth approximately $100 million—about one-third of the state's wealth. Slavery was simply too important economically to contemplate its end. And if slaves were emancipated and sent away, there would be no one left to do the work of the laboring class. Dew grimly concluded, after more pages of argument, "Virginia will be a desert."[9]

The *Review* returned to the topic of the supposed evils of slavery. Dew brought the argument back home with the suggestion that slavery was not so bad. The argument in the *Review* was an attempt to minimize the problem. He looked around, for instance, to Haiti, where slaves had freed themselves in the 1790s, and found horrible destruction of slave owners; but Dew also thought that freedom had not benefited the formerly enslaved: "The negroes have gained nothing by their bloody revolution."[10]

For one who believed slaves happy, then, it made sense to oppose the termination of such a system that brought so much good. Why should there be abolitionist agitation? Dew asked. "Why, then, since the slave is happy, and happiness is the great object of all animated creation, should we endeavor to disturb his contentment by infusing into his mind a vain and indefinite desire for liberty—a something which he cannot comprehend, and which must inevitably dry up the very sources of his happiness." More talk of abolition would just invite insurrection. And that led Dew to the conclusion that the case for slavery had been "almost as conclusive as the demonstrations of the mathematician ... that the time for emancipation has not yet arrived, and perhaps it never will." The United States had preserved liberty for some while still employing slavery. Dew's final words in the *Review* were those of opposition to change: "Let us

... learn wisdom from experience; and know that the relations of society, generated by the *lapse of ages*, cannot be altered in a *day*."[11]

Other people at William and Mary took up pieces of the defense and developed it more thoroughly, particularly the arguments about slavery's importance to politics. Dew's William and Mary colleague Nathaniel Beverley Tucker focused on the importance of slavery to white freedom. In a lecture on William Blackstone's discussion of slavery, Tucker argued that slavery makes freedom possible for whites; otherwise, whites could not abide universal democracy. Moreover, it kept the laboring class laboring and thus made it possible to have all white people above the slaves voting. Tucker, like Dew, made a bold statement about the utility of slavery: "It has done more to elevate a degraded race in the scale of humanity; to tame the savage; to civilize the barbarous; to soften the ferocious; to enlighten the ignorant; and to spread the blessing of Christianity among the heathen, than all the missionaries that philanthropy and religion have ever sent forth."[12] Two key proslavery arguments appeared in Tucker's lecture. First, slaves were taken care of by their owners, while employers of free workers did not care for them. Thus, slavery was good for the slaves. Second, slavery preserved freedom for white people. While we might think that linking freedom to slavery is paradoxical, there was a long lineage to the belief that they went hand in hand. And therein lies an unusual story.

Tucker traced the lineage of slavery's "contribution" to the idea of freedom to Edmund Burke, who was a member of Parliament during the American Revolution. Burke's "Speech on Conciliation with the American Colonies," which he delivered in March 1775—just before the outbreak of war in April 1775—summarized the reasons why the American colonies were so attached to the idea of liberty. Some of the reasons had to do with Americans' heritage of liberty and with religious attitudes in the North, and others with Americans' respect for Anglo-American law. Burke also credited the institution of slavery as another cause of Americans' respect for liberty. Slavery in Virginia and the Carolinas led the masters there to have respect for freedom because of the benefits that slavery conferred on them.[13]

The Shift to the Focus on Natural Inequality

The argument about slavery's support for white republicanism was heard right up to the Civil War. Most notably, Senator James Henry Hammond of South Carolina used it in his 1858 "mud sill" speech. But Hammond's primary point was that enslaved people provided labor and thus supported the economic life of the white ruling class. Thus, Hammond embellished the argument about the political benefits of slavery from the 1830s by emphasizing the economic and social benefits of slavery.[14] In the 1840s and 1850s proslavery political theory largely shifted away from talk of slavery's service to republican government in two ways. First, there was an expansion of the argument that slavery is good for the enslaved. Second, and closely related to the first, is the idea that there is a hierarchy inherent in nature and that not all people are fit for freedom.

In 1852 Professor William Porcher Miles of the College of Charleston delivered an address to students titled *Republican Government Not Everywhere and Always the Best; and Liberty Not the Birthright of Mankind*. Miles mocked Thomas Jefferson's statement in the Declaration of Independence that all people are created equal as a "monstrous and dangerous fallacy." Instead, Miles thought that freedom "must be rooted in the nature, manners and habits, no less than the thoughts and affections, of a People."[15] This was an indictment of universal freedom and an endorsement of slavery. Two years later, in an address to the William and Mary literary societies in 1854, lawyer John Randolph Tucker spoke in similar terms of the need to calibrate the amount of freedom a people had to their social status. He replaced the Enlightenment-era understanding that all people are created equal with another formulation: some people are not fit for freedom. This was a political theory based on inequality.

> The man who writes constitutions by the dozen, and keeps them on hand for use or distribution, without a careful investigation of the social capacities of the people for whom they are designed—he who *guesses* that our institutions would be admirably suited for China or Japan, or that our federative system of republics would work with facility and success under a President Roberts upon the coast of Africa, is a dangerous empiric—a mere pretender, whose reward should be fixed in perpetual banishment from the counsel of a wise people. And in the solitude of an asylum for political lunatics.[16]

University of Virginia professor Albert Taylor Bledsoe's 1856 treatise, *An Essay on Liberty and Slavery*, expanded on the political theory of slavery. Bledsoe argued that because some people were only fit for slavery, a restriction on them was appropriate. Slavery for people fit best for slavery was, in Bledsoe's mind, justified, and those restrictions on some led to greater freedom for the remaining free population. The rights of free people were not interfered with by the slaves.[17] This completed the southern turn away from Jefferson; after Bledsoe, it was slavery that was the natural condition of many. Far from Jefferson's aspiration that all people are created equal, there was the belief that people were inherently unequal and that their amount of personal autonomy should be calculated accordingly.

Similar ideas were promulgated in addresses of politicians to colleges as well. For instance, Robert Toombs, who served as a U.S. senator from Georgia from 1853 to 1861 (and then as a general in the Confederacy), defended slavery in an address given to the Few and Phi Gamma literary societies at Emory College in Oxford, Georgia, in 1853. He found that slavery gave more stability to the South than anywhere else. Slavery was responsible for the order of the world. Nevertheless, he understood that many disagreed with his assessment, so his purpose was to "vindicate the wisdom, humanity, and justice of the system, to show that the position of the African race in it, is consistent with its principles [and] advantageous to that race and society." Then followed an investigation of history, ranging from the American colonies, where slavery was commonplace, back to ancient Egypt, where the ancient monuments "furnish evidence both of [the African's] national identity and his social degradation before history began." Toombs depicted Africans as suited only to slavery: "We find him then without government, or laws, or protection, without letters, or arts, or industry, without religion, or even the aspirations which would raise him to the rank of an idolator." Toombs pointed to Haiti, the British West Indies, and Jamaica and claimed that experiments in freedom in those places similarly showed the incapacity of enslaved Africans for freedom. Yet when he turned to the American South he found that the slave population was increasing, a sign of the success of the institution. Toombs presented both a concise and a broad defense of slavery. His simple conclusion was that "the adoption of no other system under our circumstances would have exhibited the individual man (bond or free) in a higher development, or a society in a happier civilization."[18]

Students seemed to learn these lessons. In their literary journal, the *Virginia University Magazine*, students at the University of Virginia revealed many of the same ideas as their professors, such as James Holcombe, Albert Taylor Bledsoe, and George Frederick Holmes. The magazine attacked Jefferson's Declaration and turned to slavery's history as demonstration that hierarchy is inherent in nature and that not everyone is suited to freedom. Slavery hung over students' discussion of politics, history, and economics—as the author of a *Virginia University Magazine* article wrote, slavery "is the great problem of the nineteenth century."[19] The students wrote about history's lessons, which showed that change is difficult and would take centuries to accomplish. In addition to their discussion of slavery's history, they looked to other eras of history for lessons. They turned to the much-maligned feudal era to show that it produced positive benefits for society such as a respect for property, enabling English merchants to purchase their freedom from the Crown. But the emergence from feudalism took centuries—just as the termination of slavery would.

The Natural Law Argument in Favor of Slavery

This new political theory appeared in perhaps its strongest form in a lecture entitled "Is Slavery Consistent with Natural Law?" given in Petersburg in 1858 by University of Virginia professor James Holcombe.[20] The lecture built on Bledsoe's theory—and also on that of law professor Henry St. George Tucker, whose lectures argued for the consistency of slavery with natural law.[21] Bledsoe claimed that the Anglo-Saxon race was entitled to freedom and that people of African descent were not and might very well never be entitled to freedom. This was in distinction to those who, like Jefferson and William Blackstone, said that slavery was inconsistent with natural law. Holcombe, a supporter of natural law, argued that the common law should protect slavery. His final argument was that because slavery is consistent with natural law, the North should tolerate slavery and stop trying to abolish it.

The pieces of this theory were put together just before the Civil War by Thomas R. R. Cobb in his 1858 book *An Inquiry into the Law of Negro Slavery in the United States*. He intentionally joined history, economics, and the contemporary "science" of race to make the case for continued slavery. In fact, the first paragraph of the book begins by linking history to the cause of understanding law: "Philosophy is the handmaid, and frequently the most successful expounder of the law. History is the groundwork and only sure basis of philosophy. To understand aright, therefore, the law of Slavery, we must not be ignorant of its history."[22] Much as Dew had done nearly three decades before, Cobb synthesized the proslavery argument. The differences between those two texts illustrate how the arguments changed over time. Like Dew, Cobb dwelt on the history of slavery to show that it was nearly ubiquitous in human history and that emancipation frequently led to disastrous economic results for the community of slave-owners and sometimes disastrous demographic results. Dew and Cobb made similar points, but they also each had different points of emphasis. When Cobb wrote about enslaved people he often depicted them as childlike and thus not fit for freedom. He also claimed that they were well taken care of by their owners and thus were better off as slaves. Dew also made those arguments, but Cobb focused on slaves' limitations and the benefits of slavery for the enslaved, while Dew focused more on the benefits of slavery for white people. Thus, the later and much longer work was more in line with the recent arguments about political theory. This shift may also reflect, perhaps, the power of the antislavery critique. Proslavery writers may have felt compelled to respond to the images of black humanity and dignity that were proving so powerful for the cause of abolition.[23]

The first half of Cobb's book was devoted to an exploration of the history of slavery throughout human history, stretching from ancient Egypt, Greece, and Rome through the emancipation in the West Indies. It was an empirical study that drew on history, contemporary economics, and anthropological pseudoscience. Cobb relied heavily upon research by the contributors to Josiah Nott and George Gliddon's edited volume *Types of Mankind* (1854) to argue that Africans had been slaves since the days of ancient Egypt. Africans had always been enslaved, so the argument in *Types of Mankind* went, and seemingly should be enslaved. For instance, Cobb discussed one of Gliddon's chapters from *Types of Mankind* that referred to tomb inscriptions in ancient Egypt that supposedly showed enslaved Africans from thousands of years before. In fact, *Types of Mankind* collected data from many places, from tomb inscriptions to cranial measurements, to make a case for white supremacy and racial hierarchy. The book's argument was that Africans were inferior, always had been, and would continue to be. Nott and Gliddon asked, "Have 3400 years, or any transplantation altered the NEGRO race?"[24]

The arguments of Nott and Gliddon had obvious political and legal implications. In the introduction to *Types of Mankind*, Nott wrote about how Senator John C. Calhoun of South Carolina had met with Gliddon and had seen the relevance of the book's ideas about the "science" of racial distinctions to debates about slavery.[25] Nott, Gliddon, and others who wrote about biological differences between races were providing a "scientific" justification of racial hierarchy. In this way, science was seen as justifying the political theory that some must labor for others rather than the theory that all people are equal.

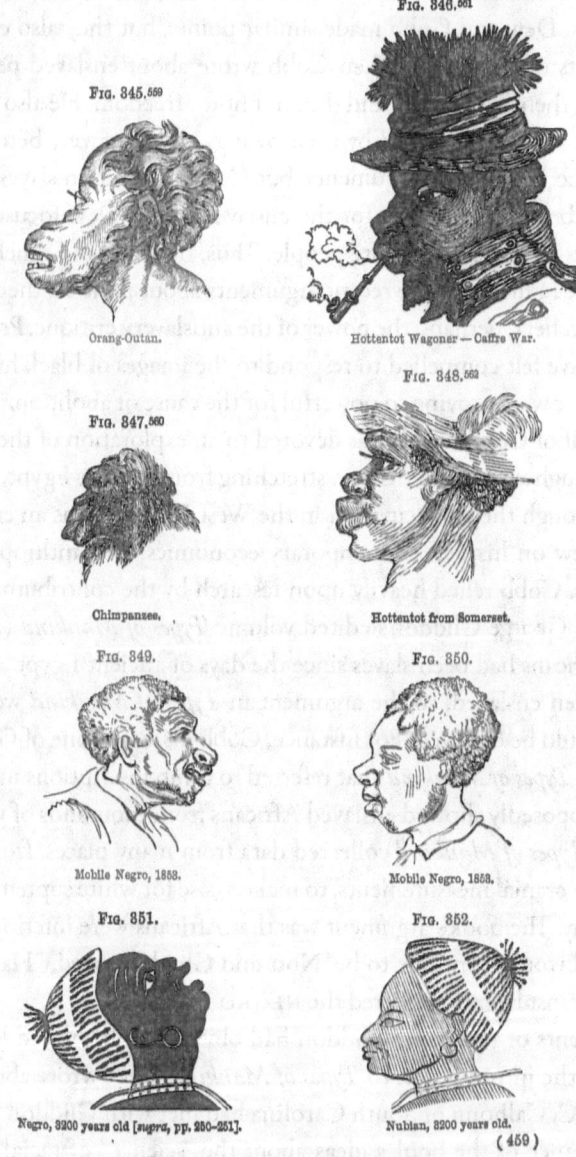

This plate was designed to show supposed physical continuities over time between people in ancient Africa and people of African ancestry in the United States, as well as point out supposed physical similarities between people of African ancestry and nonhuman primates. J. C. Nott and George R. Gliddon, *Types of Mankind, Or Ethnographical Researches* (Philadelphia: Lippincott, Grambo and Company, 1854), 459.

Hugh A. Garland, a onetime classics professor at Hampden-Sydney College and later one of the lawyers for Dred Scott's owner in the Missouri suit seeking Scott's freedom, also picked up on the theory proposed by Nott and Gliddon. Garland wrote an extensive proslavery treatise. The book, which remained uncompleted at Garland's premature death in 1854, drew explicitly from *Types of Mankind* and from the work of Samuel Henry Dickson, founder of the South Carolina Medical College, whose work included a pamphlet entitled *Remarks on Certain Topics Connected with the General Subject of Slavery*.[26] From various historical and "scientific" arguments, Garland concluded, "Wherever we find the African, at whatever point in history or at whatever place on his own continent or in America, we find the same marked physical and moral traits, and the same condition of inferiority and servility."[27] Chief Justice Roger Taney's opinion in the *Dred Scott* decision reveals the legal implications of such ideas of hierarchy. When Taney wrote that people of African descent were not citizens of the United States, he was using law to reinforce the proslavery doctrine of white supremacy. Justice Peter V. Daniel's concurrence in *Dred Scott* drew in particular upon the historical arguments made popular by works like *Types of Mankind*: "The following are truths which a knowledge of the history of the world, and particularly of that of our own country, compels us to know—that the African negro race ... has been by all the nations of Europe regarded as subjects of capture or purchase, as subjects of commerce or traffic; and that the introduction of that race into every section of this country was not as members of civil or political society, but as slaves, as *property* in the strictest sense of the term."[28] Ideas of "science" and hierarchy appeared in other judicial opinions, too. One particularly vicious opinion from Mississippi in 1859 denied the wishes of a slave owner who wanted to leave property to his formerly enslaved daughter (whom he had freed in Ohio). The opinion, which cited Cobb's *Inquiry into the Law of Negro Slavery*, refused to give effect to the emancipation in Ohio. The judge, demonstrating the influence of the "science" of race that likened Africans to apes, asked what would happen if Ohio gave citizenship rights to orangutans.[29]

Cobb not only drew on the scientific literature of race but also contributed to it through a survey of the governors of northern states in which he inquired about free people in those states. Cobb may have modeled his survey on the research of Georgia Supreme Court Justice Ebenezer Starnes, who argued that enslaved people committed fewer crimes than free people of African descent in the North.[30] Cobb used vignettes from people he knew to suggest that enslaved people were part of the family and were treated well.[31] All of this aimed to show that slavery was the natural condition of people of African descent, that it was the appropriate condition of the enslaved, and that slaves and their white owners would suffer by emancipation. In essence, slavery was the natural order of things, and the law should support this natural order. Cobb thus presented the deeply conservative argument that, to borrow Alexander Pope's phrase, "whatever is, is right."

Cobb thus brought together just about all the strands of proslavery thought. He encapsulated the ideas about history and empiricism that led southerners to think that Enlightenment truths were unsuited to their society. This focus on specific circumstances, designed to show that reform is impracticable or impossible, is common to conservative thought. It turned adherents from the idea that there might be a better future—without slavery—to the idea that slavery was indispensable to southern society. And when there were challenges to slavery, those adherents, like Cobb, felt justified—indeed compelled—to take action to protect their society.

Justifying the Academy Because the Academy Justified Slavery

The academy was thus a generator and a disseminator of proslavery political theory. In fact, one of the key justifications of southern universities was their role in teaching students to defend slavery and in generating scholarship that defended slavery. University of Virginia law professor James Holcombe's 1853 address to alumni justified the university in part because of its role in producing scholarship defending southern institutions. It was not just that schools taught slavery, such as William Smith's course on the philosophy of slavery for seniors at Randolph-Macon College in Boydton, Virginia. They also generated proslavery literature. Holcombe went further and asked the alumni society for more faculty who could produce southern literature. Until "a class of native authors, Southern born and Southern bred," arrive to explain slavery, "the rest of the world" will never understand slavery. Harriet Beecher Stowe's *Uncle Tom's Cabin* had been out for only a short while when Holcombe addressed the alumni, but already it disclosed "the most formidable danger which crosses our line of future march." Holcombe spoke in apocalyptic terms: "We shall divide the public opinion of the world, break the force of its sympathy, and by pouring through the bosoms of our people the living tide of hope, strengthen their hearts for the day of trial, and cover our land and its institutions with a shield of fire."[32]

Such themes were heard often at southern schools in the 1840s and 1850s. When Joseph Taylor, a lawyer and newspaper editor, spoke at the University of Alabama in 1847 he focused particular attention on the utility of the University to Alabama in defending southern values. Taylor saw southern colleges, the southern pulpit, and the southern press as the defenders of slavery:

> The sons of the South are its legitimate, its reliable, and its appointed defenders; and, in the Universities of the South, they must be imbued with the skill and force in the use of the weapons of reason necessary to the high encounter to which they are called. If they be educated elsewhere, may they not imbibe the doctrines of our assailants, and thus, returning to us in the guise of friends, help to drag over the walls and into the very citadel of our domestic Troy, some fatal horse pregnant with the impediments of fanatic propagandists and unreformed reformers?[33]

Prime among the justifications for studying at the University of Alabama was its support for slavery. As Taylor said, "The University is useful in enabling the State to protect the peculiar rights and institutions which belong to it, as one of the Plantation States of the South."[34] The institution of slavery was essential to southern wealth, it was protected by the Constitution, and it was morally right. But the South was under attack by those who held a "misguided philanthropy."

From Academy to Statehouse

The prevalence of these ideas in the South raises the question of which ways the arrows of influence pointed. Proslavery ideas appeared in many places—legislative halls, pulpits, courts, newspapers, and college lecture halls. Many of the arguments heard in college classrooms echoed those already appearing in the halls of Congress and in newspapers. Sometimes the colleges were the places where the ideas were put together most comprehensively, such as by Thomas Dew at William and Mary, Thomas R. R. Cobb at the Lumpkin Law School, and William R. Smith at Randolph-Macon College. Even though those arguments reflected ideas already popular outside the academy, the academy helped to unify the arguments—such as with Dew's *Review of the Debate* and Cobb's *Inquiry into the Law of Negro Slavery*—and served as a distribution point for proslavery ideas. In short, as the university generated and disseminated ideas it helped create the environment for secession.

The importance of southern academics to the proslavery cause appears in Reverend John L. Girardeau's 1860 graduation address at the College of Charleston. He feared that the "Constitution and law of the land have lost their force and commanding authority" because so many thought that the Bible commanded antislavery action. Yet Girardeau found "the institution which [the Constitution] upholds is sanctioned by that law." He invoked eight southern writers, four of whom were academics—Randolph-Macon's William Smith, the University of Virginia's Albert Taylor Bledsoe, William and Mary's Thomas Roderick Dew, and Columbia Theological Seminary's James Henley Thornwell—to establish the southern position on the lawfulness of slavery and its consistency with the Bible.[35]

Following the election of Lincoln in November 1860, academics worked along with others to make the case for a southern nation. On November 12, 1860, Cobb urged his state to take further action. Cobb's speech was both legal and political. It proceeded from a legal question: Was Lincoln's election unconstitutional? And it worked its way up to legal, moral, historical, and political arguments for secession. Cobb had a hard argument here, because Lincoln's election met the requirements of the Constitution. Yet Cobb believed that the election was unconstitutional because it violated the spirit (if not the letter) of the Constitution. The election was brought about in part by African Americans, people who were not qualified to be citizens of the United States; it imposed the antislavery majority of the North on the proslavery minority of the South. Cobb portrayed the horrors of abolition: the attack upon slavery in the churches and in Congress; the distribution of abolitionist literature through the U.S. mail; the creation of the underground railroad, which assisted slaves to escape; and John Brown's attempted slave insurrection. Cobb saw no end to the abolitionists' efforts.

In fact, history taught him there would be no end. Here again Cobb drew on historical understanding to predict that abolitionists would never voluntarily go away. He turned to examples from ancient history to modern times and from India to Great Britain to show the power of fanaticism. Fanaticism had caused Rome to destroy Jerusalem and Mary, Queen of Scots, to kill hundreds of Protestants. Cobb cited the story that in India some believers in Vishnu threw themselves under the carriage that held an image of the god, the "Idol of the Juggernaut," hoping to die and go to heaven. In a distinct echo of the first page of his treatise, Cobb concluded that fanatics frequently draw blood in the delusion that they were doing what God commands: "Such is the teaching of philosophy, and history, her handmaid, confirms its truth."[36] Cobb concluded with an appeal to Georgia to take the lead in secession.

In March 1861 James Holcombe, then a member of the Virginia legislature, urged that body to secede. He believed that Lincoln's election posed grave dangers to southern slavery. He opened his speech with the image of a ship in the North Atlantic threatened by icebergs. Slavery was central to southern society, and if it was not protected, then "all we love and value may perish." There was a threat to slavery in Lincoln's election and, therefore, to southern society. Holcombe framed the case for secession in historical and constitutional terms during his address to the legislature. These were the terms of debate that he and others had developed and promulgated.[37]

Why, though, would Holcombe, who recognized those dangers to his society, opt for war? The South had so much of what it wanted. It controlled the Supreme Court. The *Dred Scott* decision just four years before had established the constitutional principle that slavery would be protected robustly. The decision's implications were many. Congress could do nothing to hinder slavery in the territories, the states, or probably Washington, D.C., either. There was more wealth in human beings than in any other kind of property than land. The South had disproportionate voting power because of the Constitution's three-fifths compromise. Even if, as many people believed, slavery would not flourish in the territories, it was solidly protected in the southern states by the Constitution and by voters. In some places in the West, slavery continued to do well. Why go to war? The short answer was that slavery was central to southern society and needed to be protected.

> The institution of slavery is so indissolubly interwoven with the whole framework of society in a large portion of our State, and constitutes so immense an element of material wealth and political power to the whole Commonwealth that its subversion through the operation of any unfriendly policy on the part of the Federal Government, whether that operation is extended over a long or short period of time, would, of necessity, dry up the very fountains of the public strength, change the whole frame of our civilization and inflict a mortal wound upon our liberties.[38]

That is, there was a threat to slavery in Lincoln's election and, therefore, to southern society. Holcombe framed the case for secession in constitutional terms during his address to the legislature. He had spoken in similar terms in an address to voters in his home near Charlottesville in January 1860. Holcombe explained that the South was preparing for war—was "in arms"—"because recent events have convinced the most unbelieving amongst us that there is danger to our constitutional rights in the Union, and because, to a man, people are resolved to maintain those rights." In fact, the Constitution was central to his thinking; it structured his understanding of the crisis. He worried that the Constitution was the last protection for the South and that the new Supreme Court justices would be converted to antislavery principles. The result would be the abolition of slavery in the District of Columbia and the invalidation of the Fugitive Slave Act. Holcombe predicted that the changes to constitutional law would come through appointments to the executive and judicial branches: "So long as Northern sentiment upon African slavery remains unaltered, the Constitution, as it stands, furnishes us no permanent security against Northern injustice. Upon the election of a Black Republican President, the Supreme Court will be the only remaining outwork of our constitutional independence; and that, if not stormed by legislation, must crumble as rapidly as human life."[39] The southern proslavery academics emphasized a series of ideas—a turn to history and to contemporary economics, as well as the centrality of property rights, to argue for slavery. Those ideas were then used to explain the southern move toward secession. Academics' extensive writings thus help us understand how southerners themselves looked at the world and how they spoke as they moved to secession and war.

The war was brought on by the ideas of slavery and property that southern lawyers and judges—and so many others, too—believed in. In some cases, the very people who made those arguments in the academy appeared at the center of the secession movement. Some, like Thomas Cobb, went on to take up arms to defend the Confederacy. Cobb died on the battlefield at Fredericksburg in 1862. Among the many unexpected storylines of the southern academics, politicians, and jurists who developed arguments to support their proslavery world and then followed those ideas to the point of war, this one is perhaps most important. Those who went to war to preserve slavery hastened the demise of slavery and a new birth of freedom for our nation, as four million human beings who had entered the war as slaves left it as free people.

NOTES

Epigraph taken from *Report of the Board of Visitors and Superintendent of the Virginia Military Institute, July 1856* (1856), 24.

1. David W. Robson, "'An Important Question Answered': William Graham's Defense of Slavery in Post-revolutionary Virginia," *William and Mary Quarterly* 37, no. 4 (October 1980): 644–52.

2. See William Gaston, *Address Delivered Before the Philanthropic and Dialectic Societies at Chapel Hill, June 20, 1832* (Raleigh, N.C.: Jos. Gales & Son, 1832), 14.

3. Alfred L. Brophy, *University, Court, and Slave: Proslavery Thought in Southern Colleges and Courts and the Coming of Civil War* (New York: Oxford University Press, 2016), 53.

4. Ralph Waldo Emerson, "The Fugitive Slave Law: Address to the Citizens of Concord, 3 May, 1851," in *The Complete Works of Ralph Waldo Emerson* (Boston: Houghton, Mifflin and Company, 1904), 11:177.

5. *Review of the Debate in the Virginia Legislature of 1831 and 1832* (Richmond: T. W. White, 1832), reprinted as "Professor Dew on Slavery," in *The Pro-slavery Argument: As Maintained by the Most Distinguished Writers* ... (Charleston: Walker, Richards & Co. 1852), 287, 312, quote at 325.

6. Ibid., 355.

7. Ibid., 459.

8. David Walker, *Appeal to the Coloured Citizens of the World*, 3rd ed. (Boston: David Walker, 1830), 9.

9. *Review of the Debate*, 356, 357–58, 365–66, 384.

10. Ibid., 440.

11. Ibid., 459–60, 467, 489, 490.

12. [Nathaniel Beverley Tucker,] "A Note to Blackstone's Commentaries," *Southern Literary Messenger* 1, no. 5 (January 1835): 227.

13. Edmund Burke, "Speech on Conciliation with the American Colonies," paragraph 42, reprinted in *Edmund Burke's Speech on Conciliation with the American Colonies Delivered in the House of Commons March 22, 1775*, ed. William I. Crane (New York: D. Appleton and Company, 1908), 75–76; Tucker, "Note," 230.

14. James Henry Hammond, "Speech of Hon. James H. Hammond, of South Carolina, on the Admission of Kansas, under the Lecompton Constitution: Delivered in the Senate of the United States, March 4, 1858," Washington, D.C., 1858, reprinted in *Selections from the Letters and Speeches of the Hon. James H. Hammond, of South Carolina* (New York: John F. Trow & Co., 1866).

15. William Porcher Miles, *Republican Government Not Everywhere and Always the Best; and Liberty Not the Birthright of Mankind: An Address Delivered Before the Alumni Society of the College of Charleston ... March 30th, 1852* (Charleston: Walker & James, 1852), 24, 26.

16. *Address of John Randolph Tucker, Delivered before the Phoenix and Philomathean Societies, of William and Mary College, on the 3d of July, 1854. Pub. at the request of the two societies,* 11.

17. Albert Taylor Bledsoe, *An Essay on Liberty and Slavery* (Philadelphia: J. B. Lippincott & Co., 1856).

18. Robert Toombs, *An Oration, Delivered Before the Few and Phi Gamma Societies, of Emory College, at Oxford, Ga., July 1853* (Augusta: Chronicle & Sentinel, 1853), 810–11, 26.

19. "The Utility of Slavery Discussion," *University Literary Magazine* 1, no. 1 (December 1856): 25, 30. See also "Cannibals All, Or, Slaves Without Masters," *University Literary Magazine* 1, no. 5 (May 1857): 193–99; "Government a Divine Institution," *Virginia University Magazine* 4, no. 6 (March 1860): 326; "The Effect of the Holy Wars upon Civilization," *University Literary Magazine* 1, no. 6 (June 1857): 260; "Man's Rights—Man's Progress," *Virginia University Magazine* 2 (October 1857): 310–14.

20. James P. Holcombe, "Is Slavery Consistent with Natural Law?" *Southern Literary Messenger* 27, no. 6 (December 1858): 401–21.

21. John Randolph Tucker is the son of Henry St. George Tucker, and J. Beverly Tucker is Henry St. George Tucker's brother.

22. Thomas R. R. Cobb, *An Inquiry into the Law of Negro Slavery in the United States* (Philadelphia: T. & W. Johnson, 1858), xxxv.

23. See, for example, Sarah N. Roth, *Gender and Race in Antebellum Popular Culture* (New York: Cambridge University Press, 2014); Alfred L. Brophy, "Antislavery Women and the Origins of American Jurisprudence," *Texas Law Review* 94, no. 1 (November 2015): 115, 119–22.

24. Josiah Nott and George Gliddon, eds., *Types of Mankind: or, Ethnological Researches, Based upon the Ancient Monuments, Paintings, Sculptures, and Crania of Races, and upon Their Natural, Geographical, Philological, and Biblical History* (Philadelphia: J. B. Lippincott & Co., 1854), 256.

25. Ibid., 51, discussing Calhoun's use of ideas of racial differences in his letter to William Rufus King of Alabama and U.S. ambassador to France at the time.

26. Samuel Henry Dickson, *Remarks On Certain Topics Connected with the General Subject of Slavery* (Charleston: Office Press, 1845).

27. Hugh A. Garland, "Treatise on Slavery" (ca. 1854), 2:36, Garland Family Papers, Library of Virginia. See also Alfred L. Brophy, "Slaves as Plaintiffs," *Michigan Law Review* 115, no. 6 (April 2017): 895, 913 (discussing Garland's treatise).

28. Scott v. Sanford, 57 U.S. (15 How.) 393, 475 (1857) (Daniel, concurring).

29. Mitchell v. Well, 37 Miss. 235, 260 (1859) (quoting Cobb's *An Inquiry*), 264 (asking whether Mississippi would be expected to grant comity to Ohio if it granted citizenship to "the chimpanzee or the ourang-outang").

30. Cobb, *An Inquiry*, cci–ccv and note 7 on cciv (referring to Ebenezer Starnes's work,

which is reprinted in an appendix to Starnes's epistolary novel, *The Slaveholder Abroad* [Philadelphia: J. B. Lippincott & Co., 1860], 465–510).

31. Cobb wrote, for instance, that "on my father's plantation an aged negro woman could call together more than one hundred of her lineal descendants. I saw this old negro dance at the wedding of her great-granddaughter. She did no work for my father for more than forty years before her death" (*An Inquiry*, ccxviii).

32. James P. Holcombe, *Address to the Alumni of the University of Virginia* (Richmond: MacFarlane and Fergusson, 1853).

33. Joseph Taylor, *A Plea for the University of Alabama: An Address Delivered before the Erosophic and Philomathic Societies of the University of Alabama on Their Anniversary Occasion, August 9, 1847* (Tuscaloosa: M. D. J. Slade, 1847), 25.

34. Ibid., 23.

35. John L. Girardeau, *Conscience and Civil Government: An Oration Delivered Before the Society of Alumni of the College of Charleston . . . March 27th, 1860* (Charleston: Evans & Cogswell, 1860).

36. Thomas Read Rootes Cobb, *Substance of Remarks Made by Thomas R. R. Cobb, Esq.: In the Hall of the House of Representatives, Monday Evening, November 12, 1860* (Atlanta: John H. Seals, 1860), reprinted in *Secession Debated: Georgia's Showdown in 1860*, ed. William W. Freehling and Craig M. Simpson (New York: Oxford University Press, 1992), 5, 21.

37. *Proceedings of the Virginia State Convention of 1861* (Richmond: George H. Reese, 1961), 2:75.

38. Ibid., 2:76.

39. James P. Holcombe, *The Election of a Black Republican President an Overt Act of Aggression on the Right of Property in Slaves* (Richmond: C. H. Wynne, 1860), 12, 15.

CHAPTER FOUR

Negotiating the Honor Culture

Students and Slaves at Three Virginia Colleges

Jennifer Bridges Oast

His honor was at stake. In 1769 John Byrd, a student at William and Mary, had called for a slave who worked for the college, and the slave did not comply. Only an immediate show of dominance could counter this offense and save Byrd's reputation. William and Mary's faculty minutes tell the story:

> John Byrd, after calling for a Servant which was at that Time employ'd by the House keeper in the Hall, came into the said Hall with a Horsewhip in his hand and taking hold of his Servant, with his whip lifted up threaten'd to whip him if he did not immediately go with him, the Housekeeper answer'd "that he should not;" upon which the said Byrd replied, "that if she were in the Boy's Place, he would horsewhip her also;" to which she said, "It was more than he dared to do," she supposing that he threaten'd to horsewhip her.... Resolved unanimously, that John Byrd, out of regard to his general better deportment be forgiven the above very ill behavior on condition that he ask pardon of the President for... disobedience of their order and ill treatment of their Servant.[1]

Young Byrd felt he had the right to command the labor of this slave despite the fact that the slave belonged to the school, not to him. As a young man of wealth and status in the deeply hierarchical society of 1760s Virginia, Byrd would also have felt that his right to command the college's slave superseded that of the housekeeper. In this altercation, Byrd's honor and manhood were doubly threatened by both the bondsman and the lower-status woman if Byrd did not get his way. This is perhaps one reason why the faculty who looked into this incident decreed forgiveness for Byrd as long as he asked forgiveness of the college president—not, of course, the housekeeper or the slave. Submitting to the discipline of his college president would not tarnish his reputation; apologizing to the housekeeper or the slave certainly would.

Virginia before the Civil War was a society where upper-class men valued their honor very highly. One way to understand the relations between students and slaves on Virginia campuses is to examine how honor and dishonor functioned in Virginia society. This essay looks at how honor shaped the experiences of male students and male slaves at three schools, the College of William and Mary, Hampden-Sydney College, and the University of Virginia, as well as the unique economic and educational opportunities male slaves owned or employed by these schools seized despite a campus culture that sought to emasculate and dishonor them. Orlando Patterson demonstrates that "dishonor" is a key part of the definition of slavery throughout human history. The compulsion about honor that John Byrd exhibits in 1769 was driven in part by the fact that Virginia was a slave society in which the socioeconomic structures of society were based on slavery. Patterson asserts that "wherever slavery became structurally very important, the whole tone of the slave holder's culture tended to be highly honorific."[2] This was certainly the case in old Virginia, and its colleges were the proving grounds where young men of the upper class defined themselves as "honorable" men.

Slaves who were owned or hired by Virginia colleges from the colonial era through the Civil War negotiated a minefield daily as they attempted to complete work assigned them by college officials while also frequently coming into conflict with students who wanted their own honor recognized and enhanced by the obedience and humility of the slaves around them. Patterson argues that masters gained honor by wielding power over slaves, while the slaves were dishonored in return: "What was universal in the master-slave relationship was the strong sense of honor the experience of mastership generated, and conversely, the dishonoring of the slave condition." Writing of the Greek experience specifically, Patterson also asserts: "Slaves did more than help in meeting material needs, they also satisfied a psychological need to dominate."[3] Students did not own the college-owned slaves they attempted to control, but they did not need to do so in order to receive the social benefits of mastery. They could take liberties with slaves working on campus that they rarely would have with another man's slaves because institutionally owned or controlled slaves were overseen by men and women with a limited interest (economic or otherwise) in them.

In order for the students to enhance their honor, the slaves had to be dishonored. Many slaves working on campus, like all slaves, probably did act in the prescribed ways that signaled acceptance of their "dishonored" place.

However slaves presented themselves before students, other actions of many slaves on college campuses show that they worked to establish their own honor through seizing economic and educational opportunities that were available to them as slaves working at a college.

When the University of Virginia opened in 1825, the board of visitors, a group of prominent men chosen to oversee the governance and finances of the new university, also decided to hire and purchase slave labor, and the same patterns of violence and abuse that began at William and Mary were repeated on the new campus. The board of visitors hired a janitor (sometimes a slave and sometimes a free black) whose main duties were to ring the bells in the Rotunda at dawn to wake the students and then, according to a former student, to "visit the dormitories in the morning and report violations of the law requiring students to rise early. This was sufficient to make him a man of many sorrows." Why a man of sorrows? The young men at the university were often not pleased at being awakened at dawn, as the university required. As a result, the poor janitor was "often the object of the malevolent humor of the disturbed student; bucketfuls of water descended upon him from the doortops, where they had been balanced with diabolical skill, or other unwelcome attentions were bestowed upon him."[4] This former student recalled the questionable treatment of an African American janitor in a humorous tone, but the situation might have been described much differently from the janitor's point of view. A black janitor was given the responsibility to wake the young men, giving the janitor a kind of power over them, in theory. Students may have felt the need to reassert their more honorable place in campus society through these "unwelcome attentions."

While the harassment of the janitor may have been at least partially attributed to the high spirits of young men, some cases were more serious. At the University of Virginia, many slaves on campus belonged to the hotelkeepers, who housed and fed students in buildings fronting the Lawn, rather than the university itself. In 1828 one hotelkeeper, Warner W. Minor, brought an offending student, Thomas Boyd, before the faculty for an investigation into his "disorderly conduct in his [Minor's] dining room." According to Minor, Boyd asked a slave serving in the dining room for butter and then complained about its quality. Minor stated that the "servant made no reply to him but spoke to another servant in an insolent tone of voice . . . saying among other things he was surprised that Mr. B. having read so many books should not know the difference between water & butter." The slave had made these "insolent" comments after Boyd had left the room, but another student overheard them and reported them to him. The next day, when Boyd saw the offending slave in the dining room, he ordered him to leave. When the slave refused, Boyd and a friend assaulted him and tried to force him out of the room. When Minor and his wife rushed into the room because of the commotion, they found blood running freely from the slave's head and a broken stick in Boyd's hand. Boyd then stopped immediately and, honoring the code of southern chivalry, begged Mrs. Minor's forgiveness.⁵

The faculty minutes record that Boyd "expressed his astonishment and indignation at being called before the faculty for so trifling an affair as that of chastising a servant for his insolence." The faculty also apparently felt that this incident did not require their attention, because their resolution states that Minor himself was responsible for punishing Boyd's dining room misconduct. But the drama did not end there. Soon after Boyd's appearance before the faculty, Boyd challenged Minor to a duel for reporting his misconduct. A crowd gathered as Boyd threatened to shoot Minor, and another student yelled out, "Whip him, Boyd, whip him!" Minor refused to accede to the hotheaded student's demand for satisfaction and called him a "puppy" before leaving the scene. Two days later, Boyd was again summoned before the faculty. This time, Boyd was moved to a different dormitory altogether.⁶ Surely no one was happier about Boyd's relocation than the slaves he terrorized. New slaves would have to deal with his temper and his prickly concern for his honor.

These incidents reveal a great deal about the hostile social climate in which the slaves at Virginia colleges labored. Working with students could be hazardous, especially in the cultural milieu of antebellum Virginia. The upper-class young men who could afford to attend universities considered their personal honor as a most cherished possession. When a former University of Virginia student named Henry Winter Davis reflected back on this period, he observed that the students' "sense of personal dignity and self-importance was developed in an exaggerated degree."⁷ As a result, the students simply could not walk away from a perceived slight to their honor not only from slaves but also from fellow students. While he was a student at the University of Virginia in 1826, Edgar Allan Poe wrote in a letter to his guardian that "a common fight is so trifling an occurrence that no notice is taken of it."⁸ The student violence at the University of Virginia was sometimes so uncontrolled that in 1839 a professor was publicly horsewhipped by students, and in the following year another professor was fatally shot in front of his own home on the Lawn by a masked student.[9]

In this violent environment, where even faculty needed to fear for their safety, where did the slaves stand? They must have developed very good skills at conciliating the students they served every day to avoid the violence of their tempers, so easily set off by the slightest perception of "insolence." The slaves employed by the hotelkeepers at the University of Virginia did have a master to turn to for redress when they faced problems from students, but the hotelkeepers could not really save their slaves from student abuse while the slaves did their work, even when the hotelkeepers wished. These slaves were often ordered about not by their owners but by volatile students with no long-term—or even short-term—interest in the slaves' well-being. They were insufficiently protected by their masters, the hotelkeepers, whose own power to shield the slaves was compromised by the hotelkeepers' positions as university employees who were hired to keep the students happy.

Slaves in these situations must frequently have been worn out with the commands of so many "masters." One task assigned to slaves at William and Mary was running errands for students. Apparently, there had been a problem with students requiring slaves to run errands for them at all hours of the day, because in 1769 the faculty resolved that "a boy be appointed to go into the Town on errands from the young gentlemen between the hours of eight & twelve o'clock in the morning, and at no other time."[10] This attempt at limiting the time that errands could be run—which was also done at the University of Virginia—was most likely an attempt by the college faculty to assert their right to control the labor of the college's slaves. Putting a rule like this in place was meant to reduce the kind of conflict that John Byrd had with the housekeeper later that same year over who had superior rights to the labor of college slaves at any given time.[11]

Students at Hampden-Sydney were just as likely as their William and Mary counterparts to try to compel college-owned slaves to serve students personally. In the "Laws of Hampden-Sidney College," a pamphlet that appeared about 1821, the students at that school were admonished that "the college servant shall be under the sole discretion of the officers. Complaint may be made to them concerning him. No student shall be allowed to employ him in services other than his stated duty, or on any pretence to chastise him, or treat him with abusive language."[12] This passage in the "Laws" surely describes, as well as it proscribes, student behavior toward the African Americans hired by Hampden-Sydney. When students had complaints about slaves' work, students were to bring slaves to the faculty and not harass the workers themselves, either physically or verbally. Rules like this one did not do away with hostility toward slaves at Hampden-Sydney, though; an example of this enmity can be found in an 1856 letter from John S. Dyerle to his sister. Concerning the slaves who worked at Hampden-Sydney, Dyerle writes that he feels "like killing every time I see one. Half of our time we cannot get any water &c which it is their duty to bring us."[13] Despite the emotions of students like Dyerle, there are fewer recorded instances of abuse of slaves there than at William and Mary or the University of Virginia. Perhaps the more evangelical campus culture of Hampden-Sydney, a Presbyterian institution, discouraged open violence against slaves, but certainly there may have been a conflict among some students over the demands of Christianity and southern honor.[14]

In 1849 the faculty at William and Mary also found it necessary to place a statement about college slaves in a pamphlet titled "Laws and Regulations of the College." The faculty insisted that "students shall be entitled to no other services from the College servants, unless sick, than to have their rooms Cleaned up once a day; their fires lighted, and their Boots or shoes cleaned once a day, and fresh water put in their rooms twice a day."[15] This regulation raises the question of what other services the students had been asking of the college's slaves. Students who felt that they had a right to command the service of college-owned slaves created conflicts for the slaves, who had certain duties assigned to them by the housekeeper or the faculty but still had to carefully balance the daily commands of the students.

It is not surprising that students felt entitled to order the slaves about, as almost all of the students had come to college from slave-owning homes and were habituated to mastery. The earliest southern college students had a reputation for being a willful, dangerously capricious, arrogant, and sometimes violent lot; these tendencies were made worse by the fact that most of them were teenagers, younger by a few years than modern college students. In his important book, *Southern Honor*, Bertram Wyatt-Brown asserts that "by age fourteen or so many of them [elite southern boys] had learned to drink, swear, gamble at cards, fight and wrestle, and imitate the mannerisms of their older brothers and fathers."[16] They brought these "manly" habits with them to college. In her study of early southern education, Lorri Glover has noted that "drinking, gambling, sexual experimentation, and dueling and other forms of orchestrated violence were accepted and even encouraged in southern male culture. . . . This self-mastery distinguished elite men from other members of society and laid the foundations for their dominance over wives, children, and particularly, slaves." Glover goes on to state that "universities provided the proving grounds on which young southern men could adopt these behaviors and thereby move from boyhood to refined manhood."[17]

A few students came to William and Mary accompanied by their own personal slaves; in 1754, for example, 8 out of about 110 students—presumably the wealthiest and most socially prominent—paid a fee to the bursar to board their own slaves at the college.[18] Students from prosperous families also brought slaves with them to Hampden-Sydney to look after the students' needs. By 1793 there were enough student-owned slaves living on campus that the board of trustees saw them as a problem and declared, "Whereas it is represented to this Board that the servants who are allowed to attend the students at the College very often commit great abuses by going from room to room and stealing or taking the property of the students; ordered that no such servant on any pretense whatever be allowed to go into any of the rooms of [the] college but that in which his master lives."[19] While the rampant theft implied by this measure seems unlikely because of the severe punishment slaves suffered for stealing, reports of unoccupied slaves roaming the school may have sparked the board's displeasure. These sorts of concerns may explain why the University of Virginia did not permit students to bring their own slaves with them to campus; in 1824, just before the first students arrived, the board of visitors (including at that time former presidents Thomas Jefferson and James Madison) declared that no student at the new university could "keep a servant, horse or dog."[20] The situation in which some students at William and Mary and Hampden-Sydney had personal slaves to wait on them while others did not may have made those students who did not bring their own manservants more likely to want to command the labor of college-owned slaves. If they could not have a slave of their own at the college, they could still enjoy the social benefits of mastery through their interactions with college slaves and raise, if not equalize, their status with their peers who did bring manservants with them.

Fear of physical violence at the hands of ungovernable young students must have been pervasive among slaves on Virginia campuses. During the early days of the American Revolution, the faculty at William and Mary complained of a "run of ill treatment which has of late been bestow'd by the Boys upon the Servants of the College both Male & Female."[21] The students' mistreatment of college slaves during the war was possibly exacerbated by the fact that many white Virginians considered slaves natural allies of Great Britain.[22] Later, in the nineteenth century, students continued to harass and abuse the college's slaves. For example, in 1831 the faculty investigated the churlish behavior of student William Robinson. Several students had taken chairs from the Blue Room (in what is today the Wren Building) to their own chambers, which the faculty realized when they assembled there for their regular meeting. Therefore, a professor ordered a slave named Abraham to return all the chairs to the Blue Room, but the students made things difficult for poor Abraham. Eventually, he was able to obtain all the chairs except the one misappropriated by Robinson. The faculty sent Abraham up to Robinson several times with verbal and written messages demanding the return of the chair. Robinson responded to Abraham by "using very threatening language toward him" and also "threatened him with violence." Finally, Robinson himself was called down to the Blue Room to explain his impertinence toward the faculty's repeated requests. Robinson blamed his behavior on Abraham, whom he called a "somber mute." Did the slave relay to Robinson their repeated demands for the chair? the faculty asked. Robinson replied, "It is possible he may have done so in his unintelligible way, but I really did not hear him."[23] Here again is a case where a slave was caught dangerously between the demands of different "masters." Abraham could not ignore the orders of the faculty, but by following them he faced the threat of violence from a volatile student. Is it any wonder, therefore, that Abraham may have tried to protect himself by being "unintelligible" in passing on orders to the student?

The slaveholding culture in which Virginia college students grew up permitted and sometimes demanded violence toward African Americans. Therefore, when the faculty did attempt to regulate student behavior toward slaves, the students felt their rights or their honor had been compromised. This attitude is clearly expressed in a student newspaper titled *The Owl*. *The Owl* was only published once, in January 1854, but its one issue devotes considerable space to racial issues. In one particular cartoon, titled *Negroes Rejoice*, an African American man dances above this caption: "Chapter V. Sec. 13 is not abolished, which says 'no Student shall abuse strike or injure negroes. Not even if they are grossly impertinent Ahem! This law savors of Northern manufacture, or perhaps it originated in some classic author; Horace (Greely) for instance.'"[24] William and Mary had recently updated its student regulations, and apparently there had been some debate about whether the college should retain this regulation, which read in full, "No student shall, by words or blows, insult a fellow-student, nor a citizen; nor shall he abuse, strike or injure negroes."[25] Perhaps some students argued that they should have the right to physically punish a slave on campus who was "grossly impertinent." When the faculty refused to change the regulation, the writers of *The Owl* chose to paint the professors as abolitionists, comparing them to Horace Greeley, the well-known liberal editor of the *New York Tribune* who promoted the antislavery movement.

This problem of "too many masters" was common among institutionally owned slaves, who dealt with concerns uncommon to individually owned slaves. Of course, all slaves were in constant danger of poor treatment; the economic interest of the owner was not an infallible incentive for decency. Many slaves were terribly abused and some even killed by their owners. Further, the most "mild" forms of slavery still denied slaves their freedom, something more precious than the best clothes or a full stomach. But the individual slave owners' economic interest, sometimes coupled with a moral or philosophical concern for the welfare of their slaves, did usually encourage the slave owners to provide their bondsmen and bondswomen with the basic necessities of life. Historian Philip D. Morgan notes, "Slaves faced all sorts of insecurities—about whether they might be sold, or whipped, or have to endure some fresh humiliation . . . , but the one compensation for such dependence was that a slave generally could expect a minimal subsistence. The master had an obvious and real incentive to see that the slave survived."[26] In other words, slaves were too valuable a possession to be denied the necessities of life—food, clothing, shelter, and basic medical care. Masters would also shield slaves from the demands of other whites who had no legitimate claim on their labor. Again, this would all be in the owners' self-interest. In contrast, slaves who were owned by institutions rather than by individual owners often lacked even the minimal protection of an owner's pecuniary interest. In the broader context of institutional slavery, this problem arises frequently; slaves owned by church congregations, by charity schools, and by the state, as well as slaves owned by colleges, faced this problem.[27]

William and Mary's slaves were usually under the day-to-day control of a steward, housekeeper, or member of the faculty. These individuals directed the labor of their institution's slaves and controlled the quality of their lives: their food, clothing, and shelter; when and where they worked; and whether or not they would live with their families or be separated from them. Sometimes the managers of institutional slaves worked energetically to provide them with a decent standard of living; other times, they used their authority to exploit the slaves for the managers' benefit. The well-being of the slaves, therefore, depended entirely on the integrity, diligence, and compassion of those who were appointed to oversee them. The great complication at William and Mary, Hampden-Sydney, the University of Virginia, and other universities was the student body, who felt entitled to employ college-owned slaves but had no real interest in their welfare. Faculties enacted rules to protect the slaves owned by universities but had to balance the needs of slaves with the demands of students.

But if the situation of slaves at Virginia colleges was difficult in many ways, some of them also enjoyed opportunities unique to their situation. In a larger discussion of southern honor among antebellum southern men, Craig Friend and Lorri Glover write, "White male mastery and the code of honor provided a variety of practices designed to subordinate and brutalize black men . . . [but] black men resented and sometimes violently resisted such denials of manhood." They continue, "Black men sought to empower themselves through education, financial autonomy, and physical escape from slavery."[28] There are important examples of this kind of black resistance on college campuses as well. Slaves at William and Mary, for instance, achieved some "financial autonomy" by earning money raising their own produce or doing extra work. Between 1804 and 1806 Lemon was paid five times for barrels of corn, earning $20.33.[29] William and Mary must have been among those nineteenth-century owners who allotted to their slaves plots of land to raise crops that they could call their own. This was work the slaves did in their limited free time, often on Sundays. Like other such owners, the college sometimes became the slaves' customer.

At Hampden-Sydney, economic opportunity can also be seen in the case of Billy Brown, referred to in some records as College Billy, who would become one of the longest-serving employees in the history of Hampden-Sydney. Brown took advantage of his position as a hired slave at the college to make money by doing extra work for students in his free hours and ultimately was able to purchase his own freedom. In 1824 Brown petitioned the legislature to allow him to remain in the Commonwealth of Virginia as a free black man. By law, all slaves freed after May 1, 1806, had to leave Virginia within a year or petition the legislature for permission to remain. Although his petition was accompanied by a certificate that testified to his "unsullied character for probity & good demeanor" that had been signed by sixteen prominent county residents, it was denied by the legislature. Undaunted, Brown and his white supporters submitted a second petition in 1825, which also included recommendations from the leading men of Prince Edward County, who wrote that Brown had "been for many years the servant for Hampden-Sydney College & demeaned himself with great propriety & integrity." On this second attempt, the House of Delegates passed the petition, only to have it fail in the Senate.[30]

By law, then, Billy Brown was required to leave Virginia forever, but it does not appear that he did so. There are scattered references to a college servant named Billy or Old Billy from that time through 1851.[31] Billy Brown's connection with Hampden-Sydney College helped him to obtain his freedom and gain the respect of the powerful white leaders of the community. He was in a unique position to earn extra money from the students and worked among men who allowed him to be paid for work he did in his off-hours. While these opportunities for earning money were not limited to college-owned slaves, those slaves who belonged to or were hired by colleges did have numerous opportunities for earning money of their own. Brown was able to buy his freedom, and although he could never enjoy it in complete safety because of the actions of the Virginia legislature, he still had the support of his local community. Hampden Sydney supported him in a remarkably humane fashion throughout this saga; the college allowed him to keep money he earned from extra work initially and then continued to employ him as a free black for decades, despite his illegality.

Slaves at the University of Virginia also took advantage of living in close quarters with the students to make extra money. One historian of the university writes that "the students began to turn surreptitiously to the kitchens of the professors, whose cooks were always ready to earn, in this furtive way, a few dollars by providing a dinner or a supper, sometimes at their master's expense.... Breakfast was smuggled into the dormitories by a shrewd little black boy... with a covered basket ostensibly selling apples."[32] These dealings between the students and the professors' slaves benefited both parties, with only the larders of the professors being a little lighter, as the author implies. It is just as likely, however, that these cooks used the students' money to furnish these extra meals without pilfering from the slaves' owners.

As Friend and Glover state, empowerment through religious and secular education could also be an important way that slaves resisted oppression and asserted their own manhood. While African Americans were excluded from formal education on campus, those with a desire to learn could pick up more than the average slave might on a plantation or farm. For example, the large concentration of African Americans at the University of Virginia attracted many Sunday schools for the university slaves, some of which were conducted by professors, including John B. Minor and Gessner Harrison.[33] There were also many visiting preachers who were attracted to the university both for its students and its large African American population. For example, in 1834 Gessner Harrison and Eliza Harrison wrote of a Mr. Cobbs, who visited the university on Sunday nights "to meet all the coloured people of the University with a view of giving them religious instruction.... [T]hey attend very regularly and behave themselves in a decent orderly manner."[34] This letter implies that many African Americans freely chose to attend the sermons and Sunday schools brought to campus for their benefit.

Secular education was also within reach for some blacks on campus. In 1928 W. T. Greenhow wrote that his father, George Greenhow, had learned to read and write while working as a free black janitor at William and Mary before the Civil War. Terry Meyers observes that the elder Greenhow "liked to boast (with a fine sense of irony, obviously) that he was 'the only negro ever educated at William and Mary'—he had been taught to read and write by one of the students in return for Mrs. Greenhow's doing his laundry."[35] This opportunity for education was not limited to free African Americans. For example, William Gibbons was the slave of University of Virginia professor Henry Howard in the late antebellum period. His daughter later recalled that he worked hard to learn how to read and that he educated himself by being around the professor's books and by listening in on the conversations of university students. Gibbons's innate talents, combined with the education he gleaned in these ways, helped him to become the first African American minister of the First Baptist Church of Charlottesville. Later, he moved to Washington, D.C., to minister to a congregation there and took theology classes at Howard University. Gibbons and his daughter saw his long years of work at the University of Virginia as an educational opportunity.[36] His educational advantages made him a leader of the black community after the Civil War.

In conclusion, the situation of slaves who worked on Virginia college campuses in the eighteenth and nineteenth centuries differed from the experiences of more traditional slaves in important ways. In particular, slaves on campus, whether owned or hired, were often the victims of students' fragile code of honor. As elite young men usually in their teens, students at Virginia colleges before the Civil War were still developing their own reputations among their peers. Though their rights to command the slaves on campus were limited, they frequently sought power over them in order to enjoy the social benefits of mastery and to enhance their own honor among their fellow students. Because slaves on campus lived daily with young men in this developmental stage, they probably were overworked (by serving students on demand) and faced more violence than slaves owned by traditional masters or mistresses. This problem of too many "masters" was exacerbated by the fact that those who did have the official right to the labor of college slaves, whether a board of trustees or a housekeeper, had a limited personal stake in the well-being of the slaves. Even those who owned the slaves, like the University of Virginia hotelkeeper Warner Minor, still needed to balance their economic interest in shielding their slaves from abuse by students with their job requirement to please those same students.

While students enhanced their honor by exhibiting power over slaves on campus, slaves resisted the inherent dishonor of their situations. Despite the drawbacks, slaves at universities also enjoyed opportunities to earn money by doing extra work for students or for the university itself. Other African Americans found ways while working on campus to gain some education, which was both useful and a source of pride later in their lives. Under adverse circumstances, slaves made a clean, warm, and comfortable life possible for the students and faculty who lived and worked at Virginia colleges, while at the same time they resisted the honor culture that would deny their manhood and seized opportunities to improve their own lives.

NOTES

1. "Journal of the Meetings of the President and Masters of William & Mary College, November 16, 1769," *William and Mary Quarterly Historical Magazine,* 1st series, 13, no. 2 (1904): 137.

2. Orlando Patterson, *Slavery and Social Death: A Comparative Study* (Cambridge, Mass.: Harvard University Press, 1982), 79.

3. Ibid., 11, 88.

4. John S. Patton, *Jefferson, Cabell and the University of Virginia* (New York: Neale Publishing Company, 1906), 119–24.

5. Minutes of the General Faculty, 1825–1970, 151–54, Albert and Shirley Small Special Collections Library, University of Virginia, Charlottesville.

6. Ibid.

7. Charles Coleman Wall Jr., "Students and Student Life at the University of Virginia, 1825–1861" (PhD diss., University of Virginia, 1978), 113.

8. Edgar Allan Poe to John Allan, Charlottesville, Virginia, 1826, in ibid., 88.

9. Thomas Perkins Abernathy, *Historical Sketch of the University of Virginia* (Richmond: Dietz Press, 1948), 12.

10. "Journal of the Meetings of the President and Masters of William and Mary College, August 28, 1769," *William and Mary Quarterly Historical Magazine*, 1st series, 13, no. 2 (1904): 135.

11. Philip Alexander Bruce, *History of the University of Virginia, 1819–1919: The Lengthened Shadow of One Man* (New York: Macmillan, 1920), 1:209. Students at the University of Virginia were asked to make errand requests to slaves only between 2:45 and 3:00 p.m. daily.

12. "Laws of Hampden-Sidney College," pamphlet, ca. 1821, in *History of Hampden-Sydney College*, vol. 1, *From the Beginnings to the Year 1856*, by Herbert Clarence Bradshaw (Durham, N.C.: Fisher-Harrison Corp., 1976), 444.

13. James Luckin Bugg Jr., "Student Life at Hampden-Sydney in the Ante-bellum Days," 46–47, Hampden-Sydney, Virginia, ca. 1940, Eggleston Library, Hampden-Sydney College, Hampden-Sydney, Virginia.

14. Many historians have argued that the southern culture of honor conflicted with evangelical Christianity. See Anne C. Loveland, *Southern Evangelicals and the Social Order, 1800–1860* (Baton Rouge: University of Louisiana Press, 1980); Rhys Isaac, *The Transformation of Virginia, 1740–1790* (Chapel Hill: University of North Carolina Press, 1982); Mark A. Noll, *The Rise of Evangelicalism: The Age of Edwards, Whitefield, and the Wesleys* (Downers Grove, Ill.: IVP Academic, 2003).

15. "Laws and Regulations of the College," 1849, folder 5, William and Mary Papers, E. G. Swem Library Special Collections Research Center, College of William and Mary, Williamsburg, Virginia. Hereafter cited as Swem Library.

16. Bertram Wyatt-Brown, *Southern Honor: Ethics and Behavior in the Old South* (New York: Oxford University Press, 1982), 165.

17. Lorri Glover, "'Let Us Manufacture Men': Educating Elite Boys in the Early National South," in *Southern Manhood: Perspectives on Masculinity in the Old South*, ed. Craig Thompson Friend and Lorri Glover (Athens: University of Georgia Press, 2004), 29.

18. "Bursar's Book, 1754–69," Swem Library.

19. Alfred J. Morrison, ed., *The College of Hampden-Sidney: Calendar of Board Minutes, 1776–1876* (Richmond, Va.: Hermitage Press, 1912), 42.

20. "Minutes of the Board of Visitors of the University of Virginia," 73, Albert and Shirley Small Special Collections Library, University of Virginia, Charlottesville.

21. "Journal of the Meetings of the President and Masters of William & Mary College," *William and Mary Quarterly Historical Magazine*, 1st series, 15, no. 2 (1906): 138–39.

22. Virginians had good reason to suspect their slaves of favoring Great Britain, because in 1775 Virginia's last royal governor, Lord Dunmore, threatened to free any adult male slave who left his master to fight for the British. Thousands of slaves heeded Dunmore's call. Good resources on this subject are Sylvia R. Frey, *Water from the Rock: Black Resistance in a Revolutionary Age* (Princeton, N.J.: Princeton University Press, 1991); and Woody Holton, *Forced Founders: Indians, Debtors, Slaves, and the Making of the American Revolution in Virginia* (Chapel Hill: University of North Carolina Press, 1999).

23. "Faculty Minutes, 1830–36," in "William and Mary College Historical Notes," by Mary R. M. Goodwin, 360–61, manuscript report, Colonial Williamsburg Research Department.

24. *The Owl*, January 1854, Swem Library; thanks go to Professor Terry L. Meyers for bringing this newspaper to my attention in "A First Look at the Worst," background paper for the Faculty Assembly of the College of William and Mary, September 2007.

25. "Laws and Regulations of William & Mary College, at Williamsburg, Virginia," ca. 1852–53, 9, Swem Library.

26. Philip D. Morgan, "Slaves and Poverty," in *Down and Out in Early America*, ed. Billy G. Smith (University Park: Pennsylvania State University Press, 2004), 121.

27. Jennifer Bridges Oast, "Forgotten Masters: Institutional Slavery in Virginia, 1680–1860" (PhD diss., College of William and Mary, 2008).

28. Craig Thompson Friend and Lorri Glover, introduction to Friend and Glover, *Southern Manhood*, xi.

29. "Bursar's Book 1804–1806," Swem Library.

30. Legislative petitions, December 9, 1824, and December 4, 1825, Archives Division, Virginia State Library, quoted in Bradshaw, *History of Hampden-Sydney College*, 360–61; Melvin Patrick Ely, *Israel on the Appomattox: A Southern Experiment in Black Freedom from the 1790s through the Civil War* (New York: Alfred A. Knopf, 2004), 546n97.

31. Bradshaw, *History of Hampden-Sydney College*, 361.

32. Bruce, *History of the University of Virginia*, 235.

33. Gayle M. Schulman, "Slaves at the University of Virginia," 2004, 22.

34. Gessner Harrison and Eliza Harrison to Mary Jane Harrison, Charlottesville, December 13, 1834, in papers of Harrison, Smith, and Tucker in the possession of Gayle Schulman, cited in ibid., 13–14.

35. Terry L. Meyers, "Thinking About Slavery at the College of William and Mary," April 26, 2012, College of William & Mary Lemon Project Occasional Paper, http://ssrn.com/abstract=2033882.

36. Schulman, "Slaves," 1–2, 24, 33.

CHAPTER FIVE

Making Their Case

Religion, Pedagogy, and the Slavery Question at Antebellum Emory College

Patrick C. Jamieson

On a spring evening in March 1858 at Emory College in Oxford, Georgia, twenty-two-year-old George Wren listened intently to his professor lecture the class on the morality of slavery. "In the first place slavery is right per se," Professor William Sasnett told the class. "It is right ... to the slaves themselves; and it is right for the good it does the white race." He added: "Many slaves that have been brought here heathens have been sent back Christians and in this way much good [has] been done by the single act of bringing away one slave." Sasnett repeatedly returned to his argument that slavery was not simply a necessary evil, as defenders of the peculiar institution had long argued, but rather an inherently *righteous* practice that benefited both masters and slaves. "People are in necessity of this government," he said. "The government of negroes must be strong, from their inferiority and their natural instinct differing from the white race. They need superior minds to govern them, which we may learn from the state of those who live to themselves and are shut out from the authority of the white race."[1]

Sasnett's notion that slaves were in need of a "superior mind" to rule and govern them was not uncommon by 1858. White southerners and many northerners alike had long perceived blacks as inferior beings, allowing proslavery thinkers to advance an argument that blacks were in need of the protection and guidance enslavement afforded. In an analogous vein, well-known proslavery author George Fitzhugh wrote, "The weak in mind or body require guidance, support, and protection; they must obey and work for those who protect and guide them—they have a natural right to ... masters."[2] Fitzhugh, like Sasnett, believed strongly that "nature" made slaves and that law and government existed to "regulate, modify, and mitigate" the peculiar institution.[3]

Southern educators not only accepted but actively embraced a responsibility to the economically and politically powerful slaveholding class to educate the young men of the South about slavery's value and benevolence. The antebellum southern college, including Emory College, went beyond indoctrinating its students with a worldview *compatible* with slavery. It sought to influence *all* of southern society through religion, pedagogy, and print culture. William Sasnett's lecture to his students exemplifies the prevailing proslavery arguments of the late antebellum period, as well as the way in which southern educators incorporated proslavery arguments into their teachings. His lecture also sheds light on Emory's student culture and how the college's students were being prepared to become defenders of the South's most vital institution. Emory College did more than shape the lives of the few thousand students and professors who lived and studied in Oxford before the Civil War. Its faculty developed, elaborated, and propagated numerous arguments to explain and justify the peculiar institution, placing the college at the forefront of the proslavery defense.

This chapter investigates Emory's intellectual investment in the peculiar institution in three brief parts: first, by looking at the 1844 schism of the Methodist Church; next, by surveying moral philosophy and political economy classes and textbooks at Emory; and lastly, by discussing student culture as examined through wealth, social status, and participation in college debating societies.

Emory College was born in 1836 in the midst of the movement to open more church colleges to train the future clergy of the Methodist Church and the future leaders of southern society.[4] Less than a decade later, the college was already embroiled in a significant controversy over the slavery question. In early May 1844 a group of Methodist preachers traveled from Oxford to New York to attend the general conference of the Methodist Church. Among this group were Bishop James Osgood Andrew, the first president of Emory's board of trustees, and Augustus Baldwin Longstreet, president of Emory College. Almost immediately after the conference began, northern delegates called for an investigation of Andrew's ownership of slaves and his proslavery stance. While Andrew was willing to resign from his leadership post at the conference, Longstreet and other members of the Georgia delegation pressed him to stay. After efforts to reconcile their competing positions over whether a bishop could own slaves, the southerners, realizing they were in the minority, began to look for ways to secede from the church. Thus began the "Methodist Civil War" and the schism that split the church between North and South over the slavery question.

Born in Augusta, Georgia, in 1790, Augustus Longstreet was an esteemed jurist and minister in the Methodist Church prior to assuming the presidency at Emory. Shortly after the 1845 schism of the Methodist Church, he published a powerful proslavery pamphlet, *Letters on the Epistle of Paul to Philemon*, in which he set out to demonstrate the scriptural legitimacy of slavery. Longstreet based the pamphlet on the New Testament story of Philemon, particularly on a passage invoked by both proslavery and antislavery activists to demonstrate the Bible's stance on slavery—a passage that "invited fits of temper" between northerners and southerners.[5] In the story, an imprisoned Paul wrote to Philemon, a slaveholder, on behalf of Philemon's slave, Onesimus, who had apparently run away. What is clear from the letter is that Paul urged reconciliation between Philemon and Onesimus. Whether the passage endorses or condemns slavery is as unclear today as it was during the time Longstreet was writing.[6] Longstreet, however, interpreted the passage as a staunch endorsement of slavery in the Greco-Roman world, noting that the letter established that "there is no sin in holding slaves" and that "slaveholding is no disqualification for the ministry." "If Paul and his colleagues thus esteemed Philemon," Longstreet concluded, "how can you and your colleagues reconcile it to your consciences to treat Bishop Andrew as you have treated him and as you are still treating him?"[7] Though directed at northern Methodists, the pamphlet was widely republished throughout the South.[8]

Two years later, Longstreet published his most influential defense of slavery, *A Voice from the South*. The pamphlet contained a series of letters ostensibly authored by "Georgia" addressed to "Massachusetts," the state Longstreet considered the "mother of Abolitionism." Two related themes emerge from this work. First, Longstreet attempted to portray the transatlantic slave trade as an abominable and barbarous system propagated by northerners. Second, his explanation of how southerners "coped with" slavery—the manner in which he believed they managed their slaves—is, at its core, an argument rooted in the paternalist rhetoric of the Old South.

One of Longstreet's primary aims was to demonstrate to his readers that northerners were far from innocent with respect to the transatlantic slave trade. Longstreet was certainly not the first to embrace this argument. Indeed, Thomas Jefferson, in an early draft of the Declaration of Independence, attempted to lay the blame for the slave trade squarely on England, characterizing the slave trade as a "cruel war against human nature itself, violating it's [*sic*] most sacred rights of life and liberty in the persons of a distant people who never offended [the king]."[9]

Because slaves were "fasten[ed]" upon Georgia, in Longstreet's words, southerners were left with little choice but to impose Christianity and moral values on them. Thus emerges a very recognizable brand of slaveholder paternalism. "That my children, in purchasing slaves from yours," Longstreet wrote, "delivered them from the most cruel bondage that man ever groaned under, is most true—that there was pity and compassion on the side of the purchasers, and none on the side of the vendors is equally true; but for these things I give them no credit, because selfishness and not humanity urged them to traffic." In making this argument, Longstreet emphasized how the South's paternalism brought order and morality to the institution the South had inherited instead of created.[10]

During the eight years Longstreet served as president of Emory College (1840–48), he authored several other important pamphlets on the scriptural legitimacy of slavery. He also gave numerous sermons and lectures on the subject. While his works certainly influenced the Emory community, his voice carried far beyond the boundaries of Oxford. Longstreet's words continued to fan the flames of the fire over proslavery and secessionist arguments during his tenure at Emory College, ultimately contributing to the growing sectional divide of the nation.[11]

At the time of Emory's founding, both northern and southern educators were contemplating whether a curriculum based on the classics should be supplemented or replaced with a practical one. Supporters of practical education advocated replacing classical texts with modern ones and adding courses in science and mathematics. Many elite schools North and South resisted this change, however, because they "maintained primarily an elite clientele and a focus on classical literary attainments."[12] Reform at some elite southern schools did happen, albeit gradually.[13] Basil Manly, the eminent president of the University of Alabama, sought to supplement the classics with practical courses in the mechanical arts, mathematics, and science. "It is a fact that you may make the best mathematicians, and scientific scholars, generally, out of those who have learned the classics best," Manly wrote in defense of the modernized curriculum at Alabama.[14]

Emory College primarily offered a classical education throughout the antebellum period, with little variation in its course offerings from 1838 to 1861. In 1838, with just five faculty members and twenty students, the school boasted courses in ancient languages and literature and in moral and mental philosophy. The college did, however, offer courses in mathematics and the natural sciences, including chemistry, mineralogy, and geology.[15] By 1845 Emory's course offerings had expanded to include Greek Tragedies, Greek Testament, Xenophon's *Memorabilia*, Homer or Herodotus, and Virgil's *Georgics*. The college required both "composition" (writing essays) and "declamation" (oral recitation in front of a group) in all courses.[16] During their senior year of study, students were also required "to deliver original orations in the College Chapel, several times during the year, in addition to the usual exercises at commencement."[17]

The curriculum at Emory in multiple ways reinforced ideas about the essential rectitude of slavery. More than any other subjects at Emory College, moral philosophy and political economy were the primary forums in which students and professors explored prevailing proslavery theories. These courses, as part of the larger academic and theological discipline of moral science, were crucial in the intellectual development of the young southern gentleman.

The need for a strong moral foundation built on Christian theology was clear to educators. "Young Southerners, in particular the young men slated to steer southern slave society through times of mortal danger," Elizabeth Fox-Genovese and Eugene Genovese tell us, "had to be steeped in moral philosophy."[18] Southern educators increasingly sought to align their proslavery lectures with the prevailing defenses of the peculiar institution in a move that created continuity and broader appeal throughout southern intellectual circles. Indeed, the move to imbed the topic of slavery within moral philosophy courses in effect created an early social science course of study for students while further legitimizing proslavery theories.[19]

The character of any moral philosophy course depended on the professor's choice of textbook. Several moral philosophy texts dominated higher education in the nineteenth century. Anglican theologian William Paley authored one of the most notable works of the period, *Principles of Moral and Political Philosophy*, first published in 1785. The text was popular at many southern colleges, including Emory, where professors assigned it beginning in 1847, if not earlier.[20] Paley's text could hardly be considered a proslavery text at the time, however, as it condemned slavery in numerous places. Commenting on the fact that many proslavery advocates believed slavery was not prohibited in the Bible, Paley noted, "It is unjust to infer from this silence, that Christ deemed all the then existing institutions right, or that he forbade the worse to be bettered." He also called for gradual emancipation, noting that it would be the only way to truly "correct the wickedness and folly" of the institution of slavery.[21]

The available moral philosophy texts posed a unique problem for southern educators: they contained not only agreeable ideas to southerners but also elements that were difficult for southerners to digest. Both northern and southern colleges often assigned Brown University president Francis Wayland's *The Elements of Moral Science* (1835) for moral philosophy courses.[22] While many of slavery's apologists agreed with Wayland's beliefs on legitimate authority in society, they disagreed with his views on slavery.[23] Wayland's text carried inklings of antislavery sentiment. In his 1835 edition, Wayland wrote in a section titled "The Violation of Personal Liberty by the Individual" that domestic slavery is "the most common form of this violation." "Slavery ... violates the personal liberty of man as a physical, intellectual, and moral being."[24] Wayland ultimately became embroiled in a public controversy over the issue of slavery when his correspondence with Richard Fuller, a proslavery apologist, was published in 1845. Despite the controversy, Wayland largely held, as one historian has argued, a "centrist position" on the slavery question.[25] Wayland was antislavery but did not support the abolitionist movement. He believed from a pragmatic standpoint that the extremism of the abolitionist movement only further agitated the slavery debate and could have dire consequences for the Union. "Slavery in this country will yet cease, for it is wrong," Wayland wrote to a correspondent in 1837. "But it will never be made to cease by the present efforts.... They may destroy the union, plunge this country into a civil war, break us up into a half dozen different confederacies, but abolish slavery as they are now attempting to do it—they never will. You may note my words, *they never* will."[26] Basil Manly, who used Wayland's political economy text in his own class, reflected on Wayland's stance on slavery in 1845: "The truth is that his *heart is right*, his *head is wrong*."[27]

Though it is unclear whether Wayland's *Moral Science* was assigned to Emory students, his 1837 text *The Elements of Political Economy* was assigned by

1853, if not earlier, and it remained mandatory reading even after the Civil War. While Wayland grounded *Political Economy* in the classical tradition, he insisted on a connection between economics and Christian natural theology. In *Political Economy*, Wayland argued that the slave trade "caused the impoverishment of another nation." The result, he wrote, "has been the almost ultimate depopulation of the slave coast." Wayland also commented extensively on capitalism and the nature of free labor. "The accumulation of capital is more for the advantage of the laborer than of the capitalist," he wrote. "The greater the ratio of capital to labor, the greater will be the share of the product that falls to the laborer." Wayland concluded that the laboring classes, more so than the wealthy classes, were more interested in increasing the capital of the country.[28]

On the eve of the Civil War, southern academics began to adopt texts that explicitly endorsed slavery, displacing Paley's and Wayland's moral philosophy texts. In moral philosophy courses, Emory switched to Methodist preacher and educator R. H. Rivers's *Elements of Moral Philosophy* (1859). Rivers's book was divided into two sections: theoretical ethics, where the author criticized and argued against Francis Wayland's definition of moral law; and practical ethics, complete with an entire chapter devoted to the defense of slavery.

Rivers's book and its subsequent revisions were written to appease a southern audience. The southern *Methodist Quarterly Review* praised the text as possessing a "rare excellence," noting, "So far as we know it, it is the only textbook of Moral Philosophy which takes the Southern side of this question."[29] Introducing the subject of slavery, Rivers wrote, "Most of the philosophical writings of American authors are exhibitions of fanaticism rather than of sound logic or scriptural truth when they discuss the subject of slavery." Rivers divided his discussion on slavery into sections on everything from the "delicacy of the subject" to an argument that slavery was "a blessing to the slave." Above all else, Rivers argued, "slavery is not a sin . . . [because] it has done more to Christianize the African race than all else combined."[30]

Rivers satisfied the demands of southern intellectuals who desired a textbook that embraced their point of view. His argument that slavery "is not a sin" because it Christianized the African race was commonplace by the time of the book's publication. Seeking to answer abolitionist charges that slavery was immoral and un-Christian, proslavery writers stressed the positive connections between slavery and morality, arguments contributing to the widespread appeal of paternalism as *the* answer to the antislavery movement.

Exemplary of this principle is Thornton Stringfellow's argument in the proslavery pamphlet *Cotton Is King* (1860). Stringfellow emphasized that God ordained slavery and that Christian masters had an obligation to convert and baptize their slaves. "Masters give unto your servants that which is just and equal, knowing that you also have a master in heaven," he wrote.[31] The striking similarities between Rivers's college textbook and the writings of proslavery thinkers such as Stringfellow are not surprising, as Rivers was most likely influenced by many of their works when drafting his own book.

The skirmish over textbooks in antebellum southern colleges was one front in a war for ideological control over students. The choices professors made in choosing particular texts are crucial to understanding the proslavery atmosphere at Emory College. Texts, however, were often supplemented with additional lecture material from the professor.

On the eve of the Civil War, Professor William Sasnett held the ideological reins of proslavery instruction in many classes at Emory College. A lecture Sasnett delivered in 1858, later remembered by student George Wren, was typical. Invoking prevailing paternalist ideas of slavery as a boon to the enslaved, Sasnett argued that slaves, though not paid in money, were, in fact, "better paid than any other class of laborer." When ill, "they have some one to wait on them and administer their wants, while the poor class of people of the black and white have to labor much harder and with but little pay not even enough generally for sustenance."[32]

Sasnett's teachings complemented his book, *Progress: Considered with Particular Reference to the Methodist Episcopal Church, South*, published in 1855. The book served as a commentary on the functions of the Methodist Episcopal Church, South, in society and included suggestions for how it "ought to be developed." Proslavery ideology occupied an important position in the book. Sasnett considered slavery "both abstractly and concretely ... defensible on the ground of both philosophy and Scripture."[33] The author subscribed to a highly paternalistic view of slavery, arguing that masters must take care of their slaves just as parents do their children, in language and ideology that were very similar to his classroom lectures.

Both Sasnett and Rivers advanced similar arguments about slaveholder paternalism, the positive good of the institution, and slaveholders' responsibilities to Christianize and care for their slaves. The arguments also responded to antislavery propagandists by attacking free labor and factory owners in the North.

Many southerners argued that slavery was a better and more humane alternative to the North's free-labor marketplace. Factory owners did not "care" for their workers, did not protect them from the vicissitudes of nineteenth-century life, did not "save" them with Christianity, and did not provide them with job security. Slave masters, many in the South argued, did all of this.[34] The similarities between arguments for slavery in moral philosophy courses and the proslavery writings of leading southern intellectuals only further highlight the extraordinary power of slaveholder paternalism and the hegemonic attitudes of the master class. Additionally, they help highlight why secession would become so accepted by many southerners in 1860.

Throughout its antebellum years, Emory was a church college, attracting primarily the children of ministers and occasionally the children of area planters. The students at Emory College did not exclusively come from the wealthy families of antebellum Georgia. In addition to tuition being less expensive—$135 at Emory compared to as much as $171 at Franklin College (later the University of Georgia) in 1838—church colleges generally attracted students who were more likely to be the sons of ministers than the sons of planters. South Carolina College, among the most prestigious colleges in the antebellum South, attracted almost exclusively the sons of prominent planters and politicians. Some students at Emory did, however, come from prominent slaveholding families. Lewis Graves, a graduate of the class of 1845 and the son of wealthy Newton County planter and entrepreneur Iverson L. Graves, came from a household that in 1840 had thirty-two slaves, twelve of whom were under the age of ten.

A college education elevated the standing of a southern male significantly. Students came to Emory with aspirations for future prosperity. With only a minority of students becoming ministers following their graduation, many Emory students went on to careers in law, education, politics, business, or farming. Students would often move up to positions within southern society in which they could afford to purchase slaves. William W. Flewellen, a graduate of the class of 1845, for instance, had already acquired a forty-three-year-old female slave less than five years after graduating.[35] John W. Hudson, class of 1846, who moved to Putnam County, Georgia, after graduating, had thirty-seven slaves in 1860.[36] Robert W. Lovett, of the class of 1843, owned eight slaves by 1850.[37]

Gustavus John Orr, a graduate of the class of 1844, returned to Emory to become a professor of mathematics. In 1850 he had at least four slaves residing at his home in Oxford. His personal records indicate he owned at least nine slaves in 1860 on the eve of the Civil War.[38]

College literary societies were a primary forum for students to complement their classroom studies and debate the virtues of the peculiar institution with their peers. Literary societies were a mainstay of almost all antebellum colleges, and the societies were perhaps one of the few outlets for students to entertain themselves outside of their rigorous academic and devout religious lives. Emory student Joseph Addison Turner later remembered his time in the Phi Gamma literary society as productive and essential. "I gained my reputation for talent more by the speeches I made in the Phi Gamma Society than by any proficiency in my text-books," he noted.[39] Students were intensely loyal to their respective societies. The societies organized debates, usually held on Saturdays, on a variety of topics. They also hosted famous speakers and served as the intellectual and social epicenter of the college.[40] As the debate societies were perhaps the most important aspect of extracurricular life for many college students, the topics of debates reveal issues students felt were important and relevant outside of their classroom education.

Two literary societies existed at Emory throughout most of the antebellum period: the Phi Gamma Society and the Few Society. Both societies were interested in debating issues related to slavery, as well as other topics under discussion in the surrounding culture. Topics connected either to slavery or to states' rights were debated a total of 43 times between the two societies out of a total of 832 recorded debates in the antebellum period, or about 5 percent of the debates, according to the records available.[41] Other popular topics included women's suffrage, temperance, constitutional questions, and other current political topics.

Of the debates recorded in the societies' record books, twenty-four debates were directly on the subject of slavery, while nineteen were on the subject of states' rights. Within those debates on slavery, ten centered on the morality of slavery, and eight focused on whether the slave trade should be reopened or abolished. Topics on slavery varied, from the scriptural legitimacy of the peculiar institution to the morality of owning slaves. The question of whether slavery should be abolished appeared often as well—and at an increasing frequency on the eve of the Civil War. Questions debated included "Is it right for us to bring Africans over to America to become Slaves?" and

"Is Slavery justified by natural rights and the principles of human equality?" Students debated whether slavery should be abolished in October 1859 and asked whether the Union should be dissolved in 1860. The societies asked whether the slave trade was "right" and whether slavery "as it exists in the South" was a "moral evil."[42]

Antebellum students debated similar topics at other colleges as well. In 1850 in the Dialectic Society at the University of North Carolina, students argued the question, "Should slavery as it now exists in our country be justly considered a reproach?" In 1855 students debated the question, "Is southern slavery justifiable?" Topics of secession and states' rights were also common: in 1859 UNC students debated "Would disunion be profitable to the South?"[43] Slavery appeared as a topic in an increasingly frequent fashion at both institutions as the war neared. Indeed, as one historian has noted, debates on slavery "waxed and waned at intervals, but became a subject of intense interest in 1860 and 1861."[44] Students recognized the important political and social questions of the day and sought to include them in this extracurricular outpost.

George Wren, the student who transcribed William Sasnett's 1858 lecture on slavery, graduated from Emory College in 1859, ripe to join the ranks of the Confederacy. Wren joined Company G, Eighth Louisiana Infantry Regiment, just two months after war broke out. He survived the conflict and was released from Union capture after taking the oath of allegiance in June 1865. Following the war, he went on to become a teacher in Claiborne Parish, Louisiana.

Wren is truly a member of a group that historian Peter Carmichael has called the "last generation": southern men who came of age in college on the eve of the war.[45] Wren and his peers cultivated their identities as students, Methodists, and, ultimately, as Confederate soldiers during their time at Emory College. Emory's students were not simply a passive audience of the proslavery rhetoric that surrounded them in their years at the college. As future leaders, clergymen, planters, and soldiers they actively thought and wrote on the virtues of slaveholding and southern society.

What emerges from looking at Emory and its relationship to proslavery thought in this period is a microcosm for the larger political and social realities in southern society. Indeed, the college was an important center not only for the creation of proslavery thought but also for its dissemination. At a time when slavery was increasingly coming under intellectual attack, many of the students and faculty at Emory were deeply committed to preserving it. Faculty members authored proslavery treatises and lectured their students on the inherent good in slavery, nurturing a vision of southern slavery as a benign, paternalistic institution. Many students left Emory with a desire to become members of the slaveholding class, and many realized that desire. These stories reveal that the world of antebellum Emory was inextricably linked to the institution of slavery. Emory's story is that of many colleges, northern and southern, revealing rich and important connections between the institution of slavery and the university.

NOTES

1. Sasnett's lecture was recounted nearly word for word in a student's diary. See George Lovick Pierce Wren Diary, March 1858, MSS 249, Manuscript, Archives, and Rare Book Library, Emory University.

2. Here, Fitzhugh's argument adds an additional dimension to Sasnett's by inverting the prevailing rights language of the time in arguing that slaves have a *right* to a master.

3. George Fitzhugh, *Sociology for the South, or the Failure of Free Society* (Richmond, Va.: A. Morris, 1854), 178.

4. On the growing number of southern evangelicals and the slavery question, see Christine L. Heyrman, *Southern Cross: The Beginnings of the Bible Belt* (New York: Alfred A. Knopf, 1997), 3–27. On the growing number of church colleges, see Donald George Tewksbury, "The Founding of American Colleges and Universities Before the Civil War, with Particular Reference to the Religious Influences Bearing Upon the College Movement" (PhD diss., Columbia University, 1932); Ralph Eugene Reed, "Fortresses of Faith: Design and Experience at Southern Evangelical Colleges, 1830–1900" (PhD diss., Emory University, 1991).

5. Elizabeth Fox-Genovese and Eugene Genovese, *The Mind of the Master Class: History and Faith in the Southern Slaveholders' Worldview* (New York: Cambridge University Press, 2005), 518.

6. The Genoveses have highlighted the ambiguity of Philemon with respect to the slavery question, referencing both sides of the argument. See ibid., 519n24.

7. Augustus Baldwin Longstreet, *Letters on the Epistle of Paul to Philemon* (Charleston, S.C.: B. Benkins, 1845), 177, 179.

8. On Emory College's involvement in the 1844 split of the Methodist Church, see Mark Auslander, *The Accidental Slaveowner: Revisiting a Myth of Race and Finding an American Family* (Athens: University of Georgia Press, 2011), 129–32, 71–77. On the significance of Longstreet's 1845 pamphlet, see Christopher H. Owen, *The Sacred Flame of*

Love: Methodism and Society in Nineteenth Century Georgia (Athens: University of Georgia Press, 1998), 63.

9. Julian P. Boyd, ed., *The Papers of Thomas Jefferson, Vol. 1, 1760–1776* (Princeton, N.J.: Princeton University Press, 1950), 243–47.

10. Augustus Baldwin Longstreet, *A Voice from the South: Comprising Letters from Georgia to Massachusetts, and to the Southern States* (Baltimore, Md.: Western Continent Press, 1847), 6, 10, 5.

11. Lewis M. Purifoy, "The Southern Methodist Church and the Proslavery Argument," *Journal of Southern History* 32, no. 3 (August 1966): 326.

12. Jennifer Green, *Military Education and the Emerging Middle Class in the Old South* (Cambridge: Cambridge University Press, 2008), 135.

13. On the debate over classical versus practical education, see Green, *Military Education*, 130–50; Caroline Winterer, *The Culture of Classicism: Ancient Greece and Rome in American Intellectual Life, 1780–1910* (Baltimore, Md.: Johns Hopkins University Press, 2002), 77–98. See also Wayne K. Durrill, "The Power of Ancient Words: Classical Teaching and Social Change at South Carolina College, 1804–1860," *Journal of Southern History* 65, no. 3 (August 1999): 469–98.

14. As quoted in A. James Fuller, *Chaplain to the Confederacy: Basil Manly and Baptist Life in the Old South* (Baton Rouge: Louisiana State University Press, 2000), 163.

15. "Catalogue of the Officers & Students, in Emory College, GA, and the Report of the Board of Trustees to the Georgia Conference," Oxford, Ga., 1839, Emory University Archives (hereafter EU-A).

16. "A Catalogue of the Officers and Students of Emory College, 1845, Oxford, Newton Co., GA.," EU-A.

17. *Catalogue of the Officers, Students & Alumni of Emory College, Oxford, Georgia* (Macon, Ga.: Printed by Benjamin F. Griffin, 1853), EU-A.

18. Fox-Genovese and Genovese, *The Mind of the Master Class*, 566.

19. See Drew Gilpin Faust, "The Proslavery Argument in History," in *Southern Stories: Slaveholders in Peace and War*, ed. Drew Gilpin Faust (Columbia: University of Missouri Press, 1992), 80.

20. Emory College records prior to 1847 do not indicate which text was used in a particular class.

21. William Paley, *Paley's Moral and Political Philosophy (as Condensed by A. J. Valpy)* (Philadelphia: U. Hunt & Son, 1845), 111.

22. Joseph L. Blau, introduction to *The Elements of Moral Science*, by Francis Wayland, ed. Joseph L. Blau (1835; Cambridge, Mass.: Belknap Press of Harvard University Press, 1963), xliii–xlix.

23. Fox-Genovese and Genovese, *The Mind of the Master Class*, 570.

24. Francis Wayland, *The Elements of Moral Science* (New York: Cooke and Co., 1835), 103, 225.

25. Matthew S. Hill, "God and Slavery in America: Francis Wayland and the Evangelical Conscience" (PhD diss., Georgia State University, 2008), 1, 18.

26. Francis Wayland to James Hoby, December 25, 1837, as quoted in Brown University, *Slavery and Justice: Report of the Brown University Steering Committee on Slavery and Justice*, accessed September 15, 2012, http://brown.edu/Research/Slavery_Justice/documents/SlaveryAndJustice.pdf.

27. Basil Manly to Basil Manly Jr., March 15, 1845, as quoted in Fuller, *Chaplain to the Confederacy*, 216.

28. Francis Wayland, *The Elements of Political Economy* (New York: Leavitt, Lord & Company, 1837), 186, 131.

29. Methodist Episcopal Church, South, *Quarterly Review of the Methodist Episcopal Church, South* (Published by John Early for the Methodist Episcopal Church, South, 1860), 186. Interestingly, this review was written in Oxford, Georgia, most likely by an author affiliated with Emory College. Unfortunately, the publication does not indicate the reviewer's name.

30. R. H. Rivers and Thomas O. Summers, *Elements of Moral Philosophy* (Nashville, Tenn.: Southern Methodist Publishing House, 1860), xv, 329, 348, 355.

31. Thornton Stringfellow, "The Bible Argument: Or, Slavery in the Light of Divine Revelation," in *Cotton Is King, and Pro-slavery Arguments: Comprising the Writings of Hammond, Harper, Christy, Stringfellow, Hodge, Bledsoe, and Cartwright, on This Important Subject*, by E. N. Elliott (Augusta, Ga.: Pritchard, Abbott & Loomis, 1860), 461–521.

32. Wren Diary, entry for March 1858.

33. William Jacob Sasnett, *Progress: Considered with Particular Reference to the Methodist Episcopal Church, South* (Nashville, Tenn.: E. Stevenson & F. A. Owen, 1855), 11, 211.

34. See Faust, "The Proslavery Argument," 81. "The proslavery argument asserted its opposition to the growing materialism of the age and offered the model of evangelical stewardship as the best representation of its labor system" (81).

35. 1850 U.S. Census, Slave Schedules, District 8, Georgia (Muscogee County).

36. 1860 U.S. Census, Slave Schedules, District 311, Georgia (Putnam County).

37. 1850 U.S. Census, Slave Schedules, District 74, Georgia (Screven County).

38. 1850 U.S. Census, Slave Schedules, Subdivision 65, Georgia (Newton County); Auslander, *The Accidental Slaveowner*, 59–60. Following the war, Orr signed a contract with his former slaves, agreeing to provide them with some basic necessities. A copy of the contract appears in Auslander, *The Accidental Slaveowner*, 59–60. In a recent article, Royal Dumas estimated that the student body of the University of Alabama in 1845 came from families that owned at least 3,343 slaves (as recorded in the 1840 census). See Royal C. Dumas, "My Son and My Money Go to the University of Alabama? The Students at the University of Alabama in 1845 and the Families That Sent Them," *Alabama Civil Rights & Civil Liberties Law Review* 1 (2011): 77.

39. Diary entry for January 10, 1850, in "Notes on Autobiography," by Joseph A. Turner, EU-A.

40. On literary societies generally, see Thomas Spencer Harding, *College Literary Societies: Their Contribution to Higher Education in the United States, 1815–1876* (New York: Pageant Press International, 1971). On literary societies at Emory College, see Mark Swails, "Literary Societies as Institutions of Honor at Evangelical Colleges in Georgia" (MA thesis, Emory University, Atlanta, Ga., 2007). A good study on literary societies at the University of North Carolina is Timothy J. Williams, "Intellectual Manhood: Becoming Men of the Republic at a Southern University, 1795–1861" (PhD diss., University of North Carolina, Chapel Hill, 2010).

41. See the appendix in Swails, "Literary Societies."

42. For debate topics, see ibid.

43. Erica Lindermann, "The Debating Societies," in *True and Candid Compositions: The Lives and Writings of Antebellum Students at the University of North Carolina*, online exhibition, *Documenting the American South*, University of North Carolina at Chapel Hill, http://docsouth.unc.edu/true/chapter/chp05-02/chp05-02.html (accessed March 18, 2011).

44. Harding, *College Literary Societies*, 156.

45. Peter S. Carmichael, *The Last Generation: Young Virginians in Peace, War, and Reunion* (Chapel Hill: University of North Carolina Press, 2005), 6.

CHAPTER SIX

"I Whipped Him a Second Time, Very Severely"

Basil Manly, Honor, and Slavery at the University of Alabama

A. James Fuller

On March 4, 1846, Sam walked into the office of the president of the University of Alabama, where the faculty had gathered. That afternoon trouble had arisen when Sam had refused to measure or even receive a load of coal brought by Thomas G. Green, a local man contracted to deliver coal to the university. Green had not taken the refusal well and charged Sam with insolence, a very serious accusation in a society of honor where even the smallest slight might lead to violence and where the labor system rested on the obedience of slaves.

Now, walking into the room where the president and faculty waited, Sam came face-to-face with the dominant ethic of the Old South. Sam was a slave owned by the university, and he had been living and working there since March 11, 1839, when the governor had sent him to join the school's staff. The code of honor demanded that an injured party be given satisfaction. If a slight were given by a gentleman to a gentleman, and no apology followed, a duel might result. If a gentleman were slighted by a free white man beneath him in society, he might cane the culprit, beating him with a walking stick. Matters of honor at the lower levels of white society often led to the brawls for which southern poor whites were so well known. Someone might lose their sight to an eye gouging or have a finger bitten off. But if a slave slighted the honor of a white man, the punishment was whipping.

Southern ideas of democracy and equality rested on white supremacy. No slave or even free black man could be allowed to slight a white man if the community hoped to keep the racial foundations of honor, of white equality, and of white supremacy intact.[1]

On that day, Sam's first offense to the system of slavery was insolence to

The University of Alabama in 1839. Courtesy of the W. S. Hoole Special Collections Library, University of Alabama.

a white worker. Whether Sam's so-called insolence was real or imagined, whether he was right or wrong about the coal, he found himself at the complicated crossroads of southern society, where honor met slavery and where racism met democracy. He would soon be in front of white men of a higher status and face dire consequences. But he remained unbowed.[2]

Green had complained, and the matter had been referred to the faculty. The university could not afford to have its reputation among the citizenry smeared by ill will. A few complaints, some muttered rumors, and discussions in the community about such an issue could lead to larger complaints about elitism and might intersect with the strong anti-intellectual impulse of many in the predominantly rural society. In a world where symbolism mattered more than substance, where honor trumped reality, the insolence of a slave to a white working man might cause both political and social problems for a university already plagued by complaints about extravagant expenditures and tax dollars being used to educate the children of the rich at the expense of the poor. And this was a matter of order as well, for slavery required subordination. The purpose of slavery, as Justice Thomas Ruffin of the North Carolina Supreme Court stated in *State v. Mann*, "is the profit of the master, his security and the public safety." In order to achieve that end, "the power of the master must be absolute, to render the submission of the slave perfect."[3]

The president's mansion at the University of Alabama. Basil Manly was the first occupant. Completed in 1841, the building contained the president's residence and his office. Sam was most likely whipped in this building in the presence of university faculty members. This building still stands on campus, with Manly's desk on display. Courtesy of the W. S. Hoole Special Collections Library, University of Alabama.

Most of the faculty members were gentlemen and native southerners; most of them were also slave owners. They did not hesitate to take action to protect the image of the university and restore peace under honor's code. They ordered that Sam be "chastised" by the president, who was nominally Sam's master as the head of the institution that owned him. Furthermore, they ordered that the whipping be conducted in front of them. And so Sam walked into the room to receive what honor—and order—demanded. The president of the university, the Southern Baptist preacher turned educator Basil Manly, carried out his duty, whipping the slave while the faculty watched.

But honor and slavery were not finished with Sam that afternoon. He took the beating, but Sam indicated in some way now lost to history that he was not humbled by it. Perhaps Sam resented being punished because he did not think he was in the wrong. Perhaps he did not think anyone should have the right or power to whip him. Maybe he resented Basil Manly personally. Perhaps his spirit refused to be broken. One can speculate about the ideas of antislavery that were in circulation in the 1840s even in Alabama, such as in

Francis Wayland's *Elements of Moral Philosophy*, which Manly used as a textbook in his lectures to the senior class. This episode, precisely because so little is known about it, invites speculation on the ideas and impulses motivating Sam. Whatever went through his mind, Sam was, in the words that Manly recorded in his diary, "not sufficiently humbled." That reaction did not satisfy the self-righteous Baptist, who was always prickly about his honor.[4]

For Sam to show any kind of disrespect in that setting was to defy the president's authority in front of the faculty members he led. To not be humbled by the whipping defied Manly's mastery, challenged his masculinity, slighted his honor, and threatened order on the campus. Sam had slighted Thomas Green earlier in the day, and now he had slighted his master. And so, as Manly wrote in his diary, "I whipped him a second time, very severely."[5]

For Basil Manly, the faculty, and Sam, this incident was just another whipping, another day in a long period of trouble. The university faculty and administration did not forget, and Manly kept track of the record, judging on February 11, 1850, that Sam "has always been impudent and hard to manage." That day, four years after the whipping in the president's office, the faculty voted to sell Sam after he was "very impudent and insubordinate" to one of the professors. Manly did as the faculty wished: he sold the university slave the next day and sent him to his new master. But on February 16, 1850, Sam returned to campus and begged to be allowed to come back. Apparently, his new owner had agreed to allow Sam to return, and Manly referred the matter to two professors, who served as a subcommittee to decide the matter. This reference to the faculty illustrates the model of university self-governance and administrative management the University of Alabama followed at that time. The university took the advice of faculty quite regularly.

Two days later, at the Monday faculty meeting, one of the professors argued for Sam's reinstatement, saying that he thought the slave was "truly penitent." Swayed by their colleague's arguments, the faculty voted to rescind the order to sell Sam and reinstated him as a university servant. Manly thought that Sam should be sold "as a matter of policy," but Manly did not worry that he would have any problems with Sam himself. He was confident that "so far as anything that I have to order or require from Sam is concerned, I am not afraid that he will disobey or displease me, personally, in any serious degree." After all, if Manly felt that Sam was disobedient or impudent, he had options. He could choose to whip or to sell Sam.[6]

A year later, on February 21, 1851, Sam once again found himself the victim of a whipping, this time at the hands of a student or students. The university president learned that a number of the students had been involved in "combining to whip Sam." Manly investigated, discovered who the "chief actors" were, and addressed the students about the matter, warning them not to do it again and advising those who had done it to present themselves to the faculty about the matter. His initial warning did little to dissuade the young gentlemen of the student body, all of them striving to become men of honor. One way of demonstrating one's honor, of establishing one's mastery, was to have authority over slaves. Being a gentleman meant being independent, having mastery, having honor. Slaves had no independence, were subordinate, had no honor. Manly had to deal with student mistreatment of the university slaves or those owned by faculty members on numerous occasions. This time, the students were beating Sam. This illustrates the precarious position that slaves occupied on a university campus—or elsewhere in the South. They were subject to physical abuse by people who occupied a higher status, even if those people did not own them.

Despite his warning and keeping an eye on the malefactors, Manly discovered that the whippings did not stop. A month later, on March 19, 1851, the president "spoke to the students, again, about whipping Sam; and again advised them to communicate with me or with some member of the Faculty." One student came forward and confessed that he had been involved and that he knew it was wrong. Manly thought him sincere, and no punishment was given. For the Southern Baptist serving as university president, forgiveness, like equality, depended on race. And so it went, as Sam continued to live and work and suffer on the campus in Tuscaloosa.[7]

Sam's case stands as a stark symbol of the realities of slavery and the university in antebellum Alabama. Discovered by the research of Alfred L. Brophy during his passionate work during the recent "Age of Apology," the treatment became part of the argument over whether or not the University of Alabama should apologize for slavery, which it did in 2004. But Sam's case also included Basil Manly, the university president, the Southern Baptist preacher, the intellectual defender of slavery who was also the master with the whip in his hand. Looking at the ways in which Manly understood slavery, the ways he defended it, and the ways that he lived reveals the complexities and the contradictions of life in a society built on honor and slavery.[8]

Who was the man who whipped Sam twice that day in 1846? Born and raised in Chatham County, North Carolina, in 1798, Basil Manly Sr. became one of the most important Baptist leaders in the country in the years before the Civil War. Converted while kneeling in prayer with a slave in a cornfield at age sixteen, he believed that God called him to the ministry. He attended South Carolina College and established himself as a man of honor at the graduation ceremonies on December 21, 1821. Manly's grades won him the right to make the valedictory address, but the student who finished a close second was resentful and wanted to argue the point in the graduation line. The jealous student, angered by Manly's cool response, pulled a knife and rushed at Manly, who deflected the blade and wrestled the attacker to the ground. Manly nearly choked the student to death before others intervened and pulled him off the assailant. The other students cheered the young Baptist for defending his honor and demonstrating his mastery in a physical setting.[9]

He soon demonstrated his mastery in an intellectual setting—the pulpit—as well. Invited to serve as a minister in the rural Edgefield District, Manly worked hard to build several Baptist congregations, and his efforts were rewarded with a widespread religious awakening. The Edgefield Revival lasted for about two years, from 1822 to 1824, and Manly's preaching led to several hundred conversions. While revivals were widespread and frequent during the Second Great Awakening, the Edgefield Revival spilled over into surrounding areas, even reaching into Georgia. Manly's regular reports on the movement were published in Baptist periodicals as he helped define and construct the events even as they occurred. While living in Edgefield, he married the daughter of a wealthy planter and started a family. His dramatic preaching success in the backcountry led to a call to serve as the pastor of the First Baptist Church of Charleston. That congregation, considered the "mother church" by Baptists in the South, had been led by several famous ministers, including the illustrious Richard Furman, namesake of Furman University. In Charleston Manly once again enjoyed tremendous success as a preacher. He also became a public man, moving in the elite circles of the city. These activities included intellectual matters, and Manly often delivered lectures before the Literary and Philosophical Society. Some of his writings and sermons were published, and his prominence among Baptists led to wider fame and spheres of influence. In 1838 he left Charleston to take the position of president of the University of Alabama in Tuscaloosa. There he oversaw curriculum reform (somewhat reluctantly installing the liberal arts while trying to maintain a model of classical education), instituted a new system of discipline, and led the school through a period of growth amid financial difficulties.[10]

During his eighteen-year tenure as university president, Manly continued to preach and lead the Baptist denomination. He worked as an evangelist and traveled widely across the state and region to preach at revival services. In 1845 he wrote the Alabama Resolutions, which led to the breakup of the national Baptist Triennial Convention and the creation of the Southern Baptist Convention. A slave owner and staunch defender of slavery, he also worked for reform by leading statewide efforts to help the insane and those in the prison system. He also joined and led the Anti-Dueling Society, a matter that clearly revealed the tension between the ethics of honor and Evangelical Christianity. His efforts on behalf of education included helping to found Furman University and the Southern Baptist Theological Seminary. He left the university to return to Charleston and then moved to Montgomery, Alabama, where he served as a pastor and accepted the position as official chaplain to the Confederate government in 1861. A longtime proponent of separate southern institutions, he saw the Confederacy as the fulfillment of God's plan. He and his family struggled through the war years, and Manly preached many funeral sermons for soldiers and worked to help the Confederate cause on the home front. He suffered a stroke in 1864, and this forced him into retirement. He continued to preach whenever possible and tried to offer advice to younger Baptist leaders, including his sons (Basil Manly Jr. and Charles Manly), who had taken up his mantle and become preachers and educators. He died in 1868, and although his dream for a southern nation had been crushed, he held fast to his faith to the end.[11]

Throughout his career, Manly defended slavery as an institution. To Manly, slavery stood as a viable, just, and Christian institution, and he defended it as such. He had long imbibed the proslavery ideas of his society and had become a leading defender of it among Baptists. In private he engaged Francis Wayland in an exchange of letters debating slavery that foreshadowed the northern antislavery clergyman's later, published debate with Manly's good friend and fellow Southern Baptist Richard Fuller. Publicly, in sermons and addresses, Manly argued that slavery was rational, economically sound, and superior to wage labor. Further, slavery was good for the slave as well as for the master, as long as it was a Christian institution. Through it, blacks might be saved from sin and hell. Through it, a divine order for society might be established. Indeed, Manly thought of the peculiar institution in terms of his paternalism. For him, slaves were part of the family, a patriarchal structure that he thought had been created by God. To be sure, while Manly fully supported the gen-

Basil Manly, 1845. Courtesy of the W. S. Hoole
Special Collections Library, University of Alabama.

dered and racial aspects of southern patriarchy, he also hoped to reform it. In his mind, making the patriarchal family (which included slavery, he argued) a Christian order based on Christian morality and justice would improve it, restoring it to the state God had intended. As a minister, he recognized the humanity of slaves and knew that masters often abused their power. In fact, he had only to look at himself to see the violent side of slavery. At times, he was a cruel master. Yet at other times, he took actions that pushed the racial and social boundaries of his time. In his thinking, he combined Calvinism with honor in a traditional patriarchal order, creating in his sermons a full-scale defense of southern society as a whole and of slavery in particular. Two stories illustrate his complicated experiences as a master, while one of his sermons demonstrates the complexity of his thought about slavery.[12]

Manly's cruelty is demonstrated most clearly in his dealings with Claiborne, a slave he owned in Charleston. In his diary, Manly complained about the slave boy's behavior. Despite whippings and numerous attempts at persuading him to behave the way his master wanted him to, Claiborne continued to misbehave. On July 5, 1833, the preacher sent the young man "to the workhouse to be put on the Treadmill—and kept in solitary confinement." The Charleston workhouse was a hellish place where slave breakers worked fiendishly with whips to punish slaves chained like animals to the treadmill. There in the dank, dark prison, Claiborne was beaten and forced to trudge for hour upon hour, helping other poor souls to turn the grindstones attached to the treadmill. Manly insisted that this treatment was necessary because of Claiborne's "repeated and perturbing misconduct," especially since he had taken to keeping "bad company and gambling, and was fast getting into their attendants, Lying and stealing."[13]

The next day, July 6, Manly went and saw Claiborne at the workhouse. The young slave "seemed penitent" and promised his master that he would behave, so he was taken home. But Claiborne soon got into more mischief, and the Baptist worried about his own image as a minister as his slave, a member of his household, engaged in sinful activities. Drawn to various vices, Claiborne was especially fond of gambling, a difficult habit for a slave because he lacked means, which led to stealing. He also spent time on the city's waterfront, where he "got the venereal." Once, when he feared that Manly was going to whip him, Claiborne "ran away, and got in with a vagabond who kept a drunkery." Time and again, the preacher tried both "severity, and kindness," but Claiborne only "grew worse and worse."[14]

During one period in which Claiborne seemed to have gained self-control, Manly hired him out to a carpenter in the city. This afforded the young slave the opportunity to live outside his master's home and the chance to learn a skilled trade. But the plan backfired when Claiborne quit going to work and instead started going down to the waterfront, where he hired himself out as a day laborer "for a day or two at a time [and] gamble[d] and frolic[ked] with the money." To cover his tracks, he told his employer that he was sick and at Manly's, while his master thought he was at the carpenter's. When the Baptist preacher found out, he warned Claiborne that "I should flog him no more, that if he displeased me again in any respect, I would make an end of his troubling me, and sell him." Although he owned Claiborne's mother and siblings and he often preached that slaveholders should not break up slave families, on March 1, 1836, Manly decided that Claiborne was incorrigible and sold him for $1,025. Here, Manly clearly failed to maintain his paternalistic ideals.[15]

The sale of Claiborne became an issue and helped lead directly to the creation of the Southern Baptist Convention. Later in 1836, not long after selling his slave, Manly traveled to Boston. While visiting with fellow Baptist ministers in the city, he took a long drive with one of them, a man named Henry Jackson, and in the course of their conversation, the northern divine asked Manly "about all the peculiarities of Southern society, institutions, and manners." Jackson asked Manly "how many slaves I had, what their ages, how they were treated—if I had ever bought one, or sold one—and so on, endlessly." Of course, the southerner recounted the story of Claiborne, as well as other particular cases. Jackson asked "if it was really the feeling at the South that we had a right to sell them, at will." The Southern Baptist replied that "it certainly was; that however great the trial was to my feelings in other respects, I had none as to the right of property." Manly insisted that he did not like to sell his slaves "on account of family relations" but that when it came down to it, "I had no more doubt or compunction than in pocketing the price of a horse or anything else that belonged to me." Soon, antislavery Northern Baptists were talking about how Manly had said that he would sell a slave the same as he would a horse.[16]

In 1844 tensions rose in the Baptist Triennial Convention, a national organization designed to support missions. Northern Baptists argued that slavery was a sin, while southerners defended their peculiar institution. In the midst of this tension, Manly's nomination to office in the convention was defeated by northerners who raised objections to him based on the story and other information that they claimed to have about him as a slave owner. His honor slighted, Manly wrote to a Northern Baptist who had objected to his nomination and learned that the wife of John L. Dagg, a renowned Southern Baptist theologian, minister, and president of Mercer University, had said that Manly would often "go out of a morning, take off his coat, and whip, severely, every negro about his premises, just for the sake of exercise." Stunned, Manly carefully asked Dagg about it but was unable to receive satisfaction. He then turned to another means of restoring his honor: he challenged the right of Northern Baptists to question his rights as a slave owner. Manly wrote the "Alabama Resolutions," which asked the Triennial Convention to state its official position on the question of slavery, demanding to know if the convention—now controlled by a northern majority on its board—would appoint slaveholders to be officers or missionaries. Although he insisted that he had "kept my private griefs to myself," Manly's honor had been insulted. When the Triennial Convention responded by saying that they could not appoint a slave owner, the southerners walked out and in May 1845 created the Southern Baptist Convention. Manly had defended his honor, and he had defended his right to punish and sell his slaves.[17]

Such was the imperious part of Manly's personality. But in keeping with his paternalistic ideas, Basil Manly also showed kindness to slaves, especially those who were his parishioners, and he sometimes skirted the edges of social acceptance in doing so. While Manly spoke often and strongly about the virtues of slavery and the need for subordination, he also sometimes found himself caught in the context of slavery, unable to serve his African American congregants in the same way that would have helped a free white person. The case of Lydia Frierson demonstrates how the Southern Baptist preacher worked with slaves and saw them as human beings even as it also illustrates how he was unable to step outside the bounds of honor. Lydia Frierson was a slave who had been converted and baptized by Manly during his ministry in Charleston, and on June 22, 1829, the preacher reported in his diary that she had come to visit him. During these pastoral sessions, Lydia had told him why she had not been taking Communion. She feared that she had been committing a sin, because her master, John Frierson, "compels her to live in *constant* adultery with him." She was brokenhearted and did not know what to do. Furthermore, several of the white members of the Frierson family, although not John Frierson himself, were members of the congregation at First Baptist Church.

In this situation, Manly pondered his own paternalistic conception of the family and also confronted the bounds of southern honor. John Frierson, as a husband, father, and master, had power and authority as a patriarch and as a southern gentleman. If Manly slighted Frierson's authority or honor, there would be consequences. As a minister and member of Charleston's Anti-Dueling Society, Manly might be able to avoid a violent meeting, but the issue could divide the Frierson family, the congregation, and the community. Further, Lydia might become the victim of violence at the hands of her master, or perhaps Mrs. Frierson, also subordinate to patriarchal authority, might take her frustration and powerlessness out on the slave. Unsure what to do, Manly advised Lydia to "remonstrate kindly with her master" and "tell him that she could not consent to sin." But on her next visit, the slave reported that although she had tried everything she could, John Frierson continued to rape (my term, not Manly's) her and now "threatens her most dreadfully if she resists him." Both Lydia and her white minister were trapped by the context of slavery and the limits of honor. Manly assured her that he would not do what the rules demanded of him, which was to report her to the appropriate committee for church discipline. He urged her to try to resist Frierson and (easily enough for him) argued that "it is better for her to die, than to sin." Eventually, when Frierson died and the opportunity presented itself, Manly purchased Lydia and took her into his own household, where "she is now our worthy and respectable old nurse."[18]

In the case of Lydia Frierson, Manly lacked the ability to confront John Frierson. In large part that was due to Manly's own acceptance of the code of honor and of the boundaries of the owner's dominion over his slaves. Moreover, Manly's theological understanding of the patriarchal household as a sacred institution precluded an outsider from stepping in to challenge the patriarch's divinely and socially ordained authority. But he did realize the sin and urged Lydia to resist her master. As a Baptist preacher, Basil Manly believed that God had called him to save the souls of others. In the Old South, the only way to "save some souls was to buy their bodies."[19]

In the cases of Lydia and Claiborne, Manly tried to live out in complex reality his paternalistic notions. Honor, faith, and slavery all came together in Manly's conception of the family. In one of his most often preached series of pulpit discourses, he provided a blueprint for his vision of a Christian society. Manly's "Sermons on Duty" consisted of a series of twenty-one sermons, and he preached them many times, first in Charleston, then repeatedly during his years in Alabama. The first eight dealt with his conception of the family, the next six were dedicated to the Christian living as a citizen in the world, and the last five looked at the duties required of individuals living in different contexts such as wealth, old age, and poor health. Clearly, the family was foundational to Manly's thought, and honor was foundational to the family. Among those eight homilies on the nature of the family was a very long sermon entitled "Duties of Masters and Servants." In it, Manly presented a defense of slavery but also an inherent criticism of the institution, as his justification for its continuance called for it to be reformed along Christian lines. His defense of the peculiar institution in this particular sermon mustered many of the same arguments he made in many other sermons and addresses he gave in vindicating slavery. But it also stood apart from those other orations because of its place in the series and its direct connection to his patriarchal view of the family.

In "Duties of Masters and Servants" Manly argued that slavery could be more than just a necessary evil; it could also be part of a benevolent Christian social system that was a positive good for both prosperous masters and happy slaves. Quoting heavily from scriptures in both the Old and New Testaments, Manly claimed that God had divinely ordered slavery just as God had established the family structure and society as a whole. As in his other writings on the subject, he defended slavery by comparing it to the conditions of workers in Europe and the North, arguing that southern slaves "are less worked, as well fed and clothed, and liable to fewer hardships, changes, . . . and anxieties." Slavery, the Southern Baptist argued, "is a kind of Patriarchal Government—partaking in some respects of the character of Paternity." Here was southern paternalism. Slaveholders had a duty to recognize that "God has made you their masters—placed them under your protection, made you their guardians, the conservators of their lives and happiness." White masters were their slaves' "guides and counselors, their benefactors and friends." The Christian master had a duty to "make proper regulations with regard to their employment," was obligated to set up a system of discipline to govern them (one that included rewards as well as punishment), and—above all—had to make sure that his slaves had plenty of "opportunity to receive religious instruction, and to worship God." Slaves had duties, too, of course, including an obligation to obey their masters. But faithfulness, "respectfulness and teachableness," contentment, truthfulness, cheerfulness, conscientiousness, "plainness, and an humble simplicity" also went into the good slave's "religious sense of duty." Such a list smacked of simply making religion a matter of social control and was clearly the result of a master's mind working up the image of how he wanted his slaves to act. While the concept of duty allowed Manly to unite honor and his Calvinist theology in a form of Christian gentility, it did not necessarily humanize slavery. Rather, it reaffirmed both white supremacy and the power of the master.

But social criticism came into the sermon as well. Manly admitted that southerners, white and black, failed to live up to his vision of an idyllic form of slavery, complete with just, kind Christian masters and happy, obedient Christian slaves. Still, he urged them to strive to live up to that ideal. The preacher argued that both master and slave had to "remember that each has a master in Heaven" and needed to know that "the discharge of duty in these relations adorns the doctrine of God and our Christian profession." If only slavery worked as God intended, then both slaves and slaveholders would see that "mutual advantage and satisfaction arises out of the relation, and the proper discharge of its duties." If so, then all would "be led to faithfulness in duty from the prospect held out to the good of possessing in common, the inheritance and dwelling place of Heaven." While this clearly told slaves to wait for their reward in the afterlife while serving their masters faithfully in this world, it also placed an obligation upon those masters who sincerely believed and hoped for heaven. Masters had to provide for their slaves physically and spiritually. This demanded "the effort to teach and christianize our 3 millions of Africans," an effort that needed to be promoted "with the whole force of the South."[20]

Manly's rhetoric about making slavery a Christian institution clearly served as a justification for slavery. But as Eugene Genovese has argued, it also contained a threat to the institution as it really existed. By holding up their ideal of slavery being Christian and calling on masters to ameliorate the viciousness of the system with Christian duty and morality, ministers like Manly took on the role of reformer. Such reforms would necessarily mean that standards would have to change. To replace arbitrary power with a clear system of rules and discipline deprived masters of their absolute authority. To demand better conditions for slaves might mean taking away some of the masters' profits. To say that southerners did not actually live up to the ideal form of slavery was to give the lie to the very heart of the proslavery argument: that it was a positive good. In other words, saying that it *could* be a positive good was a very different thing from saying that it *was* a positive good. Here again Manly skirted the edges of social acceptance. He focused on the duty of slaves and emphasized their spiritual needs rather than the material ones. After all, if his words in defending the institution gave the lie to the proslavery argument, he would once again be pushing the limits of honor. To "give the lie" meant showing that appearance was different from reality. No gentleman could allow someone to give him the lie. It was a slap in the face. Southern preachers like Manly got away with it by couching their arguments in careful language in sermons that ultimately defended slavery. But if a northerner dared to do the same thing, those same southern ministers howled in protest and took offense. Clearly, the Christian proslavery argument was just that, a proslavery argument. That it contained internal criticism was to be taken individually and understood religiously, not to be taken as a condemnation of slavery as a whole.[21]

And so once again Manly lacked the ability to confront evil even as he denounced sin and delicately walked the social minefields of his society. He tried to reconcile evangelical Christianity and honor and hoped to reconcile slavery with Christian faith and morality. The tensions were great, and he often failed in practice. But he forged just such an intellectual reconciliation in his own mind, developing more than a defense of slavery and more than a justification for his own sin, although he provided those too. In his thinking, he brought together Calvinism and honor in a form of Christian gentility.[22] Duty was the key to that reconciliation. And duty was not always kind and was rarely gentle. A Christian patriarch did not spare the rod. He did not hesitate to take up the whip. When honor was slighted, Manly moved quickly to defend it. When authority was challenged, the Southern Baptist acted to assert and prove it.

Thus Manly as a leading Baptist minister and educator developed and promulgated a vision of slavery that both was consistent with the existing intellectual, religious, and social structure in the South and at points challenged it. He communicated such ideas in places beside the university—such as the pulpit. Thus Manly illustrates again the ways that schools like Alabama were consonant with ideas and practices in circulation throughout the South. This may in some ways show the university as a place more similar than dissimilar to the rest of the South. And it may call into question the emerging area of studies on "universities and slavery," for it shows that the practices and ideas at the university were not very different from those outside. Or it may demonstrate again how studying the ideas and practices of universities can tell us a great deal about the society that supported them and that they in turn supported through the education of the next generation of elite southern men.

So one day in March 1846 a man named Thomas Green brought a load of coal to the University of Alabama, and a slave named Sam refused to take it. A small thing, really, but it illuminates the complicated tensions that lay not only in the heart of the university president but in the university itself and in southern society as a whole.

NOTES

1. For the concept of honor and its role in southern society, see Bertram Wyatt-Brown, *Southern Honor: Ethics and Behavior in the Old South* (New York: Oxford University Press, 1982); Wyatt-Brown, *The Shaping of Southern Culture: Honor, Grace, and War, 1760s–1890s* (Chapel Hill: University of North Carolina Press, 2000); Kenneth S. Greenberg, *Masters and Statesmen: The Political Culture of American Slavery* (Baltimore, Md.: Johns Hopkins University Press, 1985); Greenberg, *Honor and Slavery: Lies, Duels, Noses, Masks, Dressing as a Woman, Gifts, Strangers, Humanitarianism, Death, Baseball, Hunt-

ing, and Gambling in the Old South (Princeton, N.J.: Princeton University Press, 1996). Two more recent accounts have continued the interpretation of honor in the old South: Ariela Gross, *Double Character: Slavery and Mastery in the Antebellum Southern Courtroom* (Princeton, N.J.: Princeton University Press, 2000); and Timothy S. Huebner, *The Southern Judicial Tradition: State Judges and Sectional Distinctiveness, 1790–1890* (Athens: University of Georgia Press, 1999).

2. Basil Manly, March 4, 1846, Record Book I (1843–1848), Manly Family Papers, William Stanley Hoole Special Collections Library, University of Alabama, Tuscaloosa (hereafter MFP); Basil Manly, March 11, 1839, Diary II (1834–1846), MFP.

3. State v. Mann, 13 N.C. 263, 264 (1829).

4. A. James Fuller, *Chaplain to the Confederacy: Basil Manly and Baptist Life in the Old South* (Baton Rouge: Louisiana State University Press, 2000), esp. 56–88.

5. Manly, March 4, 1846, Record Book I.

6. Manly, February 16, 1850, February 18, 1850, Record Book I.

7. Manly, February 21, 1851, March 19, 1851, Record Book I. For more on honor and students in the antebellum South, see Robert F. Pace, *Halls of Honor: College Men in the Old South* (Baton Rouge: Louisiana State University Press, 2004). Pace includes reports from Manly in his section on students mistreating slaves (49–50).

8. For more on the controversy over the university's apology, see Alfred L. Brophy, "The University and the Slaves: Apology and Its Meaning," in *The Age of Apology: Facing Up to the Past*, ed. Mark Gibney and Rhoda E. Howard-Hassmann (Philadelphia: University of Pennsylvania Press, 2008), 109–19.

9. Fuller, *Chaplain to the Confederacy*, 25–27.

10. Ibid., 11–129.

11. Ibid., 130–267, 287–318.

12. For a more complete discussion of Manly's proslavery thought and paternalism, see ibid., esp. chaps. 9, 10, and 11. More recent scholarship provides interesting insights into the ways in which race and slavery intersected with paternalism in the thought of southern clergy. See especially Lacy K. Ford, *Deliver Us from Evil: The Slavery Question in the Old South* (New York: Oxford University Press, 2009); Erskine Clarke, *Dwelling Place: A Plantation Epic* (New Haven, Conn.: Yale University Press, 2005).

13. Basil Manly to Basil Manly Jr., August 2, 1844, August 25, 1844, MFP.

14. Basil Manly to Basil Manly Jr., August 25, 1844, MFP.

15. Basil Manly, August 19, 1831, June 30, 1833, Diary I (1826–1833), MFP; Basil Manly to Basil Manly Jr., August 25, 1844; Manly, March 1, 1836, Diary II.

16. Basil Manly to George B. Ide, August 27, 1844, Diary II; Basil Manly to Basil Manly Jr., August 25, 1844; Basil Manly to Basil Manly Jr., August 26, 1844, MFP.

17. Basil Manly to George Ide, August 27, 1844, in Manly, Diary II, 321–25; Manly to Manly Jr., August 25, 1844, August 2, 1844; Manly to Ide, October 17, 1844, MFP; Basil Manly to Basil Manly Jr., March 31, 1845, MFP; Basil Manly to J. L. Dagg, April 8, 1845, Di-

ary II, 351–52; Manly to Dagg, May 6, 1850, in Basil Manly, Diary III (1847–1857), 137–38, MFP; Manly to E. B. Teague, March 15, 1845, MFP. For the full story of Manly's role in the creation of the Southern Baptist Convention, see Fuller, *Chaplain to the Confederacy*, 212–227.

18. Basil Manly, June 22, 1829, Church Journal, Basil Manly Papers, South Carolina Baptist Historical Collection, James Buchanan Duke Library, Furman University, Greenville, South Carolina. A margin note dated 1833 tells of Manly's purchase of Lydia. This story can be found in Fuller, *Chaplain to the Confederacy*, 72–74.

19. Fuller, *Chaplain to the Confederacy*, 74.

20. Basil Manly, "Duties of Masters and Servants," no. 8 in Basil Manly, "Sermons on Duty," in Basil Manly Sermons, James P. Boyce Library, Southern Baptist Theological Seminary, Louisville, Kentucky. I take this summary from Fuller, *Chaplain to the Confederacy*, 213–15.

21. Eugene D. Genovese, *A Consuming Fire: The Fall of the Confederacy in the Mind of the White Christian South* (Athens: University of Georgia Press, 1998), 1–33.

22. I take this conception of Manly's thought from Fuller, *Chaplain to the Confederacy*, 2.

CHAPTER SEVEN

"Two Youths (Slaves) of Great Promise"

The Education of David and Washington McDonogh at Lafayette College, 1838–1844

Diane Windham Shaw

On February 1, 1838, a white New Orleans slave owner named John McDonogh wrote to Walter Lowrie, the secretary of the Presbyterian Board of Foreign Missions in New York City, the following: "I beg leave to observe that among my Black family, I have Two Youths, (Slaves) of great promise, of the age of nineteen to twenty years, who are remarkable at that early period of life, for their intelligence, knowledge, and solidity of judgment, their pious, and tractable dispositions, whom I offer to your Society, to be given a Religious Education, preparatory to their becoming missionaries of the Gospel in the Land of their forefathers."[1] These words set in motion one of the most interesting chapters in Lafayette College's long history: the education of David and Washington McDonogh at Lafayette. It is a chapter that has not been long on our radar. Only since about 1980 has the full story of Lafayette's role in educating black students in the 1830s and 1840s begun to emerge.[2]

Lafayette College opened its doors in 1832, a very different institution from the one its founders, prominent citizens of the town of Easton, Pennsylvania, had envisioned. Caught up in the spirit of the marquis de Lafayette's "farewell tour" of America in 1824, the founders planned a school that would emphasize military science and civil engineering. It named a board of trustees that did not include a single clergyman to avoid sectarianism. Chartered in 1826, it took the trustees another six years to find someone willing to take on the presidency and open the school. The Reverend George Junkin, a staunchly conservative Presbyterian minister, agreed to bring his struggling Pennsylvania Manual Labor Academy from Germantown to Easton, if the trustees would give up military science and accept the manual labor model, which called for students to work in either the agricultural department (gardening, hauling

131

manure, cutting hay, and digging potatoes) or the mechanical department (making boxes, trunks, and agricultural implements) to make money for the college and to offset their tuition.[3]

In the first class in 1832 was an African American, Aaron O. Hoff, from neighboring Belvidere, New Jersey. Hoff remained enrolled for two years and was noted for blowing the trumpet to summon the students in from the fields to the classroom. Aaron Hoff is duly recorded in the college's records, but in 1836 a second black student arrived for whom there is no record.[4] This was Ephraim Titler, a Liberian colonist who was selected by the Presbyterian Board of Education to return to the United States for special studies to enable him to assist with the mission efforts in Liberia. The church sent him to Lafayette College early in January 1836 to study under President Junkin. In a testimonial he wrote for Titler, Junkin touted the success of the endeavor: "He [Titler] has spent part of the winter in this institution & produced a very favorable impression toward his object. We are desirous of aiding the enterprise by gratuitously instructing a few such young men & providing frames for houses & farming utensils for them to take out with them."[5] Junkin's willingness to provide such an opportunity marked his growing support of colonization and positioned Lafayette College as a hospitable site for candidates to be trained for missionary work in Liberia for the Presbyterian Church. Between 1832 and 1844 ten students of color were enrolled at Lafayette, and four of them went on to Liberia. Although a request was received from Elliott Cresson, the Quaker philanthropist and colonizationist, to enroll another black student to be prepared for Liberia in 1847, the student did not matriculate. Lafayette College did not admit another black student for the next one hundred years, until after World War II, when it admitted two students who had been Tuskegee airmen. The college did award an honorary degree in 1869 to Edward Wilmot Blyden, the noted Liberian diplomat and scholar.[6]

No records survive that reveal exactly what the arrangement was that brought David and Washington McDonogh to Lafayette. As Lafayette College archivist, I have long been intrigued by their story, and recently, with the help of a student research assistant, I have attempted to gather all known sources and documents for the Lafayette College Archives. To date, we have amassed nearly three hundred documents. By far the most valuable materials are the numerous letters preserved in various manuscript collections, particularly those in the archives, the Presbyterian Historical Society in Philadelphia, and the Tulane University Library in New Orleans. The latter institution houses the papers of John McDonogh, who was the owner of David and Washington McDonogh.

Born in Baltimore in 1779, John McDonogh was apprenticed as a young man to a mercantile firm, which sent him to New Orleans in 1800. After several years of representing the firm, he established his own mercantile business and built up a fortune, most of which he invested in real estate. He bought swampland, paying attention to the periodic flooding of the Mississippi River and purchasing tracts that would benefit from silting. He bought and sold slaves and set up plantations. He was a hard businessman, not afraid to litigate for what he felt was his due. He was pious, a Presbyterian by birth, and with age he became more concerned with things of the spirit. In 1817, as a cost-saving measure, he gave up his lavish lifestyle in New Orleans and moved from his elegant townhouse to a plainer plantation dwelling across the Mississippi River. Education for poor children and emancipation of slaves became two of his causes.[7]

McDonogh became a member of the American Colonization Society soon after its founding in 1816, and in 1825 he initiated a scheme to enable his slaves to buy their freedom on the installment plan and go to Liberia. McDonogh was already allowing his slaves to earn money by paying them for their regular work on Saturday afternoons, and under the new plan he would bank their earnings until they had enough (it took approximately seven years) to purchase their freedom on Saturday mornings. Then with the money earned on their free Saturdays, they could purchase Fridays, and little by little, in approximately fifteen years, they could purchase the entire five-and-a-half-day work week and full freedom for themselves and their children.[8]

McDonogh was very clear with his slaves that manumission was contingent on going to Africa. "It is your freedom in Liberia that I contract for," he told them. "I would never consent to give freedom to a single individual among you to remain on the same soil as the white man."[9] McDonogh ultimately believed that if he could convince other slaveholders that he did not lose money with his scheme, it would be widely adopted. Indeed, in writing about it publicly for the first time in 1842 in the *New Orleans Commercial Bulletin*, he attested to making money—enough money to "enable me to go to Virginia or Carolina and purchase double the number of those I sent away."[10]

McDonogh felt it was important to prepare his slaves for freedom in Africa, so during this period of gradual emancipation he trained slaves in various trades and provided education to many. In teaching his slaves to read and write, McDonogh was in direct violation of a Louisiana law passed in 1830 that made the crime of educating slaves punishable by up to a year in prison.[11] But McDonogh was determined, even petitioning the Louisiana legislature to allow him to educate slaves who were bound for Liberia. Even though he was unsuccessful, he continued to flout the law.[12] In fact, in his first letter to Walter Lowrie, McDonogh disingenuously denied knowledge of how his slaves had learned to read and write: "You are aware Sir, that, by our laws no owner of a slave is permitted to educate him within the State, under heavy penalties.— (By what means these two youths have learned to read—for they read well, and one of them, I am told, writes well—I do not know.)"[13]

In a subsequent letter to Lowrie, McDonogh explained his choice of David and Washington as the young men to be sent north for further education in preparation for immigration to Liberia:

> David is a Boy of bright parts—and if a high, proud, brave, and aspiring disposition (tempered at the same time with much piety), can be kept down, tempered, and made to walk humbly in the footsteps of his Lord and master, will become great among his people—he is capable of acquiring every science—in short, he may become a Madison... among his people.—Washington not so bright and imaginative, has greater solidity of character; is of mild disposition, meek, humble, full of piety, can be moulded to any form, and may be called the Monroe of his people.[14]

Both slaves used the surname McDonogh. John McDonogh told Lowrie that he had asked David and Washington what they wanted to be called in the North, and they had asked to continue to use the McDonogh surname as they had heretofore.[15] In this case, both David and Washington called John McDonogh father, as did many of his other slaves. In his letters John spoke of knowing David from his infancy, and Washington, in one of his letters, reported that John took him from his parents when he was small and brought him up in his own house "as a son instead of a servant."[16]

Little is known about the parents of David and Washington McDonogh. Washington's mother and siblings were also among John McDonogh's enslaved people in New Orleans. His parents' names, James and Fillis Watts, are noted in Lafayette College records.[17] Washington used the name Washington Watts McDonogh in his letters, and David used David Kinney McDonogh. The birthplace of David McDonogh's mother is listed as Virginia in the 1880 census, while the birthplace of his father has been left blank. David is listed as mulatto in the 1850 census and as black in the 1860, 1870, and 1880 censuses. He is identified as mulatto by Edward Byron Reuter in his *Mulatto in the United States*.[18]

The choice of Lafayette College as the institution to educate David and Washington McDonogh hinged on Presbyterian and American Colonization Society connections and the fact that the Presbyterian Church officially supported the work of the ACS. Lafayette was probably selected by Walter Lowrie, whom John McDonogh had made the legal guardian of David and Washington. Lowrie would have known of Lafayette president George Junkin's interest in colonization through his previous service to the Presbyterian Church in tutoring Ephraim Titler for mission work in Liberia. And Junkin, with his manual labor program failing about this time, would have been interested in the financial support that educating these young men would bring from the Presbyterian Church, which was funding the McDonoghs' educational expenses.[19]

Junkin's stance on slavery was a complicated one. Apparently some who favored immediate abolition considered Junkin a proslavery supporter because of an eight-hour speech he made before the Cincinnati Synod in 1843 presenting his conclusion that the Bible tolerates slavery, but he actually supported the idea of gradual emancipation.[20] At the time of the speech, Junkin was president of Miami University (in between his two terms at Lafayette), where, according to antislavery advocates, his repressive attitudes toward abolition had resulted in declining enrollments.[21] But Junkin was also pro-Union and had to leave his final post as president of Washington College (now Washington and Lee) when Virginia left the Union because he could not support secession. In his biography of his brother, David X. Junkin observes that the McDonogh "servants" were "sent to Dr. Junkin's care at Lafayette College, to be educated. ... It is a suggestive fact, that when black men were excluded from most, if not all, of the Colleges in the land, Dr. Junkin, whom his opponents tried to brand as a pro-slavery man, received them."[22]

Still enslaved when they left New Orleans, David and Washington McDonogh were listed on the slave manifest of the packet *Orleans*, bound for New York on May 2, 1838. John McDonogh had been clear on this point when writing to Lowrie: "As our Laws do not permit owners to Emancipate Slaves, before they have attained the age of thirty years, and even then, only in particular cases ... I will pray you to inform me Sir, whether there will be any difficulty under your Laws in sending them into your State, as they can only go from here to you as slaves."[23] When they boarded the ship, David and Washington carried documents that would give them their freedom—a power of attorney from John McDonogh to Walter Lowrie transferring guardianship of David and Washington to Lowrie and empowering him to emancipate them whenever he saw fit to do so, although McDonogh hoped it would be deferred until their education was finished and they had departed for Africa.[24]

Lowrie's decision to do otherwise tells us something about Lowrie's attitudes toward slavery, as well as conditions in Pennsylvania, where David and Washington were to be educated. As a United States senator from Pennsylvania from 1819 to 1825, Lowrie had opposed the extension of slavery into the western territories, and he had argued eloquently against it in the debates leading up to the Missouri Compromise.[25] Three weeks after the arrival of the McDonoghs at Lafayette College, Lowrie drafted a document that is still preserved among his papers at the Presbyterian Historical Society "emancipating and setting free from the bonds of slavery, David McDonogh and Washington McDonogh."[26] It is clear that Lowrie felt strongly about taking this action, as it was done so promptly, in spite of the wishes of John McDonogh. It was also important for him to do so before the McDonoghs had been long at Lafayette College. Slavery in Pennsylvania was virtually extinguished by 1830, although a few slaves continued to reside in the state as late as the 1840s, and it was illegal for slaves to be brought into Pennsylvania by their owners from other states for more than six months.[27]

Still, at Lafayette College, the McDonoghs' race and their recent servitude were the overriding factors influencing the way they were treated during their years on campus. At the time they were in residence, the Lafayette campus was dominated by a large four-story building, the College Edifice, which served as both classroom building and residence for the president and his family, the faculty, and all the students. But the McDonoghs were housed in a low adjacent building, the former shop of the manual labor program. Though they were required to attend all recitations of their classmates (oral presentations demonstrating mastery of a lesson), they had to sit separately. They ate their meals separately. They even received their instruction separately.[28]

The segregation endured by David and Washington McDonogh was later remarked upon by President Junkin's daughter Margaret Junkin Preston, who was a teenager during the McDonoghs' residency at Lafayette and who later became a well-known poet of the Confederacy and the sister-in-law of

Stonewall Jackson, the Confederate general. In the 1886 biography of John McDonogh written by her stepdaughter's husband, the first principal of McDonogh School in Baltimore, Preston remembered: "The Presbyterian Mission Board had asked my father to have these boys educated. They were accordingly sent to Lafayette College, where they were for several years under his care. They were a great care and trouble to him, as they were kept and taught wholly apart from the students, who would never have consented to their presence among them. For the sake of the cause the professors took them over the regular courses by themselves. David took a full diploma. I think Washington did not take the whole course."[29] Austin Craig, a member of the class of 1846, also wrote years later about the time "when college classes, Model school, and the Coloured Theological class (of one person), all came together, either to sup in the middle basement, or to attend prayers before daybreak, in the old chapel under the Society Halls."[30]

Margaret Junkin Preston's vivid description offered further details about the McDonoghs and their life at Lafayette:

> These boys were very black, of the purest African color; David lithe, graceful and handsome, with features that had scarcely a negro trace about them; and both were exceedingly well mannered. Mr. McDonogh treated them as his children. They dressed like gentlemen, both carried watches when not many students did, and had their supply of pocket-money. He wrote to them very frequently, always in French; and many a long letter of moral and religious advice they used to bring to me to read to them. I was then a schoolgirl studying French, and used to wonder at their inability to read French when their easy chatter of it made me envy them. They were always good boys, and used to come a good deal to our large, airy kitchen to talk with our servants, who were always black. All the while they were under my father's care, Mr. McDonogh kept up a correspondence with him about them. I remember well the long foolscap sheets he used to write, and he always seemed more intent upon their spiritual condition than anything else.[31]

The story of the watches is borne out in the correspondence. David had apparently lobbied for a watch, telling John that students had only three minutes between classes, and they must be on time. Suspecting that David was simply eager for a watch as a status symbol, John asked Lowrie in frustration: "Is there not a clock belonging to the College, which strikes the hour?" But admitting he had intended to get watches for David and Washington before they went to Africa, he authorized Lowrie to purchase them each an "old fashioned silver watch, with good works."[32]

Lafayette's second president, John Yeomans, writing to Presbyterian officials in 1843, also confirmed the segregated treatment of the McDonoghs: "We have had two colored youth several years, one of whom [David] is here now in junior standing. He attends the recitations of the class, but rooms and eats by himself and has a separate seat in all assemblings of the students." Yeomans paradoxically went on to say: "No student in the College mingles more freely with the other students than he. He is intelligent and popular, although not in all respects the most amiable."[33] The latter comment reflected the tensions between David and Yeomans. Yeomans had earlier commented to John McDonogh about David's temperament: "We have much more trial with David's temper & disposition than with Washington's. He is quite high minded & needs occasional checks which we endeavor in the best way we can to impose upon him."[34] David, for his part, protested to Lowrie that Yeomans "wants me to submit to all the rules and regulations of college, whereas I enjoy none of the privileges." Yeomans had put a stop to David's role as a Sunday school teacher in a local black church after David's popularity had aroused the jealousy of the pastor. David further complained to Lowrie, "All the students . . . and also our tutor, say that he has no right to stop me and that I should not obey him in that respect. Nay, even his own Brother says that he is wrong."[35]

In addition to church activities, David and Washington McDonogh had other contact with African Americans in Easton. When they arrived in 1838, they stayed for a time in the home of Aaron Hoff, Lafayette College's first black student. And in 1840 they ceased to be the only black students at Lafayette when another New Orleans African American with McDonogh connections matriculated at Lafayette. This was Thomas McDonogh Durnford, the son of Andrew Durnford, a free black planter and close compatriot of John McDonogh. In fact, John McDonogh was Thomas Durnford's godfather. Thomas McDonogh Durnford graduated from Lafayette in 1846, the second black graduate after David McDonogh. Unlike David and Washington, as a free black, Thomas Durnford was allowed to live with the other students and was even a speaker at his commencement. Two other students studied briefly at the college in the early 1840s under the auspices of the Presbyterian Board of Foreign Missions. During the 1840–41 year, Abraham Miller, a young African prince, was in residence before returning to Liberia as a teacher. In 1841 Thomas Wilson of Trenton, New Jersey, spent a year at the college preparing for service in Liberia and eventually emigrated in 1843 with his wife and six children. Three black students (Jonathan C. Gibbs, Bazel N. Goines, and John F. Wilson) entered the college in 1843 and stayed for about a year.[36] David McDonogh wrote Lowrie that they were leaving in November 1844: "Those colored young men, who have been in this college one year, are now leaving us; they contend for Equal Rights, but they cannot get it; therefore they will not stay here."[37]

Washington McDonogh was enrolled in the Preparatory Department of the college for three years, from 1838 to June 1842, when he was notified by Walter Lowrie to prepare for his immediate departure for Africa. Apparently, the shortness of the notice left little time for good-byes, but a hasty service was held in the college chapel. President Yeomans called it "a solemn and impressive scene" and went on to say that "Washington had commended himself to the generous & warm attachments of the faculty & students, by his amiable temper, honesty & steady habits. . . . His departure was the occasion of awakening in the students of the institution a lively interest in the condition & prospects of the African race."[38] Yeomans had his own parting words for Washington in a farewell letter, counseling him to "love all men & do to every one all the good you can; especially pity the ignorant & wicked natives of Africa & when you arrive among them try to instruct and convert them. The Lord be with you, Washington. . . . Your sincere friend, J. W. Yeomans."[39]

Washington McDonogh left Lafayette on June 10, 1842, and embarked for Liberia on June 16, reaching Monrovia in late August. Arriving just a few days earlier was the *Mariposa*, the ship engaged by the American Colonization Society to take the first group of John McDonogh's slaves, as well as other émigrés, to Liberia. On board from New Orleans were approximately eighty emancipated McDonogh slaves, including Washington's mother and several of his siblings. In fact, they had expected Washington to meet the *Mariposa* in Norfolk, Virginia, not realizing that he had sailed from Philadelphia several days before.[40]

Washington McDonogh was to spend the rest of his life in Liberia, working primarily as a teacher in a mission school at Settra Kroo. In 1849 he married a Christian woman who shared his work at the school. Later in life he was elected to the lower house of the Liberian legislature.[41] A number of Washington's letters from Liberia are extant. He continued to write to Walter Lowrie and his successors at the Presbyterian Board of Foreign Missions until the 1870s. He also wrote to John Yeomans at Lafayette and to John McDonogh until the latter's death in 1850. In an 1846 letter Washington told his former owner: "I should like very much, dear father, to see you once more before we leave this world, for it would be a source of great delight to me, but I will never consent to leave this country for all the pleasures of America combined together ... for this is the only place where a colored person can enjoy his liberty."[42]

David McDonogh, after completing the preparatory program, was enrolled in the regular course of study, taking a classical curriculum, in which he did very well. His letters mention some of his courses—Latin, Greek, calculus, mechanics, chemistry, optics. In preparation for Liberia, he also studied theology and medicine. As he put it in a letter to Walter Lowrie, "I will go, with a glad and overflowing heart, to that once enlightened, but now benighted country, with my box of medicine in one hand and my Bible in the other." It was the study of medicine, though, that ignited a real passion within him. He studied anatomy, surgery, and therapeutics, and he was apprenticed to a local doctor and pharmacist, Hugh Abernathy, who taught him to bleed patients and pull teeth. He told Lowrie that he would sacrifice almost anything rather than give up his medical studies.[43] And despite his differences with President Yeomans, he admitted that Lafayette offered certain opportunities that he might not have had elsewhere. He wrote to Lowrie:

> Were it not, sir, for the advantages I possess here, I would readily desire you to find some other institution for me. But, here, I have two advantages at least, which I do not [think] I could enjoy at any other College. The first is this: Here I am so situated that I can pursue the regular college studies and also my medical studies without the molestation of any one. This I consider a very great advantage.—The next is.—here, I am acquainted with, and possess the good will of, and am very kindly treated by all the students and professors. This I look upon as an advantage equal, if not greater than, the other.[44]

David McDonogh's final year at Lafayette was marked by frustration and altercations with John McDonogh over his future. Increasingly eager to continue his study of medicine, David stalled for time against his former owner's insistence that he finish up and head to Liberia. Finally, in a letter of April 5, 1844, David took a stand, telling John that he was "decidedly, utterly, and radically" opposed to going to Africa now and enumerating the reasons why. He made the same argument to Lowrie in a letter the next day, concluding, "And therefore sir, nothing that you and my father can say to the contrary, will induce me to leave this country before I complete, at least, my medical studies and receive the degree of M.D."⁴⁵ John McDonogh was furious, calling David "that ungrateful and most unprincipled man" and telling Lowrie that "this letter of his is of so extraordinary a character, that I do not know whether I shall ever write to him again." John advocated cutting off his funding and even suggested that he be allowed to think he could be put back into bondage if he did not cooperate, but John ultimately left the decision up to Lowrie, who continued his support of David, enabling him to graduate from Lafayette in September 1844.⁴⁶

David McDonogh remained in Easton after graduation, growing increasingly discouraged over his prospects for further medical education. Finally, he got word from Lowrie that none of the New York medical schools would admit him. Lashing out, David wrote to Lowrie:

> Permit me to say that the Refusal on the part of the medical faculties, and the worse than slavish treatment which I have suffered here, and from those, too, who are looked upon by their Kind as saints on Earth, have given me the strongest Reasons to distrust the fidelity of the white man. Therefore sir—with due deference to your honor, I have resolved to cover my sable Brow with a cloud of despair and never more to look up to the White man, whatever may be his profession or condition in society, as a true friend.⁴⁷

David did allow for "honorable exceptions" to this general pronouncement and, remarkably, found one in the person of Dr. John Kearney Rodgers, a professor at the College of Physicians and Surgeons in New York (now the medical school of Columbia University). Rodgers was willing to serve as a preceptor for David McDonogh and arranged for him to attend classes at the college. He was never officially admitted, nor did he receive a degree. However, he completed the full course of study and was afterward treated as a medical colleague by other doctors. Rodgers arranged an appointment for McDonogh at the New York Eye and Ear Infirmary, where it was said that "he did excellent work and was frequently in demand as a consultant." In 1875, when he was about fifty-four years old, McDonogh did receive a medical degree from the Eclectic Medical College of New York. For a time, he was also a member of the faculty of the Eclectic Medical College. His offices were in the Hell's Kitchen area of the city.⁴⁸

From the early 1850s, McDonogh was active in the Colored Conventions movement. He was first elected to the New York State Council of Colored Persons in 1853; attesters to the election were Frederick Douglass and fellow

African American physician James McCune Smith. In 1854 McDonogh attended the organization's meeting in Albany, where he was a vigorous participant. In 1855 he was elected by the Young Republican Colored Citizens of the Eastern District as a delegate to the state convention, and in September he attended the Colored Men's State Convention in Troy, New York, where he was elected a delegate to the national convention in Philadelphia, although it is not known whether he attended that meeting. Later activity included attending in 1870 the New York Colored Labor Convention in Saratoga, where he served on the vital statistics and labor committee; chairing in 1874 the meeting of the Colored Republicans of the Eighth Congressional District to ratify nominations; and serving in 1890 as delegate to the National Colored Convention in Washington, D.C., where he was elected one of the vice presidents. In 1875 he was one of the organizers, along with Henry Highland Garnet, of a memorial service for the noted abolitionist Gerrit Smith at the Shiloh Presbyterian Church, a black church in Manhattan.[49]

David McDonogh died in Newark on January 15, 1893, survived by his wife and a daughter. In his will he listed both Lafayette College and Washington McDonogh among his beneficiaries. An imposing granite obelisk was erected over his grave in the Bronx's Woodlawn Cemetery. The Lafayette student newspaper of November 10, 1893, included a three-page article devoted to the dedication of this marker, a ceremony attended by family and fifty invited guests, including a number of physicians, both white and black, some of whom had studied under McDonogh. A grandchild pulled the cord that unveiled the monument, which read:

> DAVID K. MCDONOGH, M.D.
> Born New Orleans, La., Aug. 10, 1821;
> Died Newark, N.J., Jan. 15, 1893.
> By Example and Precept a Leader
> in the Elevation of His Race.[50]

In January 1898, five years after David McDonogh's death, a new hospital was established at 439 West 41st Street in New York City. It was the first hospital in the city to be interracial in terms of both physicians and patients, and it bore the name McDonough Memorial. According to the first annual report, "The Hospital opens two new fields. The one is a Hospital in which Physicians, regardless of nationality, creed or color, can have clinical practice;

the other is a training school in which our colored girls can learn to be professional nurses. The McDonough Memorial Hospital was established to afford medical and surgical aid and nursing to sick and disabled persons of every creed, nationality and color." Among its distinctions was its selection as the treatment site of black Spanish-American War soldiers, including the famed "buffalo soldiers" who fought at the Battle of San Juan Hill in Cuba. Unfortunately, McDonough Memorial ceased operations in 1904 when funds could not be raised for a suitable building. But for the six years it existed, it was the only place in New York where African American patients could be treated by physicians of their own race.[51]

The divergent paths taken by David and Washington McDonogh to establish themselves as free men were representative of the national debate about the place of free blacks and emancipated slaves in America. Promoting emigration as a solution to the perceived problem of free blacks and whites living together in America, the colonization movement had perhaps its greatest impact in the opposition it engendered. Although not all blacks were opposed to the idea, the agents of the American Colonization Society encountered a lack of interest, resistance, and outright hostility from many of the free blacks they attempted to enlist. By the early 1830s most American blacks emigrating to Africa were, like Washington McDonogh, emancipated slaves. But among many of those who did emigrate, both free and emancipated blacks, there was the profound sense that only in Liberia could they enjoy full rights of citizenship.[52] Washington had attested to this in his 1846 letter to John McDonogh: "There exists no prejudice of color in this country, but every man is free and equal."[53] For most northern blacks by the early 1830s, however, the emergence of the radical abolitionist movement brought the principles of immediate abolition and full equality in America to the forefront. For these blacks, colonization was an anathema; they considered themselves Americans and were fiercely opposed to emigration. David McDonogh's refusal to go to Liberia and his determination to succeed as a doctor in New York reflected this prevailing attitude that freedom could and should be had in America.[54]

A century after McDonough Memorial Hospital was shuttered, Lafayette College commissioned another memorial tribute to David McDonogh. It was the result of a mention of his story in the inaugural address of Lafayette president Daniel Weiss in 2005. Lafayette professor of art and printmaker Curlee Raven Holton took note and proposed the creation of a sculpture to honor

Melvin Edwards (b. 1937), *Transcendence* (2008, stainless steel, 16 ft. high). Lafayette College Art Collection. Courtesy of Lafayette College Communications Department and Lafayette College Art Collection.

David McDonogh. In the fall of 2008, a sixteen-foot, five-ton sculpture by artist Melvin Edwards, himself a descendant of slaves from Louisiana and Texas, was erected on campus. The dedication of this powerful work, representing struggle, tension, and achievement and fittingly entitled *Transcendence*, brought great excitement to campus with the presence of some of the country's best-known African American artists and the participation of the McDonogh Network, a new organization made up of black alumni.[55]

The sculpture *Transcendence* and the remarkable life it commemorates do indeed remind us, as Clement Alexander Price has so perceptively expressed it in writing about the sculptor, that "the torment of race did not come without a countervailing effort by blacks to survive, to weld elements of their pain onto their quest for joy and aspirations and their intense desire to move forward."[56] The story of David and Washington McDonogh, played out on two continents, is a record of such survival, a testament to aspiration, will, defiance, and the transformative power of education.

NOTES

1. John McDonogh to Walter Lowrie, February 1, 1838, Board of Foreign Missions Correspondence, Presbyterian Historical Society, Philadelphia. Hereafter cited as BFMC.

2. Andrew E. Murray, "Bright Delusion: Presbyterians and African Colonization," *Journal of Presbyterian History* 58, no. 3 (Fall 1980): 224–37; Bernard R. Carman, "Also David K. McDonogh the Coloured Youth," *Lafayette Alumni Quarterly* 58, no. 1 (Fall 1986): 25–31; Russell W. Irvine, "Completing the Story of Lafayette College: The Presence of African Americans before the Civil War" (lecture, Lafayette College, February 15, 2001); Jeffrey A. Mullins, "Standing on Their Own: African American Engagements with Educational Philanthropy in Antebellum America," in *Uplifting a People: African American Philanthropy and Education*, ed. Marybeth Gasman and Katherine V. Sedgwick (New York: Peter Lang, 2005), 25–38.

3. David Bishop Skillman, *The Biography of a College: Being the History of the First Century of the Life of Lafayette College* (Easton, Pa.: Lafayette College, 1932), 22–55.

4. Ibid., 60; Aaron Hoff, Reference Files, Lafayette College Archives, Easton, Pennsylvania, includes Hoff obituary from the *Easton Daily Express* (January 30, 1902), which indicates that Hoff was most probably associated with the Manual Labor Academy of Pennsylvania as early as 1831.

5. Irvine, "Completing the Story," 5.

6. Black Students at Lafayette: 1832–1900, Reference Files, Lafayette College Archives, Easton, Pennsylvania.

7. Marc P. Blum, *John McDonogh, the Founding of McDonogh School, and the Early Leaders* (McDonogh, Md.: McDonogh School, 1998), 7–29; William Allan, *Life and Work of John McDonogh* (1886; reprint, Metarie, La.: Jefferson Parish Historical Commission, 1983), 33–35.

8. James T. Edwards, ed., *Some Interesting Papers of John McDonogh Chiefly Concerning the Louisiana Purchase and the Liberian Colonization* (McDonogh, Md.: Boys of McDonogh School, 1898), 43–71.

9. Ibid., 48.

10. Allan, *Life and Work*, 49.

11. Henry A. Bullard and Thomas Curry, comps., *A New Digest of the Statute Laws of the State of Louisiana, from the Change of Government to the Year 1841, Inclusive* (New Orleans: E. Johns & Co., 1842), 271–72, http://books.google.com/.

12. Allan, *Life and Work*, 51.

13. McDonogh to Lowrie, February 1, 1838.

14. John McDonogh to Walter Lowrie, May 2, 1838, BFMC.

15. Ibid.

16. John McDonogh to John W. Yeomans, December 6, 1841, John William Yeomans Correspondence, Lafayette College Archives, Easton, Pennsylvania; Bell I. Wiley, ed.,

Slaves No More: Letters from Liberia, 1833–1869 (Lexington: University Press of Kentucky, 1980), 141.

17. Seldin J. Coffin, *Record of the Men of Lafayette* (Easton, Pa.: Skinner & Finch, 1879), 329.

18. Edward Byron Reuter, *The Mulatto in the United States* (Boston: G. Badger, 1918), 261.

19. Irvine, "Completing the Story," 8.

20. Stacey Jean Klein, *Margaret Junkin Preston, Poet of the Confederacy: A Literary Life* (Columbia: University of South Carolina Press, 2007), 17–18.

21. Andrew E. Murray, *Presbyterians and the Negro: A History* (Philadelphia: Presbyterian Historical Society, 1966), 110.

22. David X. Junkin, *The Reverend George Junkin, D.D., LL.D., a Historical Biography* (Philadelphia: Lippincott, 1871), 442–43.

23. McDonogh to Lowrie, February 1, 1838.

24. McDonogh to Lowrie, May 2, 1838.

25. Walter Lowrie, *Memoirs of the Hon. Walter Lowrie* (New York: Baker & Taylor, 1896), 22–23.

26. Lowrie, document emancipating David and Washington McDonogh, June 13, 1838, BFMC.

27. Christopher Densmore, "Seeking Freedom in the Courts: The Work of the Pennsylvania Society for Promoting the Abolition of Slavery, and for the Relief of Free Negroes Unlawfully Held in Bondage, and for Improving the Condition of the African Race, 1775–1865," *Pennsylvania Legacies*, November 2005, 16–18.

28. The Lafayette faculty minutes for November 21, 1842, include the motion: "Resolved that David McDonogh receive private instruction from Professor McCartney in Mathematics and from Professor Nassau in Languages." Faculty Minute Books, Lafayette College Archives.

29. Allan, *Life and Work*, 52.

30. W. S. Harwood, *Life and Letters of Austin Craig* (New York: Fleming H. Revell, 1908), 30.

31. Allan, *Life and Work*, 52–53.

32. John McDonogh to Walter Lowrie, June 10, 1839, BFMC.

33. John Yeomans to M. B. Hope, August 2, 1843, Yeomans Correspondence.

34. John Yeomans to John McDonogh, November 18, 1841, Yeomans Correspondence.

35. David McDonogh to Walter Lowrie, September 13, 1842, BFMC.

36. Black Students at Lafayette: 1832–1900, Reference Files, Lafayette College Archives.

37. David McDonogh to Walter Lowrie, November 12, 1844, BFMC.

38. Yeomans, "For *The Presbyterian*: Departure for Africa," 1842 (letter book copy), Yeomans Correspondence.

39. John Yeomans to Washington McDonogh, June 10, 1842 (letter book copy), Yeomans Correspondence.

40. Arthur G. Nuhrah, "John McDonogh: Man of Many Facets," *Louisiana Historical Quarterly* 33, no. 1 (1950): 117; Yeomans, "For *The Presbyterian*."

41. Wiley, *Slaves No More*, 118, 153.

42. Ibid., 142.

43. McDonogh to Lowrie, September 13, 1842.

44. Ibid.

45. David McDonogh to John McDonogh, April 5, 1844; David McDonogh to Walter Lowrie, April 6, 1844, BFMC.

46. John McDonogh to Walter Lowrie, April 16 and 24, 1844, BFMC.

47. David McDonogh to Walter Lowrie, November 26, 1844, BFMC.

48. Russell W. Irvine, "Pride and Prejudice: The Early History of African-Americans at P&S," *P&S: The College of Physicians and Surgeons of Columbia University*, Winter 2000, 13–16; Carman, "Also David K. McDonogh," 30–31; John A. Kinney, *The Negro in Medicine* (Tuskegee, Ala.: Tuskegee Institute Press, 1912), 32–33. McDonogh at some point took "Kearney" as his middle name (replacing "Kinney") in tribute to John Kearney Rodgers.

49. *Frederick Douglass Paper*, October 28, 1853, December 9, 1853 March 2, 1954; *New York Times*, August 25, 1870; *New York Herald*, October 31, 1874; *Utica (N.Y.) Daily Observer*, January 11, 1875; *New York Weekly Press*, January 22, 1890).

50. "A Pioneer in His Race," *The Lafayette*, November 10, 1893, 51–53. Although this article cites the full middle name Kearney on the marker, it is actually only a "K."

51. Carman, "Also David K. McDonogh," 31. The spelling of McDonogh's name as McDonough by the hospital is unexplained and is possibly attributable to the fact that the name was frequently misspelled in this manner. It appears that there was an attempt to reestablish McDonough Memorial Hospital in 1918 at West 133rd Street, near Fifth Avenue. Photographs available through Corbis Images show crowds attending a ground-breaking ceremony on June 9, 1918. The image caption notes that "the institution is named in honor of Dr. David Kearney McDonough, a pioneer African American Physician."

52. Marie Tyler-McGraw, *An African Republic: Black & White Virginians in the Making of Liberia* (Chapel Hill: University of North Carolina Press, 2007), 6, 73; Eric Burin, *Slavery and the Peculiar Solution: A History of the American Colonization Society* (Gainesville: University Press of Florida, 2005), [169].

53. Wiley, *Slaves No More*, 142.

54. Leslie M. Harris, *In the Shadow of Slavery: African Americans in New York City, 1626–1863* (Chicago: University of Chicago Press, 2003), 141–42, 170; Claude A. Clegg III, *The Price of Liberty: African Americans and the Making of Liberia* (Chapel Hill: University of North Carolina Press, 2004), 35.

55. "Remembering David K. McDonogh 1844," Lafayette College news release, December 11, 2006.

56. Clement Alexander Price, "Mel Edwards' Way," in *Melvin Edwards: The Prints of a Sculptor* (Jersey City, N.J.: Jersey City Museum, 2000), 5–7.

CHAPTER EIGHT

"I Am a Man"

Martin Henry Freeman (Middlebury College, 1849) and the Problems of Race, Manhood, and Colonization

William B. Hart

> Let us send them back to their native land, and let us send with them the treasures of science and of art and the richer treasures of the gospel to be diffused through their instrumentality among their wretched fellow-countrymen. Then Africa herself will bless us. She will love us as her friends and ... will invoke heavenly mercies on us as her benefactors.
>
> REVEREND DANIEL DANA, FORMER PRESIDENT OF
> DARTMOUTH COLLEGE

On October 15, 1863, at the forty-fourth anniversary meeting of the Vermont Auxiliary Colonization Society "assembled in the brick church" in Montpelier, Vermont, Middlebury College president Benjamin Labaree (1840–66) introduced Martin Freeman, an African American alumnus of Middlebury College (class of 1849), a native of Rutland, Vermont, and the former president of Avery College (1856–63), to "a large and intelligent audience," which received him warmly. Freeman, one reporter wrote, "surpassed the expectations of all who heard him" as he spoke on the topic "the best way to elevate the African race." Speaking in "an elevated and beautiful style," Freeman used "facts, plain and palpable," to explain that "while living here [in the United States] with the ruling race of Anglo Saxons his manhood was crushed out and he had no hope for it. But in an African nationality he saw a bright future for his people." Freeman insisted that the colonization of free blacks in Liberia was the best solution for both the white and the black races. Many in the church listened with rapt attention, finding Freeman's presentation "earnest, sincere, profound and scholarly." The reporter added that any who heard him that evening would long "remember him as a man of power and culture," for surely

An undated image of Martin Freeman, Middlebury College alumnus, class of 1849. Courtesy of Special Collections & Archives, Middlebury College Library.

among "the many sons of Middlebury College, none will shine a brighter lustre upon her than Martin Freeman." Members of the audience were so moved by his and Labaree's addresses that they took up a collection totaling over $108 (supplemented by some jewelry), $100 of which they gave directly to Freeman, who accepted the gift with a "few feeling remarks."[1]

Freeman's reputation for making what many white Vermonters considered powerful, eloquent, and sensible speeches on "the Negro race" preceded him. A week later, on October 23, Mary Ann Swift, the daughter of a prominent judge in Middlebury, wrote in her journal, "Prof. Freeman, a colored student who graduated at Midd Coll. delivers an address tonight on the African race. he [sic] advocates their colonization in Liberia. Prof. F. has recently been appointed Professor of Nat. Philosophy and mathematics in Liberia College."[2] Freeman did not disappoint. In the lecture hall of the town's Congregational Church, "filled to its utmost capacity," he sketched a "perfectly drawn" picture of "the Condition and prospects of the Free Africans in America" to show that "it is morally impossible for the 'manhood' of the African race to be developed under all the discouraging circumstances that must rest upon them in a mixed society." "Every intelligent mind" in the audience, a reporter wrote, must "adopt his conclusions": that "colonization and a pure African nationality" were "the only hope of his race." It is not clear if the audience at the

An image of Liberia College from Edward Wilmot Blyden, *Liberia's Offerings: Being Addresses, Sermons, etc.* (New York: John A. Gray, 1862). Courtesy of John Shaw Pierson Civil War Collection, Rare Book Division, Department of Rare Books and Special Collections, Princeton University Library.

Congregational Church took up a collection, but one reporter remarked that those who remembered Freeman from his days as a student at Middlebury would follow his "future career with interest, and have a special regard for the Liberia College to which he is called as Professor."[3]

Freeman's visits to Montpelier and Middlebury were part of a fund-raising tour he undertook throughout New Hampshire and Vermont in 1863—a tour to raise funds for his own salary of $800 per year as professor of mathematics and natural philosophy at Liberia College in Monrovia, Liberia. His position at Liberia College was contingent on the success of his fund-raising, the consequence of the depleted coffers of the Massachusetts Colonization Society, the overseers of Liberia College, as a result of the Civil War. Freeman was not happy about this circumstance, but he agreed nevertheless to undertake the tour out of desperation to leave the United States. "If Africa needs the product of my brain," he once conveyed to a Vermont colonizationist, "well. If not, she shall have the labor of my hands."[4] A few months prior to his leaving for Liberia with his family in September 1864—the bleakest, bloodiest year of the Civil War, when many northerners lost patience and hope—Freeman affirmed his commitment to Liberia to a reporter who asked him why he was accepting a teaching position at Liberia College. "Because I am fully persuaded," Freeman replied, "that emigration to Liberia is the quickest, the surest, the best... the only way by which the Negro of the U.S. can rise to the full status of manhood.... I am a man, and by consequence... it is not only my privilege but my duty to endeavor to secure for myself and my children all the rights, privileges and immunities that pertain to humanity."[5]

In many respects, Freeman's words are surprising and unusual. The majority of African Americans had always opposed colonization, the privately funded, publicly supported program designed to transport free blacks to Liberia, first voicing their opposition less than a year after the founding of the American Colonization Society in December 1816 by a collection of white religious leaders, politicians, educators, and self-described antislavery advocates. Since that time, thousands of free blacks had rallied in cities and large towns, from Richmond to Boston, to protest this "wicked and fraudulent" scheme and its "hateful motive, diabolical in principle, and murderous in design."[6] Moreover, by October 1863 the Emancipation Proclamation had been in effect for nearly a year. Lincoln, an uneasy colonizationist, was even willing to concede citizenship to "especially intelligent" black men like Freeman. Furthermore, several Republicans in Congress and many abolitionists and social reformers had already begun to propose ways to reconstruct the southern states and to consider means by which black freedmen and freedwomen might be incorporated into the Republic.[7] Martin R. Delany and Henry Highland Garnet, both staunch black nationalists throughout the 1850s and early 1860s, now recruited black troops for the Union army, believing that black participation in the war would lift black people "from social degradation to the plane of common equality with all other varieties of men" in the United States. The Great War was a fight over freedom versus slavery. "Better even die free, than to live slaves," Frederick Douglass urged his brethren, for "liberty won by white men would lose half its lustre."[8]

Nevertheless, Freeman remained adamant that social change would never materialize in the United States. The decade of the 1850s was a bleak time for African Americans; several pieces of congressional legislation, including the Fugitive Slave Act as part of the Compromise of 1850, and "popular sovereignty," linked to the Kansas-Nebraska Act of 1854, as well as the Supreme Court's decision on Dred Scott in 1857, produced deleterious effects on the lives of both the enslaved and the free black populations. The prospects for black opportunity grew so dim at this point that Freeman and a small but vocal segment of the African American intelligentsia, including Delany, Garnet, William Wells Brown, and others, insisted that fully fledged African American citizenship in the United States was utterly unattainable and that black Americans should seriously consider emigration. Even Douglass, who viewed Lincoln's election in 1860 as perhaps signaling "the death of the modern Abolition movement," as the president-elect showed "complete loyalty to slavery in the slave States," supported migration to Haiti in the weeks following the 1860 election.[9] As one historian of colonization has implied, slavery was so deeply entrenched in the American psyche and racism was so persistent that abolition was no guarantee of freedom.[10] After all, myriad examples of freed blacks in the North and the South and even in the nation's capital, snared by the "reverse underground railroad" and sold illegally into bondage between the 1830s and the 1850s, reminded free blacks of the precariousness of their status.[11] Freeman, a member of the black educated elite and the first African American college president, held such little faith in the American concept of equality that he was willing to forsake all that he had achieved and begin anew in a foreign land that very few African Americans wished to visit.

Perhaps even more puzzling than Freeman's remarks is why white Vermonters, living in a state that outlawed adult slavery in its 1777 and 1791 constitutions and had the smallest black population per capita of any state in the Union, supported so vehemently "the colonization enterprise."[12] The simple answer is that white supporters of colonization in both the North and the South viewed the scheme as an antislavery project. Colonization not only offered a solution to the pernicious problem of slavery by relocating emancipated slaves to Liberia with their and their former owners' consent but also served as a grand, providential plan for solving the race dilemma in America. Many whites who saw themselves as well-meaning, benevolent reformers argued throughout the first half of the nineteenth century that it should be clear by the complexion and circumstances of African Americans that "this [the United States] is not their country, nor their home." Free blacks, they insisted myopically, would never be able to enjoy the "privileges from which the laws and structure of society must forever prohibit them," for they constituted "a population for the most part idle and useless, and too often vicious and mischievous."[13] An additional benefit of colonization, its proponents maintained, was to fulfill God's plan of using "coloured missionaries" to save Africa, to bring to Africans "the proposition of civilization and Christianity."[14] Thus, by one simple means, colonization could perfect American society by cleansing it racially and uplift and save the "infidels" in faraway Africa through black Protestant churches and American institutions.

Throughout the second quarter of the nineteenth century, most white northern and southern Americans who opposed slavery and the international slave trade used their institutions—most notably colleges and universities, white Protestant churches, and state legislatures—to promote colonization. This essay examines the role played by one institution of higher learning, Middlebury College, in fostering the project of colonization. Middlebury planted the seeds of colonization in Martin Freeman, a restless, studious, and prickly young black Vermonter. Although it would take nearly fifteen years of living in Pittsburgh for those seeds to fully germinate, Freeman's Middlebury education prepared the soil to receive those seeds. As the third student of color at Middlebury in its first forty-five years, Freeman endured persistent reminders, some subtle, others overt, that his future lay in Liberia. With the outbreak of the Civil War, Freeman's black nationalist thought reached full bloom, and he was ready to make the leap to Liberia. Perhaps during his recruiting trip to Avery College in 1862, Alexander Crummell, professor of intellectual and moral philosophy, English language and literature, logic, rhetoric, and history at Liberia College, convinced Freeman that a Union victory in the bloody Civil War was no guarantee of manhood for African Americans.

Writers, intellectuals, and activists have weighed in on colonization, pro and con, almost since the founding of the American Colonization Society (ACS) in December 1816. While many nineteenth-century supporters of colonization viewed the ACS's program as a benevolent antislavery plan—one that did not promote abolition outright but that provided a safety valve for uneasy slave owners and enemies of slavery—critics of the ACS voiced doubts about its benevolence. In his 1853 collection of "facts and opinions" on colonization, for example, Giles Stebbins characterized colonization as a scheme premised on "hatred to the free negro" and "friendship to the slaveholder," designed to "screen American slavery, as a system, from all imputation of moral guilt" by "holding up the free negroes as most pernicious and dangerous nuisances."[15] In other words, colonization was a scheme intended not to end slavery but to rid the nation of an unwanted race of free people of color, an interpretation affirmed one hundred years later by P. J. Staudenraus in his seminal modern study of the American Colonization Society.[16]

In recent years, scholars have reexamined Liberian colonization through multiple lenses, including that of Atlantic World studies, as well as those of slavery, race, class, religion, and gender, to arrive at various useful interpretations. For some scholars, Liberia stood as an American version of the Exodus story, in which black Americans were delivered from slavery to freedom in an imagined national homeland. For others, Liberia offered the means by which black Americans could construct a common political and cultural identity based on the commonly shared experiences of slavery and racism. For still others, Liberia carried gendered meanings in that it embodied white American women's ideals of a domestic utopia by reflecting "white evangelical, educational, and domestic values."[17]

This essay embraces the venerable perspective of colonization as an antiblack rather than merely an antislavery movement. Additionally, it shares the conclusions of those studies that view Liberia in the trope of the Exodus story: biblical language gave meaning to Liberia for many African Americans and white Americans. However, this essay also emphasizes a particular gendered aspect of Liberia with class implications. It shares with Marie Tyler-McGraw the conclusion that for professional men like Martin Freeman who were confined by their race to "narrow, restricted lives," Liberia represented a utopia where educated free black men could exercise the rights and privileges of citizenship, framed as "full manhood," and enjoy the quotidian aspects of life as good republican fathers and husbands living in dignity.[18] For white Vermonters, as well as for Martin Freeman, Liberia stood as a project for restoring black manhood and dignity—a lesson Freeman learned first at Middlebury College.

The historiography on the academy and colonization is emergent. The recent study by Craig Steven Wilder on race and slavery and the academy devotes a chapter to colonization. He astutely notes that the American Colonization Society "was born on campus." Its founder, Robert Finley, conceived of the plan to send free blacks to Africa in 1816 while teaching near Princeton University (then the College of New Jersey) and serving on the college's board of trustees. His scheme, he reasoned, would provide a "three-fold benefit" to the United States: (1) the nation would be purged of an undesirable population, (2) the black émigrés could help "civilize" and Christianize "heathenish" Africa, and (3) "our blacks themselves would be put in a better situation." Wilder identifies correctly the plan as springing from dual impulses: first, "the evangelical urge to solve the moral problem of slavery," and second, "the political and social rejection of a multiracial society."[19] Most American college and university presidents, trustees, faculty, and students in the early nineteenth century, including those at Middlebury College, shared these sentiments and endorsed colonization.[20]

Russell Irvine's study of black higher education during the pre–Civil War era argues that most American college and university presidents and trustees at this time viewed their jobs as preserving a cohesive white republic. Blacks, regarded by many as uneducable, should be trained up in black institutions like the Ashmun Institute, the precursor to Lincoln University.[21] Of course, there were exceptions, as many of these same white colleges enrolled a black man now and then whom they regarded as exceptionally intelligent and well suited to undertake the rigors of their courses of study. For Middlebury, that promising student was black Vermonter Martin Freeman, whom the college enrolled in 1845 after much pressure from the community to put into practice what it preached: abhorring slavery and endorsing Liberia as a place where black men could realize their manhood.

The few scholars who have written about Freeman, a complex and enigmatic figure, have correctly characterized him as a "black nationalist" and have submitted that he embraced his nationalistic views while teaching at Avery College near Pittsburgh. There he developed close personal and professional ties with a number of black nationalists and intellectuals, most notably Martin R. Delany. Delany mentions his friend Freeman in his landmark 1852 publication, *The Condition, Elevation, Emigration, and Destiny of the Colored People of the United States*, identifying him as "a young ... gentleman of talents," a "'Junior Professor,' in Allegheny Institute [Avery College]" who is "doing much good in his position."[22] Delany appointed Freeman special foreign secretary of the Niger Valley Exploring Party, Delany's organization created to explore the feasibility of establishing an alternative homeland to Liberia in West Africa. Moreover, Freeman, following Delany's urgent recommendation to all African Americans, bought land in Canada as a potential safe haven for himself and his family.[23]

From the 1850s onward, Freeman remained firm in his belief that black people would be better off almost anywhere on the planet than in the United States. For him, Liberia was a republican utopia. Yet he would find that his imagined utopia—translated etymologically as "no place" but homophonically as "good place"—was far from good and perfect and Christian and republican. Nevertheless, with all its known problems, flaws, and challenges, including its high mortality rate, factionalism, color prejudice, and few modern comforts, Liberia remained Freeman's imagined Eden, a lesson he first learned at Middlebury.

Middlebury College and Its Early Struggles

Middlebury College was founded in 1800 in Middlebury, Vermont, a small town in the south-central Champlain Valley, tucked between the Green Mountains and Lake Champlain. Like many small New England villages, Middlebury founded a college to prepare and educate its local and neighboring young men—all white—in the ways of the republican world so that they might "know their own rights, and the means of protecting them from violation." "Ignorance," the founding corporation declared, "[was] the bane of Republican government." To meet its responsibility of preserving the Republic, Middlebury pledged to educate its men "in the rudiments of Literature, and in the principles of Morality and Religion."[24] Jeremiah Atwater, a strict Congregational Calvinist and the college's first president, summarized the purpose of a college education as continuing to teach the restraint of passions, lessons "begun in the family" and carried on by schools, through which system they sowed "the seeds of knowledge and virtue ... in the youthful mind." A young college man, according to Atwater, was to be "constantly learning new lessons of moral instruction" and "trained to virtue and order by perpetual and salutary restraints."[25] As a result of this inculcation, most early Middlebury graduates became either lawyers or ministers. The nonsectarian college affiliated itself with the local Congregational church—local members of the church strongly supported the school, and early presidents of the college preached there—although the church neither funded nor founded the college. Nevertheless, because of its close ties to the church, Middlebury was thought to be a proper, sober-minded, moral institution—not like the state's other institution to the north, the publicly financed University of Vermont, considered by many Vermonters to be too religiously liberal.[26]

Middlebury College's reputation and popularity grew so rapidly over the next thirty-five years that its enrollment ballooned from 27 in 1801–2 to 168 in 1836–37. Yet the college limped along financially during this time, teetering on bankruptcy and fending off repeated overtures to affiliate with the University of Vermont. It suffered through two rocky, albeit short-lived, affiliations with

Antebellum Middlebury College. Courtesy of Special Collections & Archives, Middlebury College Library.

two Vermont medical schools: the Vermont Medical Institution to the south in Castleton and the Vermont Medical College to the east in Woodstock. Middlebury's curriculum remained classically oriented—Greek, Latin, and mathematics anchored the curriculum—with a limited number of courses added in the 1820s and 1830s in English, modern languages, and the sciences to compete with UVM and Amherst College as they reformed their curricula. Perhaps the thick atmosphere of morality and piety that infused learning at Middlebury College kept the college going. This was particularly true during peaks of religious enthusiasm, of which there were no fewer than ten between 1805 and 1835. None were more profound, more costly, nor more divisive and decisive for the college than the revival of 1835, when Jedidiah Burchard, a fiery, enthusiastic, theatrical evangelical, rolled into town.[27]

Burchard, a white-hot preacher in the mold of Charles Grandison Finney, the ardent and formidable evangelical minister of western New York during the Second Great Awakening, stormed through Vermont with his wife, also an evangelical, in 1835–36. The president of Middlebury College, Joshua Bates, and Thomas Merrill, the minister at the Congregational church, not only invited the Burchards to Middlebury but also literally stood by them as the minister preached in nearby towns. James Marsh, the president of UVM, criticized Bates for supporting Burchard, cautioning that Burchard undermined the authority of the

> established clergy in regard to those very questions which it is their business and duty to settle, and teaches the people to judge and decide for themselves what they are wholly unqualified to determine. When this is done, it has precisely the same effect in the church, which the prevailing radicalism of the day has in politics. It puffs up the ignorant and inexperienced with a vain confidence in their own understanding of their own fancied experience in spiritual things, and leads them to undervalue, perhaps to censure and deride, those to whom they ought to look up with humility and reverence.[28]

Marsh and the clergy who opposed Burchard considered him coarse, uncouth, and haughty, a crude outsider to whom pious Vermonters should not listen. As a consequence, because of Bates's affiliation with Burchard, Middlebury College's prestige plummeted, as most Vermonters now branded the college as radical and irregular. The University of Vermont's star now rose as Vermonters put their faith and trust in what they deemed to be a more sober, ordered, and sensible institution.[29] Suspicion over outside interlopers branded as radicals would color the local reception of non-Vermont speakers, most notably abolitionists, in the coming decades.

The college suffered for its perceived close relationship with Burchard. By 1838–39 the college had lost its president and virtually all of its faculty through dismissal or resignation (and one death). Its freshman enrollment plunged from thirty-seven in 1836 to nineteen in 1838. By the mid-1840s Middlebury College had almost shut its doors.[30]

Colonization versus Antislavery at the Town's College

The era of religious revivalism sparked anxiety about the self and society, awakening many Americans to the need for social reform. Perfectibility defined the goal of the religious movement known as the Second Great Awakening and gave rise to a number of reform movements, including temperance,

Sabbatarianism, prison reform, and immediate abolitionism.³¹ "Immediatism" called for the emancipation of the enslaved without delay and without compensation to slave owners and demanded full incorporation of freedmen and freedwomen into the body politic as citizens. People like William Lloyd Garrison and Frederick Douglass symbolized this school of thought. Immediatists rejected colonizationism and its claim that whites and blacks could never peacefully coexist as equal citizens of the United States.

At Middlebury, support for the American Colonization Society remained strong. Middlebury College presidents, faculty, and students numbered among Liberia's most visible supporters. In 1819, Vermont was the first state in the union to found an auxiliary society; Reverend Benjamin Labaree, the fourth president of Middlebury College, served as vice president and president. In 1822, Jehudi Ashmun, who attended Middlebury College from 1813 to 1816 but took his degree at the University of Vermont, journeyed to Liberia on the West African coast. The ACS had that year created the colony by forcibly purchasing land just south of Sierra Leone from a local chief for about $300 in trade goods. Ashmun served as agent for the society and helped repel insurrections led by native Liberians who sought to rid their country of Americans.³² So great was Middlebury's support of colonization that the August commencement in 1826 became a rally for the Vermont Colonization Society (VCS). The commencement speaker, Francis Scott Key, the renowned author of the poem that became the U.S. national anthem, was a founding member of the ACS and in 1826 served the society as an agent. In his commencement address, Key "demonstrated the practicability of removing the evil of slavery from the United States," safely, efficiently, and noninjuriously to both blacks and whites, by relocating free blacks to the "prosperous" colony of Liberia in West Africa. He so enthralled the Middlebury crowd that several leading members of the VCS resolved that the state's auxiliary was worthy of all Vermonters' monetary support, especially that of their churches, which they identified as ideal venues for "raising money."³³

Most members of Middlebury College's administration, faculty, and student body, as well as residents of the town, endorsed colonization, convinced that it was the best means by which to preserve the Republic. They embraced colonization as a middle ground between tolerating noxious slavery and supporting its troubling immediate, noncompensated termination because they feared that radical abolitionists would fracture the country. The debate over which antislavery project was most practicable—colonization or immediate abolition—simmered in the town and at the college in the decade before Martin Freeman arrived in 1845.

As early as the late 1820s, Vermont colonizationists began to debate how their vision differed from that of the national organization. Vermonters viewed their work as leading to the "ultimate obolition [sic] of Slavery; and the evangelization of Africa." The parent organization focused primarily on removing from the nation free blacks, whether they were freeborn or newly emancipated. Within a few years, increasing numbers of colonizationists began to embrace abolitionism and thus joined antislavery societies. Eighty-six delegates from throughout the state of Vermont, including four from the town of Middlebury and two from the college, founded Vermont's Anti-Slavery Society in Middlebury on April 30, 1834.[34] They entered into a covenant not to fight for the displacement of free African Americans "from their native land to a foreign clime, as the price and condition of their freedom," but to ensure that free blacks shall "receive the protection of law" and that "the power which is invested in every Slaveholder ... shall instantly cease."[35]

Vermont colonizationists forced Vermont abolitionists to address a number of questions about their relationship to slavery, including what business was southern slavery to Vermonters, and did abolitionists support racial amalgamation?[36] The two sides confronted each other in Middlebury in July 1843, two years before Freeman matriculated at Middlebury College. That summer, Garrisonian abolitionists launched a one-hundred-city convention tour designed to arouse abolitionist sentiments in Vermont, New York, Pennsylvania, Ohio, and Indiana. Middlebury was their first stop, and Frederick Douglass, labeled by the press "a fugitive slave," was the keynote speaker. Douglass characterized his reception in Middlebury as "intensely bitter and violent." Few in attendance "professed any sympathy in opinion and feeling" with him or the other speakers. Middlebury College men had placarded the town with posters, calling Douglass "an escaped convict from the state prison." Provoked by the show of resistance to their message, one abolitionist speaker denounced the Constitution, the Congress, and the Supreme Court, professing that the latter were "boobys" who constituted "a dishonest gang." This speaker touched a raw nerve when he called "the church and the clergy of Vermont hypocrites," as well as "the people of Vermont ... hypocrites."[37]

In response, one reporter, invoking the time when Burchard visited Middlebury, scolded the abolitionist outsiders. "We did not want itinerant lecturers," he told his readers, "to convince us of the evils of slavery, which we have so long deplored, or to urge us forward to its abolition, by neglecting all the best pecuniary interests of the country, by destroying the present political parties, by prostrating the church, by reviling the clergy, by trampling upon the laws, by leveling the pillars of the constitution, and dissolving the Union ... unless a free passage is immediately given to its progress."[38] Vermonters did not like outsiders—whether they were evangelicals or abolitionists—coming into their backyards and telling them what to think or what to question. They especially did not like outsiders criticizing their churches, the institution that 80 percent of Vermonters had come to love and trust deeply.[39] Most were content with life in Vermont, but now they were made to feel uncomfortable as abolitionists called into question their moral fiber.

Middlebury College students were not immune to such debates and encounters. In the 1830s and 1840s members of the Philomathesian Society, an early debate club, met weekly to discuss important questions that arose from their studies as well as from matters of the world, including Congress's patronage of the American Colonization Society, public support for antislavery societies, and the status and condition of free blacks versus that of newly arriving European immigrants.[40] Middlebury students took both sides of the emancipation debate; some supported colonization, others supported immediate emancipation. Nearly all believed that slavery was an evil institution that must end but without sacrificing the cohesiveness of the country. Their debates constituted an intellectual exercise carried out safely in the sheltered halls of academe, tucked safely away in the foothills of the Green Mountains, securely isolated from the actual institution of slavery, and far enough removed socially and culturally from local African Americans whose opinion students need not ask.

Middlebury men did tend to travel after college, and those who ventured south sometimes expressed their views about race and slavery. One such graduate was Edward Merrill, class of 1845, the son of the prominent local Congregational minister, Thomas Merrill. During his travels through Georgia in 1846, Edward shared with a college friend, John W. Steward (class of 1846), his impressions of the slaves he encountered there, who he thought were "a first rate piece of property." He told his friend John that it was

> as right to hold slaves as it is to eat oysters. A slave is not a person; he is a "thing" in law. You cannot send one to the state prison here. For the first offense against the

law of the land, he gets the "cat." The next time he must look out for his neck. There is one to be hung here next month for stealing. You cannot teach them anything.... First white man then Indian then dog then nigger. The idea that they are not happy is all humbug. Slavery with them is second nature.[41]

It is difficult to know if other Middlebury men shared Edward's feelings about the enslaved. But the fact that he felt he could voice such negative opinions about them so openly and casually suggests that at least one Middlebury man—John Steward, who would have been a student during Martin's first year—understood, if not shared, his perspective.

Regardless, the debates between abolitionists and colonizationists throughout the Northeast led some antislavery proponents to question the sincerity of the rhetoric of some college presidents. Many abolitionists began to demand that colleges like Middlebury, Dartmouth, and Williams do more than pay mere lip service to emancipation. They should demonstrate their commitment to ending slavery by enrolling African American youths.

During the late spring of 1845, several abolitionists criticized Middlebury's president, Benjamin Labaree, for not responding promptly to requests from black youths and their white minister in Philadelphia to admit several "poor pious young men of color." To admit the young men, the critics claimed, would "have engraven her [Middlebury College] an imperishable name which ages to come if not the present age would have mentioned with honor."[42] Labaree did not respond promptly because he did not know what to say. He was forced to justify himself that summer.

Labaree informed the corporation (the board of trustees) that he, along with the presidents of Dartmouth, Williams, Amherst, and the University of Vermont, received in the spring a letter "purporting to be written by a young man of color, inquiring if he and *three others* of the same complexion, could be admitted to the College." President Nathan Lord at Dartmouth agreed to accept those who might be qualified but added that "we should not choose to have a flood of blacks at the College." The presidents of Williams, Amherst, and UVM all rejected or discouraged the young black men from attending their schools. Labaree, debating with himself what to do, first approached the faculty. They told him that they had "no authority to exclude young men of a suitable character and qualifications on account of complexion." At the meeting of the corporation, Vermont governor William Slade, a board member, produced a letter of support from the boys' Sunday school teacher, Reverend David Gardiner. Labaree told Slade and the corporation that there was nothing in the college's by-laws prohibiting the enrollment of blacks, but enrolling four at once would "create the impression that this is the College for the resort of colored students." The corporation deliberated and concluded that "Middlebury is not designed especially for the colored race" and that the corporation was "not inclined particularly to encourage negroes from all parts of the country to resort here for education; we are disposed to do our fair proportion in educating this class of citizens, and therefore, colored young men in VT and States adjacent, who would naturally fall to us, we will cheerfully receive."[43] The corporation did not explain what it meant by "not designed... for the colored race." "Not ready" is probably the more appropriate language for Middlebury and the other elite schools of the Northeast, none of which felt it could afford to have its reputation darkened by admitting a few students of color.

Governor Slade saw a troublesome double standard in the college's admissions policy. In a letter to the boys' pastor, he worried that a "great and important principle would be compromitted [sic]": Middlebury would accept "white young men from any and every quarter of the country; that we professed to feel a desire for the improvement of the colored race, and especially for the civilization and christianizing of Africa, and should, I thought, be guilty of great inconsistency, if we shut the doors of our College entirely to colored young men from other States. From which most, if not all, of the applications would be made, as we have very few colored people in our own State."[44] Slade was concerned that immediatists might notice Middlebury's Janus-faced admissions policy.

Nevertheless, Middlebury lived up to its claim that its first task was to educate men from Vermont, regardless of color. Historically, this appears to be true; two local biracial men studied at Middlebury prior to Freeman—Alexander Twilight (class of 1823) of Corinth, Vermont, and William Haynes of Granville, New York, by way of Rutland, Vermont, who studied off and on at Middlebury in the late 1820s but did not receive a degree. Nevertheless, despite one local reporter's joy that Middlebury College had until now avoided the reputation among the public "as the favorite resort of the colored race from all parts of the Union," Middlebury would enroll its third student of color in August 1845.[45]

Reverend Mitchell, the pastor at the East Parish Congregational Church of East Rutland (1833–46) and a graduate of Yale (1818) and Union Theological Seminary (1821), was a strong supporter of the American Colonization Society, for which he became an agent after leaving his Rutland church.[46] Mitchell found in Martin Freeman such an able and bright child that he took him under his wing in 1838, when Freeman was just twelve years old, to prepare him for college. Whether Mitchell believed at that time that Freeman would help advance the cause of colonization is unknowable. However, in 1845 he and Labaree colluded to enroll Freeman at Middlebury College for just that purpose.

Martin Freeman conveniently fit the bill of helping Middlebury fulfill its charge, articulated by the corporation in 1845, to educate bright, capable, local black youths. Freeman was born in Rutland, Vermont, in 1826. His grandfather Pearson Freeman relocated the family there from Connecticut in 1793. Pearson was born a slave in Waterbury, Connecticut, in 1761 and served as a waiter in the American Revolution. This service led to his freedom at age twenty-seven and perhaps prompted him to take the surname Freeman. In Rutland the elder Freeman worked in a potash factory, a trade he acquired in Connecticut. Within a few years, he opened his own shop on North Main Street. In time, he also bought an acre of land in town and built a two-story house. It is not clear why Pearson relocated his family to Rutland. Perhaps the young state's reputation as a free state brought him and other African Americans there. Or perhaps economic opportunities beckoned. Perhaps the young black clergyman, Lemuel Haynes, who had been preaching for five years at the white Congregational church in West Rutland, gave the region the appearance of tolerance and cordiality. Regardless of the reasons, the Freeman family insinuated itself into Rutland and earned the reputation as an honest, kind, friendly, hardworking, and devout family.[47]

The family's reputation surely devolved to young Martin after the death of his reputed father, Pearson Toussaint, an accomplished musician, in 1830 at age thirty.[48] Martin, a bright, precocious, and somewhat sensitive child, captured the attention of peers and adults. Perhaps because of his race—or because of his intellect—he was bullied by schoolmates, whom he reproved for inflicting "out-door teachings" on him so that he would never forget his place.[49] Nevertheless, he developed at an early age a close, long-standing friendship with a young white girl, Charlotte Thrall, who in October 1850 married Frederick Chaffee. Martin and Charlotte corresponded as adults, exchanging good and sad news about their respective families and their lives, hers in Rutland, Vermont, his in Monrovia, Liberia. After Freeman moved to Liberia, Charlotte's father kept him apprised of news back home by sending him regularly copies of the *Rutland Herald*, the town's local newspaper.[50]

In 1845 Mitchell wrote a strong letter of recommendation for Freeman to Labaree. He believed that the young man of nineteen was now ready to matriculate into Middlebury College. Although Labaree and Mitchell tried to keep Freeman's enrollment quiet, it seems to have caused a stir in the press, and even in the Labaree household. Dr. J. E. Rankin (class of 1848), the renowned philanthropist, future chaplain of the House of Representatives, and, toward the end of his life, president of Howard University (1889–1903), was reminded years later that when he arrived at President Labaree's house to begin his sophomore year at Middlebury, he met Freeman and Reverend Mitchell. The two young men played together in the president's backyard until dinner was ready, at which time "the precise and lady-like wife of the president was at a loss how to dispose of the black boy at the table—as society has always been since, unless he will be a waiter." Rankin, who marked his introduction to Freeman as the start of his "chivalry for the Afro American race," stepped forward to save everyone from embarrassment: he—Rankin—suggested that "the others should sit down first, and afterwards the two boys should eat by themselves—both becoming waiters."[51] Freeman's "welcome" was a reminder that he was a special case, an experiment. One Middlebury resident who housed Freeman and perhaps Mitchell for a day or two, no doubt for the income, took umbrage at the press's implications that he might be seen as a good friend of African Americans. The paper apologized defensively for the impression it may have created and thanked

> Mr. Israel Stow for correcting us in stating a matter of fact in relation . . . to the colored student now in Middlebury College, by President Labaree. Upon particular enquiring of that gentleman, it turns out that this colored student when he first came to town was admitted into this family but a day or two. Afterwards at Commencement, when he presented himself for admission into the College, he was hospitably entertained for two days or more, and was furnished by President Labaree with a loan of money, and with books to enable him to pursue his studies for the next term. In some of our papers of the week alluded to by Mr. Stow, a few of the first impressions stated that there were two colored students in the College. We soon found we were mistaken, and corrected ourselves by altering the *two* to one. We can assure Mr. Stow that as to any intentional misrepresentation our conscience is clear, and that as a christian man he should repent of the uncharitableness towards us which his letter in the subject manifests.[52]

The paper felt it had done its duty to correct the record, offering a lukewarm apology to Stow and clarifying that only *one* black student had enrolled at Middlebury, not two, lest anyone think that Middlebury had now become the college of refuge for young men of color. The paper offered no apology to young Martin, nor did it demand one of Stow on his behalf.

As a college student, Freeman presented himself as very friendly but also as very serious and "very strict." He proved himself to be "most constant in the class-room; he went to classes earlier and left later than any of the others" and was "much interested in the library." One might speculate whether this eyewitness's observation meant that Freeman was a very studious loner or if he placed himself apart from his classmates either by choice or by circumstance.[53] One classmate and close friend, J. J. H. Gregory, recalled that Freeman was "almost the first negro to graduate from a New England college. He was a hard student, excellent scholar and fine man." Gregory remembered how ironic it was that Middlebury had "two or three pronounced abolitionists in college" but that in 1848, as juniors marching in procession, "their courage was hardly equal to their convictions, for poor Freeman marched alone until I took his arm." Gregory would remain Martin's life-long friend, corresponding with him long after Middlebury and mailing him American newspapers when Freeman lived in Liberia.[54]

In addition to his financial sponsorship of Freeman (he loaned the young man money to help cover the $83 comprehensive fee), President Labaree sought to support the young man morally and spiritually as best he knew how. Labaree was a man of strong moral convictions who detested injustice. "Injustice and Oppression," he once remarked, "must be ranked among our national sins." He once called slavery "that dark spot upon our national character," an "unsightly excrescence upon the body politic" whose end demanded "the calm, dispassionate and prayerful consideration of the wise and the good." As a Christian minister, educator, and colonizationist, Labaree put great faith in the ability of good Christians to find solutions to life's challenges with the help of God. He believed that "the blessings of civilization and christianity" could uplift and inspire all men, and could heal all "bleeding wounds."[55] As such, all Middlebury men, President Labaree believed, should expect to reap the full rights, privileges, and immunities of American citizenship—unless a man was African American. Labaree often said that black men possessed the necessary capacity to become good men, just not in the United States. Their "manhood," Labaree liked to say, "is not extinguished, only degraded; and that by suitable measures and exertions it can be elevated and burnished."[56] Those "suitable measures and exertions," Labaree contended, were religious, educational, and financial opportunities in Liberia. So firmly did he hold to this idea that almost twenty years after Freeman graduated from Middlebury College, after the Thirteenth Amendment to the Constitution had become the law of the land, Labaree continued to insist that Liberia represented the most "natural and desirable home for the colored man." There, men like Freeman, Labaree believed, could found and run their own republic, get a good living from the soil, engage in commerce, and do God's work of spreading the gospel to non-Christian Africans.[57]

Although Labaree never lost faith in Freeman, he saw him initially as a timid, self-deprecating, insecure student who "distrust[ed] . . . his own abilities." He neither liked nor trusted his white classmates, from whom he expected to receive insults at every turn, just as he had as a schoolboy in Rutland. Yet as far as Labaree knew, Freeman's classmates never tormented him. Labaree watched Freeman grow and develop into an accomplished and confident young man who conducted himself "in all respects with great propriety, and secured the confidence and good will of his instructors and fellow students. His scholarship was excellent in all the departments of study, and his deportment uniformly that of christian gentlemen."[58] Indeed, the Middlebury faculty assured Freeman repeatedly that he belonged there, that he was admitted as a "student in full standing, and that so long as his deportment was correct and his progress in study satisfactory, the authorities of the College would regard him as entitled to all the rights and privileges that were allowed to other students." Freeman did better than progress satisfactorily in his course of studies; he graduated as "one of the first scholars in his class." Labaree recalled, perhaps a little too rosily, that Freeman's classmates, "with a united voice, requested the faculty to give Freeman the honor of delivering the salutatory address in Latin," an honor accorded at that time to the graduate most proficient in Latin oration, who also spoke first at commencement. No copy of his oration in Latin, "Nemo sibi vivat" (Let no one live for himself), exists. However, one eyewitness noted that Freeman, "a gentleman of sterling worth and unimpeachable integrity," was in "every way worthy of distinguished regard." The reporter took pride in "seeing at least one man of color rank himself among the alumni of Middlebury College." However, Labaree seemed to betray some anxiety over the choice of the salutatorian, for he told a colonizationist audience almost two decades later that "lest the public might suppose that he [Freeman] was required to speak in Latin because he could not speak well in English, an oration in that language was also assigned him," a highly unorthodox practice. His second oration, "Utility as a Standard of Morality," was not likely a translation of his Latin oration but rather a separate oration altogether. Nevertheless, Freeman delivered both very well "to his credit, and to the satisfaction of his friends and instructors. This is probably the only instance in a New England College," Labaree added, "in which a colored man has been honored with the appointment of salutation on commencement day." The local newspaper reported that when some of Freeman's classmates learned that Freeman had "carried off their laurels," they grew shamefaced.[59]

Once Freeman graduated, he expected to reap the full rights, privileges, rewards, benefits, and immunities accorded Middlebury graduates, as promised by President Labaree. Some of his classmates would go on to study law and medicine and prepare for the ministry. Some even received offers to teach "winter school," the school term that ran from November through April. However, no offers came Freeman's way. Even "friends of the colored man were not disposed to place their children under his instruction."[60] Freeman could not even land a job as a private tutor in an immediatist abolitionist household. Over the next decade, Freeman would begin to shape his ideology around Labaree's message of "suitable measures and exertions."

In 1850, at age twenty-four, Freeman was offered the position of professor of math and science at the newly established black college, the Allegheny Institute and Mission Church, later renamed Avery College, located outside of Pittsburgh. He would remain at Avery for about a dozen years and would be named the school's second president in 1856, thereby becoming the first black college president in the nation. In addition to his success at Avery College, Freeman experienced joy in his personal life as he mingled with Pittsburgh's black elites. For example, in 1852, Freeman met Dr. David Peck, the first African American medical school graduate, who in all likelihood introduced him to his sister, Louisa Eleanor Peck, a graduate of Oberlin College. Their father, John Peck, a black abolitionist and an opponent of colonization, was one of the founders and trustees of Allegheny Institute and Mission Church. Martin and Eleanor married in September 1857. Eleanor gave birth to their first child, daughter Cora B., in 1860, and to their son, Edward P., in 1862. Life appeared good.[61]

However, despite his professional achievements and domestic accord, Freeman experienced growing unease over life in Pittsburgh. He found himself "caught between two worlds": the world of the black masses in Pittsburgh, who were not only Methodists, of whose faith Freeman, a Congregationalist, did not approve, but who also appeared to be not as committed as he to the importance of education to racial uplift, for other matters such as work, income, and autonomy seemed more pressing to them; and the world of white Pittsburghers, whom Labaree called "men of low degree," who openly insulted Freeman "in the streets [and] . . . in public conveyances, [who] degrade[d] him to the side table at hotels, and remind[ed] him that neither education nor moral excellence, neither civility of language nor courtesy of manner," could protect him from racist affront.[62] Freeman's liminal life in Pittsburgh transformed his thinking about Liberia.

From Labaree's perspective, Freeman, the Middlebury student, "for want of correct information, had become strongly prejudiced against the Colonization Society. He thought he saw in it a purpose to deprive the black man of his natural and national rights, and to expatriate him to a distant and desolate wilderness." Freeman's mentor believed that his pupil saw only "Anglo Saxon selfishness" in the ACS's activities. Now Freeman, the professor and college president, living a life restricted by racism, was able to "examine candidly the character and claims of the Colonization Society" and could see that "the native home of his ancestors presented hopes and attractions that neither America nor any other land could furnish."[63]

By the late 1850s Freeman shared Labaree's view. In 1858, while an officer of the Niger Valley Exploring Party, a black-organized association founded to compete with the efforts of the American Colonization Society, Freeman wrote to Martin R. Delaney, "I am more and more convinced that Africa is the country to which all colored men who wish to attain the full state of manhood, and bring up their children to be men and not creeping things, should turn their steps."[64] He reiterated the same at the Vermont Auxiliary convention in 1863, where he left the audience with the indelible image of his manhood crushed out of him.[65]

In 1862 Alexander Crummell, a young black Episcopal priest and a humanities professor at Liberia College, visited the United States to recruit bright black students for the college. One of his stops was Pittsburgh, where he met with Freeman. The ACS reported that during his visits to the States, Crummell "exchanged thoughts" with African American leaders, met with black clergymen and congregations, and "exhibited to them Liberia as opening to men of color advantages and prospects to be sought in vain in any other country." After his meeting with Freeman, Crummell recommended the young college president to the Massachusetts Colonization Society, the overseers of Liberia College, and the college's trustees in Monrovia.[66]

In February 1863, when the prospect of teaching at Liberia College arose—not even a job offer, just the possibility of it—Freeman quit his job at Avery College. He would not sail for Liberia, however, until September 1864. The Civil War caused the delay by disrupting the flow of funds into the coffers of the ACS and the Massachusetts Colonization Society. Moreover, few free blacks wished to emigrate. In order for Freeman and his family to sail to Liberia, the Massachusetts Colonization Society imposed another condition in addition to his fund-raising for his salary: raising a "large company" of fellow expatriates to accompany him to Liberia to make the trip cost-effective. Freeman was now furious. He feared that his reputation would be ruined. He had resigned his situation at Avery College, and now he was about to lose his "reputation as an honest man among many of my friends in the East," he declared, "who have generously given me money for an outfit supposing that I would go this fall." He felt "blameworthy," as he had "lost the respect of my own people who will not fail to proclaim that they knew that I did not mean to go, and say that my late New England tour was an ingenious device to raise a little extra funds." Nevertheless, Freeman, although feeling manipulated, wanted to assure the MCS that his desire to go was not based on self-interest. "I am not one of those Negroes," he wrote to Reverend Joseph Tracy, the secretary of the Massachusetts Colonization Society, "who are always aspiring to place themselves at the head of a crowd and act as leader."[67] He asserted that he hoped neither to get rich nor to achieve safety in security, the latter of which he could still enjoy at Avery College. In fact, he feared that Liberia might lead to his "premature suffering and death." Nevertheless, he needed to go because he believed that Liberia would "secure for myself and my posterity, this greater good, Liberty and Equality." He preferred to live in "a log hut," performing "hard labor" and living in "poverty, with political, civil and social freedom and equality," than live in the United States under "political, civil, and social slavery and degradation."[68]

Freeman and his family arrived in Monrovia in the fall of 1864. For the next twenty-four years, Freeman taught math, algebra, geometry, chemistry, natural philosophy, Latin, and Greek. His day usually ran from 7:00 a.m. to midnight. Exhaustion and the difficult climate, as well as careless teaching—he may have viewed a solar eclipse through a telescope without the proper protective lens, which led to long-term eye problems—compromised his health, causing him to return periodically to the United States for extended stays for medical treatment. In 1867 Freeman's family accompanied him on a nearly yearlong visit to Pittsburgh and other cities in search of medical care and teaching supplies. While the family was in Pittsburgh, Avery College offered to double his salary and provide a furnished house rent free. He declined the school's offer.[69]

When Freeman returned to Liberia in late 1868, he returned alone. Louisa's father, John, a harsh critic of colonization, begged Louisa not to return to Liberia. Moreover, Louisa was pregnant with their third child and too unwell to travel. Thus, she stayed behind in Pittsburgh to give birth and to care for her other two children, especially Cora, who was "very ill with Typhoid fever." Sadly, Clarence, born in August 1868, died in July 1869. In grief, Louisa and her two surviving children returned to Liberia in 1870, but only after she received assurance that Martin had secured a life insurance policy on himself.[70]

In 1870, the Trustees of Donations and the Board of Trustees named Freeman president pro tempore due to the chronic absences of Edward Blyden, the president of Liberia College. Freeman loathed the extra burden of his new administrative duties, which included submitting annual reports of the Educational Department of Liberia College to the MCS, in which he summarized the college's affairs and activities. He also had to make recommendations for hiring new faculty, propose faculty salaries, and oversee renovations and repairs to the physical plant. Over the next two decades, his administrative and teaching duties, as well as his recurring bouts of illness, wore down Freeman and forced him to ask to be replaced from time to time. Once in the late 1870s while receiving treatment in New York City for heart and kidney failure and perhaps be treated for a case of septicemia due to several tooth extractions, he was told that the society intended to replace him with a white president. Freeman replied, "I shall be glad if any man whether white, black, red, yellow, or even green is sent out to relieve me."[71] The new president, Reverend John B. Pinney, an agent for the New York Colonization Society, lasted only six months, from March through October 1878.

Ill health, personal disappointment, declining productivity, a family tragedy, and perhaps depression marked Freeman's final years at Liberia College. The family tragedy involved the poisoning of his only daughter, Cora, shortly after her marriage to a controversial local Liberian. This event marked the nadir of his time served in his adopted country.[72] In January 1889 the board of trustees of Liberia College officially appointed Martin Freeman president. Two months later, he was dead at age sixty-two. Louisa used the benefit from his life insurance policy to bury Martin in Monrovia. Following his death, his wife and son Edward returned to Pittsburgh. Little is known of Louisa's and Edward's lives after Liberia. The Records of the Allegheny Cemetery Association identify a "Louisa E. Freeman" as buried in Allegheny Cemetery in 1897. One historian believes that Edward exemplified Martin Freeman's greatest fear for black men in the United States: for a brief time before his death in 1893, he worked as a janitor.[73]

Historians celebrate Martin Freeman as America's first black college president. Yet how odd that this black native son of Rutland, Vermont, and graduate of Middlebury College should play an important, albeit unheralded, role in the colonization movement in the mid-nineteenth century. Activities at Middlebury College and in the town on the cusp of Freeman's matriculation and during his stay suggest that the young man was constantly reminded that true equality in the United States was beyond the reach of even the brightest of young black men. The discussions at the college, in the town, and throughout the region over slavery; personal slights directed at Freeman; and subliminal messages of difference led Freeman to search for a place to belong after college. He found his ideological home in the colonization movement. However, his physical home in Liberia was less than ideal. He adopted a love-hate relationship with his "Dear Old Fatherland," declaring publicly his love for this "land of the free, and land of my hope," yet complaining privately about the "Negro hate" that existed in Liberia. He detested the unhealthful climate and denounced the irritating "rivalries and jealousies" that defined Liberian society.[74] Nevertheless, Freeman remained steadfast in his belief that only in a black homeland abroad could black Americans realize their full manhood, that is, attain self-determination, self-reliance, self-sufficiency, and dignity. Freeman insisted that he never aspired to be a black leader. Rather, as a member of the black elite, he merely hoped for a life of dignity in Liberia, where he could realize his "manhood," defined as the full rights and privileges of black male citizenship, not found in the United States. Middlebury College exposed Freeman to this ideal, which he slowly embraced over time and strove mightily to realize in a black utopia of his making.

NOTES

1. *Middlebury Register*, October 21, 1863, 2, Collection of Henry Sheldon Museum of Vermont History, Middlebury, Vt. (hereafter CHSMVH); *Vermont Record* (Brandon, Vt.), October 23, 1863, 1, CHSMVH. Martin Freeman became the first black president of a college when he moved from the faculty to the office of the president at Avery College (1856–63), formerly Alleghany College, a short-lived, historically black college on the northern edge of Pittsburgh, Pennsylvania.

2. *Middlebury Register*, October 21, 1863, 2; Mary Ann Swift, Journal, vol. 8, October 23, 1863, Stewart Family Papers, CHSMVH.

3. *Middlebury Register*, October 28, 1863, 2, CHSMVH.

4. Russell W. Irvine, "Martin H. Freeman of Rutland: America's First Black College Professor and Pioneering Black Social Activist," *Rutland Historical Society Quarterly* 26, no. 3 (1996): 83; William Coppinger to Joseph Tracy, September 3, 1862, Papers of Martin Freeman, Middlebury College Special Collections and Archives (hereafter MC Archives), photocopy of original at Massachusetts Historical Society (hereafter MHS).

5. *National Intelligencer* (Washington, D.C.), September 23, 1864, Freeman Papers, photocopy of original at MHS.

6. Samuel E. Cornish and Theodore S. Wright, *The Colonization Scheme Considered, in Its Rejection by the Colored People—in Its Tendency to Uphold Caste—in Its Unfitness for Christianizing and Civilizing the Aborigines of Africa, and for Putting a Stop to the African Slave Trade: In a Letter to the Hon. Theodore Frelinghuysen and the Hon. Benjamin Butler* (Newark, N.J.: Aaron Guest, 1840), 5, Samuel L. Southard Papers, Rare Books and Special Collections, Firestone Library, Princeton University (hereafter cited as RBSC Princeton).

7. See Eric Foner, *Reconstruction: America's Unfinished Revolution, 1863–1877* (New York: Harper & Row, 1988), 35–76; Bruce Dain, "'The Power of Making Me Miserable': Abraham Lincoln and Race," in *The Struggle for Equality: Essays on Sectional Conflict, the Civil War, and the Long Reconstruction*, ed. Orville Vernon Burton, Jerald Podair, and Jennifer L. Weber (Charlottesville: University of Virginia Press, 2011), 112; Willie Lee Rose, *Rehearsal for Reconstruction: The Port Royal Experiment* (New York: Oxford University Press, 1964).

8. Frederick Douglass, "Men of Color, to Arms!," *Douglass' Monthly* (Rochester, N.Y.), March 1863; James M. McPherson, *The Struggle for Equality: Abolitionists and the Negro*

in the Civil War and Reconstruction (Princeton, N.J.: Princeton University Press, 1964), 204–5; McPherson, *The Negro's Civil War: How American Negroes Felt and Acted during the War for the Union* (New York: Vintage Books, 1965), 77–82; and C. Peter Ripley, ed., *The Black Abolitionist Papers, Vol. V: The United States, 1859–1865* (Chapel Hill: University of North Carolina Press, 1992), 261–62.

9. McPherson, *Negro's Civil War*, 173, 177, 239; Glenn M. Linden, *Voices from the Gathering Storm: The Coming of the American Civil War* (Wilmington, Del.: Scholarly Resources, 2001), 198–200; Dain, "'The Power,'" 103.

10. Eddie S. Glaude, *Exodus! Religion, Race, and Nation in Early Nineteenth-Century Black America* (Chicago: University of Chicago Press, 2000), 5.

11. The best-known individual who represents the phenomenon of the "reverse underground railroad" is Solomon Northup, who was kidnapped in Saratoga Springs, New York, in 1841 and held in bondage in Louisiana for twelve years. During his enslavement, he met other free black men who had been unlawfully sold into bondage. See Solomon Northup, *Twelve Years a Slave* (1853), ed. Sue Eakin and Joseph Logsdon (Baton Rouge: Louisiana State University Press, 1968), esp. 38, 41–42 for Robert and Arthur, two free black men caught in the reverse underground railroad. For a primary source referencing this crime, see Cornish and Wright, *Colonization Scheme Considered*, 20.

12. *Middlebury Register*, October 28, 1863, 2, CHSMVH.

13. Philip C. Hay, *Our Duty to Our Coloured Population: A Sermon for the Benefit of the American Colonization Society, Delivered in the Second Presbyterian Church, Newark; July 23, 1826* (Newark, N.J.: W. Tuttle & Co., 1826), 7, RBSC Princeton; Jared Sparks and David A. Borrenstein, *Extracts from an Article in the North American Review for January, 1824: On the Subject of the American Colonization Society* (Princeton, N.J.: Princeton Press, for the New-Jersey Colonization Society, by D. A. Borrenstein, 1824), 6, RBSC Princeton.

14. *Twenty-Sixth Annual Report of the Vermont Colonization Society, Presented October 16, 1845* (Burlington, Vt.: Chauncey Goodrich, 1845) 15, RBSC Princeton; Hay, *Our Duty*, 13.

15. G. B. Stebbins, *Facts and Opinions Touching the Real Origin, Character, and Influence of the American Colonization Society: Views of Wilberforce, Clarkson, and Others, and Opinion of the Free People of Color of the United States* (Boston: John P. Jewett & Co., 1853; repr., New York: Negro University Press, Greenwood Publishing, 1969), iii–vii.

16. P. J. Staudenraus, *The African Colonization Movement, 1816–1865* (New York: Columbia University Press, 1961; repr., New York: Octagon Books, Farrar, Straus and Giroux, 1980), vii–ix.

17. For more recent scholarship on colonization, see, for example, Glaude, *Exodus*; Claude A. Clegg III, *The Price of Liberty: African Americans and the Making of Liberia* (Chapel Hill: University of North Carolina Press, 2004); Marie Tyler-McGraw, *An African Republic: Black and White Virginians in the Making of Liberia* (Chapel Hill: University of North Carolina Press, 2007), 5 (quote).

18. Tyler-McGraw, *An African Republic*, 6.

19. Craig Steven Wilder, *Ebony and Ivy: Race, Slavery, and the Troubled History of America's Universities* (New York: Bloomsbury Press, 2013), 247–48.

20. Russell W. Irvine, *The African American Quest for Institutions of Higher Education Before the Civil War: The Forgotten Histories of the Ashmun Institute, Liberia College, and Avery College* (Lewiston, N.Y.: Edwin Mellen press, 2010), 4–6.

21. Ibid., 3–12.

22. Martin Robison Delany, *The Condition, Elevation, Emigration, and Destiny of the Colored People of the United States* (Philadelphia: King & Baird, Printers, 1852), 122. Delany mistakenly identifies Freeman's alma mater as "Rutland College, in Vermont."

23. Irvine, "Martin H. Freeman," 71–99; Irvine, *African American Quest*, 304, 354–55.

24. David Bain, *College on the Hill: A Browser's History for the Bicentennial, Middlebury College, 1800–2000* (Middlebury, Vt.: Middlebury College Press, 1999), 12.

25. David Stameshkin, *The Town's College: Middlebury College, 1800–1915* (Middlebury, Vt.: Middlebury College Press, 1985), 74.

26. Ibid., 72, 31–35, 90–91.

27. Ibid., 36–67, 77–80, 84, 299n41, 126–28; Irvine, *African American Quest*, 106, 70.

28. Stameshkin, *Town's College*, 128.

29. Ibid., 128–30.

30. Ibid., 131–43.

31. William G. McLaughlin, *Revivals, Awakenings, and Reform: An Essay on Religion and Social Change in America, 1607–1977* (Chicago: University of Chicago Press, 1978), 98–140.

32. Bain, *College on the Hill*, 28.

33. *National Standard*, August 22, 1826, 3 (microfilm), Ilsley Public Library, Middlebury, Vt. Vermont was one of fourteen states—nine northern, five southern—to organize auxiliary societies to the ACS at this time.

34. *Middlebury Free Press*, May 5, 1834, 2, and April 21, 1834, 1, CHSMVH.

35. *Middlebury Free Press*, May 26, 1834, 2, and May 12, 1834, 1, CHSMVH.

36. *Middlebury Free Press*, May 12, 1834, 1, and July 21, 1834, 3, CHSMVH.

37. *Middlebury People's Press*, July 19, 1843, 2, CHSMVH.

38. Ibid.

39. Randolph Roth, "Can Faith Change the World? Religion and Society in Vermont's Age of Reform," *Vermont History* 69 (2001): 7.

40. "Philomathesian Society Journal, Division the First, Vol. 5, 1829–1846," MC Archives.

41. Edward Merrill to John W. Steward, July 1846, CHSMVH.

42. *Northern Galaxy*, September 23, 1845, 2, Freeman Papers.

43. Ibid.; *Northern Galaxy*, October 7, 1845, 3, Freeman Papers.

44. *Northern Galaxy*, September 23, 1845, 2, and October 7, 1845, 3, Freeman Papers.

George Boardman, Middlebury class of 1847, professor of rhetoric and English (1853–59), and a trustee (1868–93), while paying homage to Labaree during the centennial celebrations in 1900, called the whole affair of enrolling black youths at Middlebury in the 1840s "someone's imagination." See George N. Boardman, "Doctor George N. Boardman's Speech," in *A Record of the Centennial Anniversary of Middlebury College* (University Press, 1901), 259.

45. *Northern Galaxy*, September 23, 1845, 2, Freeman Papers. Ironically, the editors printed in this same issue, adjacent to the story detailing Labaree's troubles, a story that began: "Nothing can be more intolerant, and we dare say unscriptural, than to withhold christian fellowship from a man on the sole ground of his being a slave holder." Many Americans at this time shared this bifurcated sentiment. Middlebury College awarded Lemuel Haynes, William's biracial father, an honorary degree in 1804 while he pastored at the West Rutland Congregational Church. Edgar J. Wiley, comp., *Catalogue of the Officers and Students of Middlebury College in Middlebury, Vermont, and Others Who Have Received Degrees, 1800–1927* (Middlebury, Vt.: Middlebury College, 1928), 75, 101, 178, 713, MC Archives; Bain, *College on the Hill*, 56–57, 95.

46. *History of Rutland County*, 366–68.

47. "Biography of Freeman," *Rutland Herald*, September 30, 1996; Marvel G. Swan and Donald P. Swan, comps., and Dawn D. Hance, ed., *Early Families of Rutland, Vt.* (Rutland, Vt.: Rutland Historical Society, 1990), 142–44; Irvine, "Martin H. Freeman," 71.

48. Sources disagree over the names of Freeman's parents. Some say his parents' names were Charles and Patience. Others offer that his father's name was Pearson Toussaint Freeman, named perhaps after the Haitian revolutionary. See *Early Families of Rutland, Vt.*, 142–144.

49. M. Freeman, "The Educational Wants of the Free Colored People," *Anglo-American Magazine*, April 1859, Freeman Papers.

50. M. H. Freeman to Mrs. Charlotte Chaffee, August 22, 1883, Freeman Papers.

51. *Middlebury Register*, October 14, 1863, 2, CHSMVH; *The Undergraduate* (Middlebury College) 24, no. 1 (October 1898): 1, MC Archives; obituary, *The Undergraduate* 20, no. 7 (May 1895): 102, MC Archives. Rankin believed that this embarrassing moment took place in August 1844, but Freeman enrolled in August 1845. For Rankin's standing as a sophomore in 1845-46, see *The Catalogue of the Officers and Students of Middlebury College for the Academic Year 1844–1845, with the Course of Study* (Troy, N.Y.: Press of Kneeland & Co., 1844) 8, which lists Rankin as a member of the freshman class.

52. *Northern Galaxy*, October 21, 1845, 3, Freeman Papers.

53. *The Undergraduate* 20, no. 7 (May 1895): 102, MC Archives.

54. James J. H. Gregory to President J. W. Thomas, October 27, 1908, Freeman Papers; Freeman to Chaffee, August 22, 1883.

55. M. H. [Freeman] to Rev. Joseph Tracy, October 23, 1863, Freeman Papers, photocopy of original at MHS; Irvine, "Martin H. Freeman," 72. Fourteen years after gradua-

tion, Freeman still had yet to fully repay Labaree. Rev. Benjamin Labaree, *A Sermon on the Death of General Harrison, Delivered in Middlebury, Vermont, on the Day of the National Fast* (Middlebury, Vt.: E. Maxham, 1841), MC Archives.

56. Address of Rev. Benjamin Labaree, D.D., Late President of Middlebury College, from "51st Annual Report of the American Colonization Society," January 21, 1868, 37–42, MC Archives; Wilson A. Farnsworth, *Personal Reminiscences, 1822–1844* (printed by their children, 1902, the golden wedding anniversary of Dr. and Mrs. Farnsworth), MC Archives.

57. Labaree address, January 21, 1868.

58. B. Labaree to Rev. F. Butler, September 15, 1863, Freeman Papers, photocopy of original at MHS.

59. Labaree address, January 21, 1868; *Middlebury Register*, October 14, 1863, 2, CHSMVH; *National Era* (East Poultney), July 30, 1849, Freeman Papers; Irvine, "Martin H. Freeman," 91; *Middlebury Galaxy*, July 31, 1849, 2, SCHSMVH. Many thanks to Jane Chaplin, professor of classics, Middlebury College, for help with the Latin translation.

60. Labaree address, January 21, 1868, 39.

61. Russell W. Irvine, "Martin H. Freeman of Rutland: America's First Black College Professor and Pioneering Black Social Activist," *Rutland Historical Society Quarterly* XXVI (no. 3) (1996): 79–81; "Departure of Emigrants," *The African Repository* 1864, vol. 40 (no. 11) 314. Irvine cites the son's name as "Edwin P." while the *African Repository* identifies him as "John P." The Records of the Allegheny Cemetery Historical Association lists the son's name as "Edward."

62. Ibid.; Bernard Morris, "Avery College—Symbol Worth Preserving," *Carnegie Magazine* (January 1969): 21–24; Saul Sack, *History of Higher Education in Pennsylvania* (Harrisburg: Pennsylvania Historical and Museum Commission, 1963), 1:167–69; Wm Coppinger to Rev. Joseph Tracy, September 3, 1862, Papers of Martin Freeman, MC Archives, photocopy of original at MHS.

63. Larabee address, January 21, 1868, 39.

64. Letter cited in *Rutland Herald*, October 31, 1996, Freeman Papers.

65. *Middlebury Register*, October 21, 1863, 2, CHSMVH.

66. *Forty-Sixth Annual Report of the American Colonization Society, with Proceedings of the Annual Meeting and of the Board of Directors* (January 20, 1863), 6. The Trustees for Donations for Education in Liberia, a Boston-based philanthropic group whose members were also members of the Massachusetts Colonization Society, managed the fiscal and academic needs of Liberia College. Reverend Joseph Tracy, the secretary of the MCS between 1842 and his death in 1874, was the go-between between the two organizations.

67. Freeman to Tracy, November 7, 1863, Freeman Papers, photocopy of original at MHS.

68. In *Auxiliary State Colonization Societies* 39, no. 11 (1863), MC Archives; *National Intelligencer*, September 23, 1864, Freeman Papers.

69. M. H. Freeman to Rev. Sir [Tracy?], August 9, 1867, Freeman Papers; *African Repository* 40, no. 2 (February 1864): 37; Irvine, "Martin H. Freeman," 95.

70. M. H. Freeman to Rev. J. Tracy, October 17, 1867, Papers of Martin Freeman, MC Archives, photocopy of original at MHS; M. H. Freeman to Rev. J. Tracy, April 6, 1868, Papers of Martin Freeman, MC Archives, photocopy of original at MHS; Louisa E. Freeman to Rev. J. Tracy, May 25, 1869, Papers of Martin Freeman, MC Archives, photocopy of original at MHS; M. H. Freeman to Rev. J. Tracy, March 7, 1870, Papers of Martin Freeman, MC Archives, photocopy of original at MHS; Records of the Allegheny Cemetery Historical Assocation.

71. Irvine, "Martin H. Freeman," 95.

72. Freeman to Chaffee, August 2, 1880.

73. Irvine, "Martin H. Freeman," 96; Records of the Allegheny Cemetery Historical Association.

74. M. H. Freeman to Mr. Coppinger, Esq., July 14, 1863, Freeman Papers, photocopy of original at MHS; Martin H. Freeman to Rev. J. Tracy, January 30, 1864, Freeman Papers, photocopy of original at MHS; Freeman to Chaffee, August 2, 1880.

CHAPTER NINE

Towers of Intellect

The Struggle for African American Higher Education in Antebellum New England

Kabria Baumgartner

James Easton embodied "mechanical genius and mental ability," recalled abolitionist and historian William Cooper Nell.[1] Born to free black parents in eastern Massachusetts in 1754, Easton served in the Revolutionary War and then moved to North Bridgewater, where he operated an iron factory. In conjunction with his factory, he established a manual labor school in the early 1820s to equip African American male youth with a mechanical trade as well as literary skills. Approximately twenty youth attended yearly, including Easton's own son, Hosea, until the school closed in the late 1820s due to racial threats.[2] Recalling this incident years later, Hosea, an abolitionist in his own right, declared that "prejudice is destructive to life," particularly black life.[3] Like his father, the younger Easton espoused black intellectual vitality and improvement through education. In his writings, he affirmed black civil rights and citizenship in the United States and pushed for the emancipation of slaves; for him, education was crucial, a "sign of life" for African Americans in the face of racial animus.[4]

The story of antislavery leaders who championed black education dates back to at least the eighteenth century, but the radical abolition movement in antebellum New England ushered in a revolutionary platform that called for the immediate, uncompensated emancipation of slaves. African American and white abolitionists articulated a politics of elevation that linked black self-improvement, primarily through education, with racial advancement and equality.[5] Given these twin goals, African American abolitionists sought to establish institutions of higher education, from seminaries to colleges, to serve black communities. They believed that higher education charted a path to empowerment. And white abolitionists concurred and joined forces with them. Over a ten-year period, from 1830 to 1840, these radical abolitionists tried three times to establish educational institutions in New England: first, a manual labor college for African American men in New Haven, Connecticut; second, a seminary for young African American women in Canterbury, Connecticut; and third, a coeducational and interracial academy in Canaan, New Hampshire. Though each institution held a different function and served a diverse group of students, together they represented what I call "towers of intellect," a distinct abolitionist vision of higher education that celebrated the black desire, pursuit, and embodiment of knowledge as well as the fight for a multiracial democracy. These institutions, however, were short-lived. They all shared the same fate: destruction.

Historians have debated why a black college, an all-girls black seminary, and an interracial and coeducational academy became targets of white antagonism and violence: was it the fear of labor competition; racial prejudice; abolitionist agitation; resentment of black elevation; or some combination thereof?[6] This essay reorients the debate to focus on the initiative of and cooperation between African American and white abolitionists who fought for black educational opportunity in the New England region. In doing so, this essay reveals how radical abolitionists turned a local issue, higher education, into a significant regional issue centered on combating racial prejudice and slavery in the United States.

New England was not immune to the institution of slavery; on the contrary, slavery actually shaped the region economically. Historian Joanne Pope Melish explains that the enslaved population "remained quite small" in the seventeenth century before growing slowly but steadily in the eighteenth century.[7] Melish estimates that at the start of the American Revolution, the population of African-descended people in New England hovered at around sixteen thousand, making it the smallest black population by region in North America. Though early census records fail to differentiate between enslaved and free persons of color, it is likely that the majority of African-descended people in New England were slaves who lived near coastal areas or commercial port towns like Boston.[8] States such as Rhode Island and Connecticut depended heavily on the labor of slaves, who were put to work in skilled trades and as domestic servants. Black labor enabled the region to expand commercially.[9] Though New England was a society with slaves, to borrow historian Ira Berlin's term, and hence did not depend economically on slave labor, slavery itself fueled the ideology of white supremacy.[10]

The Age of Revolution witnessed enslaved and free black people arguing for their equality and liberty.[11] In New Hampshire, for instance, nineteen enslaved blacks petitioned for their God-given right to "life and freedom, upon the terms of the most perfect equality with other men."[12] In addition to petitioning, many enslaved blacks fought on the side of the Patriots in the American Revolution, while others defended the Loyalists, who promised enslaved blacks manumission in exchange for military service. The radical activism of African Americans and the emergence of antislavery discourse, coupled with the disruptions brought on by the war, led New England states to enact gradual emancipation laws, which eroded the institution of slavery in the region. The free black population stood at 137,506 in 1830, with approximately 21,310 free blacks residing in the New England area. Free blacks had established autonomous institutions, from mutual aid societies to schools, and thus shaped an ideology of racial uplift. This ideology was partly ameliorative, in the sense that African Americans could gain respect through education, and partly practical, as African Americans could acquire knowledge and realize upward social mobility, wealth, and citizenship.

Many white New Englanders tackled this rapidly changing environment by reconstructing a distinct New England regional identity that depended on the removal and erasure of African Americans. White writers, travelers, and inhabitants spoke of the fine churches and stately buildings that dotted the picturesque New England landscape.[13] Rarely did these inhabitants mention the riches that had been gained from slave labor and the African slave trade, nor did they recognize African Americans as free.[14] Rather, they boasted about the region's industrious white citizens, even the poor farmer, as well as the republican and Protestant ideals as represented in its institutions, particularly colleges like Harvard and Yale. Stephanie Kermes argues that these colleges "signified the region's high level of education, which New Englanders saw as an essential precondition for a good republican people and, therefore, in the New England mind, justified the region's feeling of superiority."[15] At the same time that Harvard and Yale welcomed young elite white men and stood as exemplars of New England virtue and hard work, higher education in the region expanded and, with it, ideas about self-improvement.

Dubbed the Age of Improvement, the early decades of the nineteenth century witnessed the steady growth of colleges that primarily served white male youth from various class backgrounds.[16] Even though less than 2 percent of the total population received a collegiate education in the antebellum era, these institutions were, according to Kenneth Nivison, the "largest and most important institutional prize of the new republic."[17] For some families, sending their twenty-year-old son to college made sense for professional opportunity, self-improvement, and economic and social advancement.[18] The influx of older, poorer students in search of upward social mobility, however, transformed student life in New England, leading to an increase in student revolts and bureaucratic control.[19] This transformation also coincided with the increase in the number of colleges: there were twenty-five degree-granting institutions in 1800 and fifty-two by 1820.[20] Amherst College is one such example. Founded in 1821, it aimed to provide a "classical education for indigent young men of piety and talents for the Christian ministry."[21] The student population at Amherst College grew quickly: the inaugural class of 1821 included 47 students, and enrollment rose to 211 by 1828. Many students at this and New England's other hilltop colleges received financial assistance through charity or self-help, which enabled them to matriculate and eventually graduate, having acquired significant cultural and social capital.[22] According to historian John Thelin, these hilltop colleges allowed white male youth of varying means "entrée into a new, educated elite."[23]

Notably, the earliest African Americans to earn baccalaureate degrees were men who graduated from New England's hilltop colleges, but they did not share the same opportunities as white male students. These early African American pioneers included Alexander Twilight, who graduated from Middlebury College in 1823; Edward Jones from Amherst College in 1826; John Russwurm from Bowdoin College in 1826; and Edward Mitchell from Dartmouth College in 1828. Born in Jamaica in 1799 to a white English father and a black mother, John Russwurm, for instance, had been educated at New England academies and entered Bowdoin College in Brunswick, Maine, at the junior class level in 1824. Chartered in 1794, Bowdoin College promoted "virtue and piety, and the knowledge of... languages and... the useful and liberal arts and sciences" among its student body. Russwurm was one of thirty-two graduates in 1826.[24] Winston James, a biographer of Russwurm, notes that while Russwurm may well have experienced racism in college, Bowdoin College itself boasted some of "America's most distinguished progressive, anti-racist, and abolitionist intellectuals."[25] Other colleges were not as progressive. In fact, some faculty and students at hilltop colleges openly opposed the antislavery movement; and some, like John Hough, a white professor of languages at Middlebury College, concluded that African Americans were a

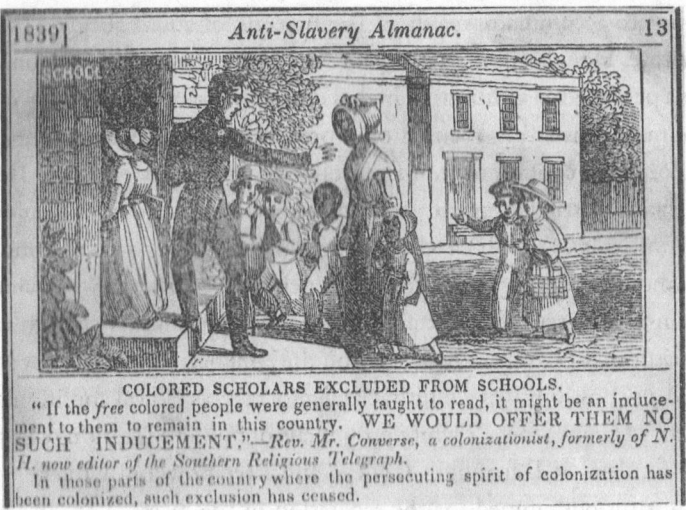

Publications such as *The American Anti-Slavery Almanac* often criticized the exclusion of children of African descent from educational institutions. Image courtesy of Kabria Baumgartner.

"despised and hopeless race."[26] While New England's hilltop colleges occasionally enrolled African American men, these institutions neither catered to them nor served their needs. By 1860 only twenty-eight African Americans had earned degrees from recognized colleges.[27]

Despite the formidable achievement of a few African Americans who earned a collegiate education, myths about the degraded, debased, and inferior free black population seemed to prevail. From broadsides and pamphlets to sermons, propaganda circulated that portrayed the supposed degraded condition and innate inferiority of African Americans. The aforementioned John Hough delivered such a sermon in October 1826 at a meeting of the Vermont Colonization Society, an auxiliary society of the American Colonization Society, an organization founded in 1816 that aimed to send African Americans to Africa. In his condemnation of African Americans, he asserted that "the state of the free colored population of the United States, is one of extreme and remediless degradation," implying that no amount of education could change their status—it was uniform, undeniable, and fixed. Moreover, Hough surmised that African Americans had no desire for education anyway, since they "evince no solicitude to acquire knowledge or, by diligence and economy, to accumulate wealth."²⁸ The Eastons, of course, begged to differ. In any case, Hough's position was not atypical; racism and procolonization factions pervaded institutions of higher education in New England.

Colonizationists thus focused on a project of black emancipation, if enslaved, or black containment, if free, followed quickly by removal. They believed that repatriation greatly benefited free blacks, who would enjoy new opportunities in West Africa while engaged in missionary work to bring civilization and Christianity there. The real beneficiaries, however, were whites invested in a white republic. Certainly, most colonizationists wished to abolish the institution of slavery, a great stain on the American Republic, but they all rejected any possibility of a multiracial democracy, as radical abolitionists envisioned.²⁹ Calvin Stowe, a white proponent of public education who served on the faculties at Dartmouth College and later Bowdoin College, among other institutions, argued for the separation of the races: "I am in favor of colonization, because I suppose it to be right, and agreeable to God's design, that the different races of men should continue to be distinct, and each reside in the climate best adapted to their physical and intellectual development."³⁰ In fact, most families who sent their sons to college believed in colonization. Margaret Sumner asserts that these families "imagin[ed] Liberia as one more educational community for their world, a distant place where 'black' genius might be cultivated."³¹ White New England families thus constructed free white educational institutions symbolic of a free white republic completely devoid of African Americans.

African American abolitionists rejected claims of innate black degradation and inferiority and instead promoted black self-improvement. In Boston, African American abolitionist David Walker penned a radical treatise, *An Appeal to the Coloured Citizens of the World* (1829), that accused colonizationists of plotting to perpetuate slavery with free African Americans gone, unable to aid their brethren. Walker asserted that African Americans were natives of the United States, and he encouraged them to gain intellectual and religious knowledge.³² Similarly, African American abolitionist Maria W. Stewart, a neighbor and friend of Walker's, lectured her audience of African American men and women to "turn their attention to knowledge and improvement."³³ In contrast to colonizationists who connected black removal to the abolition of slavery, radical abolitionists, from Walker to Stewart to Easton, linked the acquisition of knowledge to black emancipation and freedom in the United

States. In other words, for abolitionists, higher education promised feasible and immediate solutions to improve black life and unfetter enslaved African Americans.

For abolitionists, higher education held productive and reproductive qualities in regard to both knowledge and activism. In 1827 African American abolitionists John Russwurm and Samuel Cornish touted the importance of education to community uplift in their newspaper, *Freedom's Journal*. Similarly, ten years later, the *Colored American*, a black newspaper run by Charles B. Ray, an educated African American man from Massachusetts, featured editorials on the politics of elevation and the abolition of slavery. One editorialist proclaimed that an African American man could "cultivate a reading habit[,] know his own condition better... [and] become conversant with the world and prepared to lend an influence, to give a right direction and tone, to the habits of all within his reach."[34] Though editorialists in black newspapers tended toward androcentrism in discussions on education, they did acknowledge the particular role of African American women in gaining and imparting knowledge. "Teach one, teach many" seemed to be the motto. This view arguably inspired white abolitionists like William Lloyd Garrison, a Massachusetts native who started his own newspaper, *The Liberator*, in 1831. Supported largely by black subscribers, *The Liberator* published articles linking knowledge to emancipation. "Knowledge is power. A people generally enlightened cannot be enslaved," one correspondent opined.[35]

Peter Osborne and other like-minded abolitionists imagined the development of educated black communities and the cultivation of black intellect not in distant Africa but right in New England. However, the racial violence occurring in northern cities, from New Haven, Connecticut, to Providence, Rhode Island, in the 1820s and 1830s, often perpetrated by white mobs against black and white abolitionists, compelled activists like John Russwurm to advocate for black immigration to Africa.[36] Some abolitionists, however, discouraged that. In an address to an audience of African American churchgoers in New Haven in 1832, African American abolitionist Peter Osborne affirmed that the United States was "our native country." He continued, "It becomes every colored citizen in the United States to step forward boldly, and gallantly defend his rights," which included the right to an education.[37] High schools, academies, and colleges represented the spatial realization of the black pursuit of knowledge as well as intellectual culture. African American and white abolitionists thus articulated a central tenet within the fight for black education: to cultivate black intellect and to work toward black equality and a multiracial democracy.

The issue of African American higher education became a point of concern at black organizational meetings. At the First Annual Convention of the Free People of Colour, held on June 6, 1831, African American abolitionists from New York to Virginia assembled at Wesleyan Church in Philadelphia to discuss a handful of serious issues, from deadly race riots to discriminatory "Black Laws" that suppressed the political, social, and economic elevation of African Americans. In the face of this turmoil, delegates identified three principles for black elevation: education, temperance, and economy.[38] This convention was more than just an exchange of declarations, however. Following earlier school-building initiatives by James Easton in the 1820s and African American abolitionist Peter Williams in the 1830s, Simeon Jocelyn, a white pastor and abolitionist from Connecticut, and five other white leaders, including William Lloyd Garrison, proposed to establish a manual labor college for African American men in New Haven. The manual labor system, popular at this time at places like Beriah Green's Oneida Institute in New York, promised to train African American male youth for skilled labor jobs. For Garrison, the benefits multiplied after that: "When [African American men] once get trades, they will be able to accumulate money; money begets influence, and influence respectability. Influence, wealth, and character will certainly destroy those prejudices which now separate you from society."[39] Unfortunately, this narrative of progress failed to account for racism and its destructive effects on people and communities. Nevertheless, the proposal, which the delegates endorsed, represented the fight for collective black educational opportunity in the Age of Improvement. Delegates closed their convention address by reiterating the maxim, "Knowledge is power."[40]

In addition to promoting educational opportunities for African American male youth, the plan for a manual labor college appealed to abolitionists, who viewed it as a much-needed corrective to racism and slavery. "The *form* of slavery does not exist among us [in the North]," wrote white New England abolitionist Lydia Maria Child, "but the very *spirit* of the hateful and mischievous thing is here in all its strength."[41] Charles B. Ray felt it firsthand. After completing his studies at Wesleyan Academy in Wilbraham, Massachusetts, Ray applied for and was admitted to Wesleyan University in Middletown, Connecticut, making him the first African American student there. Wilber Fisk, president of Wesleyan University and a colonizationist, likely admitted Ray because he believed in educating African Americans for missionary work.[42] After Ray's arrival, the white student body petitioned to have Ray dismissed from the university, but he left of his own accord. The Wesleyan University board of trustees then passed a resolution that "none but male white patrons shall be admitted as students at this institution."[43] That resolution represented the destructive nature of racism in the North and in New England specifically. The solution was to work toward building high schools, academies, and colleges for African Americans. The cooperation and collaboration between African American and white abolitionists to build a manual labor college became a turning point in interracial activism.[44]

When white New Haven residents learned of this educational proposal, many of them expressed disapproval. The specific complaints fell along class lines. The white New Haven elite, which included David Daggett, a Yale College professor of law, argued that the manual labor college would promote immediate emancipation, which interfered with the institution of slavery in various states. Daggett also contended that the very presence of African American men threatened Yale's prosperity. The mayor of New Haven, Dennis Kimberly, a white Yale graduate, called a city meeting, where residents not only voted 700 to 4 to reject the proposal but also vowed to "resist the establishment of the proposed college in this place, by every lawful means."[45] Historian Hilary Moss finds that white middle-class and working-class New Haven residents objected to the proposed college partly because they "feared for their socioeconomic stability," particularly in the form of labor competition.[46] Furthermore, some white New Haven residents, both elite and working class, denounced African American higher education altogether because it undermined the progress that had been made by the local chapter of the American Colonization Society to send African Americans back to Africa. The weight of opposition, at times violent, in New Haven did not push proponents to abandon the project immediately; rather, they continued to explore alternatives.

Though the manual labor college plan collapsed, the larger fight for African American higher education did not. African American and white abolitionists redoubled their efforts by supporting another school. In 1833 Prudence Crandall, a white woman from Rhode Island, attempted to integrate her all-white seminary in Canterbury, Connecticut, when she admitted Sarah Ann Harris, a twenty-year-old free African American woman from the area. Harris aspired to gain a practical education to become a teacher. Some white parents threatened to withdraw their daughters if Crandall did not dismiss Harris. Crandall forestalled their actions by closing her school and reopening it to serve African American women. Compared to the proposed manual labor college, this female seminary served a different population, African American girls and women, with a different objective, teaching. However, this seminary had what the proposed manual labor college did not: infrastructure—a building, curriculum, and instructors. Garrison's *Liberator* advertised the seminary as "a seasonable auxiliary to the contemplated Manual Labor School for Colored Youth," thus annexing Crandall's school as part of the push for black education.[47] Crandall's school replaced the proposed manual labor college because the central tenet of the struggle for African American higher education remained intact: to cultivate black intellect and work toward black equality and a multiracial democracy.

Abolitionist support for Crandall's school rolled in from Arthur Tappan, Peter Williams, Samuel Cornish, Simeon Jocelyn, and William Lloyd Garrison, among others. These men advised her on the feasibility of recruiting African American students, acted as informal trustees, and publicized the school. A newcomer to the radical abolition movement, Crandall actually requested Garrison's help in particular to recruit African American girls and women. Garrison had gone on record at the newly organized American Anti-Slavery Society echoing what African American abolitionists had proclaimed years earlier, namely, that educating African Americans could counter proslavery and antiblack claims about degradation and inferiority while forging learned and moral identities.

The opposition to Crandall's seminary reflected white antagonism to the African American presence in New England.[48] Many white elites, like Andrew Judson, a Connecticut state attorney, promoted black removal, not building seminaries for African American women to become teachers in the United States. Samuel J. May, a white abolitionist and ardent defender of Prudence Crandall, recalled that Judson uttered the following words: "There shall not be a school set up anywhere in our State. The colored people never can rise from their menial condition in our country; they ought not to be permitted to rise here."[49] Unlike colonizationist John Hough, Judson admitted that there might be potential for black advancement, but he did not wish for that to occur in the United States. Indeed, he made it clear that Crandall and her school threatened the process of removing African Americans from the nation. Echoing prevailing myths about the "menial condition" of African Americans was not a point of clarification; rather, Judson was suggesting that racism was a temporary organizing system for dealing with free blacks in "his country" until colonization could take root and remove African Americans.

The African American pursuit of higher education also unsettled some white New England inhabitants who appreciated the link between education and equality. What troubled opponents was the possibility that educated African Americans could destabilize the racial and social order. One opponent of African American education apparently confessed, "The blacks of the town [Canterbury] . . . would begin to look up and claim an equality with the whites; and if they were all placed upon an equal footing *property and life* would no longer be safe!"[50] Safety here likely refers less to white male physical well-being and more to the idea of livelihood. Oftentimes an institution of higher education increased property values in the surrounding area; some opponents predicted a decline in property values and hence a decline in their livelihood if black schools remained. Just as African American and white abolitionists recognized the impact of black education, so too did opponents who, for all of their claims about innate black degradation and inferiority, feared a rising class of free, educated African Americans in the United States.

Like the proposed manual labor college, Crandall's seminary occupied physical space in the Connecticut landscape and hence interfered with the ideal of a free, white New England. Prudence Crandall was put on trial multiple times for violating Connecticut's Black Law, a hastily enacted law that forbade the "instruction or education of colored persons" who did not reside in Connecticut.[51] If there were any doubts about Judson's belief in white supremacy, his remarks at Crandall's trials provided clarity: "America is ours—it belongs to a race of white men."[52] Amid the ordeal, Crandall kept her school open until violence erupted on September 9, 1834, when a mob attacked the school building. At that point, she decided to close her seminary. The criminal prosecution and then extralegal violence that Crandall and her students endured represented an attack on abolitionists; on their principles of immediate emancipation, black equality, and a multiracial democracy; and on their strategies, like building institutions of higher education.[53]

After the closure of Crandall's seminary, the fight for African American higher education reanimated when abolitionists threw their support behind Noyes Academy, an interracial and coeducational institution in Canaan, New

Hampshire. George Kimball, a white Massachusetts native and Dartmouth College graduate, spearheaded the effort to procure funds for the academy and to secure a charter from the New Hampshire state legislature, which was granted on July 4, 1834. Noyes Academy became one of thousands of academies in the United States. Kim Tolley notes that an academy was the "prevailing institution of higher schooling in eighteenth- and nineteenth-century America."[54] It served different functions, from socializing youth to training them for skilled labor positions; however, only a few academies were coeducational, let alone racially integrated. Noyes was to be different. A slight majority of the proprietors, some of whom sympathized with the plight of African Americans, voted to enroll African American students. The board of trustees, elected by the proprietors, issued a circular to the "American republic," emphatically stating: "We proposed to afford colored youth a fair opportunity to show that they are capable, equally with whites, of improving themselves in every scientific attainment, every social virtue, and every Christian ornament."[55] The principles of educational equity and black equality resembled earlier remarks on education by abolitionists like William Lloyd Garrison and Simeon Jocelyn. Besides, Garrison had converted at least two of the trustees at Noyes to radical abolition and, apparently, black education: David L. Child, husband of Lydia Maria Child, and Samuel Sewall, a Harvard graduate and lawyer and also the cousin of Samuel J. May. Though neither Garrison nor Jocelyn became trustees, their presence was felt.

Many white Canaan residents denounced the decision to admit African Americans for reasons that appear all too familiar: fear of labor competition, the equalizing effect of education, and abolitionist fanaticism, as well as the desire to expel African Americans from New England and the nation. The composition of the student body, however, introduced one latent issue: interracial socializing, or as opponents called it, "amalgamation."[56] Soon after Noyes opened its doors in March 1835, fourteen African American students, including Henry Highland Garnet and Thomas Paul, both of whom would become ardent abolitionists, studied alongside twenty-eight white students. The local press incited anger by publishing an article that detailed the "spectacle ... of *colored gentlemen* walking arm in arm with what ought to be respectable *white females*."[57] For opponents, the trouble with the abolitionist brand of education was its transformative power: it plunged otherwise respectable white females into disrepute. By the summer of 1835 one anonymous writer had expressed a readiness "to act in any capacity, even at the head of a mob," to destroy Noyes.⁵⁸ On the Fourth of July, a year to the day after the approval of the academy's charter, at least seventy men from Canaan and its environs gathered with their weapons drawn, ready to attack the schoolhouse. Timothy Tilton, a white magistrate, forced the mob to retreat by threatening legal action. And the mob retreated, but only temporarily, because "amalgamation" was too crucial an issue for them to cede ground.

While opponents in Canaan plotted to bring ruin upon Noyes Academy, abolitionists convened in Boston in May 1835 and pledged to continue to work diligently in the cause for black education. In attendance were George Kimball and Samuel Sewall, who heard and perhaps voted to pass a host of resolutions, including Samuel J. May's, which called for "more efficient efforts" to fund a manual labor school as well as "public patronage" for Noyes Academy.⁵⁹ *The Liberator* published a committee report by Sewall in which the board of the Massachusetts Anti-Slavery Society, an auxiliary of the American Anti-Slavery Society, sent one hundred dollars to Noyes Academy on behalf of British abolitionists. The board of the Massachusetts Anti-Slavery Society also appealed to individual donors for money, since the academy, which explicitly served "the colored people in New-England," could also provoke other institutions to accept African Americans and thus, over time, achieve an end to racial prejudice.⁶⁰

The academy's detractors wished to put an end to any financial or public support. On July 31, 1835, a committee appointed by outraged white citizens of the town voted to get rid of the school.⁶¹ Over a week later, three hundred people gathered, according to one account, and "forcibly demolished the yard fences" and, with the aid of nearly a hundred yoke of cattle, removed the building "into the highway."⁶² African American students, all of whom appeared to be from out-of-state, fled New Hampshire. Jacob Trussell, a white opponent, fancied himself a patriot; the ruined schoolhouse, in his mind, was a "monument of the *folly* of those living spirits, who are struggling to destroy what our fathers have gained."⁶³ A tower of intellect for African Americans represented for Trussell a "monument of folly." The opposition, then, at Canaan was as much about destroying Noyes Academy as it was about disrupting the New England abolition movement.

Decrying white opposition, African American and white abolitionists concluded that New England was inhospitable to black institutions of higher education. The 1836 annual report from the Massachusetts Anti-Slavery Society surmised that the "most relentless spirit of hostility to any plan for the improvement and elevation of the people of color" existed in New England despite its tradition of education. A hostile New England found Samuel J. May, among others, supporting Oneida Institute in New York, but this institution did not animate the fight for black education as Noyes Academy did, perhaps because of sheer distance.[64] Others like Reuben Ruby, an African American abolitionist from Maine, inquired about establishing a high school, academy, or college in the Midwest.[65] Still others floated alternative ideas. Simeon Jocelyn recommended the establishment of educational societies, while Samuel Cornish used the *Colored American* to publicize black self-improvement efforts, particularly in creating literary societies, reading circles, and libraries. By the late 1830s African American and white abolitionists had differing approaches to strengthen African American higher education. Consequently, the struggle for African American higher education in New England lost cohesion and began to ebb.

Three institutions of higher education expressly for African Americans rose and fell in New England. No distinctly African American college, academy, or seminary would ever come to be in any state in antebellum New England. Still, this fight for African American higher education was influential. First, African American abolitionists linked and denounced both slavery and racial prejudice and in doing so asserted their presence and intellectual vitality. Second, the cooperation between African American and white abolitionists set the stage for future alliances. Third, the educational vision of these abolitionists impacted New England high schools, academies, and colleges, which began to debate radical abolition, desegregation, and racial integration. In fact, the efforts of abolitionists had desegregated, either directly or indirectly, at least four colleges and universities in the New England area, including the University of Vermont, where Andrew Harris became the first African American graduate in 1838.[66] Radical abolitionists brought awareness to the cause of black education, which would be fought over for years not just in New England but throughout the United States.

NOTES

1. William Cooper Nell, *The Colored Patriots of the American Revolution with Sketches of Several Distinguished Colored Persons: To Which Is Added a Brief Survey of the Condition and Prospects of Colored Americans* (Boston: Robert F. Wallcut, 1855), 33.

2. George R. Price and James Brewer Stewart, "Introduction: Hosea Easton and the

Agony of Race," in *To Heal the Scourge of Prejudice: The Life and Writings of Hosea Easton*, ed. Hosea Easton, George R. Price, and James Brewer Stewart (Amherst: University of Massachusetts Press), 8–9.

3. Hosea Easton, *A Treatise on the Intellectual Character and Civil and Political Condition of the Colored People of the United States; and the Prejudice Exercised Towards Them: With a Sermon on the Duty of the Church to Them* (Boston: Printed and Published by Isaac Knapp, 1837), 43.

4. Ibid., 39.

5. For more on antebellum black protest, see especially Patrick Rael, *Black Identity and Black Protest in the Antebellum North* (Chapel Hill: University of North Carolina Press, 2002).

6. Hilary J. Moss, *Schooling Citizens: The Struggle for African American Education in Antebellum America* (Chicago: University of Chicago Press, 2009); Leon Litwack, *North of Slavery: The Negro in the Free States, 1790–1860* (Chicago: University of Chicago Press, 1961), 123; Benjamin Quarles, *Black Abolitionists* (New York: Oxford University Press, 1969), 106. For other studies on abolition and education in the United States, see especially Carter G. Woodson, *The Education of the Negro Prior to 1861: A History of the Education of the Colored People of the United States from the Beginning of Slavery to the Civil War* (New York: G. P. Putnam's Sons, 1915); Carleton Mabee, *Black Education in New York State: From Colonial to Modern Times* (Syracuse, N.Y.: Syracuse University Press, 1979); and Milton C. Sernett, *Abolition's Axe: Beriah Green, Oneida Institute, and the Black Freedom Struggle* (Syracuse, N.Y.: Syracuse University Press, 1986).

7. Joanne Pope Melish, *Disowning Slavery: Gradual Emancipation and 1780–1860* (Ithaca, N.Y.: Cornell University Press, 1998), 15.

8. Ibid., 51.

9. Lorenzo J. Greene, *The Negro in Colonial New England* (New York: Columbia University Press, 1942), 123.

10. Ira Berlin, *Many Thousands Gone: The First Two Centuries of Slavery in North America* (Cambridge, Mass.: Harvard University Press, 1998), 10.

11. For an excellent analysis on black radicalism and revolutionary thought, see Manisha Sinha, "To 'Cast Just Obliquy' on Oppressors: Black Radicalism in the Age of Revolution," *William and Mary Quarterly* 64, no. 1 (January 2007): 149–60.

12. "Petition from Slaves, 1779," in *The State of New Hampshire: Miscellaneous Provincial and State Papers, 1725–1800* (Manchester, N.H.: John B. Clarke, Public Printer, 1890), 18:705.

13. Stephanie Kermes, *Creating an American Identity: New England, 1789–1825* (New York: Palgrave Macmillan, 2008), 33.

14. Melish, *Disowning Slavery*, 107.

15. Kermes, *Creating an American Identity*, 36.

16. Daniel Walker Howe, *What Hath God Wrought: The Transformation of Amer-*

ica, 1815–1848 (New York: Oxford University Press, 2007), 244; John R. Thelin, *A History of American Higher Education* (Baltimore, Md.: Johns Hopkins University Press, 2011), 69.

17. Kenneth Nivison, "'But a Step from College to the Judicial Bench': College and Curriculum in New England's 'Age of Improvement,'" *History of Education Quarterly* 50, no. 4 (November 2010): 470.

18. Thelin, *A History of American Higher Education*, 53.

19. David F. Allmendinger, *Paupers and Scholars: The Transformation of Student Life in Nineteenth Century New England* (New York: St. Martin's Press, 1975), 107–9.

20. Thelin, *A History of American Higher Education*, 41.

21. William Seymour Tyler, *A History of Amherst College During the Administrations of Its First Five Presidents, from 1821 to 1891* (New York: Frederick H. Hitchcock, 1895), 5. The emphasis on classical education, which followed the curricular model at Yale College, would later be defined in the 1828 Yale Report, which defended the classical curriculum in American colleges and become the standard at many eastern colleges for a while.

22. Roger L. Geiger, "Introduction: New Themes in the History of Nineteenth-Century Colleges," in *The American College in the Nineteenth Century*, ed. Roger L. Geiger (Nashville, Tenn.: Vanderbilt University Press, 2000), 3.

23. Thelin, *A History of American Higher Education*, 69.

24. *Charter of Bowdoin College, Together with Various Acts of the Legislature, and the Decision of the Circuit Court, and the By-Laws of the Overseers* (Brunswick, Maine: Printed by J. Griffin, 1850), 7; *General Catalogue of Bowdoin College and the Medical School of Maine, 1794–1912* (Brunswick, Maine: Published by the College, 1912), 74–76.

25. Winston James, *The Struggles of John Brown Russwurm: The Life and Writings of a Pan-Africanist Pioneer, 1799–1851* (New York: New York University Press, 2010), 17.

26. John Hough, *Sermon Delivered before the Vermont Colonization Society at Montpeleir [sic], October 18, 1826* (Montpelier, Vt.: E. P. Walton–Watchman Office, 1826), 9.

27. Leon Litwack, *North of Slavery: The Negro in the Free States* (Chicago: University of Chicago Press, 1961), 139.

28. Hough, *Sermon Delivered*, 8–9.

29. Craig Steven Wilder, *Ebony & Ivy: Race, Slavery, and the Troubled History of America's Universities* (New York: Bloomsbury Press, 2013), 6. For more on the American colonization movement, see Beverly C. Tomek, *Colonization and Its Discontents: Emancipation, Emigration, and Antislavery in Antebellum Pennsylvania* (New York: New York University Press, 2011).

30. "Professor Stowe on Colonization," *African Repository and Colonial Journal* (Washington, D.C.) 10 (1834): 301–2.

31. Margaret Sumner, *Collegiate Republic: Cultivating an Ideal Society in Early America* (Charlottesville: University of Virginia Press, 2014), 12.

32. The full title of David Walker's treatise was *Walker's Appeal, in Four Articles; To-*

gether with a Preamble, to the Coloured Citizens of the World, but in Particular, and Very Expressly, to Those of the United States of America. Written in Boston, State of Massachusetts, September 28, 1829. Third and Last Edition, with Additional Notes, Corrections, &c. (Boston: Revised and Published by David Walker, 1830).

33. Maria W. Stewart, "Address Delivered at the African Masonic Hall," *Liberator*, March 2, 1833.

34. "Elevation of Our People," *Colored American*, November 23, 1839.

35. "Education," *Liberator*, January 1, 1831. Hilary Moss argues a similar point in her book *Schooling Citizens*.

36. For a firsthand account of racial prejudice and violence as experienced by free African Americans in New England, see William J. Brown, *The Life of William J. Brown, of Providence, Rhode Island, with Personal Recollections of Incidents in Rhode Island* (Providence: Angell and Company, 1883).

37. "Address of Mr. Peter Osborne," *Liberator*, December 1, 1832.

38. *Minutes and Proceedings of the First Annual Convention of the People of Colour*, June 1831 (Philadelphia: Published by Order of the Committee of Arrangements, 1831), 5.

39. William Lloyd Garrison, *An Address Delivered Before the Free People of Color* (Boston: Printed by Stephen Foster, 1831), 10.

40. *Minutes and Proceedings*, 18.

41. Lydia Maria Child, *Appeal in Favor of That Class of Americans Called Africans* (Boston: Allen and Ticknor, 1833), 208.

42. For more on Charles Ray and Wesleyan University, see David E. Swift, *Black Prophets of Justice: Activist Clergy before the Civil War* (Baton Rouge: Louisiana State University Press, 1989).

43. Minutes, October 10, 1832?, Nineteenth Century Administrative Records, General Records, Joint Board of Trustees and Visitors, 1830–70, Wesleyan University Special Collections and Archives, Olin Library.

44. James Brewer Stewart, *Abolitionist Politics and the Coming of the Civil War* (Amherst: University of Massachusetts Press, 2008), 178.

45. Simeon S. Jocelyn, *College for Colored Youth: An Account of the New-Haven City Meetings and Resolutions* (New York: The Committee, 1831), 5.

46. Moss, *Schooling Citizens*, 46.

47. "High School for Young Colored Ladies and Misses" (advertisement), *Liberator*, March 2, 1833. I examine this case in more detail in my forthcoming article in the *Journal of Social History*.

48. Historian Joanne Pope Melish advances this argument in her brilliant study, *Disowning Slavery: Gradual Emancipation and "Race" in New England, 1780–1860* (Ithaca, N.Y.: Cornell University Press, 1998).

49. Samuel J. May, *Some Recollections of Our Anti-Slavery Conflict* (Boston: Fields, Osgood & Co., 1869), 47.

50. "George Benson to William Lloyd Garrison," March 5, 1833, *Liberator*, March 9, 1833.

51. *Report of the Arguments of Counsel in the Case of Prudence Crandall Plff. in Error vs. State of Connecticut Before the Supreme Court of Errors at Their Session at Brooklyn, July Term 1834* (Boston: Garrison & Knapp, 1834), iii.

52. Ibid., 22.

53. Wilder, *Ebony and Ivy*, 266.

54. Nancy Beadie and Kim Tolley, "A School for Every Purpose: An Introduction to the History of Academies in the United States," in *Chartered Schools: Two Hundred Years of Independent Academies in the United States, 1727–1925*, ed. Nancy Beadie and Kim Tolley (New York: Routledge, 2002), 4.

55. "To the American Republic," *Liberator*, October 25, 1834.

56. For an interesting analysis of interracial socializing and sex, see Leslie Harris, "From Abolitionist Amalgamators to 'Rulers of the Five Points': The Discourse of Interracial Sex and Reform in Antebellum New York City," in *Sex, Love, Race: Crossing Boundaries in North American History*, ed. Martha Hodes (New York: New York University Press), 191–212.

57. "Colored School at Canaan," *New Hampshire Patriot and State Gazette*, August 17, 1835.

58. William Allen Wallace, *The History of Canaan, New Hampshire* (Concord, N.H.: Rumford Press, 1910), 258.

59. "New England Anti-Slavery Convention," *Liberator*, May 30, 1835.

60. S. E. Sewall, "Manual Labor School," *Liberator*, July 4, 1835.

61. Wallace, *The History of Canaan, New Hampshire*, 271.

62. Jacob Trussell, "Colored School at Canaan," *Liberator*, September 5, 1835; John H. Harris, "Exposition of Affairs Connected with Noyes Academy," *Liberator*, October 3, 1835.

63. Trussell, "Colored School at Canaan."

64. *Fourth Annual Report of the Board of Managers of the Massachusetts Anti-Slavery Society*, January 20, 1836 (Boston: Published by Isaac Knapp, 1836), 28.

65. *Minutes of the Fifth Annual Convention for the Improvement of the Free People of Colour in the United States*, June 1835 (Philadelphia: Printed by William P. Gibbons, 1835), 10.

66. "Verdict of Colored Citizens of Boston," *Liberator*, April 3, 1840.

CHAPTER TEN

"I Have At Last Found My 'Sphere'"

The Unintentional Development of a Female Abolitionist Stronghold at Oberlin College

J. Brent Morris

On August 1, 1846, the abolitionists of Oberlin, Ohio, gathered to celebrate the anniversary of West Indian independence. The First of August was the only Independence Day celebrated in Oberlin, since July 4 marked the birth of a nation fundamentally entangled with slavery. This particular occasion featured the first public antislavery address by Lucy Stone, an Oberlin student who would go on to become one of America's foremost abolitionists and women's rights advocates. In 1846, however, her career as an accomplished reformer was years in her future, and in the lead-up to the event, the gravity of what she was about to do set in. Here she was, a woman, and she was to speak publicly on the most explosive issue of the day. A "siege of terrible headaches" betrayed her trepidation, yet when the time came for Stone to address the crowd, she did so with a confidence that impressed her audience, including a Cleveland newspaperman. Stone's speech, he reported, "gave evidence that a mind naturally brilliant had not been dimmed, but polished rather, by classical studies and the higher mathematics." He recognized her as "one of those who believe that neither color nor sex should deprive of equal rights."[1]

Stone's abolitionist brilliance was the logical result of an Oberlin education thoroughly steeped in moral duty, perfectionism, and a certainty of the sinfulness of slavery. However, Oberlin women were never meant by the school's leaders to venture into the public sphere, much less become outspoken abolitionist lecturers. Their education was designed to prepare them for the domestic life of a supportive wife—"to *bridle the tongue*" while their husbands made their mark in the world.[2] However, Oberlin women took many of the same classes as budding male reformers, were taught by the same abolitionist professors, and were instilled with the same moral imperative to fight sin in all its forms. Unexpectedly but unavoidably, Oberlin women trained toward domesticity became some of the most articulate and effective social reformers, male or female, of the nineteenth century.

From its founding in 1833, the town of Oberlin and its organically connected college of the same name formed one of the most significant communities in the American abolitionist movement. It achieved this distinction because of unique circumstances in its early years that gathered an unprecedented multiracial and cohesive abolitionist population that maintained a fever pitch of reform agitation throughout the antebellum period. Oberlin was founded as a utopian community whose sole mission was to save souls and prepare the world for the coming millennium of Christ. Within two years, the community of only a few hundred had become the most radical academic environment in the nation, perhaps the world. Oberlin was the first college in America to admit men and women of all races, and as more conservative schools persecuted outspoken student-abolitionists, Oberlin welcomed them with open arms. The school became a beacon for the nation's most progressive students, and together with a thoroughly abolitionist faculty and community, they set about the mission of ridding America of its greatest and most pressing sin: slavery.[3]

Oberlin's distinction in becoming the first coeducational college in America, however, is a more complicated story. Scholarship on women during this period presents it as a time in which women's roles were being transformed, yet not necessarily to their benefit. This period witnessed the increasing glorification of "true womanhood": the woman who represented piety, purity, obedience, and domesticity.[4] Although the veneration of the "feminine" sphere by contemporaries was often used as an apology for its constraints in the public sphere, many of the women aspired to nothing short of the purification of America through the liberal application of their moral influence as wives and mothers and, increasingly, as teachers.[5] This trend also led to an extension of formal educational opportunities for American girls. A handful of educational theorists agreed that to circumscribe the education of women was "at least problematic."[6] These reformers argued for the necessity of more thorough education of females and stressed the republican project of educating America's youth as virtuous citizens.[7]

In the early decades of the nineteenth century, women's academies sprang up with alacrity. These schools offered their female students a curriculum that included not just elements of a classical education but also instruction in etiquette and refinement, a strong emphasis on moral and religious education, training in domestic science and economy, and preparation for teaching. This early vanguard of educators, which included several women among its ranks, believed that if women were to be prepared to mold the nation's infant minds, bring about the salvation of mankind through education, competently oversee their traditional domestic realm, and fill the role of pious and intelligent helpmeet to their husbands, then they needed to be taught more than traditional "ornamental" pursuits such as embroidery and drawing.[8]

The combination of the need for literate women to provide religious instruction to their children, a growing recognition of the desirability of an educated citizenry, and, at least in Oberlin's case, simple fairness became the opening wedge for women in American higher education.[9] In Oberlin's first circular of 1834, founder John Shipherd announced that a primary goal of the institution was to bring "within the reach of the misjudged and neglected sex, all the instructive privileges which hitherto have unreasonably distinguished the leading sex from theirs."[10] Philo Stewart, Shipherd's earliest Oberlin associate, agreed that "the work of female education must be carried out in some form, and in a much more efficient manner than it has been hitherto, or our country will go to destruction. For I believe that there is no other way to secure success in our great moral enterprises, than to make prevalent the right kind of female education."[11]

Accordingly, they established Oberlin as America's first coeducational college. Yet despite the founders' otherwise progressive stance, many Oberlin professors initially welcomed the experiment for the effects it would have on young men, not their female classmates. James Fairchild articulated the Oberlin position: in a coeducational environment "the animal man is kept subordinate.... We have found it the surest way to make men of boys, and gentlemen of rowdies. It must be a very poor specimen of masculine human nature that is not helped by the association, and a very poor specimen of a woman that does not prove a helper."[12]

To be sure, women were receiving an education on a level previously unavailable to them, but women's involvement in the Oberlin experiment was rarely viewed by college officials independent of their "refining" influence on Oberlin men. Coeducation, then, radical as it was, was not undertaken as a revolutionary reform but as a practical measure firmly embedded in popular notions of women's work and proper sphere.[13] At the same time, however, Oberlin did knowingly and intentionally provide its female students with "all the instructive privileges" it made available to its young men, opportunities and didactic processes that were explosive in their potential and revolutionary in their results.[14]

As late as the 1850s, many of Oberlin's professors appeared to remain in the dark as to the dynamic potential that coeducational collegiate training at Oberlin could offer America's young ladies. In a reply to the question "Is 'the woman question,' so called necessarily involved in your experiment?" the editor of the *Oberlin Evangelist* replied, "Not at all. . . . The first and greatest right of women—the right to be educated, as being endowed with intelligence equally as man,—is fundamental to the system; beyond this it goeth not."[15] However, where the Oberlin system dared not officially go, Oberlin women boldly marched independently. Their admission to Oberlin brought them under the same radical instruction and exposed them to the same revolutionary ideas as the young men, and they made the most of what they were grudgingly given. In an atmosphere that made concerted action a moral duty for men, many Oberlin women leaped at the chance to fulfill their own duty by speaking out in public on behalf of the abolition of slavery.[16]

A defining aspect of the liberal education of Oberlin men was their training and regular practice in public speaking. There were practical grounds for thorough training in oratory, since most graduates went on to become either ministers or lawyers, or they engaged in some vocation that required skill in public declamation. Women in the early nineteenth century found nearly all approaches to public speaking closed to them, since almost no one expected "proper" women to attempt to enter any of the learned professions.[17] Moreover, as one male Oberlin professor pointed out, women might not speak in public assemblies "without violating the natural sense of propriety which God has given us."[18] Thus at Oberlin, men were trained in the arts of debate and oratory; women learned to write essays.[19]

Still, Oberlin had opened a Pandora's box when it decided to offer its women the same education as its men. Instruction that was calculated to encourage independent thought in young men, lead them to confront the world in its sins, and rebuke unrighteousness at every opportunity could not help but instill the same emotions in the women who fell under its sway. Even as a professor declared, "It is a thing positively disagreeable to both sexes to see a woman a public character," women in his audience were already on their way down a path never fully intended by Oberlin's founders.[20]

Lucy Stone's tenure at Oberlin was, as one historian puts it, "one long protest" against the faculty's reticence.[21] She enrolled in 1843 specifically to prepare herself for a public life, and she did not mean to be a passive recipient of reluctant instruction. Rather, she and other ambitious Oberlin women met the challenge head-on. Stone made no attempt to hide her intentions and ruffled feathers in the process. "Lucy Stone was the topic of conversation . . . in all the boarding houses in town," one male student wrote. He recalled that others believed "'she was a woman who wanted to be a man'; others said in derision 'she was a hen who wanted to crow.'"[22] When Antoinette Brown first traveled to Oberlin, she was warned of this notorious student who was "much too talkative." Brown was advised "to be very careful of her opinions, not to be influenced by her or to become intimate with her." However, Brown, who would soon consider Stone her best friend, "resolved then and there to know more of Lucy Stone."[23]

Despite their criticism of Stone, no one at Oberlin could deny that "she was the most brilliant woman of her age they had ever met."[24] In 1846 she was able to convince Professor James Thome to allow her and Brown to participate in a debate in his rhetoric class (which they had only been allowed to audit). Word of the novel event spread quickly across campus, and a crowd gathered on the appointed day to witness the debate, later described by observers as "exceptionally brilliant."[25] For their efforts, Stone and Brown were called before the Ladies' Board and rebuked. Thome was warned against repeat performances.[26]

Stone later remarked that "I was never in a place where women are so rigidly taught that they must not speak in public."[27] This prohibition extended even to Oberlin commencement ceremonies, where graduating men were allowed to give orations, yet women who chose to take the college course were forced to write theirs as essays to be read for them by a professor.[28] Stone never composed a commencement essay, since doing so would have been "a public acknowledgment of the rectitude of the principle which takes away from women their equal rights, and denies to them the privilege of being co-laborers with men in any sphere to which their ability makes them adequate."[29]

It was not naked ambition that drove these women; it was a conviction, legitimately obtained through their education, that they were obligated by a higher power to agitate the public mind for the sake of righteousness. To follow their consciences into the public arena, Brown, Stone, and a handful of other determined women formed the Oberlin Young Ladies' Literary Society, an organization meant to provide a forum for female debate and "to improve its members in *Writing, Discussion, & Declamation*."[30] The society's meetings, which initially were held secretly, soon emerged as one of the most popular spectator events in Oberlin. One Oberlin man realized the potential results of this training and encouraged one young abolitionist woman that "when [she had] a little experience," she could "beat Abby [Kelley] to nothing." "You would make a glorious speaker," he said, concluding that "I'd rather meet a tropical tornado & Niagara Falls to boot than meet you as a public adversary."[31]

The literary society experience, combined with the religious training and moral instruction the women received from their formal education, resulted in Oberlin sending a great cadre of women into battle among the various social reform movements of the day. At a certain level, even college officials seem to have given a grudging consent to women who, officials had to concede, were only acting on impulses most of them developed while studying at Oberlin.[32] John Morgan admitted to one eager student that he would try to convince her to remain silent in public if he thought he would be successful, but, realizing that she was determined to speak her mind in public anyway, he would "try to do [his] best" to teach her.[33]

So taught, Oberlin women set out to save the world, and their most notable target was the abolition of slavery. Many first directed their efforts toward the mission to reform and save "fallen women" and to combat the "licentiousness" that was so notoriously the result of many slave owners' lechery. Lydia Finney, wife of Oberlin's famous professor and evangelist, Charles Grandison Finney, was elected "First Directress" of the National Moral Reform Society, with Oberlin's Alice Cowles serving as the society's first vice president.[34] The following year Oberlinites founded two moral reform societies of their own: the Young Men's Moral Reform Society of the Oberlin Collegiate Institute and the Oberlin Female Moral Reform Society. These societies soon merged into a single organization.[35]

However, Oberlin women did not limit their attack on slavery to the problem of sexual licentiousness. Many arrived with a broad abolitionist background, and they were instrumental in shaping the antislavery ideology of the other female students. For instance, Betsey Mix Cowles, who like many other Oberlin women first arrived on campus in her late twenties, had spent many of her pre-Oberlin years lecturing on behalf of antislavery through the Ashtabula Female Anti-Slavery Society.[36] Stone was an ardent supporter of William Lloyd Garrison by the time she enrolled at Oberlin, and she kept a picture of him by her bedside and promoted antislavery periodicals on campus.[37] Others arrived at Oberlin with unimpeachable abolitionist family pedigrees. Sallie Holley's father, Myron, had been a founder of the antislavery Liberty Party in 1839.[38] Frances Russwurm's father, John, had been the abolitionist editor of *Freedom's Journal*, the first newspaper owned and operated by African Americans in the United States.[39] Rosetta Douglass, daughter of Frederick Douglass, assisted his abolitionist efforts at home and at the *North Star* before she enrolled at Oberlin.[40]

Perhaps one reason for the extra zeal and effectiveness of the Oberlin women in their antislavery efforts came from their unique and intimate contact with former slaves. Many members of Oberlin's women's organizations were positioned in ways that allowed them direct access to survivors of slavery. The Young Ladies' Literary Society held its first meetings in the home of a former slave, the mother of one of Stone's pupils.[41] Stone was also a teacher in Oberlin's Liberty School, established in 1844 for the elementary education of black adults, most of whom had begun their lives in bondage.[42] Stone recalled of her pupils, "When I saw how they were *dehumanized*... I wondered, that in the wide universe of god, one tongue could be found, that failed to utter its indignant rebuke against all that pertains to so execrable a system."[43] In addition to the Oberlin Female Moral Reform Society and the Young Ladies' Literary Society, other groups such as the Oberlin Maternal Association, the Oberlin Female Anti-Slavery Society, and the Oberlin Young Ladies' Anti-Slavery Society demonstrated their empathy with the persecuted bondsmen, going to great lengths to assist self-emancipating slaves who passed through the town on their way to freedom.[44]

Since Oberlin was long the only college open to young women in America, many fathers had no choice but to enroll their daughters there if they wanted them to receive the most thorough education possible.[45] This included southerners and even a handful of slaveholders. Oberlin, for its part, did not turn away any qualified students, especially those impressionable young women raised in the midst of slavery. On the other hand, southern fathers could only have sent their daughters to "notorious" Oberlin with the full knowledge of the ideologies to which they would be exposed and perhaps ultimately accept as their own. One of Lucy Stone's Oberlin roommates was a sixteen-year-old slaveholder's daughter from South Carolina. Despite strict instructions from her father to avoid any talk about slavery, Stone's prominent display of Garrison's likeness and near-constant agitation of the slavery question would have made following the injunction impossible.[46] Another student, Harriett Keys, recounted the story of her family's slave "Aunt Lydia," who had been exposed to the "dark and malignant passions which the system of slavery is peculiarly adapted to foster and which were constantly exhibited around her."[47] Rather than diluting Oberlin's antislavery mission with conservatism, these southern women added a firsthand knowledge of the institution of slavery and an intimate understanding of the mind of the master class. As did the testimony of their professor James Thome, son of a Kentucky slaveholder, the women's ties to slavery and their witness to its brutality helped keep the object of Oberlin's opposition from becoming an abstraction.[48]

The "malignant passions" referred to in Keys's testimony clearly included the sexual abuse of enslaved women by white men. This was a common theme of abolitionist discourse, and the admittedly delicate and provocative nature of the topic was not shied away from in Oberlin's coeducational environment. As historians Ruth Bogin and Jean Fagan Yellin point out, many women's commitment to abolitionism was informed by the knowledge that such sexual abuse was widespread. However, they also note that in antebellum America, the very mention of sexual impurity might shock audiences or sully the reputation of the female speaker.[49] Oberlin's unanimity of opinion on slavery-related issues, however, allowed the school and town to offer themselves as forums where even the most controversial topics could be discussed freely and methodically. With little fear that their deliberations would be sensationalized or exploited by critics bent on disruption, the school and town left no issue off the table. In fact, all Oberlinites felt a moral obligation to give a voice to the voiceless while following their founder's injunction to "be not conformed to this world."[50]

Particular Oberlinites who could never have shied away from such a topic were the women of the student and town population who had been enslaved themselves.[51] For these abolitionists, as historian Shirley Yee points out, the issues of slavery and racism struck much closer to home.[52] There were, most especially, those Oberlin women whose very existence could be traced to their former masters' abuse of power: the mixed-race children of slave owners.

Though their being sent to Oberlin may have resulted from their biological fathers' sense of indulgence or as a last means of assuaging a guilty conscience, students like Martha Mason, Mary Townsend, and Laura Minor were constant reminders of the transgressions against which other Oberlin women spoke out.[53]

These formerly enslaved women contributed to the aggressive stance of Oberlin's female abolitionists as well as to their overall effectiveness. Just as former slaves like Frederick Douglass and Henry Bibb brought an added degree of authenticity to the abolitionist rostrum, Oberlin women who had begun their lives in chains brought a sense of urgency that others could not fully express. Not only did they "perform" abolitionism through the very fact of their participation in the daily life of the college, as historian Carol Lasser argues, African American women at Oberlin also spoke for those enslaved people who remained in the South.[54] Fanny Jackson remembered that each time she opened her mouth to speak while at Oberlin, she felt the weight of her entire race upon her shoulders.[55] No doubt students Mahalia Mcguire and Sara Margru Kinson, the youngest of the captives freed from the *Amistad* slave ship in 1841, and Mary and Emily Edmondson, both rescued from the slave ship *Pearl* in 1848, brought the extraordinary perspectives of victims of the vicious slave trade to Oberlin debates.[56] The effect was profound. Freeborn women, who could only describe at second hand the horrors of slavery, were moved to truly empathetic tears and propelled into action through the influence of their formerly enslaved sisters.[57]

As mentioned earlier, Oberlin women were conspicuous in the town's annual First of August celebrations. The town's African American community leaders planned the day's festivities, and the proceedings were very often a chance for black leaders and Oberlin women to demonstrate the "reciprocal supportive relationships" that they had developed in their close connections over the years.[58] It was clear to the organizers that some of the most zealous advocates of the cause in Oberlin were, in fact, those women who were busy breaking the traditional mold of the woman's sphere in the cause of the slave. Black leaders like William Howard Day and Daniel Seales extended invitations to Oberlin students like Stone, Brown, Emiline Crooker, and Mary Crabb to address the First of August crowds on antislavery topics. On platforms that sometimes included only a single white male participant, several Oberlin women passionately spoke out against the iniquities of American bondage.[59]

These speeches revealed a chink in the armor of the Oberlin proscription of women's public speaking. To speak at the independence celebration, these women, like any other Oberlin student, would have had to ask for and be granted permission to do so by the faculty. Both the platform and audience would have been "promiscuous," or mixed gender, a circumstance that in any other instance would likely have led to a spirited refusal by the faculty and Ladies' Board to a young woman's request to speak in public.

So why was there no chorus of disapproval for these women's requests for permission to participate in an activity their professors otherwise considered "a thing positively disagreeable to both sexes" and openly discouraged?[60] Essentially, the answer is that Oberlin's reputation and stance on the antislavery issue were sealed. At Oberlin, abolitionism trumped all other concerns. Although the antislavery activity of Oberlin women mostly occurred after the abolitionist "schism" of 1840, ostensibly over the role of women in the movement, Oberlin refused to participate in the infighting. Town and gown had a long shared history of nonsectarian reformism, and they encouraged diversity in antislavery thought. Rather than falling into a distinct abolitionist "camp," Oberlinites took the field as men and women devoted to emancipation by any means necessary, even if that was through unconventional methods or by an abandonment of strict ideological consistency. Their philosophy had always been a composite of various schools of antislavery thought aimed at providing the best hope of success.[61]

Oberlin's abolitionist pedigree, then, would have precluded the denial to any person, man or woman, the opportunity to speak on behalf of the millions of enslaved Americans. After all, even *"man woman"* Abby Kelley was allowed to present her arguments multiple times before Oberlin audiences, hostile as they were to many of those beliefs.[62] All voices in favor of the slave would be given a hearing, regardless of what social taboos they might tread upon. Moreover, in Oberlin, nearly everyone was already a committed abolitionist; there would be no risk of offending or turning away a potential "convert" over women speaking in public to a mixed audience.[63]

Oberlin officials even countenanced women's entry into the all-male club of antislavery electoral politics. The literary society paved the way by priming its members' debate arsenals with such topics as "Should Women Vote?" and "Was the Liberty Party Wise in Electing Their Candidate This Fall?"[64] Just when many abolitionists were debating the propriety of antislavery political action, Oberlin women pressed their case to cast their own ballots on behalf of freedom.⁶⁵ At times, it seemed as if the women in Oberlin were more genuinely concerned with practical politics than the men. Delegates to a Whig county convention in 1840 remarked on the notable presence of Oberlin women among the crowd. In a year when the town was struggling with the question of voting for the nominally antislavery Whig candidates or for the newcomer abolitionist Liberty Party, one man wrote, "You see the *ladies* are not backward in the good cause."⁶⁶ Even some of the professed Garrisonians among the Oberlin women got in line behind those who sought to promote antislavery through the ballot.⁶⁷ Lucy Stone, as fierce a "nonresistant" as there was in Oberlin, looked hopefully upon the efforts of Oberlin political antislavery. She was "glad to have *anything* done for the poor, downtrodden slave, and [she did] not care whether it is by the Old Organization or New Organization, for the oppressed."⁶⁸

Groups composed exclusively of black women, their own disenfranchisement more obvious than that of their white sisters, were just as active in the political realm. It was not uncommon for black women from Ohio to attend male-dominated protest gatherings or conventions, and though they did not participate as recognized delegates, they often contributed songs or toasts to the already spirited proceedings. In 1849 the women at the State Convention of the Colored Citizens of Ohio submitted a biting resolution to Oberlin graduate and business committee chairman William Howard Day that declared, "We the ladies have been invited to attend the Convention, and have been deprived of a voice, which we the ladies deem wrong and shameful. Therefore, RESOLVED, That we will attend no more after tonight, unless the privilege is granted."⁶⁹ Their threat was taken seriously, and after some debate, the resolution was adopted, and they were welcomed into the convention. This further opened the door to participation in the state conventions by Oberlin women to pressure their men to "be true, be courageous, be steadfast in the discharge of your duty."⁷⁰

However, Oberlin women were not content to limit themselves to playing a supporting role to that of their male counterparts. Despite many of the wishes of Oberlin's faculty and community leaders, the women of the college and community developed their own "sphere" of antislavery influence. It was an enlargement of the role intended for them, for while they were trained in the cult of domesticity and taught the skills necessary for a supporting role in domestic life, they were also brought under the academic influence of their abolitionist professors, taught to become critical and independent thinkers, imbued with the imperative to fight sin in all its forms, and steeped in the radical antislavery environment that was Oberlin. For many Oberlin women, the only logical and morally responsible outcome of this experience was for them to become antislavery agitators in their own right. As Sallie Holley was fond of saying when pleading for her enslaved sisters, "While woman's heart is bleeding, shall woman's voice be hushed?"[71] Immediately upon completing her degree at Oberlin in 1851, Holley undertook an abolitionist lecturing tour of the northeastern states. One of her contemporaries remarked that "it was with the clearest consciousness of the nature of the situation and the principles involved that Sallie Holley chose her path and entered on it with a courageous and trembling heart."[72] Not long thereafter, Holley reported her successes to another Oberlin alumna. "You cannot know," she effused, "how richly rewarded I feel, how full my enjoyment is, in going about with these anti-slavery friends." "It does seem to me," she concluded, "that I have at last found my 'sphere.'"[73]

NOTES

1. Lucy Stone to "Dear Father and Mother," August 16, 1846, RG30/24, box 10, folder 2, Oberlin College Archives (hereafter OCA).

2. Alice Cowles, "A Complete Finish," n.d., RG30/24, box 4, folder 17, OCA.

3. See J. Brent Morris, *Oberlin, Hotbed of Abolitionism: College, Community, and the Fight for Freedom and Equality in Antebellum America* (Chapel Hill: University of North Carolina Press, 2014).

4. See Barbara Welter, "The Cult of True Womanhood, 1820–1860," in *Dimity Convictions: The American Woman in the Nineteenth Century*, ed. Barbara Welter (Columbus: Ohio University Press, 1976), 21–41.

5. Alice Rossi, "Coeducation in a Gender Stratified Society," in *Educating Men and Women Together*, ed. Carol Lasser (Urbana: University of Illinois Press, 1987), 12.

6. Judith Sargent Murray, *The Gleaner* (Boston: J. Thomas and E. T. Andrews, 1798), 68.

7. For discussion of the idea of "republican motherhood," see Linda Kerber, *Women of the Republic: Intellect and Ideology in Revolutionary America* (Chapel Hill: University of North Carolina Press, 1980). On the rise of women's schools during this period, see Linda Kerber, "'Nothing Useless or Absurd or Fantastical': The Education of Women in the Early Republic," in Lasser, *Educating Men and Women Together*, 37–48; and Patricia Palmeri, "From Republican Motherhood to Race Suicide: Arguments of the Higher Education of Women in the United States, 1820–1920," in ibid., 49–64.

8. Annie Meyer, ed., *Woman's Work in America* (New York: Henry Holt and Company,

1891), 66–67, 69; Palmeri, "From Republican Motherhood," 52; Ronald Hogeland, "Coeducation of the Sexes at Oberlin College: A Study of Social Ideas in Mid-Nineteenth Century America," *Journal of Social History* 6, no. 2 (1972–73): 167.

9. Rossi, "Coeducation," 12.

10. *Circular, Oberlin Collegiate Institute*, March 8, 1834, RG30/24, box 12, folder 14, OCA.

11. Philo Stewart to Levi Burrell, April 10, 1837, Oberlin Collegiate Institute Letters Received, microfilm roll 1, OCA.

12. James Fairchild, *Coeducation of the Sexes* (Oberlin: Biblioteca Sacra, 1871), 390–95; Trustee Minutes, March 9, 1836, RG30/24, box 15, folder 7, OCA.

13. James Fairchild, *Oberlin: The Colony and the College* (Oberlin: E. J. Goodrich, 1883), 174.

14. Circular, Oberlin Collegiate Institute, March 8, 1834, RG30/24, box 12, folder 14, OCA; Frances Hosford, *Father Shipherd's Magna Charta: A Century of Coeducation at Oberlin College* (Boston: Marshal Jones Company, 1937), 31.

15. *Oberlin Evangelist*, December 3, 1851.

16. The past twenty years have seen the publication of a wealth of scholarship on women in the abolitionist movement. See, for example, Julie Roy Jeffry, *The Great Silent Army of Abolitionism: Ordinary Women in the Antislavery Movement* (Chapel Hill: University of North Carolina Press, 1998); Kathryn Kish Sklar and James Brewer Stewart, eds., *Women's Rights and Transatlantic Antislavery in the Era of Emancipation* (New Haven, Conn.: Yale University Press, 2007); Beth Salerno, *Sister Societies: Women's Antislavery Organizations in Antebellum America* (Dekalb: Northern Illinois University Press, 2005); John R. McKivigan, ed., *Abolitionism and Issues in Race and Gender* (New York: Garland, 1999).

17. Hosford, *Father Shipherd's Magna Charta*, 71–72.

18. *Oberlin Evangelist*, May 25, 1859.

19. Fairchild, *Oberlin*, 182.

20. Ibid., 18.

21. Robert Fletcher, *A History of Oberlin College: From Its Foundation through the Civil War* (Oberlin: Oberlin College, 1943), 291–92.

22. *Woman's Journal*, June 5, 1902.

23. Antoinette Brown Blackwell, "Antoinette Brown Blackwell: The First Woman Minister," 1–2, RG30/24, box 4, folder 3, OCA.

24. *Woman's Journal*, June 5, 1902.

25. Andrea Moore Kerr, *Lucy Stone: Speaking Out for Equality* (New Brunswick, N.J.: Rutgers University Press, 1992), 37.

26. Ibid., 37; Antoinette Brown Blackwell to George Jones, January 6, 1907, Antoinette Brown Blackwell Alumni File, folder 1, OCA.

27. Alice Stone Blackwell, *Lucy Stone: Pioneer of Woman's Rights* (Boston: Little, Brown, 1930), 60–63, 71–72; Fletcher, *History of Oberlin College*, 292.

28. Fairchild, *Coeducation of the Sexes*, 387; Meyer, *Woman's Work in America*, 69.

29. Blackwell, *Lucy Stone*, 67–73.

30. "Constitution and Bylaws of the Young Ladies' Literary Society," April 10, 1850, RG30/24, box 12, folder 3, OCA.

31. Timothy Hudson to Betsey Mix Cowles, March 5, 1846, RG30/24, box 5, folder 9, OCA. Abby Kelley was a prominent Garrisonian lecturer in the 1830s and 1840s.

32. Fairchild, *Coeducation of the Sexes*, 395–96; Antoinette Brown Blackwell, "Reminiscences of Early Oberlin," February 1918, 2, and "Oberlin College" (clipping), *University Quarterly* (1860), in RG30/24, box 18, folder 17, OCA.

33. Azariah Root, "Antoinette Brown Blackwell and Oberlin," 1, n.d., Antoinette Brown Blackwell Alumni File, folder 1, OCA.

34. Lewis Tappan, *Life of Arthur Tappan* (New York: Hurd and Houghton, 1870), 111–14; Catherine Rokicky, "Lydia Finney and Evangelical Womanhood," *Ohio History* 103 (Summer–Autumn 1994): 178.

35. *Advocate of Moral Reform*, August and September 1835, July 15, 1845.

36. See Betsey Mix Cowles Alumni File, OCA.

37. Charles Hambrick-Stowe, *Charles G. Finney and the Spirit of American Evangelicalism* (Grand Rapids: William B. Eerdmans Publishing Company, 1996), 269–70; Lucy Stone to "Dear Mother and Father," 1845, RG21, series II, box 2, A, OCA.

38. Sallie Holley, *A Life for Liberty: Antislavery and Other Letters of Sallie Holley* (New York: G. P. Putnam's Sons, 1899), 27.

39. Ellen Lawson and Marlene Merrill, "The Antebellum 'Talented Thousandth': Black College Students at Oberlin before the Civil War," *Journal of Negro Education* 52, no. 2 (Spring 1983): 145.

40. Ibid.; see also Rosetta Douglass Alumni File, OCA.

41. Kerr, *Lucy Stone*, 37; Blackwell, "Reminiscences of Early Oberlin."

42. Lucy Stone to Francis Stone and Harriet Stone, February 15, 1846, RG30/24, box 10, folder 2, OCA; "Expenses of Teaching in the Various Departments of the Oberlin Collegiate Institution for the Year 1844–1845," Lucy Stone Alumni File, OCA.

43. Lucy Stone to Francis and Harriet Stone, February 15, 1846, RG30/24, box 10, folder 2, OCA.

44. *Advocate & Family Guardian*, June 15, 1855; Oberlin Maternal Association Minutes, April 2, 1845, OCA; *Oberlin Evangelist*, August 15, 1855. The Young Ladies' Antislavery Society and the Female Antislavery Society were established in 1835. The former was mostly made up of college women, while the latter was intended mainly for older women in the community. Membership in the much larger Oberlin Antislavery Society, founded in February 1835, was open to everyone. However, after only a few years, all of these groups largely ceased to function as formal organizations. Historian Robert Fletcher notes that the term "antislavery society" was sometimes applied "to the whole unanimously antislav-

ery community (college and colony) when gathered in the frequent mass meetings held for the discussion of anti-slavery matters" (Fletcher, *Oberlin College*, 237).

45. John Shipherd also founded the second coeducational college in America in Olivet, Michigan, in 1844.

46. Kerr, *Lucy Stone*, 32.

47. *Oberlin Evangelist*, September 29, 1852.

48. See Carolyn Williams, "The Female Antislavery Movement: Fighting Against Racial Prejudice and Promoting Women's Rights in Antebellum America," in *The Abolitionist Sisterhood: Women's Political Culture in Antebellum America*, ed. Jean Fagan Yellin and John C. Van Horne (Ithaca, N.Y.: Cornell University Press, 1994), 167.

49. Ruth Bogin and Jean Fagan Yellin, introduction to *Abolitionist Sisterhood*, 5.

50. See Morris, *Oberlin*, 7, 491.

51. See Mahalia McGuire, Mary Jane Edmondson, Emily Edmondson Alumni Files, OCA; M. B. Luckens to "Mr. Harkness," October 12, 1912, Frances Josephine Norris Alumni Record File, OCA. Precise figures for African American enrollment at Oberlin and formerly enslaved Oberlinites are unavailable. Officials did not begin recording the race of Oberlin students until 1900, and contemporary and more modern lists, often compiled from memory, are incomplete. From the sources available, I have argued elsewhere that African American students at Oberlin (preparatory and collegiate departments) comprised between 3 and 5 percent of the entire student population in the years preceding the Civil War. Of 1,311 students enrolled at Oberlin in 1862, African Americans made up approximately 4 percent. The census of 1860 listed 442 African Americans in the town of Oberlin (approximately 21 percent of the total population of 2,114). See Morris, *Oberlin*, 67.

52. See Shirley Yee, *Black Women Abolitionists: A Study in Activism, 1828–1860* (Knoxville: University of Tennessee Press, 1992), 2–3.

53. See Marc R. Matrana, *Lost Plantations of the South* (Jackson: University Press of Mississippi, 2009), 41; Alfred Bushnell Hart, *Salmon Portland Chase* (Boston: Houghton, Mifflin and Company, 1899), 81; Fletcher, *Oberlin College*, 528–29.

54. See Carol Lasser, "Enacting Emancipation: African American Women Abolitionists at Oberlin College and the Quest for Empowerment, Equality, and Respectability," in Sklar and Stewart, *Women's Rights*, 319–45.

55. Fanny Jackson Coppin, *Reminiscences of School Life* (Philadelphia: L. J. Coppin, 1913), 15.

56. See C. E. Stowe to Henry Cowles, July 20, 1852, and Harriet Beecher Stowe to Mary Cowles, July 8, 1852, August 4, 1852, RG30/24, box 4, folder 21, OCA; Mahala Mcguire Alumni File, OCA.

57. Antoinette Brown Blackwell Alumni File, folder 1, OCA; Lucy Stone to Francis and Harriet Stone, February 15, 1846, RG30/24, box 10, folder 2, OCA.

58. William Cheek and Aimee Lee Cheek, *John Mercer Langston and the Fight for Black Freedom, 1829–1865* (Urbana: University of Illinois Press, 1989), 110; Kerr, *Lucy Stone*, 37–38.

59. See *Oberlin Evangelist*, July 17, 1844, August 19, 1846; "Program of First of August Celebration," 1846, RG21, series XI, box 2, OCA.

60. Fairchild, *Woman's Rights and Duties*, 18.

61. For the development of Oberlin's composite antislavery ideology and its response to the abolitionist "schism," see J. Brent Morris, "'All the Truly Wise or Truly Pious Have One and the Same End in View': Oberlin, the West, and Abolitionist Schism," *Civil War History* 57, no. 3 (September 2011): 234–67.

62. "Nothing masculine about her," Alive Cowles wrote, "except that she walks on the ground, which men have occupied alone." Alice Cowles to Henry Cowles, July 19, 1840, RG30/24, box 4, folder 18, OCA.

63. See Aileen Kraditor, *Means and Ends in American Abolitionism: Garrison and His Critics on Strategy and Tactics, 1834–1850* (New York: Pantheon Books, 1969), 46–47.

64. See Young Ladies' Literary Society Minutes, November 24, 1847, June 2, 1853, OCA.

65. Young Ladies' Literary Society Minutes, November 24, 1847, October 9, 1850, June 2, 1853, OCA.

66. Edmund West to Cornelia Johnson, September 19, 1840, RG30/24, box 3, folder 26, OCA.

67. Blackwell, *Antoinette Brown Blackwell*, 6.

68. Lucy Stone to Francis and Harriet Stone, February 15, 1846, RG30/24, box 10, folder 2, OCA. After the abolitionist "schism" of 1840, the American Antislavery Society was often referred to as the "Old Organization" and the rival American and Foreign Antislavery Society as the "New Organization."

69. "Minutes and Address of the State Convention of the Colored Citizens of Ohio, Convened at Columbus, January 10th, 11th, 12th, & 13th, 1849," in *Proceedings of the Black State Conventions, 1840–1865*, ed. Philip Foner and George E. Walker (Philadelphia: Temple University Press, 1979), 1:227.

70. John Ernest, *A Nation within a Nation: Organizing African American Communities before the Civil War* (Chicago: Ivan R. Dee, 2011), 125.

71. Holley, *A Life for Liberty*, 93.

72. Ibid., 76.

73. Sallie Holley to "The Porters," September 30, 1851, in ibid., 80.

PART TWO

Remembering and Forgetting Slavery at Universities

CHAPTER ELEVEN

Slavery and Justice at Brown

A Personal Reflection

Ruth J. Simmons

Over fifteen years have passed since the inauguration of the Brown University Steering Committee on Slavery and Justice. Launched against the backdrop of a surging national debate over slavery reparations, the committee was asked to investigate and disclose Brown's historical relationship to slavery and the transatlantic slave trade and, more broadly, to organize academic events and activities that might help our university community to think deeply and rigorously about the complex historical, moral, political, and legal questions raised by the reparations issue. When we undertook the work, none of us anticipated its international visibility or its potential to inspire so many similar studies on other campuses. Reflecting on the initiative today, I still find myself surprised by the many ways in which Brown's investigation aroused public interest (and sometimes consternation), spurred self-reflection, uncovered forgotten individual and institutional histories, and found an important place in the ongoing national effort to deal with the legacy of slavery.

At the time of my election as president of Brown in 2001, I was serving as president of Smith College. After my appointment but while still at Smith, I was informed by Brown's interim president, Sheila Blumstein, that an uproar over free speech had erupted on the campus. The controversy began with the publication of a paid advertisement written by conservative activist David Horowitz deriding the idea of slavery reparations. In the March 13, 2001, *Brown Daily Herald* ad, Horowitz asserted, in essence, that African Americans were fortunate that their ancestors had been taken from Africa, since they today enjoy a per capita income greater than the modern inhabitants of the nations from which their ancestors had been taken. He further claimed that, "if not for the anti-slavery attitudes... [and] sacrifices" of white Americans, "blacks in America would still be slaves."[1] These claims, and several more in the advertisement, seemed not only to exhibit strangely contorted reasoning but also to offer an unusually blatant defense of the manifest immorality of slavery. The publication of the advertisement sparked controversy on several campuses around the nation, but what transformed the dispute at Brown into a national firestorm was the decision by a group of outraged students to retaliate against the *Brown Daily Herald* by stealing a day's press run of the paper. Given that I had not yet assumed office, I chose not to voice publicly my opinions about the controversy, but the episode gave me an indication of what awaited me as a great-granddaughter of slaves heading an institution of Brown's history and stature.

The slavery issue resurfaced at Brown a short time later. In March 2002, less than a year after my tenure as president began, the Reparations Coordinating Committee, a group headed by Harvard Law Professor Charles Ogletree, publicly identified Brown, Yale, and Harvard as "probable targets" of reparations lawsuits. The *Brown Daily Herald*, reporting the story, noted that "researchers" had already established that Brown did not in fact have ties to slavery—an assertion that was, in retrospect, patently untrue. The threat of litigation was also widely reported in national media, prompting questions from many alumni. What was Brown's relationship to slavery, they asked?

In thinking about how to resolve conflicting assertions about Brown and slavery, I pondered an uncomfortable dilemma. To simply ignore the question seemed not only irresponsible but also unworthy of a university, whose fundamental mission is the pursuit of knowledge. At the same time, I understood that any action I took to address the issue could easily be misunderstood or deemed compromised because of my race and origins. It is a peculiar consequence of the history of slavery and race in this country that African American perspectives on these vital issues are routinely discounted, derided, and dismissed. Where I stood on racial matters large and small, whether I had a reparations "agenda," would be recurrent questions during my time as president, even as I faced and fulfilled all the other responsibilities of a university presidency.

After discussing the matter with members of my cabinet, I concluded that this was an issue best addressed as a scholarly project, driven by faculty, without my involvement or oversight. The approach of Brown's 250th anniversary celebration seemed to offer an ideal occasion not only to set the record straight about the role of slavery in the institution's founding but also to offer a helpful model of how universities might address controversial questions with the most rigorous academic standards. Further, with the approach of the bicentennial of the abolition of the transatlantic slave trade by the British Parliament and U.S. Congress and the worldwide observances planned for the occasion, the venture promised to place Brown in a leadership role in interpreting the lessons and obligations of this history. Finally, I imagined that my own history offered Brown a singular opportunity to tell its story in a different light from peer institutions slow to acknowledge similarly compromised racial histories.

Appointing a committee to examine the university's historic ties to slavery and the slave trade thus promised several benefits. It offered Brown a leading role in addressing a pressing national issue. It provided an opportunity for the university to confront and in some fashion to redress a historic wrong and to do so in a way that could be instructive for others confronting large-scale human rights abuses, present as well as past. Last but not least, it offered an opportunity for every person who cared about Brown to learn the truth of its past. It has always struck me as odd that a university so loved by grateful alumni would evade the truth about itself. Would not a university's unwillingness to examine the facts of its own history impinge upon its scholarly credibility? What of a university's ethical identity? Do not the same obligations to openness and transparency that prevail in the realm of research and teaching apply also to the university's accounting of its own history?

Having appointed a scholarly committee and put its work sufficiently beyond my reach, I thought this would be a fairly straightforward undertaking. In retrospect, this assumption was naive. Confronting massive human rights violations that have privileged some and disenfranchised others is, at its heart, a divisive undertaking. As the committee's report noted, such exercises run up against not only powerful vested interests but also a natural human "impulse to evade, extenuate, or deflect the full burden of the past."[2] This impulse is perhaps most acute in societies that have promoted forgetting as the best way to deal with the wounds that such violations inevitably leave behind. Thus the initial announcement of the committee's appointment was greeted with predictions of a disastrous outcome: fund-raising would decline, the university's reputation would be sullied, and I would be personally attacked and ridiculed, if not dismissed. Such concerns, I should note, came not only from those angered and aggrieved by the very idea of such an inquiry but also from supporters and advocates, friends and loved ones. Indeed, on the day of the first news report about the committee's existence I received a phone call from an eminent scholar and dear friend expressing concern that I had perhaps "lost my mind" in taking on such a controversial subject.

Thankfully, none of the dire predictions came to pass. Today we can affirm that the steering committee's work enhanced rather than sullied Brown's reputation while bequeathing to the university and its students a legacy of truth telling that may continue to inspire excellence in stewardship and citizenship for decades to come. Perhaps most important, the successful work of the committee has disproved the assertion that confronting the history and legacy of gross historical injustices can only come at a severe cost to social harmony and institutional reputation.

For me, as for many other members of the Brown community, the history unearthed by the steering committee provided abundant opportunities for self-reflection. As the committee's report pointed out, we live, work, study, and teach amidst artifacts and potent remnants of grievous injustice, most of which pass unnoticed. Perhaps the most potent remnant for me was a pair of portraits that hung in my office depicting James Manning, the university's founding president, and his wife, Margaret. A minister, Manning came to Rhode Island from Pennsylvania in 1764 to found North America's first Baptist college. Slavery was a pervasive institution in Rhode Island at the time. About one in eight of the colony's population was enslaved. Shipowners and shopkeepers, merchants and manufacturers participated in the institution in myriad ways, most notably through distilling rum for slave ships bound for West Africa. As the steering committee report disclosed, some thirty members of the Corporation, the college's governing board, owned or captained slave ships. The roster included John Brown, the school's treasurer and a member of the university's namesake family, and Cyprian Sterry, the school's chancellor, whose Providence merchant house mounted some twenty West African slaving voyages. In such a context, the fact that Manning arrived in Rhode Island accompanied by a personal slave aroused little comment.

Undoubtedly devout and committed to setting the young men of the college on the path to righteousness, Manning left little evidence for posterity of opposition to the inhumane, illicit, and sadistic trade in human beings. Sitting before the portrait of this man, who could never have imagined a successor like me, inspired reflection on many things: on the course of my own life, on the life of institutions, and on the wrongs so easily done in conformity with one's times.

Though over two centuries separated our tenures as president of Brown, Manning and I are very much part of the same continuum. My grandparents, though born free, bore the indelible marks of slavery's legacy. Until her last days, my grandmother transported heavy loads on her head and dressed in long dresses reminiscent of the coarse clothing manufactured for the specific use of slaves. (As the steering committee report noted, much of the clothing worn by southern slaves was manufactured in Rhode Island mills, including several owned by Brown trustees and benefactors.) My parents continued the work of their parents, toiling in cotton fields for much of their lives for the enrichment of plantation owners. Born on a hillock overlooking those fields, I came along too late to be fully vested in the sharecropping system but soon enough to experience firsthand the long days that my parents and siblings spent dragging cotton sacks down the long, unforgiving rows, sunup to sundown. There was no overseer with whip in hand, to be sure, but low wages and brutal living conditions were an effective means of keeping poor farmers from escaping the system.

Historian Douglas Blackmon, in his book *Slavery by Another Name*, suggests that the era in which my grandparents lived is inappropriately named the Jim Crow era. Instead, he writes, "Let us define this period of American life plainly and comprehensively. It was the Age of Neoslavery. Only by acknowledging the full extent of slavery's grip on U.S. society—its intimate connections to present-day wealth and power, the depth of its injury to millions of black Americans, the shocking nearness in time to its true end—can we reconcile the paradoxes of current American life."[3] The nearness of my own life to the true end of slavery holds me and obligates me. Would that one could simply set aside such realities and, turning to a new day, decree that all that is past shall never be revisited. But knowing and understanding our history is as vital to the improvement of our lives as nourishment is necessary to our physical survival. Furthermore, ignoring massive violations of human rights or minimizing their scope and cruelty can all too easily enable future atrocities. Hence, my belief in disclosing historical injustices as fully as possible, a belief that has been deepened by my experience at Brown. While focusing on blame is not productive, it is neither futile nor unimportant to acknowledge what took place and to consider how to create an environment in which similar injustices are less likely to recur.

Many complain that present-day efforts to judge the behavior and actions of those from a distant time are themselves unjust. This is certainly true to a degree. The decisions one makes for the benefit of so worthy an enterprise as a college are inevitably limited to the array of choices available at the time. But viewing past beliefs and actions through the lenses of what we believe and wish for ourselves today is both inescapable and, if done with care and humility, morally instructive, not least because of the way it compels us to imagine how successive generations may judge our beliefs and actions. Just as Manning and his cohort found ways to live comfortably with the injustices of their time, so are all of us capable of finding our way to similar compromises. Through the inspiration of his visage, I was better able to recognize the mandate to stand up to the injustices of my own times, no matter how commonplace or well accepted they might have become. I was also better able to recognize the close relationship between the predominating injustices of Manning's era and those of my own, both of which rest on a fundamental denial of the dignity and equality of all human beings.

Sitting in the presence of President Manning was sometimes uncomfortable, but the discomfort taught me much about who I am and how much I can bear. It connected me in a much stronger way to those who placed me on my path through their suffering and their hope. And it helped me better understand my responsibilities to history and to those who come after me. The journey to these recognitions was longer than it should have been, but I would not finally have wanted it to be any different.

Let me close with a few observations about the legacy and lessons of the Slavery and Justice initiative for Brown and for universities generally. This is not an easy time for American universities, which face mounting public distrust of their mission, structures, and fairness. They are hardly alone. In the case of public and private institutions alike—government, churches, media companies, health care providers, public schools, police forces, financial institutions, the criminal justice system, corporations—a deep gulf has developed between institutions' professed values and goals and the public perception of them. This skepticism bridges the normal divides of American politics: it is evident on the left as well as the right, among the religious as well as the agnostic, the young as well as the old. Indeed, while one can say that our nation is deeply divided in so many respects, it is unified in its mistrust of institutions.

The fact that universities are coming under widespread public attack in spite of the immense public good that they do is a product of many factors. But I believe that much of the problem reflects universities' own failings, including our adoption of some of the worst habits of large organizations: elitism, predominating self-interest, failure to uphold our stated values, and a mystifying reluctance to stand up to entrenched power and question the status quo. If we truly believe that the Academy exists to promote human welfare and follow the path of truth, then our first task is confronting our own compromises and corruption.

In saying this, I do not mean to suggest that universities should exhibit self-righteousness or standoffish tendencies. Far from it. I believe that universities, as living communities of learning, should continually interrogate their own values. They should examine where they stand on the most difficult questions of our time. When they detect threats to fundamental values of freedom, equality, and justice, they have a duty to engage the debate and even to wage battle against practices that would divide, exclude, or constrain freedom of thought. Last but not least, universities must ensure the ability of community members, faculty, students, and staff to participate in the process of protest, which remains an all-important avenue for disclosing corruption, challenging oppression, and perfecting our union.

One practical way that universities can help to entrench these principles is by creating structures for broad, authentic, and inclusive university governance. Modern American university governance has changed significantly as a result of the activism of the 1960s; decisions once made in secret by small groups of individuals are now often the province of a wider array of campus bodies, many of them deliberately, if cautiously, representative. There is no doubt that this change has complicated and slowed decision making on many campuses. But what has been lost in speed and simplicity has been more than compensated for by an enlarged pool of experience, greater diversity of perspective, and community ownership of challenging issues. This broad participation is, I believe, one important means of protecting institutions from the significant moral and political lapses to which more insular groups can be prone. It is also consistent with bedrock principles of good scholarship, which insist on exposing presumed facts and findings to the scrutiny and criticism of others.

Finally and most importantly, universities must fiercely defend freedom of speech and thought. This is not an easy task today, when many on our campuses, including many of our students, dismiss appeals to free speech as a screen to license hate speech, preserve privilege, and placate those who disdain activist efforts. The first precipitant for appointment of the steering committee, recall, was an uproar over the boundaries of campus speech. I believed then and I continue to believe today that all members of a campus community should feel able to express their views, even views that strike others as heinous, hurtful, hateful, and misinformed. It should go without saying that protecting the right of some to challenge what they see as violations of basic human and civil rights also requires defending the right of those who would seek to justify or defend such practices. How can we have one without the other? We must teach our students the clarifying power of opposing views, even views that seem hollow or self-interested. The one thing we should not be questioning is the importance of free speech as the underpinning of our freedom, rights, and dignity.

These reflections have particular resonance today. In these perilous political times, when some seem bent on rolling back our hard-won freedoms, when demagogues and racists come to power with the support of substantial numbers of voters, when entire communities are harassed, demeaned, and threatened, what could be more precious than our right to dissent? And dissent we must, raising our resonant voices to challenge hateful and divisive rhetoric, denouncing exclusionary practices that threaten further to divide a nation already riven into segregated enclaves of thought and identity. In the midst of the political turmoil around us, there is no greater mission for a university than to disclose facts, confront untruths, and uphold traditions of democracy, openness, and inclusion. The legacy of excellence that so many universities represent is built not on lies and secrets but on truth telling, not on narrowness of thought but on the robust exchange of ideas. Efforts by universities and other organizations to disclose truthfully their historical origins are consistent with these values and are thus to be applauded.

Because of the work of the Steering Committee on Slavery and Justice, I have a fuller understanding of the historical legacy that I and other members of the Brown community inherited. That knowledge in no way compromises my esteem for the institution. To the contrary, I am immensely proud of the legacy of Brown, a legacy entangled with slavery but also defined by independence of thought and action, a respect for dissent, and a commitment to diversity. Perhaps most important, it is a legacy that affirms and confirms the human capacity to learn, change, and grow.

NOTES

1. David Horowitz, "Ten Reasons Why Reparations for Slavery Is a Bad Idea—and Racist Too," *Brown Daily Herald*, March 13, 2001, 6.

2. Brenda Allen et al., *Slavery and Justice: Report of the Brown University Steering Committee on Slavery and Justice* (Providence, R.I.: Brown University, 2006), 45.

3. Douglas A. Blackmon, *Slavery by Another Name: The Re-enslavement of Black People in America from the Civil War to World War II* (New York: Doubleday, 2008), 402.

CHAPTER TWELVE

Harvard and Slavery

A Short History

Sven Beckert, Balraj Gill, Jim Henle, & Katherine May Stevens

When one thinks of Harvard University and its history, the names Alfred, Delia, Renty, Fassena, Drana, Jack, and Jem do not come to mind. Professorial chairs were not named for them; their names do not adorn Harvard institutions or buildings; they were not professors, graduates, or donors. Instead, they were the property of slaveholders in and around Columbia, South Carolina. The lives of these two women and five men—some African born—intersected briefly with Harvard in 1850 when they were brought to the studio of daguerreotypist Joseph Thomas Zealy. There they were individually positioned in front of Zealy's camera—sitting or standing, stripped to the waist or fully naked—and photographed from the front, from the side, and from the rear. Commissioned by Harvard professor Louis Agassiz, one of the leading natural scientists of the era, the fifteen daguerreotypes of these enslaved people were part of an arsenal of evidence Agassiz assembled in an attempt to support his claim that people of European origin were superior to other so-called races and that peoples of African descent came from a separate species. Alfred, Delia, Renty, Fassena, Drana, Jack, and Jem were photographed as a "Negro type," dehumanized specimens of a supposedly inferior race, in the advancement of ethnology and "race science"—what Frederick Douglass called "scientific moonshine."[1]

For countless years the daguerreotypes of these seven women and men were tucked in a drawer in the cluttered attic of Harvard's Peabody Museum of Archaeology and Ethnology. They resurfaced in 1976 when museum employees stumbled upon them while looking for something else.[2] Appearing since in books and exhibitions, the images have stirred controversy. For some, they are haunting; for others, infuriating.[3] While they have secured a place in the history of photography and in the study of race and racism in the United States, they are not mentioned in the standard narrative of Harvard's history. This is not surprising. Until recently, a deafening silence surrounded Harvard's historical relationship with slavery. This relationship included its role in manufacturing an intellectual defense for slavery by producing scientific claims of the alleged existence of natural racial hierarchies and black inferiority. These claims played a particular role in undermining the advances of Reconstruction after the Civil War. Confronting this legacy in a meaningful way is a project the university has only begun to undertake.

When the public thinks of Harvard and slavery, it most likely thinks of the university's contribution to the Civil War and the destruction of slavery in the United States. This association is fostered by the cathedral-like Memorial Hall, the campus's most prominent edifice, built to commemorate the sacrifice of Harvard's Union soldiers. The hall features in official publications that mark the war's anniversaries with effusive praise to Harvard enlistees.[4] Two hundred forty-six Harvard men died in the Civil War (including seventy on the Confederate side), while well-known graduates—Ralph Waldo Emerson, Henry David Thoreau, Thomas Wentworth Higginson, Wendell Phillips, among others—made important contributions to antislavery thought and action.[5] Yet even Samuel Eliot Morison, as close to an official historian as Harvard has had, conceded: "The dominant sentiment in the College in the critical winter of 1860–61 was for Union and conciliation.... It is difficult for anyone who knew Harvard [later] ... to understand the cool attitude of the College toward the Civil War." Moreover, in the years leading up to the war, Morison noted, "the abolitionists and the other reformers of the day were in a continual state of irritation because the University did not promote their pet theories."[6] Harvard as an institution was not the pioneer of antislavery it might later have wanted to be. In fact, Harvard was complicit with slavery, benefiting both directly and indirectly from slave labor.

We now know this history because of the research undertaken by a group of dedicated Harvard students. Their historical investigations began in the fall of 2007, when four undergraduates enrolled in a research seminar offered by Sven Beckert entitled Harvard and Slavery. Following Ruth Simmons's pathbreaking work to uncover Brown University's relationship with slavery, the seminar sought to engender a better understanding of Harvard's relationship to slavery and to help students understand how deeply slavery was embedded within the fabric of American life—and how that powerful legacy continues to endure today.

The students had no idea what they would find. Quickly, however, their curiosity and rapid mastery of the art of historical detection uncovered a treasure trove of findings, many disconcerting. The thirty-two students who participated in the first seminar and the three subsequent seminars scoured Harvard's archival records, drew countless volumes from its library, made careful inspections of nearby colonial graveyards, and scrutinized Harvard's oldest buildings. Much of what they found surprised them: Harvard presidents who brought their slaves to live with them on campus, significant endowments drawn from the exploitation of slave labor, Harvard's administration and most of its faculty favoring the suppression of public debates on slavery. A quest that began with fears of finding little ended with a new, more troubling question: How was it that the university had failed for so long to engage with so large a part of its history?

In retrospect, the only surprising thing was the students' surprise. Until its abolition in 1865, slavery was a core institution of colonial North America and the United States. Perfectly legal in Massachusetts until 1783, slavery stood at the center of the United States' wealthiest and most dynamic regional economy, the plantation belt of the South. And it was not contained below the Mason-Dixon Line: Boston merchants, manufacturers, and others benefited from the trade in slave-grown agricultural commodities and the processing of these commodities in New England's cities. Supplying the slave economies of the Caribbean was another profitable branch of local enterprise. It was entirely implausible to assume that the oldest and in many ways most influential institution of higher learning in the United States would not have been involved with slavery. And, indeed, the students' research established that Harvard was maintained in part by slave labor; that it benefited from profits accrued directly or indirectly from slavery; and, more broadly, that Harvard not only accommodated slavery but also helped sustain it.

The students' surprise becomes more intelligible if we take into account that for too long the history of slavery has been taught as the history of just one region, the South. While schools and universities in recent decades have made great strides in teaching the history of slavery, they too often have discussed the role of the North only as the gathering ground for the political forces that led to the abolition of the "peculiar institution." The students' surprise at their findings was fed by the peculiar version of the nation's history that they, and we, grew up with.

Over its first five years, the Harvard and Slavery Research Project began to rewrite this history. So dedicated were the seminar participants that many continued working on the project even after they fulfilled their academic obligations. In 2011 the group published its findings in a report written by Sven Beckert and Katherine Stevens entitled "Harvard and Slavery: Seeking a Forgotten History," a narrative of the connections between Harvard and slavery over the three centuries of the university's existence.[7] The group created a website with a map that linked places on and around Harvard's campus to video interviews in which students explained the significance of those sites to the history of Harvard and slavery. As Harvard celebrated its 375th anniversary in the fall of 2011, students from the seminars came together to form the Harvard and Slavery Research Project and make a sustained effort to publicize their findings. Although Harvard's official celebrations were silent on the university's ties to slavery, the group worked hard to make the intersecting history of Harvard and slavery part of the institution's shared memory. In 2016 President Drew Gilpin Faust convened an advisory committee on Harvard and slavery, unveiling a plaque commemorating four enslaved Harvard workers—Titus, Venus, Bilhah, and Juba—and in 2017 sponsored an international conference at Radcliffe Institute on the question of "universities and slavery."

Harvard and Slavery: Some Findings

When the students began, they had little to build on. Though the literature on Harvard's history is voluminous, barely anything had been said about the university's relationship to slavery. Yet it did not take students long to establish that Harvard's involvement in slavery was sustained and important to the survival of both the university and slavery. Begun in 1636 as a small Puritan outpost of learning, Harvard was founded to uphold the traditions of English universities and provide ministers for the Massachusetts Bay Colony. As the college for men of the pulpit, Harvard provided the social and political leadership during Massachusetts's early years as a religious colony. Over time, as the colony's requirements for governance became more specific and variegated, Harvard began to supplement the training in religious stewardship with instruction for the new caste of political and judicial leaders.

As the colony managed to secure a toehold in the unforgiving New England setting—at the expense of the Native population—it looked toward the prosperous slave colonies of the Caribbean for its livelihood. Massachusetts Bay was one of the key points in the "triangle trade," importing sugar, molasses, and other slave-produced goods from the Caribbean islands in exchange for fish, lumber, ships, and rum—and trading directly in slaves. New England merchants and Puritan rulers prospered from the labor of enslaved workers.

The presence of slavery in the Massachusetts Bay Colony brought slavery to Harvard's doorstep. We know, for example, that Harvard presidents Increase Mather (1685–1701) and Benjamin Wadsworth (1725–37) owned slaves, as did William Brattle, the minister who addressed the Harvard community every Sunday at the First Church of Cambridge. It is, moreover, likely that slaves did some of the cooking and cleaning for students, toiling for the Boardman family, the college stewards. And a number of former students, from Cotton Mather to John Hancock, became slave owners after graduation, particularly as the eighteenth century matured. Using gravestone markers, diaries, and personal papers, among other forms of evidence, student researchers traced the presence of enslaved Africans at Harvard who performed vital services to sustain the college community.[8]

The absence of a plantation regime in New England did not necessarily make slavery benign. Slaves were still chattel and assigned the lowest status in society. As early as 1639, when schoolmaster Nathanial Eaton was accused of mismanagement of the college, one of the offenses acknowledged by his wife was that he had allowed "the Moor" (presumably an African slave) to sleep and eat along with students, who objected to sharing the table with him.[9] Such a reaction would only grow more extreme, and at times more brutal, as African slavery became increasingly common in eighteenth-century Massachusetts and racial lines more rigid.[10]

Here too, Harvard played a role. As a key institution of the colonial elite, Harvard was central in constituting the colonial regime, which included sustaining and enforcing slavery. One incident provides a telling example of Harvard's role in sustaining slavery. In 1755 two slaves, Mark and Phillis, were accused of murdering their master, John Codman of Charlestown. Beyond the murder itself, which struck at the intimate nature of householders' slavery, the slaveholding elite was alarmed to learn that the slaves had a network of friends and acquaintances who helped them move about, gain information, and acquire resources, including—possibly—even the poison that killed Codman. The white community feared that the slaves, and the incident itself, were not as isolated as they first appeared.

For their crime of "petit treason," or social insubordination, Mark and Phillis were tried in the highest colonial court, the Supreme Court of Judicature, and executed at the Gallows Lot, now on Avon Hill in North Cambridge. Prosecuted by Harvard graduate Edmund Trowbridge, Mark was hanged and Phillis was burned at the stake. This immolation stands out for its brutality in the annals of Massachusetts; not even the Salem witches were put to the torch.[11] Three of the four judges, including presiding chief justice Stephen Sewall, were Harvard graduates, and two of them were slave owners. As the slave population grew—as much as 8 percent of Boston's population at that time was enslaved—any threat of instability or insubordination was met with the brutality endemic to slaveholding societies.[12] The Harvard-educated elite helped to uphold this regime.

Further evidence of the tenor of racial thinking in the mid-eighteenth century appeared in a brief but unsettling Harvard record. Among the items listed in the inventory of the university's collection of artifacts lost in the Harvard Hall fire of 1764 was "a piece of tanned negro's hide."[13] Even without any knowledge save that it existed, this artifact evokes the less than human status accorded to peoples of African descent at a time when racial ideology was in the process of formation.[14]

Slavery affected Harvard in more subtle ways as well. Historian Samuel Eliot Morison noted the increase in Harvard's class size after the War of Spanish Succession ended in 1713: "The increase came largely from the seaports, which reaped the first harvests from land speculation and West India commerce, and the rum business; and where the influence of court manners was most quickly felt. The new crop of young men came to be made gentlemen, not to study."[15] Harvard's growth, even at this early stage, was intimately connected to the slave trade, slave-grown agricultural commodities, and the provision of supplies for the plantations of the American South and the Caribbean.

Slaveholding was common in the upper echelons of society, and it was not controversial. U.S. president and Harvard graduate John Adams made note of having "lived for many years in times when the practice [of slavery] was not disgraceful, when the best men in my vicinity thought it was not inconsistent with their character."[16]

Nowhere is the connection of Harvard and colonial slavery more palpable than at the site of Elmwood, now the official residence of the president of Harvard. Bequeathed to the university in 1933, the estate was built in 1767 by Harvard graduate Thomas Oliver, the heir of a prominent Antiguan sugar planter and slave owner. A Tory lieutenant governor of the Massachusetts

Bay Colony, Oliver fled the country during the Revolution. But in his brief tenure at Elmwood, he lived with slaves whom he had purchased. It is not clear what slave labor went into Elmwood's construction, and research still needs to be done concerning the living situation of Elmwood's slaves. Student researcher Kaitlin Terry, however, did establish that Oliver, part of a larger movement of the colonial elite, transplanted Antiguan practices and slaves to Cambridge.[17] Also part of this migration was the Royall family, who amassed their fortune at a "classic Caribbean sugar estate" on the island of Antigua.[18] They soon established themselves as one of the city's leading names; their bequest established the teaching of law at Harvard, and their coat of arms was incorporated in the Harvard Law School emblem, where it remained in use until 2016.[19]

Large slaveholding families such as the Olivers, Royalls, and Vassalls, a closely connected elite, were a living link to the West Indian slaveholders whose exploitation of enslaved workers was crucial to the expansion of the British imperial realm.[20] Their resources contributed to Harvard's capital. More directly, Harvard invested in enterprises connected to slavery by providing interest-bearing loans to merchants. Until the emergence of a formal banking system in the late eighteenth century, Harvard was one of the colony's few institutional sources of capital.[21] Its borrowers included merchants who invested in slave plantations or were involved in shipping slave-produced commodities.[22]

Some of this changed at the end of the eighteenth century. In the wake of the Revolution, slavery was effectively eliminated in Massachusetts by court judgments in the Elizabeth Freeman and Quock Walker cases. Walker's case was presided over by a Harvard graduate, Chief Justice William Cushing.[23] The revolutionary winds also blew through Harvard. In 1773, for example, the college commencement included the "Forensic Debate on the Legality of Enslaving the Africans." One student, Theodore Parsons, upheld the morality of slavery because of the alleged inferiority of Africans, while another, Eliphalet Pearson, later Harvard's acting president (1804–6), rebuked slavery as contrary to the "natural rights of mankind."[24] Pearson's arguments pointed the way toward the expanded vision of rights that was later evident in the Walker case. According to Werner Sollors and his coeditors, the debate "elicited so much comment" that it was "immediately printed and published."[25]

Harvard students like Pearson and alumni like Cushing helped eliminate slavery in Massachusetts, but slavery remained important in the lives of New England's elite.[26] This fact, however, like the slaves themselves, was kept at a distance in the collective memory of most of the members of the institution and its recorded histories. As New England moved away from enslaving laborers, it also erased the presence of slaves from its historical narrative.[27]

In the early nineteenth century, the governance of Harvard changed hands from Calvinists to Unitarians, reflecting the split in the Congregational Church and the shift from a doctrine focusing on original sin to a more liberal one. This coincided with the maturing of merchant capitalism in New England and the eventual emergence of a new Boston elite tied to overseas trade, domestic commerce, industry, and finance. With this changing of the guard, Harvard branched out beyond its theological roots and began to emerge as a modern university. It became a place where the new elite sent its dollars and sons in a conscious effort to create an institution in its image—"reflecting the banker's mentality and the rhythms of modern industry"—and where succeeding generations could be nurtured.[28] The wealthiest among this elite were merchants, financiers, and lawyers involved in all manner of trade and commerce.

Yet amid these changes, Harvard's connection to slavery remained. The university's growth in stature and resources came in part from donations from merchant families who had made their fortunes trading slave-produced commodities like sugar, coffee, and cotton; they sometimes also traded in slaves. The Perkinses were one such merchant family. Harvard president Josiah Quincy (1829–45) compared the character of James Perkins to the merchant house of which Perkins was the elder partner. Both were, Quincy wrote, "formed on the noblest and purest model of professional uprightness; without guile and without reproach."[29]

Perkins, however, began his career as a commodities broker in Saint-Domingue—present-day Haiti—where hundreds of thousands of enslaved men and women produced sugar, cotton, and coffee for European and North American markets. Quincy's homage also failed to mention that among the commodities in Perkins's consignments were African slaves brought to cultivate sugar and other agricultural commodities. Student researcher Robert Mann found that as the Perkins firm accumulated capital, it invested in ships and slaves and established commercial relationships in the slave markets of Charleston, New Orleans, and Havana. In the wake of the Haitian Revolution in 1791, the Perkinses fled the island but later returned. The firm finally closed its West Indian business in 1804 when it began garnering higher profits from its trade in Asia. Even then the Perkinses occasionally looked to the slave trade to generate quick cash, which they used to fund that Asia trade. One such instance appears in papers dating from 1810 when the firm sought insurance for slave cargoes and the two ships that would carry them.[30] The Perkins family's involvement in the slave trade provided the foundation for its business activities in the eighteenth century, including for the firm's involvement in quarries, textile mills, and railroads in the nineteenth century.[31] Other major Harvard benefactors who profited from West Indian trade included Israel Thorndike, Benjamin Bussey, and Peter Chardon Brooks.

Starting in the 1840s, New England textile mill owners were another source of donations for Harvard. These mills depended on cotton produced by slaves in the U.S. South, and in turn cotton plantation owners used credit from northern and English banks to purchase slaves and supplies. Harvard donor Abbot Lawrence, for example, gained much of his wealth from the textile industry. He owned and operated cotton factories in Massachusetts, along with a trading firm that sold the products of his mills. In 1847 and 1849 he donated $100,000 (the equivalent of $2,816,266 in 2016) to the university.[32] Northern bankers and textile mill owners were an essential part of the cotton-plantation economy, and their donations and services helped transform Harvard from a colonial academy to a leading university with national and, eventually, international influence. Of course, it is also an example of the many ways that slavery was profitable to northerners who may never have personally bought or sold a slave.

Perkins, Thorndike, Brooks, Bussey, and Lawrence were a minority among the twenty-five individuals who made major personal donations to Harvard between 1800 and 1850. Their combined contribution of $497,400, however, accounted for 50 percent of all major individual donations in this period. Harvard honored them by naming buildings, professorships, and schools after them, and their legacies are still visible in some of Harvard's most well known institutions.[33] Lawrence's gift created the Lawrence Scientific School (now the John A. Paulson School of Engineering and Applied Sciences). While Bussey's envisioned agricultural school struggled to find a place at the university, eventually merging with other schools in the biological sciences, his estate in Jamaica Plain became part of Harvard's research resources as the Arnold Arboretum. James Perkins left Harvard $22,000 to endow the Perkins Professorship in Mathematics, still extant today. Perkins's brother and business partner Thomas Handasyd Perkins provided most of the funds to build the Harvard College Observatory, and the Perkinses contributed to the establishment of Massachusetts General Hospital, where scores of Harvard medical students were trained. In fact, the hospital's first board of trustees meeting was held in the home of Thomas Handasyd Perkins. While members of wealthy merchant families sought social standing by affiliating themselves with institutions like Harvard, they were also active participants in transforming the institutions to which they donated time and money—the latter the product of slave labor.[34]

It was not just money: Harvard could not avoid entanglement in the politics of slavery, which were particularly contentious in the 1830s. As radical abolitionists demanded the immediate emancipation of slaves, William Lloyd Garrison emerged as one of their Boston-area leaders. The university's donors, comprised of conservative businessmen, considered the Garrisonians a fringe movement, assuring their southern slaveholding business partners that abolitionists carried no weight in the political and social affairs of the North. Various Harvard professors and students, however, joined antislavery organizations, prompting the administration to try to undermine the movement's influence at the university.

Three incidents reveal how the backlash against abolitionists affected Harvard policy in the 1830s. The first two involved Professors Charles Follen and Henry Ware Jr., activists in the abolitionist movement who were attacked by Boston newspapers. "It is to be regretted," wrote the *Boston Gazette*, "that any portion of the Professors at Harvard College should countenance the wild and mischievous schemes of the antislavery agitators, who are imprudently meddling with property of the planters and others of the southern states." The *Gazette* singled out "foreigners" like Follen, who had fled political persecution in Germany. Members of the clergy like Ware, the paper suggested, "should be severely rebuked for their impertinence and folly."[35] In 1835 Follen left Harvard when the endowment for his chair expired and the Harvard Corporation did not renew his professorship. He remained a staunch abolitionist until his untimely death in 1840. After much pressure from friends and colleagues, Ware resigned as the president of the Cambridge Anti-Slavery Society and continued teaching at Harvard. While the corporation may not have issued an ultimatum to either, it is hard to imagine that Follen's and Ware's decisions were unaffected by the public backlash against them.

In the third incident, in 1838, President Josiah Quincy intervened directly to quell discussion on abolition. When Quincy learned that the Philanthropic Society at the Divinity School was holding a debate on slavery that would be open to members of the community beyond Harvard, he wrote to the dean of the Divinity School, John Gorham Palfrey, suggesting that the discussion not take place. "Whatever may be your or my private opinion on the main question [of slavery]," he wrote, "I think there can be but one in the minds of prudent men, that, in the state of excessive excitability of the public mind on this topic abroad, it is desirable not to introduce it obtrusively into a seminary of learning, composed of young men from every quarter of the country; among whom are many whose prejudices, passions, and interests are deeply implicated and affected by these discussions and who feel very naturally and strongly on the subject."[36] Within a few months, the corporation passed a resolution barring anyone who was not a member of the Harvard community from appearing on campus without a faculty vote, a rule that blocked well-known abolitionists from speaking. Harvard would not allow itself to be seen as a staging ground for abolitionist agitation, especially not by the press or potential or current donors. The university continued working to mitigate the influence and presence of antislavery organizing on campus until the late 1850s, when northern views on slavery and abolition began to shift dramatically.[37]

Boston was a stronghold of abolitionism, and a number of Harvard graduates joined and became leaders of the movement. These men, however, became abolitionists well outside the confines of the university. Among the best known were Samuel J. May, Edmund Quincy, Wendell Phillips, Thomas Wentworth Higginson, Henry and William Ingersoll Bowditch, and Oliver Wendell Holmes Jr.—all from wealthy Boston families.[38] Antislavery alumni from humbler origins included Charles Sumner and Transcendentalists Theodore Parker, Henry David Thoreau, and Ralph Waldo Emerson.

The men entered the movement at different moments and for various reasons. Henry Ingersoll Bowditch was troubled by the attempted lynching of William Lloyd Garrison in 1835 by a mob comprised of "fifteen hundred or two thousand highly respectable gentlemen . . . of property and standing" from various parts of Boston; he joined the Massachusetts Anti-Slavery Society the following year.[39] Wendell Phillips was of a deeply conservative temperament until he married abolitionist Ann Greene. He became increasingly sympathetic to the cause and joined the abolitionist movement after the mob killing of antislavery newspaper publisher Elijah Lovejoy in 1837.[40] Like many of his abolitionist comrades, Phillips became a life-long reformer, critiquing the emerging contours of American capitalism and fighting for racial equality and the rights of women, workers, and Native peoples. Thomas Wentworth Higginson was an organizer of the Massachusetts Kansas Aid Committee and an agent of the National Kansas Aid Committee, both parts of the effort to ensure that Kansas and Nebraska entered the Union as free, not slave, states. Higginson, along with Theodore Parker, was part of abolitionist John Brown's "Secret Six" group of funders. Brown waged battles in Kansas against proslavery forces in 1856 and led the raid of a weapons arsenal in Harpers Ferry, Virginia, in 1859 as part of an attempt to initiate a slave insurrection. Oliver Wendell Holmes Jr. edited *Harvard Magazine*—then a student-run publication. He wrote articles opposing slavery and advocating free will in religious matters. The president of Harvard at that time, Cornelius Felton, admonished young Holmes for what Felton regarded as the magazine's disrespectful tone.[41] On the eve of the Civil War, Holmes also served as the bodyguard for Wendell Phillips at a mass rally. During his senior year at Harvard, he enlisted in the Union army. Charles Sumner, senator from Massachusetts, spoke energetically against slavery and the power of the slave states. As part of the radical wing of the Republican Party, he consistently drew attention to the "unhallowed union" between "the cotton planters and flesh mongers of Louisiana and Mississippi and the cotton spinners and traffickers of New England, between the lords of the lash and the lords of the loom."[42]

Acting on their consciences made these activists outcasts in Boston society. Speaking to Harvard alumni in 1842, Supreme Court justice and fellow of the Harvard Corporation Joseph Story said the main danger of the day was "the tendency to ultraism of all sorts, and in all directions." He lamented the emergence of "a restless spirit of innovation and change—a fretful desire to provoke discussion of all sorts, under the pretext of free inquiry, or of comprehensive liberalism." He stressed that the "movement is to be found not merely among illiterate and vain pretenders, but among the minds of the highest order, which are capable of giving fearful impulses to public opinion."[43] Former Harvard professor and cynosure of Boston intellectual life George Ticknor described abolitionism as "a virus that was a disease fatal to the republic, and must be quarantined."[44] That some of Boston's "minds of the highest order" were entangled with abolition alarmed much of the city's elite, who rebuked and censured the abolitionists.

Present and former members of the Harvard administration and faculty not only worked to thwart antislavery organizing on campus but also diligently isolated the abolitionists in their elite class. Sumner was excluded from literary gatherings in Boston, publicly attacked by his close friend, Cornelius Felton (president of Harvard 1860–62), and passed over twice for a professorship at the Law School, even though he was a protégé of Joseph Story.[45] Higginson, who led a congregation in Newburyport and preached against slavery from the pulpit, was forced to resign by his wealthy parishioners.[46] Phillips was isolated by his family members, who thought he had gone insane. Emerson was "hissed and hooted" by Harvard law students when he spoke at Cambridge City Hall against Daniel Webster's defense of the Fugitive Slave Act of 1850.[47]

Influential Harvard affiliates were also busy bolstering slavery at the national level, with members of the Harvard Corporation and the board of overseers involved in passing the Fugitive Slave Act.[48] Congressman Samuel A. Eliot, Harvard's treasurer, voted for the bill—the only representative from Massachusetts to do so. Overseer and U.S. Senator Daniel Webster was a central figure in the Compromise of 1850, which included the Fugitive Slave Act. Corporation fellow Benjamin Curtis organized a rally at Faneuil Hall to honor Webster after the bill was passed; Harvard president Jared Sparks and future president Cornelius Felton were in the audience. Meanwhile, law school professors Theophilus Parsons and Joel Parker endorsed the Fugitive Slave Act in their classes.[49]

At the same time, in the 1850s, eight out of around thirty-five Harvard faculty members were involved to varying degrees with the antislavery movement. Among them was Charles Beck, who had fled from Germany to the United States with his friend Charles Follen in 1824.[50] He became a member of the Free-Soil Party (a short-lived party of the late 1840s and early 1850s dedicated to stopping the spread of slavery into western territories) upon leaving Harvard. His home, today part of Harvard's campus, was likely a stop on the Underground Railroad.[51] Henry Wadsworth Longfellow not only wrote poetry about the horrors of slavery but also aided fugitive slaves. Before joining Harvard's faculty, poet James Russell Lowell edited an abolitionist newspaper and later edited the influential magazine the *Atlantic Monthly*, which featured abolitionist articles. These faculty members were nonetheless "cautious by temperament and opposed to unnecessary controversy," particularly while they were at Harvard.[52]

In 1854 the mood shifted dramatically, making previously hushed antislavery sentiments publicly speakable. That year, the nation, and Massachusetts in particular, was shaken by the Anthony Burns case, which was pivotal in pushing northern opinion toward abolition. Burns, an escaped slave from Alexandria, Virginia, was living and working in Boston when he was remanded back to his owner under the terms of the Fugitive Slave Act. The decision was made by Judge Edward G. Loring, a member of Harvard's law faculty. Burns's capture became a rallying point for members of the antislavery Boston Vigilance Committee, which immediately distributed handbills opposing his arrest and urging noncompliance with the Fugitive Slave Act. The committee held a rally at a packed Faneuil Hall during which Wendell Phillips challenged Bostonians to show they were "worthy of liberty" by making sure Burns was not sent back to slavery.[53] A group including abolitionists Lewis Hayden and Thomas Wentworth Higginson attempted to rescue Burns from the courthouse.[54] After two U.S. marshals were killed in skirmishes, President Franklin Pierce sent in federal troops to make certain the act was upheld.

In *A Boston Ballad*, poet Walt Whitman admonished the gentlemen of Boston for inviting "government cannon" and "Federal foot and dragoons" to their city during the Burns incident. "You have got your revenge, old buster," he wrote. "The crown is come to its own / and more than its own." Old buster was King George III, and his revenge, according to Whitman, was that Boston gentlemen had come to embody and commit the kinds of high-handed injustices from which they had declared independence in 1776. By this time, Harriet Beecher Stowe's novel *Uncle Tom's Cabin* (1852) had filled the northern consciousness with images of the horrors of slavery, and the citizens of Massachusetts could imagine the fate that awaited Burns in Virginia. They were outraged by Loring's decision.

This outrage spilled over to Harvard: when Loring held class at the Law School, antislavery students hissed him, while southern students cheered him. A student from Georgia, Charles C. Jones, wrote to his father, "I could scarcely refrain from leaving my seat and forcibly ejecting from the room, by a stout application of boot leather, a puny scoundrel who was hissing in one corner of the room. But my respect for the school and myself forbade such a course."[55] In fact, Jones, along with other southern law students, served as bodyguards for Burns's master, Charles Suttle, during the trial.[56]

The indignation of Massachusetts's citizens over Loring's decision became so pervasive that within a year Harvard's board of overseers voted not to reappoint him at the Law School, despite the recommendation of the law faculty and the corporation that he be given a permanent lectureship. Unlike the corporation, which was controlled by a conservative Boston elite, the board of overseers had broader representation from across the state, including several antislavery members, a result of the political ground gained by the antislavery Free-Soil Party and the nativist Know-Nothing Party during the 1850s.[57] Passions over the board's decision ran so high that fistfights broke out among Harvard law students who were participating in a model congress.[58] The overseers also refused to confer an honorary degree on Samuel A. Eliot, Harvard's treasurer from 1842 to 1853, because of his vote in favor of the Fugitive Slave Act. Indeed, so quickly did Harvard's position shift that by 1859 it awarded honorary degrees to abolitionists Henry Wadsworth Longfellow and Charles Sumner.[59] As the prospect of disunion loomed, Harvard could no longer continue to appease southern slaveholders.

Even as antislavery sentiment built inside and outside the college, students from slaveholding states continued to be part of the undergraduate intellectual and social scene. Thomas Wentworth Higginson recalled from his undergraduate days at Harvard that "southern students were a noticeable element in the college" and favorites among Cambridge society: "They usually had charming manners, social aptitudes, imperious ways, abundant leisure, and plenty of money."[60] Like the elite families of Boston, many of South Carolina's first families sent their sons to Harvard. Charleston, South Carolina, a center of the slave trade and home to an elite class of planters, sent more than sixty-nine students between 1797 and 1845.[61] Before the abolition of the transatlantic slave trade, the majority of enslaved Africans came through the port of Charleston, and even after the trade was outlawed Charleston continued to be one of the main markets for the purchase and sale of American-born slaves.

The families that sent their sons to Harvard were among the upper echelons of Charleston society. One historian notes that these families wanted their sons to be "an ideal of an individual who was classically and liberally educated and who was supported economically by agricultural or liberal pursuits."[62] Harvard enjoyed the reputation of being one of the foremost educational institutions in the country and was considered superior to southern colleges. South Carolinian William H. Barnwell, for example, encouraged his cousin James B. Heyward to join him at Harvard: "They can teach more here in a year than they teach you there all your life." By 1850, almost twenty years after their graduation, Barnwell owned 671 slaves on four properties, and Heyward owned 378 slaves.[63]

As student researcher Hilary May discovered, Harvard not only provided the education that slaveholding families expected for their sons but also afforded an opportunity for them to forge relationships with northern elites. If southern students at Harvard were criticized or shunned because their families owned slaves, it was rarely written about. Instead, the records generally show students from slaveholding and nonslaveholding families sharing meals and housing and coalescing into one student body.[64] Only briefly in the contentious 1830s did students form a special southern club. Otherwise, southern students were less remarkable for their region than for their success on Harvard's social scene. Each year two or more of the eight to ten students selected to be part of Harvard's most exclusive social club, the Porcellian, came from southern families. Between 1797 and 1845 thirty-nine Porcellians called Charleston home.[65]

Southern students' successes do not implicate Harvard as an advocate of slavery. Rather, they reveal that for most of Harvard's history, slaveholding was not taboo. For many students, even those from the North, slaveholding was not a reason to cut off friendships, eat at separate tables, or join separate clubs. Slave owners were part of the nation's elite, and for members of that elite, the ownership of human property was unexceptional. After all, it had not been so long since members of the highest echelons of northern society had themselves owned slaves.

While Harvard's administration worked to quell debates on slavery, not least to accommodate the large population of student slave owners on campus, some of its professors worked diligently on an intellectual apparatus that helped justify slavery: the race science that claimed to prove black inferiority. While the American slave population had once been a mixture of Africans and Native Americans, slaves in the United States gradually became almost exclusively African, and blackness came to be seen as the basis for enslavement. In the nineteenth century, race was viewed as a biological category that marked people of African descent as inherently inferior to or fundamentally different from people perceived as white. Slaveholders and nonslaveholders alike believed that black people were inferior. In the 1850s these beliefs were inscribed into the field of natural science by a coterie of scholars. One of the most prominent was Harvard professor Louis Agassiz.

Agassiz wrote as a scientist, not as an advocate for slavery, yet his theories clearly legitimized slavery and were embraced by slaveholders. His 1850 article, "The Diversity of Origin of the Human Races," addressed a central concern of theorists of black inferiority by solving a vexing religious question. Slaveholders were endlessly conscious of the differences they perceived between themselves and their slaves, but they could not answer a recurring question: "If black people were inferior to, and fundamentally different from, white people," they were asked, "how could both races be descended from Adam?" Agassiz answered this by arguing that descent from Adam applied only to white people and that God had created other races to fit different climates, regions, and ecosystems.[66] Agassiz's theory was known as polygenesis, the idea that the human race had multiple origins. It derived its strengths not only from its preservation of Christian tenets but also from its association with Agassiz's renowned work on the origins of animal species. Agassiz used the prestige he had gained from his research on animal taxonomy to classify humans.[67]

Racial theories, however, were never solely about physical difference. As practiced by Agassiz, his peers, and later his students, race science turned personality traits, aptitudes, and morality into biological characteristics of "race." Agassiz's analysis of physical differences included his conclusions about the "negro disposition." "Human affairs with reference to the colored races," wrote Agassiz, should be "guided by a full consciousness of the real difference existing between us and them . . . rather than be treating them with equality."[68] Among these differences were an African "pliability . . . a proneness to imitate those among who he lives" and a "peculiar apathy, a peculiar indifference to the advantages afforded by civilized society."[69] These "traits" were considered to exist independently and objectively, somehow unrelated to the situation in which Africans and African Americans sold into slavery lived and worked.

Agassiz's ideas about natural history, particularly his theories about black difference, remained influential for almost a century after his death and set the tone at Harvard for decades after slavery's abolition. In 1869 Agassiz's student Nathaniel Shaler became a professor at Harvard and continued his mentor's study of the differences between "African and European races."[70] Like Agassiz, Shaler popularized his science, writing articles for magazines like the *Atlantic Monthly*. In one 1890 article Shaler argued against interracial marriage.[71] In another piece he cautioned against reformers who considered black people equal to whites. "They are charmed by their admirable and appealing qualities, and so make haste to assume that he [*sic*] is in all respects like themselves." This was risky, Shaler warned, because as black children entered adulthood, their "animal nature" emerged.[72] Shaler did not advocate a return to slavery, but his writing came during the Jim Crow era, when many of the rights extended to black Americans after the Civil War were being denied or annulled. Shaler was not an isolated or powerless voice; he counted among his associates Theodore Roosevelt, a former student who stayed in close touch after graduating from Harvard.[73]

Agassiz's Harvard contemporary, botanist Asa Gray, opposed Agassiz and lent his scientific name to the idea of the unity of all races. An early and insightful defender of evolution, Gray welcomed Charles Darwin's evidence for the common origins of human populations. His famous controversy with Agassiz over Darwin had a lasting impact on American science. However, as the more captivating and glamorous personality and someone who used the prestige of his Harvard post to great advantage, Agassiz had more impact on popular attitudes.[74] Agassiz's theories of racial distinctions appeared in both general and scientific writing, as well as in popular culture, which ensured and extended their afterlife. Ideas about a "negro disposition" and inherent lack of interest in civilized life lingered, making images like the Zealy daguerreotypes not artifacts of a long-ago past but the long shadows of events that still trouble the present.

Slavery in Memory

In 1880 abolitionist and Harvard alumnus Thomas Wentworth Higginson delivered an oration at the 250th anniversary celebration of the founding of Cambridge in Harvard's recently built Memorial Hall. In considering the execution of the slaves Mark and Phillis, Higginson remarked, "When we think that this fearful tragedy took place but one hundred and twenty-five years ago, and that it does not seem to have created a protest or a ripple in public opinion, shall we not be charitable to those communities in which the virus of slavery has worked far more profoundly and more recently than with our fathers?"[75] While Higginson's remark reflects the reconciliatory spirit that buried Reconstruction, it makes an important point: the North was complicit with slavery, and casting stones at the South did not address this. Yet the silence around northern slavery and Harvard's part in it persists to this day. Student researcher Robert Mann, for example, found that Harvard president

Josiah Quincy's fulsome encomium for the business integrity of slave trader James Perkins still graced the benefactor's biography in the 1991 official *History of Named Chairs*, with no mention of Perkins's slave trading and opium trafficking.[76]

Like the nation, Harvard bore the stamp of slavery long after its abolition. When in October 1903, for example, Harvard botanist Oakes Ames arrived at the former Cuban slave plantation Soledad, fifteen years had passed since that country's slaves gained their freedom.[77] The nine-hundred-acre plantation, a gift to Harvard from Edwin Farnsworth Atkins, would become a biological research station for the university. In future years, scholars and students would test different varieties of sugarcane there as they tried to eradicate plant diseases that destroyed cane fields.[78] In 1903 Ames was inspired to reflect on the plantation's past. While gazing at the sunset, he heard the plantation bell toll "one single, musical but dull note." Disquiet stole over Ames as he imagined how the bell would have sounded to a plantation slave, calling him to "the awful reality of his existence." What upset Ames was the incongruity between the beauty of the plantation, its new scientific future, and the raw injustice that had cleared its lands and secured its owner's fortune. In a letter to his wife, Ames eased his burden by scolding his predecessors who did not protest the "atrocities of holding in bondage one's fellow man . . . aided by the stinging lash, which injures one far deeper than bronze or steel."[79]

Ames tried to dispel the ghost of slavery by neatly separating Soledad's past and present, but many of the people who worked on the plantation's grounds then remembered the days of slavery. Contravening Ames, the student researchers in the Harvard and Slavery seminars proved how futile—at best—and disingenuous—at worst—attempts to consign slavery to the past are. Slavery's long and deep legacy accumulated in resources and institutions that extended well beyond individual lifetimes. Slavery, the student researchers realized, played a significant role in Harvard's development, just as it did in American history more generally.[80] And perhaps it is exactly slavery's importance that underlies the many decades of silence around Harvard's connections to it. Harvard is arguably the flagship university of the United States. If it is entangled with the practices of slavery and benefited financially from slave labor, what long-lived American institution has not? How do we understand this, especially as we begin to consider what steps could redress this terrible inheritance?

The Harvard and Slavery Research Project has uncovered some of the buried truth of the university's history and begun to examine the silence surrounding it. Student researcher Kaitlin Terry found that Elmwood, the Harvard president's residence, has been recognized as a historical site, yet its slavery connections are left out of its history. Brandi Waters found that Warren House, the Harvard-owned building that may have been a stop on the Underground Railroad, was unmarked; indeed, until 2016 there was no marker of any kind on Harvard's campus that acknowledged slavery or the historical presence of slaves. Though the Civil War had everything to do with slavery, only one modest inscription—added to the exterior of Memorial Hall well after its completion in 1891—mentioned slavery.[81]

Student researchers have struck veins that must be mined further. More archival research could be done, for example, on how the campus was built, where slave labor was employed, and which Harvard affiliates owned slaves.[82] A more sustained study on Harvard's role in enforcing colonial slavery—through the offices and influence of its graduates in trade, in government, or in the pulpit—would contribute much to understanding Harvard's ongoing role as an elite institution working on behalf of the elites who sustained it. Gary Staudt's work on the origins of the endowment could be expanded to answer the question of how dependent Harvard was on the slave trade and slavery to amass its capital. While historian Ronald Story has shown how Harvard was supported by merchant profits in the early nineteenth century, further research is needed to tease out the specific weight of slavery and the slave trade in that financial boon. Eric Williams, Joseph Inikori, and other scholars have made the argument that the West's great advantage in accumulating wealth was partly the result of the profits from slavery. Could this be true of Harvard's vast endowment as well?

There are also many questions surrounding the Civil War. Eric Andersen engaged Harvard's contribution to defining the legacy of the war by studying Memorial Hall.[83] Post facto, Harvard claimed a part in Unionist and even abolitionist sentiment, but as other students' work revealed, Harvard was anything but abolitionist before the war.[84] And the documented incidents surrounding abolitionist faculty, antislavery debates, and North-South contentions in the period are probably not the only incidents that reveal Harvard's attitude toward slavery. More could be done, for instance, to trace Harvard's equivocal stance before the war, the economic and social roots of that stance, and its influence on contemporary opinion.

Hilary May's paper on Charlestonians at Harvard offers another way to think about Harvard's influence. The relatively large number of antebellum planter elites who attended Harvard opens the question of Harvard's influence on southern opinion, as Harvard graduates occupied the strata of South Carolina society in which secession was most thoroughly and purposefully developed. Zoe Weinberg's important work on Louis Agassiz's "race science" raises broader questions about Harvard's mixed record in furthering racism after slavery. These research efforts—and many more—enhance our understanding of Harvard's role in the complex social, economic, and cultural impact of American slavery and slavery's role at Harvard.

The Harvard and Slavery Research Project has been more than a scholarly endeavor. From the start, many of the students worked to engage the Harvard community with what they were learning about the university's history. And they succeeded, engaging broader audiences, audiences that included the leadership of Harvard. They have also raised the question of what happens next. If an acknowledgment can be made that slavery played a role in Harvard's development, what consequences flow from that acknowledgment? Should Harvard publicly recognize its complicity in slavery in some way? What programs or educational centers might be developed to research and focus attention on these questions? What forms of restitution, if any, might be appropriate? We have formed no easy consensus on these questions.

Harvard has tremendous prestige and resources. We have seen that these advantages were in part accrued from a relationship with the institutions and practices of slavery: slave labor was employed; land and other endowments were derived from slavery's bounty; the ideas of slaveholders were tolerated, legitimized, and furthered by the university's intellectual capital. Harvard has at times played a role in sustaining the institutions and legacy of slavery. The Harvard and Slavery Research Project has worked to illuminate the university's and the country's troubling past and to find ways to come to grips with this history. Perhaps these efforts, along with those at other universities, will bring us closer to a broad recognition of the central role slavery played in building the United States and thus closer to an understanding of our collective responsibilities and obligation to seek justice.[85]

NOTES

1. See Molly Rogers, *Delia's Tears: Race, Science, and Photography in Nineteenth-Century America* (New Haven, Conn.: Yale University Press, 2010); Frederick Douglass, "The Claims of the Negro Ethnologically Considered, Address Delivered at Western Reserve College, July 12, 1854," in *The Life and Writings of Frederick Douglass*, ed. Philip S. Foner (New York: International Publishers, 1950), 2:289–309.

2. Rogers, *Delia's Tears*, 5.

3. See *Gletscherforscher, Rassist: Louis Agassiz, 1807–2013*, exhibit, Museum Grindelwald, Grindelwald, Switzerland, 2012; Mary Carmichael, "Louis Agassiz Exhibit Divides Harvard, Swiss Group," *Boston Globe*, June 27, 2012; "Harvard Should Openly Discuss Louis Agassiz and His Racial Attitude," editorial, *Boston Globe*, July 5, 2012.

4. For the sesquicentennial observation, see Corydon Ireland, "Blue, Gray and Crimson," *Harvard Gazette*, March 21, 2012.

5. Samuel Eliot Morison, *Three Centuries of Harvard* (1936; Cambridge, Mass.: Belknap Press of Harvard University Press, 1964), 303.

6. Ibid., 302–3, 287. As this quotation indicates, Morison himself was contemptuous of radical abolitionists. His mid-twentieth-century U.S. history textbooks have become notorious as well for dismissing and misrepresenting the experiences of enslaved people.

7. Parts of this essay are drawn from the report, which can be downloaded at www.harvardandslavery.com/wp-content/uploads/2011/11/Harvard-Slavery-Book-111110.pdf.

8. See the student paper by Shelley Thomas, "Chains in the Yard: A Discussion of Slave Owners and Slave Life on Harvard's Campus between 1636 and 1780"; and Sven Beckert, Katherine Stevens, and students of the Harvard and Slavery Research Seminar, "Harvard and Slavery: Seeking a Forgotten History" (Cambridge, Mass., 2011), 37 pp., http://www.harvardandslavery.com/wp-content/uploads/2011/11/Harvard-Slavery-Book-111110.pdf.

9. See the references included in Beckert and Stevens, "Harvard and Slavery," especially reference 7.

10. Ira Berlin, *Generations of Captivity: A History of African American Slaves* (Cambridge, Mass.: Harvard University Press, 2003).

11. For details of the trial, see Abner Cheney Goodell Jr., *The Trial and Execution for Petit Treason of Mark and Phillis, Slaves of Capt. John Codman* (Cambridge, Mass.: John Wilson and Son, University Press, 1883). See also the student paper by Jim Henle, "Harvard and the Law of Slavery: The Execution of Mark and Phillis, 1755," henle@fas.harvard.edu.

12. A. Leon Higginbotham, *In the Matter of Color: Race and the American Legal Process; The Colonial Period* (New York: Oxford University Press, 1978), 81.

13. Morison, *Three Centuries of Harvard*, 96.

14. See Barbara J. Fields, "Ideology and Race in American History," in *Region, Race, and Reconstruction: Essays in Honor of C. Vann Woodward*, ed. Morgan J. Koussar and

James McPherson (New York: Oxford University Press, 1982), 143–77; "Slavery, Race and Ideology in the United States of America," *New Left Review* 181 (May/June 1990): 95–118.

15. Morison, *Three Centuries of Harvard*, 60.

16. As quoted in George H. Moore, *Notes on the History of Slavery in Massachusetts* (New York: D. Appleton & Co., 1866), 110.

17. Student paper by Kaitlin Terry, "Elmwood and Slavery: Confronting Harvard's Hidden History with Full Authenticity"; see also Beckert and Stevens, "Harvard and Slavery."

18. C. S. Manegold, *Ten Hills Farm: The Forgotten History of Slavery in the North* (Princeton, N.J.: Princeton University Press, 2010), 143.

19. See the student paper by Gary Pelissier, "Harvard's Royall Legacy: Slavery and the Origins of the Harvard Law School"; see also Beckert and Stevens, "Harvard and Slavery."

20. The fortune of Henry Vassall, whose mansion on Brattle Street's Tory Row was commandeered by the rebels during the Revolutionary War, came from sugar plantations on Jamaica. He married Penelope Royall in 1742. Manegold, *Ten Hills Farm*, 175.

21. See the student paper by Gary Staudt, "Slavery and the Early Investment Strategies of Harvard University's Endowment"; see also Beckert and Stevens, "Harvard and Slavery"; Margery Somers Foster, *"Out of Smalle Beginnings...": An Economic History of Harvard College in the Puritan Period (1636–1712)* (Cambridge, Mass.: Belknap Press of Harvard University Press, 1962), 28–29, 158–59; Gary Staudt, "Slavery and the Early Investment Strategies of Harvard University's Endowment" (ALM thesis, Harvard University, 2013).

22. Staudt, "Slavery," 18.

23. See Emily Blanck, "Seventeen Eighty-Three: The Turning Point in the Law of Slavery and Freedom in Massachusetts," *New England Quarterly* 75 (2002): 24–51.

24. "A Forensic Debate on the Legality of Enslaving the Africans, Held at the Public Commencement in Cambridge, New England (Boston 1773)," in *Blacks at Harvard: A Documentary History of African-American Experience at Harvard and Radcliffe*, ed. Werner Sollors, Caldwell Titcomb, and Thomas A. Underwood (New York: New York University Press, 1993), 11–19.

25. Ibid., 11.

26. Not all, of course. In 1771 the Tory governor of Massachusetts Bay Colony, Thomas Hutchinson, vetoed "a bill prohibiting the importation of Negro slaves into Massachusetts" on the grounds that such slaves were not qualitatively different from indentured servants; see Bernard Bailyn, *The Ordeal of Thomas Hutchinson* (Cambridge, Mass.: Belknap Press of Harvard University Press, 1974), 378.

27. Joanne Pope Melish, *Disowning Slavery: Gradual Emancipation and "Race" in New England, 1780–1860* (Ithaca, N.Y.: Cornell University Press, 1998).

28. Ronald Story, *The Forging of an Aristocracy: Harvard and the Boston Upper Class, 1800–1870* (Middleton, Conn.: Wesleyan University Press, 1980), 56.

29. Josiah Quincy, *The History of Harvard University* (Cambridge, Mass.: John Owen, 1840), 2:429.

30. L. Vernon Briggs, *History and Genealogy of the Cabot Family, 1475–1927* (Boston: C. E. Goodspeed & Co., 1927), 410; see also the student paper by Robert G. Mann, "Money and Memory: The Perkins Family Legacy," 13.

31. Mann, "Money and Memory," 2.

32. "The Late Abbott Lawrence," *Daily National Intelligencer*, August 23, 1855, 257.

33. The value of total major individual donations comes from Samuel A. Eliot, *A Sketch of the History of Harvard College and of Its Present State* (Boston: C. C. Little and J. Brown, 1848); Harvard University, gifts and bequests, 1638–1870, comp. A. T. Gibbs, 1877, Harvard University Archives, Cambridge, Massachusetts; see also the student paper by Meike Schallert, "The Forging of a University: How Harvard Benefited from the Slave-Economy, 1800–1850," 7, 32.

34. Mann, "Money and Memory," 22.

35. *Boston Gazette* excerpted in *Gloucester Telegraph*, July 3, 1834.

36. Josiah Quincy to John Gorham Palfrey, May 25, 1838, Josiah Quincy Papers, Harvard University Archives.

37. See the student papers by Balraj Gill, "Harvard and Its Abolitionists: How Debates on Slavery and the Emergence of Radical Abolitionism Shaped Policy at the University in the 1830s," and Learah Lockhart, "The Apprehensions of the President: President Josiah Quincy's Interference in a Debate on Abolition in Harvard's Divinity School," cited in Beckert and Stevens, "Harvard and Slavery."

38. Wendell Phillips's family tree included Samuel Phillips Jr., founder of the elite private school Phillips Academy, and John Phillips, founder of Phillips Exeter Academy; his father was John Phillips, the first mayor of Boston, who served from 1822 to 1823. Thomas Wentworth Higginson was the son of merchant and philanthropist Stephen Higginson, the steward of Harvard from 1818 to 1838. Henry and William Ingersoll Bowditch were the sons of Nathaniel Bowditch, a member of the Harvard Corporation from 1826 to 1838 and one of the highest paid business executives in the country during his tenure as actuary and investment manager at the Massachusetts Hospital Life Insurance Company. Edmund Quincy was the son of Josiah Quincy, the second mayor of Boston (1823–28) and president of Harvard from 1829 to 1845.

39. *Boston Commercial Gazette*, October 22, 1835, as quoted in Theodore M. Hammett, "Two Mobs of Jacksonian Boston: Ideology and Interest," *Journal of American History* 62, no. 4 (March 1976): 846.

40. Elijah Lovejoy (1802–37), originally from Maine, was the editor of the *St. Louis Observer*, a Presbyterian newsletter, and published his antislavery writings in it. He was killed by a mob in Alton, Illinois, that had gathered to destroy his printing press. No one was convicted of the murder.

41. Louis Menand, *The Metaphysical Club: A Story of Ideas in America* (New York: Farrar, Straus and Giroux, 2001), 25–26.

42. Charles Sumner, "Union among Men of All Parties against the Slave Power and the

Extension of Slavery, Speech before a Mass Convention at Worcester, June 28, 1848," in *The Works of Charles Sumner* (Boston: Lee and Shepard, 1875), 2:81.

43. As quoted in R. Kent Newmyer, *Supreme Court Justice Joseph Story: Statesman of the Old Republic* (Chapel Hill: University of North Carolina Press, 1986), 356.

44. Menand, *The Metaphysical Club*, 11, as quoted by Carla Bosco, "Harvard University and the Fugitive Slave Act," *New England Quarterly* 79, no. 2 (June 2006): 233.

45. John T. Cumbler, *From Abolition to Rights for All: The Making of a Reform Community in the Nineteenth Century* (Philadelphia: University of Pennsylvania Press, 2008), 47.

46. Ibid., 38.

47. Morison, *Three Centuries of Harvard*, 290.

48. Carla Bosco, "When Harvard University Came to Support the Abolitionist Cause," *Journal of Blacks in Higher Education* 54 (Winter 2006–7): 76–77.

49. Bosco, "Harvard University and the Fugitive Slave Act," 237.

50. As university students, Beck and Follen were involved in the Burschenschaft, a student association and movement that came out of the wars against the Napoleonic occupation of Germany. They agitated for a German republic and liberal freedoms and increasingly came under political persecution. Unable to find work because of his views, Follen went to Paris in 1819 and eventually to Basel, Switzerland, where he met Beck. Beck, also unable to find work, had joined his stepfather, Wilhelm de Wette, at the University of Basel in 1824. When the German Confederation demanded Follen's extradition because of his revolutionary activity, the two left for the United States in November 1824.

51. See the student paper by Brandi Waters, "Interstitial Memory: Exploring the Underground Railroad in Harvard's Warren House."

52. Story, *The Forging of an Aristocracy*, 78.

53. Gordon S. Baker, *The Imperfect Revolution: Anthony Burns and the Landscape of Race in Antebellum America* (Kent, Ohio: Kent State University Press, 2010), 11.

54. Lewis Hayden was a fugitive slave and a militant abolitionist in Boston's black community on Beacon Hill.

55. Charles C. Jones to Rev. and Mrs. C. C. Jones, June 13, 1854, in *The Children of Pride: A True Story of Georgia and the Civil War*, ed. Robert Manson Myers (New Haven, Conn.: Yale University Press, 1972), 45, as quoted in Bosco, "Harvard University and the Fugitive Slave Act," 244.

56. Ibid.

57. See Earl M. Maltz, *Fugitive Slave on Trial: The Anthony Burns Case and Abolitionist Outrage* (Lawrence: University Press of Kansas, 2010), 108–33.

58. Bosco, "Harvard University and the Fugitive Slave Act," 227.

59. Bosco, "When Harvard University Came to Support," 81.

60. As quoted in ibid., 75, 76.

61. Harvard University, Faculty Records, copies of minutes, vol. 9, 1814–22, Harvard University Archives; *Catalogue of the Honorary and Immediate Members of the Porcel-*

lian Club, Harvard University, Cambridge: Instituted in 1791 (Cambridge, Mass.: Hilliard, Metcalf & Co., 1828); student paper by Hilary May, "A True Southern Gentleman: Charlestonians at Harvard in the Antebellum Period," 1.

62. Maurie D. McInnis, *The Politics of Taste in Antebellum Charleston* (Chapel Hill: University of North Carolina Press, 2005), 10.

63. William Kauffman Scarborough, *Masters of the Big House: Elite Slaveholders of the Mid-Nineteenth-Century South* (Baton Rouge: Louisiana State University Press, 2003), 66, 443, 437.

64. See, for example, James Clark, "An Undergraduate's Diary," *Harvard Graduates' Magazine*, March and June 1913, 641; see also the student paper by Matthew Chuchul, "Camaraderie and Complicity: The Role of Harvard in Forging Bonds of Friendship between Northern and Southern Harvard Students in the Decade before the Civil War," 19.

65. *Catalogue of the Honorary and Immediate*, 18–19; May, "True Southern Gentleman," 11–12. Southern students typically made up around 10 percent of Harvard students, meaning they were slightly overrepresented at 20 to 30 percent in the Porcellian.

66. Louis Agassiz, "Diversity of Origin of the Human Races," *Christian Examiner and Religious Miscellany* 49, no. 2 (1850): 138.

67. Agassiz was a staunch opponent of Darwinian evolution.

68. Agassiz, "Diversity of Origin," 144.

69. Louis Agassiz to Samuel G. Howe, August 9, 1863, in *Louis Agassiz: His Life and Correspondence*, by Agassiz and Elizabeth Cabot Cary Agassiz (London: Macmillan, 1885), 597–98; see also the student paper by Zoe Weinberg, "The Incalculable Legacy: Race Science at Harvard in the 19th and 20th Centuries," 10–11.

70. *Harvard Gazette*, May 18, 1906.

71. Nathaniel Southgate Shaler, "Science and the African Problem," *Atlantic Monthly*, July 1890, 66, 37.

72. Nathaniel Southgate Shaler, "The Negro Problem," *Atlantic Monthly*, November 1884, 54, 698; Weinberg, "The Incalculable Legacy," 16.

73. "Last Tribute Paid," newspaper unknown, 1906, Nathaniel Southgate Shaler Biographical Folder, Harvard University Archives.

74. For background on Agassiz's scientific views, see Ernst Mayr, "Agassiz, Darwin, and Evolution," *Harvard Library Bulletin* 13 (1959): 165–94. Mayr notes that Agassiz's scientific upbringing in Romanticism-influenced Germany predisposed him against evolution and encouraged the search for ideal types, not historical links. If this was the case, it is certain that Agassiz's ideal type of human was "whites." A summary of the reception of his ideas can be found in Elaine Claire Daughetee Wolfe, "Acceptance of the Theory of Evolution in America: Louis Agassiz vs. Asa Gray," *American Biology Teacher* 37 (1975): 244–47. The late Harvard professor Stephen Jay Gould wrote a definitive critique of scientific racism in *The Mismeasure of Man* (New York: Norton, 1981).

75. Thomas Wentworth Higginson, "Oration by Thomas Wentworth Higginson," in

Exercises in Celebrating the Two Hundred and Fiftieth Anniversary of the Settlement of Cambridge, Held December 28, 1880 (Cambridge, Mass.: Charles W. Sever, University Bookstore, 1881), 55.

76. Harvard University, *History of Named Chairs: Sketches of Donors and Donations* (Cambridge, Mass.: Secretary to the University, 1991).

77. Rebecca Scott, "A Cuban Connection: Edwin F. Atkins, Charles Francis Adams, Jr., and Former Slaves of Soledad Plantation," *Massachusetts Historical Review* 9 (2007): 7–34.

78. The gift of the plantation is recorded in "Treasurer's Statement 1926–1927 Gifts for Immediate Use," Annual Reports of President/Treasurer of Harvard University (1826–1995), Harvard University Archives online, http://hul.harvard.edu/huarc/refshelf/AnnualReports.htm. On cane disease, see Mrs. Edwin F. Atkins to Tom Barbour, Botanic Garden in Cuba Directors Correspondence (1898–1946), Harvard University Archives; see the student paper by Alexandra Rahman, "'A Very Plain Business Man': Edward Farnsworth Atkins and the Birth of the Harvard Botanical Station Soledad," 16–18.

79. Oakes Ames to Blanche Adams, January 11, 1903, Papers of Oakes Ames, Letters to His Family and Autobiographical Writing (MSS) (1902–49), Harvard University Archives; Rahman, "Harvard Botanical Station," 1, 18.

80. There is a series of important debates as to the exact nature and extent of the contribution. See Eric Williams, *Capitalism and Slavery* (1944; Chapel Hill: University of North Carolina Press, 1994); Joseph Inikori, *Africans and the Industrial Revolution in England* (Cambridge: Cambridge University Press, 2002).

81. The class of 1844 had a shield added in honor of their classmate Brigadier General Edward A. Wild. The inscription says, "A faithful and gallant soldier in the war that preserved the Union and destroyed slavery."

82. Student researcher Mona McKinley's inventory of slave owning in "In Ignorance of Their Own Power: Slave Owners, Slave Merchants, and Abolitionists at Harvard College, 1636–1790" is an important contribution to this history.

83. Eric Andersen, "Harvard's Memorial Hall and the Committee of Fifty: Conservatism, Abolition and Preserving the Union" (master's thesis, Harvard Extension School, Harvard University, 2015).

84. See student papers by Balraj Gill, Justin Harbour, John Kennebeck, Learah Lockhart, Robert G. Mann, Meike Schallert, and Liane Speroni, cited in Beckert and Stevens, "Harvard and Slavery."

85. See also Sven Beckert and Seth Rockman, eds., *Slavery's Capitalism: A New History of American Economic Development* (Philadelphia: University of Pennsylvania Press, 2016).

CHAPTER THIRTEEN

Scholars, Lawyers, and Their Slaves

St. George and Nathaniel Beverley Tucker
in the College Town of Williamsburg

Ywone D. Edwards-Ingram

St. George Tucker and Nathaniel Beverley Tucker taught law at the College of William and Mary in Williamsburg, Virginia, with tenures covering the years 1788–1804 and 1834–51, respectively, following the American Revolution and before the American Civil War. A review of the case of these two professors, judges, and lawyers, St. George (1752–1827) and his son Nathaniel, commonly called Beverley (1784–1851), demonstrates how the focus on the individual achievements of great white men and the priority given to the years around the American Revolution influence public history and representations of slavery at the college and the adjacent living-history museum of Colonial Williamsburg. It also provides a perspective to examine how practices in commemorations surrounding the selective nature of preservation, restoration, and nomenclature have contributed to the virtual invisibility of the African American cultural heritage on Williamsburg's built historic townscape.[1]

The built landscapes of American heritage are employed predominantly to visualize and promote knowledge about the accomplishments of notable whites. There is far less emphasis on informing the public about the involvements of other groups of people and in making their lifeways known within their own rights. This is the case for the college's historic campus, the site of three major historical buildings, and the situation is similar for the St. George Tucker House, where the Tuckers lived with enslaved people, now a restored property in Colonial Williamsburg.[2]

Both the college and Colonial Williamsburg invoke American heritage through literary genres, performances, and built spaces, with specific references to illustrious white men like St. George Tucker (but less so to Beverley Tucker); Thomas Jefferson, an American founding father and president who

St. George Tucker (1752–1827) by Bethuel Moore (1902–65), after Charles Balthazar Saint-Mémin (1770–1852). Courtesy of Special Collections Research Center, William and Mary Libraries.

Nathaniel Beverley Tucker (1784–1851) by Bethuel Moore (1902–65), after Joseph Wood (probably 1778–1830). Courtesy of Special Collections Research Center, William and Mary Libraries.

attended the college; and George Wythe, its first professor of law, who was a signer of the Declaration of Independence. Jefferson and St. George Tucker studied law with Wythe, whose restored home is near the Tucker House. With the focus on the deeds of white men, like these famous students and teachers of the college and their links to the American Revolution, public history in Williamsburg has inspired the preservation and re-creation of historic landscapes that have underrepresented the complexities of the social and material world of slavery and, consequently, have resulted in interpretations that have minimized the histories and cultural heritages of lesser-known individuals and groups.[3]

In *Representations of Slavery: Race and Ideology in Southern Plantation Museums*, Jennifer L. Eichstedt and Stephen Small provide an insightful discussion about the strategies and settings that have framed knowledge about the American past and diminished the contributions of specific groups of people. They identify individualism as a major concept in historical narrations that continues to perpetuate a guarded history: "The idea that the hard work and effort of individual (white) Americans is what made them successful is foundational to American mythology. Individualism demands that individuals create their own destiny from the sweat of their own brow; if we openly discuss or challenge this notion by pointing out that most of America's great white heroes in fact made their wealth from the theft of land from Native Americans and the forced labor of African Americans, then the mythological status of individualism is seriously undermined." Following Eichstedt and Small, what is usually suppressed at many historical sites is the information that "African Americans provided wealth for many great historical figures and lesser-known individuals alike." Many historical sites and museums are challenged in their efforts to provide interpretations that balance the individual and the community, and perhaps this, too, is at the heart of the ongoing struggles in universities to deal with their own histories and legacies of slavery.[4]

Until recently, William and Mary resembled historic universities and colleges that largely have ignored their histories and legacies of slavery and predominantly have omitted such links from their profiles. The college has changed its apathetic position, especially since 2009, when it publicly acknowledged its ties to slavery and started seeking ways to deal with its legacies. Its historic campus came under particular scrutiny as an important place associated with slave labor. This core boasts the college's main historic building, dating from 1695, called the Sir Christopher Wren Building (the Wren),

WILLIAM AND MARY COLLEGE AT WILLIAMSBURG.

This image of the historic campus by Thomas Millington includes the Brafferton, the Sir Christopher Wren Building, and the President's House. It is known as the Millington Print and was completed sometime in the 1840s or in 1850. Courtesy of Special Collections Research Center, William and Mary Libraries.

named in recognition of its putative designer. This imposing brick structure served as residence, dining area, office, and classroom for over three centuries. It is still being used for classroom and office spaces. The Wren keeps company with two other historic structures: the Brafferton (1723), which was an Indian school in the eighteenth century, and the President's House (1732), which has served as the residence for the college's presidents over the years. These three buildings are venerated for their historic and ongoing significance to the college.[5]

The historic campus's association with slavery is still not fully articulated in these acts of acknowledgment. For example, tours of the Wren present the college's history as strongly focused on its imposing architecture, functions, and contents. This information is imparted within a landscape where there are few secondary structures to incorporate with the primary ones in presentations about slavery. In the eighteenth and nineteenth centuries, there were several outbuildings in the college yards.[6]

The interpretive narratives vested in stories and displayed portraits of individuals pertinent to William and Mary's history and development overwhelm any attention given to enslaved people who belonged to the college, worked there as hired laborers, or were personal servants of the students or the faculty. The visual displays at the Wren mainly represent illustrious figures like the college's first president, James Blair, who served from 1693 to 1743; the British royals for whom the college is named; American presidents who attended the institution; and other famous Virginians buried in the crypt of its chapel. In April 2018 the college moved to diversify this space by adding two plaques on the Wren's back portico. One honors Lynn Briley, Karen Ely, and Janet Brown Strafer, who were in residence at the college in September 1967 and became the first African Americans to graduate from there. The second plaque pays tribute to the twenty-four women whose enrollment in September 1918 made the institution the first coeducational university in Virginia.[7]

The Wren was among the earliest buildings to be reconstructed in the late 1920s as part of the restoration of the core area of eighteenth-century Williamsburg to the time when it was the capital of Virginia. The restoration tied the historic campus to the newly created Colonial Williamsburg. This heritage development was realized through the vision and work of the Reverend W. A. R. Goodwin, a local clergyman, and the enterprise and dedication of John D. Rockefeller Jr., a philanthropic millionaire. Colonial Williamsburg was designed to teach and advance knowledge about patriotism and nation building in its interpretation of the townscape, which was restored to represent the time around the American Revolution. From its early years, Colonial Williamsburg has involved representations of slavery and its legacies. These dotted exemplifications were partly directed through the largely unacknowledged but highly visible African American presenters and interpreters in exhibition areas such as kitchens and trade shops and through coachmen on the streets manning carriage rides, as well as the many representatives of this group working in hospitality, construction, and maintenance. Notwithstanding, the major buildings and the wider landscape were not used effectively to tell about the most distinguishing factor of the eighteenth-century town, namely, slavery. The museum did not treat this as a priority in its public history.[8]

From the 1960s but with far more impetus toward the late 1970s, the museum started to systematically develop stated goals, invest resources, and institute programs giving more attention to "community" and "lesser-known people" of the past. It not only promoted interpretations of slavery through character portrayals, vignettes, and music programs but also featured these offerings at a slave quarters, opened in 1988, at the Carter's Grove Plantation about seven miles from the town. More provocative programming in town included the reenactment of an estate sale featuring a slave auction in 1994 and a year-long Enslaving Virginia Storyline interpretive initiative in 1999.[9]

By 2003 Colonial Williamsburg had launched Great Hopes Plantation as an interpretive space on the outskirts of its main historic core. It includes offerings similar to those of Carter's Grove Plantation, which was no longer in operation. Within the created rural landscape of Great Hopes, Colonial Williamsburg introduced structures like slave quarters, a corn crib, and a barn and areas of fields and pastures directed to interpreting middling planters and their slaves. This built landscape contrasts with the adjacent urban setting of the museum's main historic area, which strongly visualizes the white gentry's history. However, the museum achieves varying levels of inclusion of slavery through interpretations at selected sites and within different programs, especially the presentations of the African American interpreters. The Revolutionary City program, which started in 2006, has revitalized the interpretations in the historic core of the museum. Its street theater and auxiliary offerings provided a broader representation of the town's eighteenth-century inhabitants and an affecting way to understand the main issues and events surrounding the American Revolution. More recently, the museum has presented its programs without such encompassing programming.[10]

Colonial Williamsburg's eighteenth-century priority influences the college's public history, resulting in the latter's strong focus on this period, too. During the years leading up to the American Civil War, the college had strategically fueled proslavery and secessionist thoughts and defenses, especially through the teachings and writings of professors like Thomas Roderick Dew, president from 1836 to 1846 (who started teaching there in the 1820s), and Beverley Tucker. The attention given to colonial history mostly trumps consideration of the antebellum period. Beverley is best known for his secessionist novel, *The Partisan Leader* (1836), which described events similar to the Civil War. The novel "predicts that the South one day will secede from the Union because of the growing tyranny of a northern-dominated federal government." His story represents another approach to the rhetoric of equality, liberty, and justice.[11]

William and Mary and Colonial Williamsburg are invested in presenting a comprehensive and knowable history of Williamsburg. This study of the Tuckers and their slaves is encapsulated in this realm. The Tuckers outlined their views of slavery in speeches and writings formed in the crucible of the college, albeit from different perspectives: St. George proposed steps to abolish slavery, while Beverley agitated to keep it in place. Nevertheless, their dealings with people of African descent exhibited profound similarities. Both owned, sold, and managed slaves as they expounded education at the college and at the Tucker House.

The College, the Town, and Slavery

The history of William and Mary, founded in 1693 by a British royal charter, typifies the central role of slavery in educational institutions. The finances for its establishment and upkeep for many years, including scholarships for students, came from payments on tobacco and other products gained through slave labor. Well into the nineteenth century, the college perpetuated slavery and derived benefits from slave labor on campus and at a college-owned plantation, as well as through hiring out and selling enslaved people. Both anti- and proslavery sentiments at the college and in its adjacent town were predicated on the expectations that slavery would provide both the foundation and the pathway to economic wealth and social prestige.[12]

The symbiotic relationship of the college and the town started before Williamsburg was designated the capital, replacing Jamestown. This move was strongly predicated on economic and social benefits for both entities. Some of the college students were involved in the movement to persuade the colonial legislature to relocate its seat of government to the nascent town. One student pointed to the growing interdependency in the social and economic relations of these two entities, with each potentially supporting the well-being of the other. It was probably widely assumed that slavery would guarantee the growing vibrancy of this locality. For the next two centuries, the town and the college twined as together they experienced disasters and triumphs, including military invasions, occupations, and victories, and as they fought for preservation in war and peace.[13]

Nowhere is the association with the town more evident than in the college's historic campus, especially at the Wren. The Wren, built between 1695 and 1700, dates to the period when Virginia was developing into a full-fledged slave society. Therefore, this building was most likely built with slave labor. Following the arrival of the twenty or more Africans in the colony in 1619, Africans and their descendants gradually became the colony's main labor force. The growth of the college and the town paralleled that of slavery and stringent race relations in Virginia, including the push for separate living and working spaces for enslaved blacks. Many early slave quarters in Virginia that have been uncovered through archaeology date to this period.[14]

In first half of the eighteenth century, Hugh Jones, a professor who was working and living at the Wren, called for quarters to be built to accommodate the service people: "The Negroes and inferior servants belonging to the College ... not only take up a great deal of room and are noisy and nasty, but also have often made the President, me, and others apprehensive of the great danger of being burnt with the College, through their carelessness and drowsiness."[15] His fear of fires was not unfounded, because the building had burned in 1705. It was destroyed by fire twice again, in 1859 and 1862. Each time it was rebuilt.[16]

Whether the slaves had contributed directly to the college's misfortunes is difficult to prove, but perhaps they contributed to these incidents indirectly by supplying materials for the fires. They had the perpetual job of providing firewood for the college's use; as a result, the wooded areas of its grounds and wider property areas were cleared. In August 1768 or soon thereafter, the slaves were joined by hired help in this activity, because the college's president was authorized "to hire two Negroes and order such other Preparations as shall be necessary for Cutting and Carting Wood on the College Lands for the Use of the said College."[17]

These workers may have strengthened the ties between the college and the town, helping to fashion a landscape to facilitate ongoing communication, governance, and trade between these two intertwined entities. Slaves in the town most likely worked to level areas by removing earth and filling in ravines, shore up and replace eroded areas, build drains and bridges, and repair roads. In 1722 the same Hugh Jones who had advocated for separate housing on the campus commented on an accomplishment that undoubtedly involved slave labor. He observed that "it is now a pleasant, long dry walk, broad, and almost level from the College to the Capitol," still a characteristic of the landscape. Colonial Williamsburg's archaeological study a little west of the Capitol in the spring of 2014 uncovered evidence of deep ravines and the many layers of building materials used in leveling this main area and street of the town.[18]

The demand for the slaves to provide firewood for the college remained high in the nineteenth century during Beverley Tucker's tenure, which started in 1834. In 1837 a man named Joe was given the arduous task of cutting "four cords of wood weekly" while the school was in recess. He was probably the same Joe who had the job of "whitewash[ing] and clean[ing] the College chambers and Lecture rooms." This was the venue Beverley used to nurture and promote his proslavery teachings, assuring his students of their rights to slave labor and expounding the positive good of slavery.[19]

Interestingly, while the college literally extended into the town, it considered itself a geographically separate place. This required language and behavior stipulating that one had to go to the town, a place seen as beneficial, as well as fraught with negative enticements and distractions. The campus had complemented the town in a vista from the latter's main street, looking west. The additions of the Brafferton and the President's House before the mid-eighteenth century oriented the campus eastward toward the town. Members of the college who did not reside in the town frequented it for its services. To control students' trips to the town, the administration provided a boy to run errands in the mornings for "the young gentlemen" of the college. This individual, most likely a slave, was probably a well-known person in Williamsburg and may have suffered exhaustion in carrying out his tasks. To control the behavior of its staff, the college restricted visits to the town. In 1763 the college asked its white housekeeper to reduce her trips to the town because her absence was having a negative impact on the productivity of the blacks who needed her supervision, "especially in so large a Family as the College."[20]

The college formulated and administered directives to ensure that the slaves did not work unsupervised and to prevent them from having access to its stores. As auxiliary buildings proliferated on the campus, including ones that served as slave living areas, the enslaved people continued to labor for staff, faculty, and students. Students without their own personal attendants sought to incorporate the college's slaves in these duties, much to the displeasure of the administration. The slaves had to balance the demands for their time and labor from several individuals. The college also issued directives to protect slaves from abuse. The administration admonished students on the consequences for mistreating slaves, obviously overlooking its own indulgences in similar practices.²¹

Archaeological studies within the historic campus have uncovered objects such as cowrie shells and a stone marble with an incised cross mark. Historical and archaeological studies have linked these items with slave medicinal and ritual practices. That the college slaves had strong reasons to pursue their well-being through such measures can be surmised from evidence about their health. A listing of slaves at the college dating to the late eighteenth century shows that the institution hired out many of its enslaved people, and the ones that remained on the campus were classified as invalids or in poor health. At the time, the college was experiencing disruptions caused by the American Revolution, including problems acquiring funding; it resorted to selling some of the slaves to help with revenue for repairs to the buildings.²²

By the time St. George Tucker established his household in Williamsburg in the late 1780s, the town had suffered a considerable decline in politics and commerce and even as a prime residential area. In 1780 the town lost its capital status, as the center of the Virginian government was moved to Richmond, about sixty miles away. This was the Williamsburg of St. George when he taught at the college and nurtured his children, including Beverley and Henry St. George, who, like their father, studied at William and Mary. Williamsburg remained in decline up to the time of St. George's death in 1827 and Beverley's death in 1851.²³

The Tuckers and Slavery

Historical interpretations at the Tucker House in Colonial Williamsburg are concentrated on the house and to a lesser extent on its grounds. There is a remarkable absence of the many auxiliary buildings that served as either working or living areas, or both, for slaves. The achievements of the Tuckers, especially St. George, are represented in the restored house, its furnishings, the re-created gardens, and in the narratives about these spaces. Although a few programs are about slavery and freedom, they do not focus on the Tuckers and their slaves. Overall, these representations of the past do little to interpret what actually happened on the property.²⁴

Williamsburg remained home for St. George and Beverley Tucker, although as judges and lawyers they traveled, worked, and lived elsewhere. A

A List of Negroes at College

Winkfield
Daniell
Dick — almost a invalid
Pompey
Adam
Nedd
Old Lucy — a invalid
Old Kate a invalid
Nanny a invalid
Iffy — not much Better

Negroes Hired outt

Lemon   Mr Bellini's three
James
Letty   Molly
Charlott   Nass
Frankey   and Lucy
Betty
and two Gerrels

List of slaves owned by the College of William and Mary ca. 1780. Courtesy of Special Collections Research Center, William and Mary Libraries.

Bermudian born and bred, St. George fought on the American side in the Revolutionary War and had a more illustrious career than his son. He is famous for his 1803 five-volume edition of William Blackstone's *Commentaries*, a legal work that Tucker analyzed in the contexts of the American Revolution and American and Virginian laws. Tucker's *Commentaries* was "the first major legal treatise on American law" and was cited in the United States Supreme Court. His edition became "one of the most influential legal works of the early nineteenth century and the most comprehensive treatise on American constitutional law until around 1820."[25]

St. George's achievements contrast with Beverley's less prominent military and judicial career. Aside from an imposing obelisk in Bruton Parish Church cemetery in Colonial Williamsburg, which marks his gravesite and honors his life with an elaborate epitaph, there is no other explicitly named reference to Beverley in the built landscape. Nevertheless, the Tucker House articulates his history, for it was his home.[26]

Like many of William and Mary's faculty and students, chiefly individuals of elite and upper-middle-class backgrounds, the Tuckers expected deference from people they considered of lower social and economic standing, such as poor whites, Indians, and especially enslaved and free blacks. Slave-owning practices offered both economic and social prestige to whites and helped explain why a man like St. George, who was very much influenced by the ideals of liberty and the American Revolution, was unwilling to free his slaves. To his credit, he "taught his students that slavery was at the least a moral wrong" and described America as essentially a graveyard for the aspirations of blacks and not the land of promise as conceived and experienced by whites. As an early proponent of abolition, St. George crafted a proposal in 1796 for the demise of slavery even as he admitted his prejudices about blacks' inability to live successfully among whites as freed people. He developed this "complicated and prejudicial" plan, called a dissertation, during his lectures at the college.[27]

St. George Tucker's abolition plan would not have deprived him or his slaveholding contemporaries of their slaves, because it would be a very long and gradual scheme. On the other hand, it would have deprived freed blacks of many basic rights and rendered them landless, despised, working-class peasants limited to marrying their own kind. St. George's own actions betrayed the limits of the plan. On December 2, 1796, just two days after he submitted his proposal to the Virginia Assembly (which rejected it), St. George tried to sell four slaves. He encouraged his agent to seek the best price in the transaction. In spite of his advocacy for freedom, he had little belief in the competence of free blacks to direct their own lives.[28]

Like the college, the households of the Tuckers were large, blended ones. St. George, for example, managed slaves he had purchased himself, as well as others from his two marriages. On his first marriage, to Frances Bland Randolph in 1778, he became responsible for three stepsons and "three large plantations and more than one hundred slaves." This wife was Beverley's mother, and after her death in 1788 Tucker left rural Virginia with his children and some enslaved people for Williamsburg, influenced by his desire to have his children educated at the college.[29]

Between 1788 and the 1820s, many of St. George's family members, including some of his children, stepsons, and grandchildren, died. Beverley himself lost two wives and two children, who died before he started teaching at the college in 1834. By then he was in his third marriage, and his wife, Lucy Ann Smith from Missouri, came with him to Williamsburg. Enslaved people dealt with death in their own families and community and perhaps had shared times of grief with the Tuckers.[30]

Slaves came to the Tucker House after St. George's second marriage, to Lelia Skipwith Carter in 1791, and their arrivals augmented his large domestic household in Williamsburg. In the mid-1790s his household had over twenty enslaved people and no fewer than ten slaves in any given year through the early nineteenth century. St. George and later Beverley not only sold slaves but moved them around to near and distant places. While some moves were temporary as the Tuckers practiced law, vacationed, and visited one another, other leave-takings were more permanent, as when St. George provided his children with slaves as wedding gifts. While a few slaves went with relatives on these moves, some had to leave their loved ones behind, and probably never saw them again. These factors characterized Beverley's move to Missouri in 1815, as well as his return to Virginia in 1833.[31]

The mobility of the Tuckers and their slaves engendered a communication network of messaging. St. George's children, who left Williamsburg with slaves to live elsewhere, sent messages to the Tucker House on behalf of their enslaved people to inform their relatives of the welfare of loved ones. In 1804 Henry St. George wrote about his slave Bob, who was with him as he practiced law in Winchester, Virginia. The boy was missing his enslaved mother and the sister he had left in Williamsburg. In his letter to St. George, Henry St. George informed his father about Bob's concerns: "Poor fellow, thought I, and is it not then cruel to part you from those friends. Yet must we all do our duty in that state of life to which it has pleased God to call us: and am not I too separated from all my friends."[32]

St. George's children also wrote about missing the slaves they left behind at the Tucker House. Henry St. George's letter also referred to meals St. George's cook, Gabriel, had served him in Williamsburg. After his daughter Anne Frances had established her own household, St. George tried to purchase a slave of a similar disposition as Gabriel to serve her. In the early nineteenth century, both Anne Frances and Beverley regularly mentioned with affection an elderly enslaved woman named Phillis; they called her Granny. Granny Phillis eventually moved with Beverley to Missouri and apparently died there.[33]

Beverley Tucker and His Slaves

After practicing law in Missouri for almost seventeen years, Beverley returned to Williamsburg in the 1830s. He acquired the Tucker House for his own household sometime around the time of the passing of his stepmother in September 1837. Beverley resided there with his family and his slaves until his death in 1851. His daughter Cynthia Beverley Tucker Coleman called the slaves "servants" when she described them in her remembrances of the 1840s. This group included a nursemaid named Polly Valentine (Mammy Polly), a butler named Robert, and some children.[34]

In 1840 Professor Beverley Tucker was in his sixth year of teaching at the college and had as many as twenty enslaved people at his house. Even a professor of the college, Charles Minnigerode, was living at the Tucker House, undoubtedly allowing for more connections between slaves and the college's professors. Minnigerode is credited with introducing an early version of the Christmas tree at the Tucker House in 1842, based on his German tradition. Beverley's slaves probably participated in the birth of this new practice in Williamsburg.[35]

From an early age, Beverley was closely associated with enslaved women such as his mother's maid, called Granny Aggy, and other nursemaids such as Granny Phillis and Mammy Polly. Apparently, like her father, Cynthia became attached to Mammy Polly, remembering her as an elegant and faithful woman. Beverley even had a house built for her at the back of the Tucker property.[36]

Polly Valentine's house was built during a flurry of construction activities at the Tucker property in the 1840s, when Beverley had the house repaired and added a study. There was at least one slave quarters at the site prior to April 1835. It burned around that time, allowing Beverley to grade the slaves' performances during this catastrophic event. He commented that they "worked like Beavers" to save things from a number of auxiliary buildings, including a smokehouse and a stable, which were also destroyed by this event. Like their counterparts at the college, the Tucker slaves had to deal with burned buildings and losses; they lost everything in the 1835 fire, but the Tuckers had insured the structures.[37]

Colonial Williamsburg's archaeological excavations in the late 1980s uncovered evidence for a pier-supported house believed to be the remains of the 1840s home of Polly Valentine. Remnants of five piers helped to determine that the structure measured fifteen by twenty-five feet. It also had a substantial brick fireplace and a raised foundation, elements that appear to have met the recommendations of proslavery masters who advocated for better-built cabins and other changes to improve slave living and working conditions. Beverley likely followed such recommendations. Like many proslavery advocates, he believed that slaves benefited from their ties to their masters and from enslavement.[38]

The archaeological findings for the Valentine house at the back of the Tucker House, though remarkable, did not lead to its reconstruction in Colonial Williamsburg. This nineteenth-century asset in the built historic landscape joined other invisible properties of African American heritage in Williamsburg. It was not selected for restoration, a situation rather similar to that of the 1855 First Baptist Church, which was destroyed in 1957. But unlike the Valentine House, the church is remembered in the built landscape. It is commemorated in an exhibition on African American religion in a carriage house and also with a historic marker not far from the Tucker House. The church's present-day congregation meets in a structure that was dedicated in 1956 and is located outside Colonial Williamsburg but near the college.[39]

Toward More Inclusive Representations

Appreciation for Beverley Tucker's contributions to America's history has been overshadowed by veneration of his father. The college has immortalized St. George Tucker's judicial and professorial career in practices of remembrance at its law school and at the St. George Tucker Hall. Both Tuckers are featured as past deans on the law school library's website, indicating that St. George served in this capacity from 1790 to 1804 and Beverley from 1834 to 1851. Including Beverley's story in commemorations, especially at Tucker Hall, would bring more attention to slavery, inviting comparisons of the views of the father and those of the son. A space could be provided at Tucker Hall for an exhibition, a memorial, an extensive storyboard, a panel of artwork, or other interpretive formats that could broaden knowledge about the Tuckers and include more representations about slavery and its legacies at the college. The hall is adjacent to the historic campus, and this would make for easier associations between displays there and public interpretations of the Wren.[40]

William and Mary's steps to break through silences about slavery in its historic landscape are demonstrated explicitly in its digital public education. Swem Library's Special Collections Research Center webpages feature articles, exhibition materials, and guides to the archival resources about the college's history and legacies of slavery. Biographies and bibliographies about professors, including St. George and Beverley Tucker, who had strong ties to slavery are available for preview and research. Such materials bring visibility to these facets of the college's history and ameliorate the impact of the somewhat limited interpretation of slavery and African American history in its built historic landscape.[41]

In 2009 the college founded "The Lemon Project: A Journey of Reconciliation" (the name credits one of the college's slaves) to promote scholarship and other activities that illuminate its history of slavery and its relations with African Americans. In 2012 the college and Colonial Williamsburg started the Bray School archaeological study, centered on excavations at the college's Brown Hall. This facility for black children operated from 1760 to 1774 and was affiliated with the college. Enslaved children from both the college and the town attended the school, which had a curriculum mainly based on religious education. The excavations at Brown Hall uncovered several fragments of slate pencils and other artifacts such as ceramics and marble, evidence for the eighteenth-century slave quarters that predated the school, as well as other structural features relating to different phases of occupation at the site.[42] In February 1773 the college stipulated that "four Loads of Wood to be sent to Mrs Wager, who has the care of some young Negroes belonging to the College," undoubtedly a task for the college's slaves or hired enslaved workers.

In April 2018 William and Mary apologized for its slavery past and legacy of discrimination, noting in a resolution that "the Board of Visitors acknowledges that William & Mary enslaved people, exploited them and their labor, and perpetuated the legacies of racial discrimination. The Board profoundly regrets these activities, apologizes for them, expresses its deep appreciation for the contributions made by the African American members of its community to the vitality of William & Mary then, now, and for all time coming, and commits to continue our efforts to remedy the lingering effects of past injustices."[43] The board also vowed to continue its support of the collaborative work of the Lemon Project, which has been shedding light on enslaved and free blacks connected to the college's history and fostering collaborative activities with descendant individuals and communities. The project influenced the college's decision in 2016 in naming two residence halls, one honoring Lemon and the other the late Carroll Hardy, an administrator who contributed to diversity and student affairs. The director of the Lemon Project and a member of the history department faculty, Jody Allen, is championing efforts to have a memorial for the enslaved people of the college's past be placed on the campus.[44]

Colonial Williamsburg for a long time has featured programs about the Bray School, including performances by historical interpreter Antoinette Brennan. Brennan portrays Anne Wager, who served as the headmistress of the school. As Wager, Brennan also presents information about the school at the Tucker House.[45] Colonial Williamsburg also has a group of interpreters called Nation Builders (with reference to historic individuals with distinguished accomplishments like Thomas Jefferson, George Washington, and a few figures that are not as well known in the historical records) who role play historical characters at the Tucker House. As Nation Builders, historical interpreters James Ingram Jr. (who performs as a formerly enslaved black preacher and pastor named Gowan Pamphlet, one of the founding ministers of the First Baptist Church) and Emily James (who performs as a free black woman of mixed ancestry called Edith Cumbo) present information about slavery and African American history in their programs at the site. Occasionally, Ingram and James mention the Tuckers in their programs, although the Tuckers are not the focus of their interpretations.[46]

The Tuckers and their enslaved people probably knew Pamphlet and Cumbo. Pamphlet's Baptist congregation in late eighteenth-century Williamsburg was about five hundred members strong, and during the nineteenth century the group met in a structure not far from the Tucker House. Edith Cumbo was likely the sister of Solomon Cumbo, a carter and waterman who delivered building materials like garden pales to the Tucker property in the late eighteenth century.[47]

It is interesting to speculate what St. George and Beverley would have thought about the almost total exclusion of information about enslaved people in programs at the Tucker House, since they encouraged communication from them. When the Tuckers were away from Williamsburg, they relied on enslaved people to inform them about affairs at their house. St. George, for example, relied on two enslaved man, Phil Anthony and Robert Edmondson, to help in the management and general upkeep of the property. Their letters told of their labor at the Tucker House and on its grounds, including in its gardens. The enslaved men also informed the Tuckers about the activities and welfare of the other enslaved people and even the conditions of the white neighbors, with descriptions of illnesses, broken fences, and the sharing of garden produce. What might have provoked the Tuckers' dismay, and perhaps even their ire, are the ways their own thoughts and agitations about slavery have now been silenced in their own house.[48]

For Colonial Williamsburg, the Tucker House is a special place; it is a reception center for donors. Here, significant financial contributors to (public) history can find rest and revitalization in the comfort of this restored home as staff and volunteers serve them coffee, cookies, lemonade, and light refreshments. These guests are welcomed as if they are on a visit to someone's actual home. They are introduced to the architecture and furnishing and entertained with the life stories of the Tuckers. Images of the Tuckers are displayed on walls throughout the interpretive spaces. Like at the Wren, the visual displays and the narratives about individual illustrious whites overshadow references to slavery and enslaved people. The programs of Brennan, Ingram, and James are not directed to impart any vital information about the Tuckers' association with slavery or about enslaved people associated with the property. The museum could work to remedy this situation by providing detailed information at the house and on the site's webpage.[49]

African American visitors with a memorial of Thomas Jefferson in Merchant's Square, Williamsburg, Virginia. Courtesy of the Colonial Williamsburg Foundation.

Colonial Williamsburg has to continue its efforts to democratize its historical interpretations and broaden representations of its heritage landscape. While evidence for geographically separate structures for historic African American home life within the museum's core is limited, and while the interpretive priority of depicting eighteenth-century Colonial Williamsburg partially justifies not reconstructing known nineteenth-century sites, there are still opportunities to interpret the landscape in more inclusive ways. A stronger focus should be on digital reconstructions and increased efforts directed to diverse and holistic programming both within and outside extant historic structures, as well as reconstructed ones.

The museum could construct markers and memorials in places where such testaments would not compromise its interpretive-period priority. For example, areas at the main visitors' center and also at a shopping section next to the college called Merchants Square offer strong potential for such activities. A sculpture of Thomas Jefferson is already sited in a strategic location in this square, and it bears an affinity to another monument venerating him at the college.

The college's memorials to great white men in its landscape also include a bronze statue of Virginia's governor Norborne Berkeley, baron de Botetourt, who served the colony from 1768 to 1770. A reproduction made in 1993 of the statue is located at the front of the Wren Building. It is based on an original that was placed at the Capitol in 1773 and later installed in the college yard in 1801, where it stood for over 150 years before it was relocated to the Swem Library's basement. Yet there are equally key places where markers or other memorials about slavery could be placed, including areas within and near the historic campus. Likewise, the texts of extant markers on campus could be revised to include the roles of specific individuals and the history of specific buildings as they relate to the college's slavery past.[50]

Conclusion

The historic campus and the Tucker House not only represent the achievements of illustrious white men but also register and showcase the contributions of other individuals, groups, and communities. Slavery and the stories of enslaved people are integral to this heritage and cannot be omitted or sidelined without compromising commitments to sound scholarship and without endangering activities to strengthen inclusion. Commemorations should continue to involve more creative interpretations of the tangible historic properties and, at the same time, to provide more individual testimonies related to the neglected history of enslavement. In the case of the Tuckers and their slaves, there is strong evidence to support a more diversified appreciation of this heritage in Williamsburg.

NOTES

1. The Tucker-Coleman Collection at the College of William and Mary's Earl Gregg Swem Library Special Collections Research Center (Swem SCRC) is a rich source of information on the Tuckers and their slaves. Transcripts of selected items from the collection are available at the John D. Rockefeller Jr. Library, the Colonial Williamsburg Foundation. For biographical data on the Tuckers, see materials on the Tuckers at http://scdb.swem.wm.edu/wiki/index.php/St._George_Tucker and http://scdb.swem.wm.edu/wiki/index.php/Nathaniel_Beverley_Tucker_(1784-1851). Materials from Swem SCRC collated from my own research visits and those of Alexander Gebhard, a Colonial Williamsburg intern during the summer of 2010, are used in this present study of the Tuckers and their slaves. For an early publication on this topic, see Mrs. George P. Coleman, collector and ed.,

Virginia Silhouettes: Contemporary Letters Concerning Negro Slavery in the State of Virginia (Richmond: Dietz Printing Co., 1934). Key works on the Tuckers include Phillip Hamilton, *The Making and Unmaking of a Revolutionary Family: The Tuckers of Virginia 1752–1830* (Charlottesville: University of Virginia Press, 2003); articles in *William and Mary Law Review* 47, no. 4 (2006); and Robert J. Brugger, *Beverley Tucker: Heart over Head in the Old South* (Baltimore, Md.: Johns Hopkins University Press, 1978). For a discussion of the history and restoration of the town, including the college, see Robert P. Maccubbin, ed., *Williamsburg, Virginia: A City before the State 1699–1999* (Williamsburg: City of Williamsburg, distributed by the University Press of Virginia, 2000).

2. "College of William and Mary," http://scdb.swem.wm.edu/wiki/index.php/College_of_William_and_Mary; Roberta G. Laynor, Carl R. Lounsbury, and Mark R. Wenger, "St. George Tucker House: An Architectural Analysis; Block 29, Building 2," Colonial Williamsburg Foundation Library Research Report Series (2003); "St. George Tucker House," http://www.history.org/almanack/places/hb/hbtucker.cfm

3. *Vital Facts: A Chronology of the College of William and Mary* (1921; Williamsburg, Va., 1999), https://digitalarchive.wm.edu/handle/10288/17231; Michael Wallace, "Visiting the Past: History Museums in the United States," in *Public History Readings*, ed. Phyllis K. Leffler and Joseph Brent (Malabar, Fla.: Krieger Publishing Company, 1992), 429–55; Richard Handler and Eric Gable, *The New History in an Old Museum: Creating the Past at Colonial Williamsburg* (Durham, N.C.: Duke University Press, 1997); Davison M. Douglas, "Foreword: The Legacy of St. George Tucker," *William and Mary Law Review* 47, no. 4 (2006), http://scholarship.law.wm.edu/wmlr/vol47/iss4/2; Paul Finkelman, "The Dragon St. George Could Not Slay: Tucker's Plan to End Slavery," *William and Mary Law Review* 47, no. 4 (2006), http://scholarship.law.wm.edu/wmlr/vol47/iss4/5; Laynor, Lounsbury, and Wenger, "St. George Tucker House"; "St. George Tucker," http://www.history.org/almanack/people/bios/biotuck.cfm; Terry L. Meyers, "A First Look at the Worst: Slavery and Race Relations at the College of William and Mary," *William and Mary Bill of Rights Journal* 16 (2008), http://scholarship.law.wm.edu/wmborj/vol16/iss4/8; Carl Lounsbury, "Ornaments of Civic Aspiration: The Public Buildings of Williamsburg," in Maccubbin, *Williamsburg, Virginia*, 25–38; Thaddeus W. Tate Jr., "Town and Gown through Three Centuries: William and Mary in the Life of Williamsburg," in Maccubbin, *Williamsburg, Virginia*, 137–56.

4. Jennifer L. Eichstedt and Stephen Small, *Representations of Slavery: Race and Ideology in Southern Plantation Museums* (Washington, D.C.: Smithsonian Institution Press, 2002), 165.

5. Alfred L. Brophy, "Considering William and Mary's History with Slavery: The Case of President Thomas Roderick Dew," *William & Mary Bill of Rights Journal* 16 (2008), http://scholarship.law.wm.edu/wmborj/vol16/iss4/7; Meyers, "A First Look"; Slavery and Universities, http://slavery-and-universities.wikispaces.com/; Sven Beckert, Katherine Stevens, and the students of the Harvard and Slavery Research Seminar, *Har-*

vard and Slavery: Seeking a Forgotten History (Harvard University, 2011), http://www
.harvardandslavery.com/wp-content/uploads/2011/11/Harvard-Slavery-Book-111110
.pdf; The Lemon Project: A Journey of Reconciliation, http://www.wm.edu/sites
/lemonproject/?svr=web; http://scholarship.law.wm.edu/wmborj/vol16/iss4/8; Brian
Whitson, Erin Zagursky, and WYDaily Staff, "William & Mary Apologizes for College's History of Slavery, Discrimination," *Williamsburg Yorktown Daily*, April 20, 2018, https://wydaily.com/local-news/2018/04/20/william-mary-apologizes-for-colleges-history-of-slavery-discrimination; *Vital Facts*; College of William and Mary, "Wren Building," http://scdb.swem.wm.edu/wiki/index.php/Wren_Building.

6. Meyers, "A First Look," 1145.

7. *Vital Facts*; Lounsbury, "Ornaments"; Tate, "Town and Gown"; "Wren Building: Oldest Academic Structure in America," http://www.history.org/almanack/places/hb/hbwren.cfm; "James Blair," http://scdb.swem.wm.edu/wiki/index.php/James_Blair; Whitson et al., "William & Mary Apologizes."

8. Ywone Edwards-Ingram, "Before 1979: African American Coachmen, Visibility, and Representation at Colonial Williamsburg," *Public Historian* 36, no. 1 (February 2014): 9–35.

9. Handler and Gable, *The New History*; Cary Carson, "Colonial Williamsburg and the Practice of Interpretive Planning in American History Museums," *Public Historian* 20, no. 3 (Summer 1998): 11–51; Carson, "The End of History Museums: What's Plan B?," *Public Historian* 30, no. 4 (Fall 2008): 9–27; Dan Eggen, "In Williamsburg, the Painful Reality of Slavery," *Washington Post*, July 7, 1999.

10. "Great Hopes for Great Hopes," *Colonial Interpreter* 24, no. 2 (Summer 2003): 1; Carson, "The End of History Museums"; Scott Magelssen, "Revolutionary City," review, *Theatre Journal* 59, no. 1 (March 2007): 117–19.

11. Brophy, "Considering"; also see Terry Meyers, "If At First You Don't Secede . . . ," *Williamsburg Magazine*, January 2010, 52–53; Hamilton, *The Making*, 203.

12. Jennifer Bridges Oast, "Forgotten Masters: Institutional Slavery in Virginia, 1680–1860" (PhD diss., College of William and Mary, 2008); also see Meyers, "A First Look." This discussion of the college's history of slavery draws heavily from these two sources.

13. Jennifer Agee Jones, "The Very Heart and Centre of the County: From Middle Plantation to Williamsburg," in Maccubbin, *Williamsburg, Virginia*, 15–24; "Speeches of Students of the College of William and Mary Delivered May 1, 1699," *William and Mary Quarterly*, 2nd ser., 10, no. 4 (October 1930): 323–37. Also see Lounsbury, "Ornaments"; Tate, "Town and Gown"; and Meyers, "A First Look."

14. See "The Wren." The observation about slave housing is based on my 2001 research for the exhibition *The Evolution of the Slave Quarter in Tidewater Virginia* (opened February 2002), Yorktown Victory Center, Jamestown/Yorktown Foundation, Virginia.

15. Oast, "Forgotten Masters," 173.

16. "Wren Building."

17. "Journal of the Meetings of the President and Masters of William and Mary College," *William and Mary Quarterly*, 1st ser., 13, no. 1 (July 1904): 15–22, 16; Oast, "Forgotten Masters," 177.

18. M. Kent Brinkley, "The Topographic Evolution of Williamsburg over Three Centuries," in *Taking Possession Storyline Resource Book* (Williamsburg: Colonial Williamsburg Foundation, 1999), 193; personal communication with Andrew Edwards, Colonial Williamsburg's staff archaeologist and observations, spring 2014; Mark St. John Erickson, "Colonial Williamsburg Archaeologists Unearth Lost Landscape of America's 'Most Historic Avenue,'" *Daily Press*, April 20, 2014.

19. Oast, "Forgotten Masters," 178; Meyers, "A First Look," 1150.

20. Lounsbury, "Ornaments," 28–30; Tate, "Town and Gown," 137–44; Oast, "Forgotten Masters," 176–79; and Meyers, "A First Look," 1146.

21. Oast, "Forgotten Masters," 175, 179–86; and Meyers, "A First Look," 1145–46.

22. Oast, "Forgotten Masters," 174–75, 190–96; "List of Slaves Owned by the College of William and Mary, circa 1780," Swem SCRC, https://digitalarchive.wm.edu/handle/10288/16261; Mark P. Leone and Gladys-Marie Fry, "Conjuring in the Big House Kitchen: An Interpretation of African American Belief Systems Based on the Uses of Archaeology and Folklore Sources," *Journal of American Folklore* 112, no. 445 (1999): 372–403; Tate, "Town and Gown," 140.

23. Tate, "Town and Gown," 140–44; Laynor, Lounsbury, and Wenger, "St. George Tucker House," 15; see also Ralph H. Brown, "St. George Tucker versus Jedidiah Morse on the Subject of Williamsburg," *William and Mary Quarterly*, 2nd ser., 20, no. 4 (October 1940): 487–91; Stephen Bonsol, "D'Aucteville's Description of Williamsburg, and of the American Troops near Williamsburg, in 1781," *William and Mary Quarterly*, 2nd ser., 20, no. 4 (October 1940): 502–3.

24. "The St. George Tucker House," http://www.history.org/foundation/development/tucker.cfm. This definition of history draws on Michel-Rolph Trouillot, *Silencing the Past: Power and the Production of History* (Boston: Beacon Press, 1995).

25. Douglas, "Foreword," 1112–14, see page 1114 for the quote.

26. Mary Haldane Coleman, *St. George Tucker, Citizen of No Mean City* (Richmond, Va.: Dietz Press, 1938); Meyers, "If At First"; Robert Doares Jr., "The Life and Literature of Nathaniel Beverley Tucker," *Colonial Williamsburg* 23, no. 3 (Autumn 2001): 66–71; Brugger, "Beverley Tucker," 196.

27. See Coleman, *Virginia Silhouettes*. Finkelman, "The Dragon," provides an in-depth analysis of the dissertation; the quote is on page 1216. More analysis is in Phillip Hamilton, "Revolutionary Principles and Family Loyalties: Slavery's Transformation in the St. George Tucker Household of Early National Virginia," *William and Mary Quarterly*, 3rd ser., 55, no. 4 (October 1998): 531–56.

28. Finkelman, "The Dragon," 1230–38; Hamilton, *The Making*, 83, 50, 151; and Hamilton, "Revolutionary Principles," 536–37. Apparently, these slaves belonged to his daughter,

and Tucker later invested the proceeds from the sale in bank shares for her; document by St. George Tucker, December 2, 1796, Tucker-Coleman Collection, transcribed by Alexandria Gebhard. Also see St. George's letter to John Coalter (his daughter Anne Frances's husband), February 21, 1801, in Coleman, *St. George Tucker*, 133–34.

29. Hamilton, "Revolutionary Principles," 533; Hamilton, *The Making*, 43–64, 79, as well as the genealogical chart in the introduction; Laynor, Lounsbury, and Wenger, "St. George Tucker House," 15; Mary A. Stephenson, "Tucker House, Block 29, Colonial Lots 163, 164, 169, Tucker House Historical Report, Block 29 Building 2 Lots 163, 164, 169" (1947), Colonial Williamsburg Foundation Library Research Report Series, RR. 1562 (1990), see the appendix, "1815 List of Taxable Property."

30. Information compiled from Laynor, Lounsbury, and Wenger, "St. George Tucker House," app. 1, 81–105; and from Doares, "The Life and Literature."

31. Stephenson, "Tucker House Historical Report," appendix, illustration no. 5, 2–3; Meyers, "A First Look," 1510; Coleman, *Virginia Silhouettes*, 10; John Blassingame, ed., *Slave Testimony: Two Centuries of Letters, Speeches, Interviews, and Autobiographies* (Baton Rouge: Louisiana State University Press, 1977), 8–12. For Tucker's gift to Beverley on his marriage, see St. George Tucker to John Coalter, December 4, 1808, Richmond, Tucker/Coleman Collection, Colonial Williamsburg, original at the Swem Library. Also see St. George Tucker to John Coalter, February 21, 1801, in Coleman, *St. George Tucker*, 133–34; Brugger, "Beverley Tucker," 46, 86–97; Hamilton, *The Making*, 152, 188.

32. Blassingame, *Slave Testimony*, 8–12. See Coleman, *Virginia Silhouettes*, 10, for the quote.

33. See Coleman, *Virginia Silhouettes*, 8; Coleman, *St. George Tucker*, 160; Hamilton, *The Making*, 152, 188; Brugger, "Beverley Tucker," 46, 224; Laynor, Lounsbury, and Wenger, "St. George Tucker House," 95.

34. Brugger, "Beverley Tucker," 45–195; Laynor, Lounsbury, and Wenger, "St. George Tucker House," 101; Tate, "Town and Gown," 141; Meyers, "A First Look," 1150; Meyers, "If At First"; Coleman, *Virginia Silhouettes*, 53–59.

35. Meyers, "A First Look," 1150; Doares, "The Life and Literature"; Will Molineux, "Millennial Moment: Virginia's First Christmas Tree," *Daily Press*, December 16, 1999.

36. Coleman, *Virginia Silhouettes*, 28, 53–59; Ywone Edwards, "Master-Slave Relations: A Williamsburg Perspective" (master's thesis, College of William and Mary, 1990); Coleman, *St. George Tucker*, 133–34; Hamilton, *The Making*, 152, 158; Hamilton, "Revolutionary Principles," 550–51; Blassingame, *Slave Testimony*, 10; William Cabel Bruce, *John Randolph of Roanoke 1773–1833* (New York: Octagon Books, 1970), 2:700–701.

37. Edwards, "Master-Slave Relations," 107–9; Stephenson, "St. George Tucker House Historical Report," appendix, illustration no. 3, 1835–43.

38. Edwards, "Master-Slave Relations," 108–16; James O. Breeden, ed., *Advice among Masters: The Ideals in Slave Management in the Old South* (Westport, Conn.: Greenwood Press, 1980); Brophy, "Considering"; Meyers, "If At First."

39. Edwards, "Master-Slave Relations," 122–23; Ywone Edwards-Ingram, "More Than Memory: Representing an African American Neighborhood at the Ravenscroft Site," *Colonial Williamsburg Interpreter* 30, no. 1 (Spring 2009): 1–6; "Gowan Pamphlet," http://www.history.org/almanack/people/bios/biopam.cfm; Patricia Samford, "First Baptist Church Archaeological Report, Block 38, Building 33," originally entitled "First Baptist Church Archaeological Briefing" (1985), Colonial Williamsburg Foundation Library Research Report Series 1621 (Colonial Williamsburg Foundation Library Williamsburg, Virginia, 1990).

40. Law School Deans, http://scholarship.law.wm.edu/deans/; Tucker Papers Project Information, http://oieahc.wm.edu/tucker/project.html; Tucker Hall, http://scdb.swem.wm.edu/wiki/index.php/Tucker_Hall; Tucker Hall (Renovation), http://www.wm.edu/about/administration/senioradmin/adminoffice/construction/projects/tucker/index.php.

41. Swem SCRC Wiki, http://scdb.swem.wm.edu/wiki/index.php/Main_Page.

42. "The Lemon Project"; Robert Engs, "The College, Race, and Slavery: Report to the Provost and Faculty, December 1, 2008 / February 12, 2009, the College of William and Mary," http://slavery-and-universities.wikispaces.com/file/view/The+College,Race+%26+Slavery.pdf. For historical information on the Bray School, see Terry L. Meyers, "Benjamin Franklin, the College of William and Mary, and the Williamsburg Bray School," *Anglican and Episcopal* 79, no. 4 (December 2010): 368–93. Terry Meyers, an English professor at William and Mary, has conducted a relentless search for information about the location of the Bray School, and his findings directed the location for the archaeological study. See "Slavery and the School: The College's Forgotten Past," podcast, November 18, 2013, http://podcast.history.org/2013/11/18/slavery-and-the-school-the-colleges-forgotten-past/; Joseph McClain, "Search for 1760 Bray School Turns Up Something Even Older," August 7, 2013, http://www.wm.edu/news/stories/2013/bray-school-search-finds-something-even-older-123.php; personal communication with Colonial Williamsburg's staff archaeologist, Mark Kostro, spring 2014.

43. Whitson et al., "William & Mary Apologizes."

44. Ibid.

45. Meyers, "A First Look," 1146; Oast, "Forgotten Masters," 187–88; "The Bray School, September 29, 2008," http://www.history.org/media/podcasts/092908/TheBraySchool.cfm; "The St. George Tucker House," http://www.history.org/foundation/development/tucker.cfm.

46. "The St. George Tucker House"; Gowan Pamphlet; Linda H. Rowe, "Gowan Pamphlet: Baptist Preacher in Slavery and Freedom," *Virginia Magazine of History and Biography* 120, no. 1 (January 2012): 2–31; "Edith Cumbo," http://www.history.org/almanack/people/bios/bioedithcumbo.cfm.

47. Stephenson, "Tucker House Historical Report," 9, 12.

48. Ibid.

49. "The St. George Tucker House," http://www.history.org/foundation/development/tucker.cfm. For more on the personal nature of historic house presentations, see Jessica Adams, "Local Color: The Southern Plantation in Popular Culture," *Cultural Critique* 42 (Spring 1999): 163–87.

50. Norborne Berkeley, 4th Baron de Botetourt (1718–70), https://scdbwiki.swem.wm.edu/wiki/index.php?title=Norborne_Berkeley,_4th_Baron_de_Botetourt_(1718-1770); "Lord Botetourt Statue, Constructed 1770–1773," http://tribetrek.wm.edu/items/browse?search=botetourt&sort_field=relevance.

CHAPTER FOURTEEN

The "Family Business"

Slavery, Double Consciousness, and Objects of Memory at Emory University

Mark Auslander

This essay explores forms of memory work engaged in by families who trace their histories back to slave owners and enslaved persons associated with Emory University. My title is taken from a phrase sometimes used by such families in reference to the historically white-dominated institution of higher learning with which their families have long been associated. Stella Perkins, an African American woman descended from slaves owned by one of the founders of Emory College, whose family has continued to work at Emory through six generations, remarked sardonically, "I suppose you can say Emory has been the family business, practically forever!" After pausing a beat, she added with a mischievous smile, "Of course, for Emory, *we* were the family business, bought and paid for!"

Descendant families, who often trace their lineages back to both slaveholders and the enslaved, negotiate at times ambivalent relations to educational institutions. Under what circumstances are pride, resentment, and disappointment expressed toward the institution? What kinds of family narratives are invoked or repressed when descendants are students or faculty at institutions at which their ancestors were enslaved (or which are named for the person who enslaved their ancestors)? How, in short, does Du Boisian "double consciousness," the sensation of simultaneously being within and outside of a dominant narrative, function when family histories, academic institutional histories, and enslavement intersect?

In this essay, I approach this tangled ideological and emotional web through a range of physical objects and geographic locations, ranging from trees to headstones, that are sites of profound ambivalence for persons descended from enslaved families closely intertwined with the history of Emory College. As W. E. B. Du Bois long ago suggested, the "veil" of double consciousness is not experienced continuously but "descends," often with sudden abruptness, when an outrageous incident or image disrupts the quotidian flow of experience, forcefully exposing the subject to the raw edges of structures of oppression.[1] What is the nature of these abrasive memory prompts, and how do they operate in the context of educational institutions, ostensibly devoted to the universal celebration of knowledge and human dignity?

Writing as a sociocultural anthropologist, I take as my point of departure the foundational work of symbolic anthropologist Victor Turner on the "polyphony" or "multivocality" of symbolic forms.[2] A single symbolic form may speak in many voices, carrying a range of emotional charges and ideational content that might be variously activated in different contexts. Thus, a physical object that in one context may evoke pleasure or exuberance may in other contexts trigger pain or despair. Our experiences of the past and our contemplation of a potential future are in many respects built up through our dynamic engagement with these "multivalent" symbolic elements that constitute the physical, meaningful environment that we continually negotiate in our everyday lives.

Headstones and the "Family Business"

I begin with Stella Perkins's half-humorous characterization of Emory University as the "family business." She made the utterance on a warm spring afternoon in 2000 as she was assisting my students and me in a class project to document and restore the historically African American cemetery in Oxford, Georgia, where Emory College was founded in the late 1830s. Within this burial ground were interred hundreds of persons of color who in slavery and in freedom had worked in one way or another for Emory and for the leading white families associated with the institution. In 1965, soon after the passage of the Civil Rights Act and the Voting Rights Act, the Oxford city white leadership had acted, in effect, to privatize the historically white section of the city cemetery as a private "historical foundation." From 1965 until 2000 the white-dominated city council transferred all burial fees, including those collected from African American families, to the private foundation, which only disbursed funds for the care of the white cemetery. The African American cemetery had become, in consequence, overgrown with privet hedges and littered with fallen tree limbs. Many families of color were thus unable to reach the burial sites of their loved ones. Compounding these insults, in 1990 the city council authorized the clear-cutting of the oldest section of the black cemetery by an unscrupulous white pulpwood merchant. Scores of headstones were damaged or plowed under. Hundreds of trees that had functioned as informal burial markers for the African American matriarchs of the community were cut down.

As my students learned of these multilayered injustices, they became committed to partnering with the African American community to help restore the cemetery and to document, whenever possible, the location of the burial sites of enslaved persons and their descendants. We worked with local church congregations each weekend through the spring, clearing paths, repairing erosion damage, unearthing headstones, and planting flowerbeds. Stella Perkins was one of our principal community historians, decoding difficult-to-read inscriptions on weathered headstones and recalling the unmarked burial sites of her kith and kin.

On that March afternoon, as she stood surveying a dozen newly uncovered headstones, Stella was in a rather meditative mood. She motioned to me and several of my students as they paused from raking and pruning and remarked,

> You know, just about everyone you see here was connected to Emory. A lot of the menfolk brought in the crops that fed the students and the professors. The ladies here, a lot of them were my aunts. They took in laundry and cooked for the Emory boys in those boardinghouses. I guess that goes all the way back to slavery times. Not that we had a choice back then, but we were working for the college even then, when it owned the whole town. I suppose you can say Emory has been the "family business," practically forever!

Then, to my students' great delight, she added with a wink, "Of course, for Emory, *we* were the family business, bought and paid for! . . . Hard to say where our families stopped and the college began."

Significantly, her ambiguous commentary was inspired by a series of aged headstones marking the final resting places of many of her ancestors and collateral relations, a number of whom had been born in slavery. As she spoke, she was gazing down the slope of the African American cemetery, still scarred by erosion and scattered with downed tree limbs, toward the broad expanse of the historically white cemetery, its pristine marble headstones and neatly mowed lawns bathed in the soft golden glow of the afternoon sun. The visual tableau in front of her thus perfectly encapsulated the ironies of the labor history she sought to characterize through humor. In the foreground were the traces of those who had labored, as bondspeople in the antebellum era and as underpaid laborers under Jim Crow, on behalf of the white Methodist bishops and Emory faculty and presidents buried in the carefully conserved pastoral background.

Although framed in playfully ironic terms, her wording expressed a degree of pride in the contributions she and her family had made to the college across the generations. Like most present-day African American residents of Oxford, Georgia, Stella is a descendant of George Sims (ca. 1830–ca. 1900) and his wife, Angeline Sims (ca. 1840–ca. 1910), who were enslaved in Oxford.[3] George and Angeline were the property of Richard L. Sims (ca. 1795–1856), a prominent white landowner and political figure. He in turn willed them to his daughter Sarah Lee Sims in 1856. In 1836 Richard was one of the founding commissioners of the city of Oxford. In 1840 he was listed as a founding trustee of Oxford Female Academy, closely tied to Emory College; he also represented Newton County in various state political gatherings. Among his children were a prominent Covington lawyer and a Confederate brigadier general.

George and Angeline Sims, community members recall, had four daughters, who in turn bore a total of forty-nine daughters. Most of the Sims granddaughters married locally, and "for that reason, we are all related here," remarks Stella. Soon after the cemetery restoration project, Stella served on the program committee for Homecoming service at Rust Chapel United Methodist Church, the congregation her great-grandfather Thomas Anderson (the son-in-law of George Sims) had helped to found in the late 1860s. She designed the cover of the program, featuring an elaborate tree boasting thirteen branches, each branch bearing the name of one of the thirteen major African American families of Oxford, including the Sims and Anderson lines. As she proudly showed me and my students the cover, she remarked, "And remember, every one of these families worked for Emory, in one way or another. So even in the old days, you could say it was as much ours as anyone else's."

Several weeks later, however, Stella's life took an unfortunate turn. She was abruptly informed by the corporation to which Emory had contracted all food service that she was being laid off permanently, effective immediately. With the assistance of concerned students and faculty, Stella appealed her dismissal, arguing that she had worked for the college food service for twenty-five years and that her family had in one way or another worked for Emory since the institution's founding in the era of slavery. All these entreaties fell on deaf ears. The university administration insisted they had no say over personnel decisions made by a private corporation. Corporate officials in turn stated they were under no obligation to discuss personnel matters with any third parties.

Stella was mortified both by her termination and by the refusal of anyone in authority to discuss the matter with her. "We've worked so long for the college, we practically brought up all these generations of students. . . . Now we can't even get anyone to return my phone calls. Everyone says this doesn't have anything to do with them, that it is 'just business.'" To her mind, at least, a moral economy that had existed since the time of slavery in Oxford in which the college, however resented it might have been at times, could at least be counted on to "look after its people" had been irretrievably ruptured.

Stella was unemployed for several months until she was hired by the local Wal-Mart, where she continues to work until this day. She and many family members remain rather embittered toward Emory. One of her cousins remarked, "Well, the school likes to say it is one big community. But you could still say it is the Big House, after all these years. . . . Only difference is when they don't want to count you as a member of that community, they don't have to put you on the [auction] block anymore. They just 'outsource' you. Then you're not their responsibility anymore." A century and a half after legal emancipation, the legacy of enslavement continues to infuse popular perceptions of the institution.

The 1966 Marker

The disquieting legacies of slavery and Jim Crow are also, at times, brought to conscious awareness through the only visible memorial to African Americans in the Emory University system, a tree on the central quadrangle of the original Emory College grounds in Oxford, Georgia, now termed Oxford College of Emory University. Planted in 1966 by representatives of the class of 1913 in honor of two of Emory's most celebrated African American employees, the tree is marked at its base by a small plaque:

> The members of the class of 1913
> In loving appreciation
> Dedicate this tree to the memory of
> Bob Hammond
> 1858 to 1923
> and
> Billy Mitchell
> 1886 to 1958
> Who together contributed 95 years
> Of faithful and efficient service to "Old Emory"
> Dedicated June 12, 1966

The 1943 Emory at Oxford College yearbook was dedicated to Henry "Billy" Mitchell, longtime chief janitor and groundskeeper of the college. At his 1958 funeral, eight years before the tree planting, he was eulogized by college dean Virgil Eady Sr., who stated, "Billy Mitchell's friends included people in many stations of life—Congressmen, U.S. Senators, Methodist Bishops, great and influential business and professional men and women." Other white speakers referred to his family's "long service" to Emory.[4]

The meanings of the plaque and the tree to Oxford's African American residents are a good deal more complex, conditioned by intricate family histories that stretch far back into "slavery times." As is widely known in the local black community (although less appreciated by their white counterparts), Henry "Billy" Mitchell was descended on both his mother's and father's sides from persons owned by the white founders of Emory College. On his mother's side, his lineage stretched back to the family of Ellen and Cornelius Robinson, enslaved by the physician and natural scientist Alexander Means, longtime member of the Emory College faculty who for a time served as college president. Cornelius (b. 1836) and Ellen (b. 1835) were married to one another and were allowed to live in a small house behind the Means mansion, Orne Villa, on present-day Emory Street in Oxford. Cornelius, a Native American, was Means's valet. Ellen was the personal maid of Means's wife. As such, they seemed to have occupied the highest status among all those enslaved in the Means household. After emancipation, Cornelius and Ellen formed an independent household, which by 1870 consisted of their children Cora (b. 1857), George (b. 1859), Sarah (b. 1861), John (b. 1863), and Thaddius (b. 1867).

Sarah Robinson married Robert, the son of Thomas Mitchell, who had been enslaved by Bishop James Osgood Andrew, first president of Emory's board of trustees. The circumstances of Bishop Andrew's ownership of slaves, many African American residents of Oxford note, were for a time of considerable national importance. Bishop Andrew acquired Thomas's father, James Mitchell, and approximately fourteen other enslaved persons through his marriage to his second wife, Ann Leonora Mounger Greenwood, in January 1844. Her first husband, Thomas Greenwood, had died in 1825, leaving her with dower rights over some of his slaves and supervisory rights over his other slaves destined for his minor children. These included four children by his previous 1805 marriage to Nancy Mitchell, daughter of the slave owner and Revolutionary War veteran Jacob Mitchell, an established Greene County planter who also passed away in 1825.

In May 1844, the fact that Bishop Andrew owned the fourteen Mitchell slaves, as well as the enslaved woman Miss Kitty and the enslaved man Billy, a former slave of the bishop's mother-in-law, became a matter of national controversy. Northern delegates to the national conference of the Methodist Episcopal Church protested Bishop Andrew's ownership of slaves. The resulting controversy triggered the national schism of the Methodist Church and the creation of the proslavery Methodist Episcopal Church, South, a breach that remained unhealed until 1939. The dispute, sometimes termed a "dress rehearsal for the Civil War," highlighted the intimate intersections of religious faith and the slavery question in antebellum America.

In any event, after the death of his second wife, Ann Leonora Greenwood Andrew, in 1855, Bishop Andrew transferred most of the "Greenwood" slaves to Ann Leonora's surviving children. Many of the Mitchell/Greenwood slaves were thus returned to Greene County, Georgia, where they were rented out for agrarian labor until emancipation. However, the enslaved young man James Mitchell and his son Thomas Mitchell were transferred to Ann Leonora's daughter Mary Elizabeth Greenwood, who married Emory faculty member Luther M. Smith. After Mary Elizabeth's death in 1859, her property, including her slaves, all passed fully to Professor Smith, who became Emory's president after the Civil War. The enslaved Mitchell family thus remained in Oxford after emancipation, and some continue to reside there until this day.

One of the sons of Robert and Sarah was Henry "Billy" Mitchell, memorialized by the quadrangle tree, who served as chief janitor of Emory at Oxford for much of the first half of the twentieth century. His daughter, Sarah Francis Mitchell Wise, and grandson Billy Wise were close friends to many faculty and students at Oxford College.

For four decades the tree has been subject to wry observations by members of the Oxford African American community, many of whom have been employed at the college and who are mindful of the complex family history noted above. Several years ago, I stood in front of the tree in the company of Mrs. Emogene Williams, one of the most respected African American community historians in Newton County, Georgia. She herself is a direct descendant of Reverend Toney Baker, owned and sired by a prominent white member of Emory College's founding board. The leading white faculty and board members at Emory had sponsored Reverend Baker's education and supported him as he founded Bethlehem Baptist Church, now the oldest African American church in the county.

As we gazed at the tree, Mrs. Williams sighed and quietly remarked,

> How they loved Billy, their best friend, they called him. But 1966, you know, that was two years before they even admitted the first black student to study on this campus. They'd happily plant a tree dedicated to us. They just wouldn't let us in the front door.... And the amazing thing is, it was in part because of Billy's family being held as slaves that these same white folks here at Emory went and created the Methodist Episcopal Church, South. They just couldn't bear being told by northerners that a bishop couldn't own slaves. So they up and left the church so they could keep Billy and all his kin in slavery! And then they go and erect a monument to him for being so loyal. Honestly, when I look at this plaque and at this tree, I don't know whether or not to laugh or cry!

She noted in turn, in reference to Bob Hammond, that after his death his widow donated one hundred dollars, a significant amount in 1923, to the Emory building fund, supporting the institution that he so deeply loved but that his relatives could not legally attend.

It is important to emphasize that Mrs. Williams is devoted to Emory and to Oxford College, even as she remains a pointed critic of much of its history during slavery times and Jim Crow. Her daughter, Reverend Avis Williams, one of the first African Americans to matriculate at Oxford, holds undergraduate and postgraduate degrees from Emory University. Emogene and Avis have lectured to Emory students and faculty on numerous occasions and have been close collaborators and consultants in my own research for over a decade. They have been repeatedly honored by the institution, yet they are conscious of the many ways in which they continue to stand outside of its mainstream embrace. "Every time I walk by that tree," remarks Avis, "I remember my first week at the college as a freshman when my room was made by a maid who was an aunt of mine. Was I inside at last, or was I still outside, looking in?"

The Family Reunion Photograph

I next turn to an enigmatic photograph in the possession of John P. Godfrey Jr. (known as JP), one of Oxford's most prominent African American citizens. JP's paternal grandfather, Israel Godfrey (1849–1929), was owned in slavery times by Jeptha M. Cody, a wealthy Covington planter who had close ties to the Emory board members and faculty. After emancipation, Israel worked in various capacities for Emory College, serving in the mid-1870s as chief stonemason for the college's day chapel, which stands to this day. He was primarily compensated in land by the cash-poor postbellum college; most of that land remains within the Godfrey family. Israel's second marriage was to Sallie Sims, daughter of George and Angeline Sims, the great-grandparents of Sallie Perkins.

Israel had close ties to the leading white families of Oxford, including the Candlers and Branhams, who loom large in Emory's official "white" history. Warren Candler, a prominent bishop in the Methodist Episcopal Church, South, served as Emory College's president and later as chancellor of its successor institution, Emory University, an entity made possible through a substantial gift from his brother, Asa Candler, the Coca Cola magnate.

The photograph in question, taken around 1920, depicts a reunion of the white Candler-Branham extended family in Oxford. On the extreme left of the image sits Israel Godfrey; six to his right sits his wife, Sally Sims Godfrey, who through her mother, Angeline, traced her descent to a Native American Creek community in eastern Newton County along the Alcovy River.

The photograph has long been perplexing to JP and to other African American and white residents of Oxford. How was it in the 1920s that two African Americans, in the depths of the Jim Crow era, are seated, not standing, in the family reunion photograph of one of the most powerful white families in Georgia? Israel, many have noted, sits stolidly, "like he owns the place." His wife, Sally, does not look at the camera but gazes to her right, perhaps at her husband. What was going through her mind at that moment?

JP regards the image with considerable ambivalence. He wonders at times what it was that led his grandfather to be held in such high esteem among the white leadership of Emory and Oxford. How, immediately after the Civil War, did he manage to convince Emory's white leaders to donate land for the African American community Methodist church, even after the community broke with the white-dominated Methodist Episcopal Church, South, and affiliated with the northern Methodist Church? Had he perhaps done something to betray his people? Was he perhaps used as a "stud" or breeder back in slavery times, impregnating enslaved women against their will?

In any event, JP is well aware that he and his family have benefited across the years from the special standing Israel had in powerful white eyes. He recalls that during the 1954–55 school year he had to suspend his studies at Clark College to care for his ill father. The dean of Oxford College at that time, Virgil Eady Sr., hired him that year as a janitor; however, "that whole year," Mr. Godfrey recalls, "I never saw a mop or a broom." He was allowed informally to attend college classes, albeit in the rear of the classroom, so that he did not fall behind in his premedical studies.

Forty years later, Mr. Godfrey returned to settle in Oxford and was elected to the city council, where he led successful struggles to desegregate the city's cemetery and its police force. He now finds himself, as the "elder statesman" of the city, in the curious position of regularly defending Oxford College at city council meetings in the face of residents who wonder why the college has special municipal tax and financial advantages. "I always have to tell them," JP says laughingly, "that there wouldn't be an Oxford city if it wasn't for Emory. Pretty funny, if you think about it, that we are the ones safeguarding Emory's interests, though!" Yet he still finds himself wondering about the photograph. "Just what kind of hold did grandfather have on those white folks? And what does that mean about the rest of us?"

Miss Kitty's Headstones: Old and New

Next, consider a deeply contested headstone on the other side of the cemetery from where Israel Godfrey and the other African American pioneers of Oxford are interred. This simple stone marker poignantly illuminates the contradictory and enduring legacies of slavery in Emory University's self-conception. Dedicated in 2000, the stone honors the enslaved woman known as Kitty, owned by Methodist bishop James Osgood Andrew. Standard white accounts hold that according to the terms under which he had inherited Kitty as a girl, Bishop Andrew attempted to emancipate her in 1841 (when she turned nineteen) by offering to send her to Liberia, where many freed slaves had been resettled. According to a legal document produced by Augustus Baldwin Longstreet, then president of the college, Kitty refused to go to Liberia. Bishop Andrew, it is said, then built her a small cabin behind his own in which she resided "as free as the laws of Georgia would admit."[5]

White authors further state that she married a free black man named Nathan Shell, had children by him, and continued to live in Oxford until her death in the early 1850s. It is asserted that on her deathbed, Kitty exulted that she would soon see "Miss Amelia," the late first wife of Bishop Andrew, "in the better land."[6]

As noted above, Bishop Andrew's ownership of Kitty and fifteen other slaves became a matter of national controversy in 1844, when his slave-owning status was publicly debated at the annual conference of the Methodist Episcopal Church, held in New York City that year. Northern abolitionist bishops requested that Andrew resign from the episcopacy, a move denounced by Longstreet and Andrew's other southern supporters, who asserted that Andrew was only "accidentally" a slaveholder. The next year, the Methodist Church formally split over the issue of slavery and was not reunited until 1939.[7]

Oxford's African American residents contest nearly every detail of the above account. Many older residents of the community assert that Miss Kitty was the coerced mistress of Bishop Andrew and that he fathered at least one of her three children. They note that the historical record is ambiguous on Miss Kitty's origins. Although Bishop Andrew repeatedly asserted that he had been "willed" Kitty by a rich woman in Augusta, an exhaustive search of antebellum probate and deed records in Richmond County, Georgia, has failed to unearth any such bequest. Newton County, Georgia, tax records give no record of any antebellum freedman by the name of Nathan or Shell. The identity of Kitty's parents remains unknown; since Kitty was light-skinned and comparatively privileged among Oxford slaves, it is widely assumed that her father was a prominent white man. (Some elderly Oxford African Americans recall their parents and grandparents asserting that Bishop Andrew himself was Kitty's father rather than her lover.) All doubted that a free man of color named Nathan Shell, Kitty's alleged husband, ever existed.

In any event, the century and a half since Miss Kitty's passing have seen repeated symbolic struggles over the meaning of her life and her death in Oxford. Buried within the Andrew family plot, she is the only person of color generally acknowledged to be interred within the city's long-segregated white cemetery. In the late 1930s, on the eve of the reunification of the northern and southern denominations of the Methodist Church, the wealthy Atlanta businessman and Emory University trustee H. Y. McCord arranged to transport the former slave cabin from the land once owned by Bishop Andrew to Salem Campground, at the time an all-white religious campground about twelve miles away. McCord simultaneously erected a large stone tablet near Kitty's grave in the Oxford City Cemetery on which was inscribed the standard white account of Kitty's life, emphasizing Bishop Andrew's blamelessness in the matter.[8]

Meanwhile, the old cabin, renamed the Kitty's Cottage Museum, served as a memorial to the Lost Cause of the Confederacy at Salem until it was returned in 1994 to the city of Oxford, where white members of the nearly all-white Oxford Historical Shrine Society labored to restore it. Most Oxford African Americans have refused to enter the cabin, which remains a considerable site of controversy. "For us," an older African American man explained, "this building is a place of violation, not of love." Local families even debated the meaning of the fact that Miss Kitty, interred in Bishop Andrew's family plot, was the only person of color known to be buried in the historically white section of the Oxford city cemetery. Many whites saw this a sign of the close bonds of friendship between the bishop's family and his enslaved "servants," whereas most African Americans argued that, even in death, the bishop sought to control his former slaves. Many questioned if Bishop Andrew or any slaveholder could ever be said to have owned other human beings "accidentally," as his defenders claimed.

In 2000, as African Americans in Oxford became increasingly vocal in their protests over the enduring segregation of the city cemetery and over the failure of the city police department to hire any African American patrol officers, the white leadership of the city sought to appease them by placing a small headstone to Kitty in the Andrew family plot. The headstone read, "Kitty Andrew Shell, 1822–c. 1850." No African Americans were consulted in the wording of the stone, which offended nearly all members of the local black community. As J.P. observed, "We have known plenty of black families connected to Emory across the generations, but no one has ever heard of a black family named Shell! . . . And there [are] no tax records of a free man of color named Nathan in Newton County. . . . It is just another one of those fantasies, we think."

In the course of researching my book, *The Accidental Slaveowner*, I learned that there had in fact been an enslaved man who referred to himself as "Nathan Boyd" and who had considered himself married to Kitty, although in bank records he referred to her as Catherine. This discovery led me in time to locate the descendants of Catherine Boyd's eldest son, Alford Boyd, who escaped from slavery in April 1865 and who became an ordained minister in the African Methodist Episcopal Church, serving in Iowa and Illinois. Over the past several years, I have become close to Catherine Boyd's great-great-great-granddaughters, Cynthia and Darcel Caldwell, who reside in Philadelphia.

The Caldwell sisters visited Emory and Oxford in February 2011 to participate in an international conference on slavery and universities. Their trip was eased by an official declaration issued by the Emory board of trustees several weeks earlier of a "Statement of Regret" for the university's historical connections with slavery: "Emory acknowledges its entwinement with the institution of slavery throughout the College's early history. Emory regrets both this undeniable wrong and the University's decades of delay in acknowledging slavery's harmful legacy. As Emory University looks forward, it seeks the wisdom always to discern what is right and the courage to abide by its mission of using knowledge to serve humanity."[9]

On the conference's final day, hundreds gathered in a talking circle in Oxford to reflect on the legacies of enslavement at the university and in the wider community. A beautiful quilt created by community members to welcome home the descendants was unrolled. The sisters were handed a proclamation by the city's mayor, declaring that the day was devoted to Catherine and Nathan Boyd's descendants. Darcel stood before the assembled crowd and pointed to a pin Emory's vice president had recently given her marking the university's 175th anniversary. "At first I thought this morning, oh, I shouldn't wear this, since this is Miss Kitty's day. But then I thought, wait, this is her university, this is *your* university!" The applause was tumultuous.

It was a beautiful homecoming in so many ways. Many remarked that the 175th anniversary pin, which might have seemed a bit alienating, had been skillfully recuperated by Darcel. Alice Williamson, an elderly African American resident of Oxford, noted approvingly, "She just turned that pin right around. It doesn't just belong to the administration or official Emory. It belongs to all of us!" As an object of memory, the pin was effectively reclassified as a symbolic instrument of inclusion, even liberation.

Double Consciousness and the Memory Quilt

On center stage during the homecoming and reconciliation ceremony was the memory quilt, itself a complex dramatization of double consciousness in Du Bois's sense. This artwork had been produced by Atlanta-based artist Lynn Marshall-Linnemeier working in close collaboration with members of Grace United Methodist Church in Covington, a historically African American congregation that counts among its members many of the families long ago enslaved at and around Emory College. Entitled *Unraveling Miss Kitty's Cloak*, the work was expressly developed to welcome Miss Kitty's descendants back to Newton County and to honor more broadly all the African American families historically bound to Emory from the time of slavery onward.

In this striking, multifaceted work, Marshall-Linnemeier drew upon the spiritual Ifa traditions of the Yoruba peoples of West Africa, as well as African American quilting traditions of the American South. Marshall-Linnemeier initially proposed that the work be shaped like an *agan*, the swirling ancestral mask used in the Yoruba Egungun ceremony of ancestral veneration. Yet as the project developed, it became clear to the artist and her community collaborators that the work needed to be structured more as a large quilt than as a three-dimensional masquerade costume. As Alice Sanderson, a senior member of Grace, remarked, "Miss Kitty's children were just ripped out of this community, like so many other thousands gone. We need to help put them back in our family stories. A quilt seems a good way to do that, don't you think?" Other women spoke of the power of quilts to evoke and "stitch together" family stories of struggle and endurance, and they emphasized ways in which the honored dead have long been remembered through quilts incorporating elements of clothing they wore during their lives.

Listening to these thoughts, Marshall-Linnemeier came to feel that the work needed to emphasize the general figure of the "Ancestral Mother" without limiting itself to any one maternal figure in particular. She thus flanked the upper cutout image of a great tree with outward-facing silhouettes of a woman's profile. Anna Lockley, who helped sew the final work, nodded approvingly: "That could be any one of our mothers, any strong black woman." Janet Porter chimed in: "When I look at those profiles, I am reminded of the great line of women we come from." After discussion with the "ladies of the church," Lynn placed a striking red oval in the tree's trunk to evoke a hollow, signaling the hidden mysteries of lineage and ancestry that had for so long been obscured in the county.

Although the dominant tone of the work is celebratory, some of the images are avowedly painful. On the base of a photographic image of two young African American girls dressed in slave clothing, the artist has written the ambiguous word "Gifted," signaling both their God-given gifts and the painful fact that like so many enslaved persons they were transacted as dowry gifts at the time of their white owners' marriages. One church member recently told me, "I can't take my eyes off of that picture. Those were some woman's daughters, taken away from her, never to be seen again. And they are somebody's sisters. . . . Just given away as presents, as gifts. . . . So much was lost to us. But here and now, we give honor to them still." She drew particular connections with the fate of several of the young female slaves owned by Alexander Means, who gave them away as dowry presents when his daughters were married: "Those children were torn away from their own family so Dr. Means's white daughters could start their own family. . . . We need to think on them and all those who once were lost and now are found."

Similar ambivalent sentiments of loss and restoration informed the community's discussion over whose face should be visible near the top of the work. Marshall-Linnemeier had initially wanted a female figure associated with Kitty or an Afro-Caribbean "mambo" priestess behind a wedding veil. Yet in keeping with community wishes, she placed behind the veil a treasured photograph of Reverend Willis Jefferson King (1886–1976), a Methodist bishop who at one point pastored Grace United Methodist Church. This was a rather poignant choice, linked in a subtle way to the story of Miss Kitty and Bishop Andrew: Bishop King had been president of Samuel Huston College and Gammon Theological Seminary and had been honored in 1975 as the longest-serving United Methodist bishop. He had, significantly, been an early bishop elected in the so-called Central Jurisdiction, a segregated "all-negro" entity created in 1939 when the northern and southern wings of the Methodist Church were united, in principle healing the schism that had originated in 1844 caused by Bishop Andrew's status as a slave owner. As one older member of the congregation remarked,

> That great man should have been a bishop of the whole reunited Methodist Church, not segregated off in the Central Jurisdiction.... You know, the whole reason for the Central Jurisdiction was that white southerners in 1939 couldn't get over their version of the Bishop Andrew and Miss Kitty story: they just wanted our people kept in "their place," you know. And our northern brothers, to be perfectly frank, just sold us out.... So I think it is right and fitting that Bishop King is honored right up there at the top of our whole family tree!

The structural violence done to African American respect and dignity within the Methodist community and the wider world is redressed through this elaborate tapestry, in which a long-excluded patriarch is given his full due in the restored lineage of this community of faith. Marshall-Linnemeier had initially conceived of the veil in terms of Yoruba imagery of the priestess as bride of the orisha. Yet for community members the more salient associations were Du Bois's discussion of double consciousness and the "veil" of racial distinction. Hence, the appropriate subject beyond the veil is not a female initiate but a male bishop who was long forced to labor "behind the veil" of W. E. B. Du Bois's "color line."

As the great quilt descended, backlit by the afternoon sun streaming in through the church's great windows, it was hard not to think of the final lines of Du Bois's book *The Souls of Black Folk*: "If somewhere in this whirl and chaos of things there dwells Eternal Good, pitiful yet masterful, then anon in His good time America shall rend the Veil and the prisoned shall go free. Free, free as the sunshine trickling down the morning into these high windows of mine."[10] (Indeed, when one local African American woman saw the quilt unveiled, she nodded her head and remarked, "Ah, the souls of black folk.")

Next to Bishop King's visage was sewn in a reproduced photograph of Miss Kitty / Catherine Boyd's eldest children, Reverend Alford Boyd and his wife, Malvina. Congregants found great meaning in the positioning of Reverend Boyd, who had left the proslavery Methodist Episcopal Church, South, of his enslaved boyhood to seek ordination in the African Methodist Episcopal Church, next to the veiled image of Bishop King, who had served first in the northern Methodist Church and then in the reunited Methodist Church. As Emma Horne, the Grace United Methodist Church historian notes, "Right there, you see the whole remarkable history of race and Methodism in America, of the schism that started here at Emory and which we are still dealing with today."

A New Headstone

The quilt and the homecoming ceremony were deeply meaningful to all the descendants present. Yet the "Kitty" headstone in the Andrew plot still rankled for the Boyd-Caldwell descendants and other African American residents of Newton County. "She's still identified by her slave name," remarked Oxford resident Reverend Avis Williams. Following the Slavery and University conference in February 2011, the Oxford City Council debated the matter and decided to make things right by commissioning a new headstone inscribed with words that had been approved by the family members and the local African American community's representatives: "Catherine 'Kitty' Andrew Boyd, c. 1822–1851. Beloved wife, mother and member of the Oxford and Emory communities." The headstone was dedicated on Sunday, October 23, one week after the dedication of the Martin Luther King Jr. memorial on the National Mall in Washington, D.C. As a number of Oxford residents remarked, in its own small way, this local act of rededication was a significant chapter in building the "Beloved Community" that Dr. King so longed for.

During this period, the Emory University administration developed plans to celebrate the university's 175th anniversary. To mark the celebrations on December 7, the university recognized 175 "history makers," individuals, living and dead, who had made profound contributions to the institution and to humanity. Among the 175 was Catherine "Miss Kitty" Boyd; her great-great-great-granddaughters, Darcel and Cynthia Caldwell, were invited down to Atlanta to receive a medal in Miss Kitty's honor. Also present at the award luncheon was a great grandson of Bishop James Osgood Andrew, the owner of Miss Kitty. Bishop Andrew's descendant warmly greeted Darcel and told her mischievously, "You know, we might be cousins!" A few minutes later Darcel remarked with a laugh that the day was turning into a "regular family reunion."

Toward Reparations?

Meanwhile, a campaign has gradually developed to establish a scholarship at Emory for descendants of families enslaved at Emory and in Oxford. The idea was first publicly proposed in 2000 by Eugene Emory, an African American professor of psychology at Emory University who traces his ancestry back to the white family of Bishop John Emory, for whom Emory College was named. Dr. Emory participated in the opening ceremony for an exhibition curated by me and my students at Oxford College on Emory and Oxford's early African American history. In front of a hushed audience in the Oxford College Day Chapel, built by former slave Israel Godfrey in 1875, Eugene Emory spoke about his complex family history, including the likelihood that he is a direct lineal descendant of Bishop Emory, who had been a slave owner in the state of Maryland. He discussed his own sense of moral ambivalence walking across the main Emory campus, where each day, in his words, he encountered signs "bearing my name, or at least the name I bear, but not acknowledging our real history." From family oral history, he explained, he had inferred that his ancestral mother was most likely an enslaved woman who was coerced into a sexual relationship with Bishop Emory. Some years ago, Dr. Emory traveled to a point near Reisterstown, Maryland, where Bishop Emory died in a carriage accident on December 17, 1835. At the spring 2000 ceremony, Dr. Emory shared with the audience his torn emotional reactions, standing on that charged spot: "Was I supposed to feel remorse over the loss of my likely paternal ancestor? Was I supposed to mourn the death of the man who may well have raped my ancestral mother?" He then proposed that the best way to honor the memory of those who had labored as chattel on and around the Emory campus was to establish a full tuition scholarship for their descendants. The idea was received with applause.

Over the subsequent decade, J. P. Godfrey Jr. has continued to campaign for the concept. In the wake of the trustees' statement of regret and the various festivities honoring the descendants of Catherine "Miss Kitty" Boyd, the idea seems to be gradually gaining traction. As of this writing, a formal proposal is being developed for a tuition scholarship at Emory for which descendants of the Emory and Oxford enslaved community might compete.

Conclusion

Where do such objects and such moments leave us as we ponder the "family business" of slavery and universities? The photograph of the Candler-Branham reunion, marked by the puzzling presence of Israel and Sally Godfrey, is hardly a sign of serious fracture in the regional edifice of Jim Crow: Israel and Sally and their children were thoroughly excluded by law and custom from nearly all white-dominated institutions in the region, except in the capacity of servants. The memory quilt and the October 2011 rededication of a headstone, as moving as they are, hardly constitute a full measure of restorative justice or reparation. Having said that, many are heartened by ongoing discussions to establish a scholarship at Emory for descendants of enslaved families, perhaps to be named for groundskeeper Robert Hammond, honored, ambiguously, by the tree in the quadrangle, or for Catherine "Miss Kitty" Boyd, whose former slave quarters remain a sensitive political flashpoint in Oxford.

Taken together, these elements—the restored African American burial ground, the memorial tree, the photograph, the successive headstones to Kitty/Catherine Boyd, the rebuilt slave cottage, the memory quilt, and the as-yet-unrealized promise of a university scholarship—serve as haunting testimony to the unfinished business of slavery in the university and in the United States. They remind us of the curious twists and turns in American apartheid, of the enigmatic slippages and transpositions that characterized the peculiar institution and its successor systems of racialized domination. Above all, they function as a complex kind of looking glass in which conventional distinctions between self and other are simultaneously dissolved and reinforced. Thus the tree dedicated to the Jim Crow–era chief janitors can be viewed by present-day African American staff members as signs of alienation and of pride. Thus, the great image of Bishop King behind the "veil" of the memory quilt can be simultaneously viewed as an implicit condemnation of the racist formation of the Central Jurisdiction of the Methodist Church in 1939 and a celebration of the accomplishments of African Americans within the organization from 1940 until 1968. Thus Darcel Caldwell, Miss Kitty's fifth-generation descendant, can simultaneously distinguish herself and her family from the dominant narrative of Emory while declaring of her ancestral mother, by means of the anniversary pin, "This is *her* Emory." Thus Ms. Perkins can, in tragicomic vein, declare that her enslaved ancestors were Emory's "family business" even as she claims the institution as her "family business" and then, six months later, learn to her shock that neither the university nor its contractor proxy recognizes the slightest sense of moral responsibility toward her, her kin, or her fellow workers.

Universities, it has long been noted, are mythic, even sacralized, utopian spaces. The university claims to stand outside of conventional space and time, allowing its denizens the luxury of walking among the Eternals. How fitting, then, that these objects of memory remind us, in so many different ways, of eternal truths that we are so eager to forget—of the long histories of oppression, exploitation, and struggles for liberation that underlie our continuing quest for knowledge—in the university and in the world at large. They speak, as Du Bois long ago reminded us, of the enduring veil of "two-ness," of the uncanny "second sight" born of being simultaneously within and without the temple, as well as the enduring promise that someday our land "shall rend the Veil and the prisoned shall go free."

NOTES

This chapter is based on field research conducted in Newton County, Georgia, between 1999 and 2018. Most conversations and interviews were undertaken in 2001, 2002, and 2003.

1. W. E. B. DuBois, *The Souls of Black Folk: Essays and Sketches* (Chicago: A. C. McClurg, 1903).

2. Victor Turner, *The Forest of Symbols: Aspects of Ndembu Ritual* (Ithaca, N.Y.: Cornell University Press, 1967).

3. Angeline Sims, family members recall, was Native American, probably Creek. Her Native American relatives continued to reside along the Alcovy River into the 1940s; there, they were often visited by their African American kin from Oxford.

4. Eady family papers, in private hands, Oxford, Georgia. Consulted by the author in 2002.

5. Albert Henry Redford, *History of the Organization of the Methodist Episcopal Church, South* (Nashville: A. H. Redford, 1875), 160.

6. George Gilman Smith, *The Life and Letters of James Osgood Andrew: Bishop of the Methodist Church South* (Nashville: Southern Methodist Publishing House, 1883), 314.

7. For a detailed exploration of white and African American retellings of the stories of Miss Kitty and Bishop Andrew, see Mark Auslander, *The Accidental Slaveowner: Revisit-*

ing a Myth of Race and Finding an American Family (Athens: University of Georgia Press, 2011).

8. McCord was strongly influenced in these actions by Bishop Warren Candler, former president of Emory College and first chancellor of Emory University. McCord and Candler, committed segregationists, were deeply concerned that the reunification of the Methodist Church would lead to the appointment of Negro bishops in the South and to the desecration of Kitty's Cottage, which Candler described as "the most interesting building in Georgia." Mark Auslander, *The Accidental Slaveowner: Revisiting a Myth of Race and Finding an American Family* (Athens: University of Georgia Press, 2011), 104.

9. Ron Sauder, "Emory Declares Its Regret for Historic Involvement with Slavery," *Emory Report*, January 17, 2011. http://www.emory.edu/EMORY_REPORT/stories/2011/01/campus_regret_for_historic_involvement_with_slavery.html.

10. Du Bois, *The Souls of Black Folk*, 263.

CHAPTER FIFTEEN

Engaging the Racial Landscape at the University of Alabama

Ellen Griffith Spears & James C. Hall

The University of Alabama pierced the national consciousness when Vivian Malone and James Hood swept past Governor George Wallace and through the unassuming ground-floor portal of Foster Auditorium in 1963 to register as the school's first African American students.[1] However, focusing only on that one iconic moment, the frozen image of Wallace's last stand, not only distracts from the significant victory won by Malone and Hood but also neglects the long institutional history that preceded that day. Since the school opened in 1831, the University of Alabama has been a place supported and defined by race and exclusion—and the contested presence—of African Americans. Slaves owned by the university and granted to individual professors upon their arrival rest in the vicinity of a small graveyard next to the Biology Building, finally acknowledged in an apology by the Faculty Senate in 2004. "Rented slaves" constructed university buildings, including the Little Round House, the octagonal munitions building guarded by Confederate officers in training on the campus during the Civil War. Confederate markers adorn the front steps of the Amelia Gayle Gorgas Main Library. As elsewhere, the naming of buildings is fraught. Nott Hall, for example, is named for Alabama physician Josiah Nott, one of the primary slavery era proponents of polygenesis, who led the development of the Medical College of Alabama.[2] The evidence of slavery inscribed on the landscape of the university provides a significant site for launching a critical exploration of political struggle—in the past and over the past—embodied in the places students pass casually on the way to class.

As two professors who teach and write about race on the university's campus, we suggest multiple avenues of inquiry and clarification of the university's history and the nature of its current engagement with race. Our insistence is upon understanding the complex continuity between narratives of implication in slavery and slaveholding and twentieth-century university practices of racial exclusion. Place-based pedagogies are rich in opportunities to let students discover the hidden transcript of race absence and presence. In the larger national project of sorting out the relationship between the emergence of U.S. higher education and the system of slavery, the Alabama story is an important one in its physical embodiment and symbolic entangling of black human capacity, social resistance, and cultural performance of the ever-evolving racial order.

The renovation in 2010 of Foster Auditorium, where Alabama governor George Wallace stood in an attempt to block desegregation in 1963, as the women's basketball gym reopened the conversation about race and university history, making freshly evident the rich educational landscape that the campus provides. Universities and colleges that are either tentatively or boldly tackling their institutional histories of involvement with slavery are doing so in multiple ways using the standard academic tools of scholarly research and publishing and of curriculum and course development. Others are extending the scholarly mission into the life of the university community by establishing dialogue groups, such as the Crossroads Community Center's Sustained Dialogue Project.[3] Others are expanding the educational mission into activist projects carried out by scholars, mobilizing faculty and students, pressing administrators and trustees to extend apologies to the descendants of enslaved persons, such as the 2004 movement steered by law professor Al Brophy and others at the University of Alabama.[4] Still others pushed for the renaming of buildings once christened for owners of slaves or staunch segregationists, such as the campaign undertaken at the University of Texas at Austin in 2010.[5]

All of these approaches are intertwined: research is essential to designing curriculum; dialogue is necessary to creating openness and political will; activism emerging from that research and conversation is critical to institutional recognition and change. Unearthing institutional ties to slavery undergirds each of these strategies. This work links memory and landscape, with the recognition that all history takes place in space.

Rooted in the work of critical spatial theorists such as Henri Lefebvre, David Harvey, Doreen Massey, and Edward Soja, this approach also draws on the scholarship of critical pedagogy of place, in which historical memory, place, and pedagogy are interwoven.[6] David Gruenewald, a leading scholar in this field, suggests that a critical pedagogy necessitates both "decolonization," that is, "learning to recognize [both] disruption and injury and to address their causes," and "rehabitation," that is, "learning to live well socially and ecologically in places that have been disrupted and injured."[7] Making these disruptions visible through rereading the landscape serves the aim of decolonization; identifying new ways of inhabiting these spaces promotes rehabilitation, justice, and healing.

A blend of landscape studies and critical studies of race aids in exploring the visible and invisible racial ecologies on the campus. In doing so, we are hoping to link a reenvisioned environmental education, which often lacks a critical edge, with the study of racial histories of place. This process of reframing the racial ecology of the American landscape has a long history rooted in abolitionist writing of the slavery period. The abolitionists' project, as described by literary historian Ian Finseth, involved, in part, a conversation about nature and rights, a basic argument about the humanity of persons of African descent. The failure to legally vest African Americans with the unalienable rights celebrated at independence was the inherent contradiction at the nation's founding, based in a conception of nature that argued for separate origins of "races." The antislavery advocates argued, however inconsistently, against received notions that naturalized racial hierarchies. "Inevitably," Finseth argues, "what it means to be 'human,' and therefore to claim certain privileges or rights as a human being, is closely bound up with cultural perceptions of 'nature' and the 'nonhuman.' . . . [T]he meanings of 'race' depend on social definitions of 'humanness' and 'the human family.'"[8]

"In talking about race or nature, therefore," Finseth argues, "we are always working within and against the conceptual legacies of the eighteenth and nineteenth centuries."[9] We are, in effect, arguing against Josiah Nott. As one of the present authors has argued elsewhere, "In nineteenth century debates over evolutionary biology, redefining nature impelled the redefinition of race. Arguments against racial essentialism and racial hierarchy undergirded rights to legal personhood, rights to mobility, control over one's labor, and ownership of one's own body. Claims to justice, to equal political and civil rights, flowed directly from claims to a common origin in nature."[10] We are concerned today with pedagogies that illuminate this connection between nature, race, humanity, and justice.

The teaching strategies that flow from this approach stress the importance of engagement with place—a connection to one's habitus, one's physical surroundings—in shaping transformative higher education, in defining a course of study that not only informs but also allows students to envision new ways of being in the world. In ways suggested by the links between place and historical memory, we envision place-based studies that engage with sites of slavery and racism on the UA campus. The campus landscape itself presents multiple opportunities for the teaching of slavery history, highlighting those acts of memory and forgetting that illuminate or obscure responsibility and justice.

Indeed, part of our engagement with the campus landscape is to insist that any full accounting of the university's entanglement with slavery will by necessity involve a reconstruction of willful acts of forgetting in the postemancipation era. While the period of slaveholding on our campus was seminal, it was brief relative to the now 140 years of shaping and reshaping a landscape that disguises that breach. The question of "the university and slavery" can never be one of simply accounting and accumulating recoverable knowledge about the black presence. It is perhaps more energetically the story of a continuity of racial hierarchy, invented structures of discrimination, and the vexed question of southern identity. At the University of Alabama, we find in the physical landscape of the campus a hidden transcript that reveals a codependence between the image of the "modern" institution of higher education, the difficult work of racial reconciliation, and more discreet practices of forgetting and disavowal.

Nineteenth-century presidents of the university well understood the critical role of the pedagogy of place and, we might argue, anticipated the permanent bond between landscape and memory we seek to unpack. In the midst of a campus beautification project in 1887–88, President Henry Clayton wrote in his report to the trustees about the Civil War rubble that remained on the campus quadrangle: "I respectfully request and urge that the remains of the destroyed buildings be permitted to remain as historic monuments," wrote Clayton. "They constitute a chapter in the life of this university more eloquent than words, and if permitted to remain, will teach a lesson to our young men which they can learn in no other way."[11] The lesson Clayton hoped to teach involved the campus's Civil War destruction by Brigadier General John T. Croxton's Union troops in April 1865 because the institution served as "a military institution in the enemy South."[12]

President Clayton understood as well the significance of physical geography in creating alternate histories. Seeking to establish the campus landscape as a locale for Lost Cause pedagogy, Clayton opined, "It will be a sad day when our children shall believe that they are the descendants of a nation of drones and slave drivers, as is industriously being taught, while we are folding our arms in too much indifference."[13] Clayton uttered this statement with no apparent reflection on the fact that even before opening the doors to the first students in 1831, the University of Alabama trustees made their "first recorded purchase of a slave [known to us now only as Ben] ... in 1828."[14]

With "the Mound," a self-conscious decision was made during the reconstruction of the campus (a reconstruction paid for by federal reparations) to protect and gather rubble so that the conflict between the states would be remembered in distinctly heroic terms.[15] Much of the rubble remained until 1910, when, over alumni and student protests, several mounds of destroyed buildings were hauled away during a campus modernization project. However, the remains of Franklin Hall, a dormitory, and the barracks that had housed the cadets in the former Confederate Officer Corps, one of four buildings that ringed the original campus rotunda, were retained as a symbolic act that honored the Confederacy.

Maintaining the mounds as sacred space naturalized Lost Cause history. We have to excavate that history. Campus archaeologist Jerry Oldshue, who holds all three of his degrees from the university, did excavate one of the former mounds, Madison Hall. Only a small remnant of the brick building, the southwest corner, remains. Much of what Oldshue found was to be expected on a campus that at the time served Alabama's aristocratic young white elite: a beer stein, a whiskey bottle, a derringer, a desk. He also identified books that were burned: "You could still read [the titles]—*Much Ado about Nothing, Geography of Africa, Plane Geometry*—but they soon crumbled after being exposed to air." He also found "an idol of Sheba, the Union goddess."[16]

The "Mounds of Beauty" that Henry Clayton sought to preserve as sacred space held continued salience. In the first decade of the twentieth century, the campus practice began of informally using the space for initiation into honoraries and secret societies. Student Sidney Bland Gorchov described the "grass-covered oblong remnant of earth" in a school newspaper editorial entitled "The Mound" on the occasion of the university's centennial in 1931. "Its appearance suggests the dimensions of some immense coffin preserving the remains of some giant in legend," *Crimson White* staffer Gorchov wrote. "How many students at Alabama are even partially acquainted with the identity, the historical background, this hidden eeriness, and the suggestive aspects attributable to the Mound?"[17] From a distant vantage point, his question resonates today.

The mound created from that Civil War debris remains a significant site of campus rituals at which events bestowing campus honors to students and

The remains of Civil War–era Confederate cadet dormitory Franklin Hall, memorialized as "the Mound," with cadets during World War I. Courtesy of the Eugene Allen Smith Collection, W. S. Hoole Special Collections Library, University of Alabama.

faculty, called "tapping" ceremonies, take place. It was largely unmanicured space and at least since the 1970s, in the shaping of an informal counternarrative, was colonized in a way by students maintaining the modern counterculture practice of the drum circle, a key ritual in the cross-racial performance of many a young white man.

In 2006, two years after the faculty apology for slavery, the space was "rededicated"—landscaped, fenced, marked with a more formal historical marker, and now further designated by the sign Keep Off the Mound. The rededication narrative has never been especially explicit—and the reconstruction (that word again) of the space did at least partially have to do with managing feared Americans with Disabilities Act (ADA) challenges to its status as official campus ceremonial space—and the transformation and evolution of its potential meanings has largely passed without campus comment.

In analyzing how the civil rights movement inhabits our memories over time, Vanderbilt sociologist Larry Isaac reminds us that "social memory is cohort or generation-dependent."[18] Generations on a college campus are particularly short, with turnover every four years or so. Inscribing memories on a landscape promotes intergenerational memories.

Just as important as understanding how landscapes make memory is knowing how the forgetting of the university's history of slavery took place. Again, Isaac is thinking of the civil rights years, but the parallel is relevant. "Understanding the forgotten culture of the civil rights movement story, and how that forgetting took place," Isaac writes, "is important for what it can tell us about the political struggle over the past as well as envisioning and moving toward a new and more just future."[19] Such "collective memory studies," Isaac argues, show "how memory can be a vehicle by which movements of the past move to us in the present and presage alternative futures."[20]

The relationship between slavery and the University of Alabama must be recovered in the context of the Lost Cause narrative that marked the institution's return to public viability and brokered and complicated its self-image and embrace of modernity. The narrative is retrospective—a series of partially unearthed facts that detail the African American presence on our campus from its birth moment—and a more complicated process still of discerning patterns of attentiveness, of turning away, and of the shaping of formal structures of exclusion. The look back also includes gestures of reconciliation, friendship, and insight, but it remains unclear whether that more informal narrative and set of actions is able to sustain itself.

Al Brophy did a remarkable job summarizing the history of slavery at the University of Alabama in his important essay "The University and the Slaves: Apology and Its Meaning" and even more remarkable work in brokering, inciting, grounding, and guiding the 2004 faculty apology for UA's involvement with slavery. Much of what we describe here is deeply indebted to his groundbreaking work. Brophy directed people's attention to the totality of the institution's entanglement with slaves and slavery and the intellectual and economic foundations for both. There is—it must be stated in the most direct way possible—no University of Alabama without slavery and the enslaved:

- We know that black labor in enslavement was fundamental to the initial physical construction of the campus in the 1820s and that it involved both university-owned and university-hired slaves. We know that enslaved labor remained an important dimension of the everyday operations of the institution throughout the antebellum period, indeed until the very day federal troops entered the campus grounds.

- We know that faculty, students, and university presidents owned, hired, and disciplined slaves in the course of their scholarship, study, and administration of the University of Alabama. Students brought slaves with them to campus. Key figures in the development of the University of Alabama—most notably Basil Manly and William Garland—were major slaveholders.
- We know that Alabama faculty and administrators played a key role in managing the evolving justification for slavery in its biblical, political, economic, and natural scientific manifestations. Basil Manly and Josiah Nott, in particular, are not only key figures in the development of southern higher education but also absolutely central to the narrative by which the slaveocracy shaped an ever-evolving narrative of defense.[21]

The destruction of the university by Union troops on April 4, 1865, did not make inevitable the forgoing of a process of reconciliation and evaluation, but it certainly became the emotional grounding of a narrative of heroic loss. It also required the shaping of a new physical environment—literal building from the ground up—that both left traces of a lived past and more self-consciously marked an ideology that insisted upon the preservation of honor—and, of course, what Walker Percy liked to call "the venerable tradition of keeping Negroes out."[22] Both the immediate rebuilding of the Alabama flagship and the extended modernization of a twentieth-century university involved shaping and maintaining physical markers of place that hid the African American presence, valorized a distinctly martial ideal, and looked to ritually socialize insiders and outsiders into the embrace of a truncated history.

The physical landscape constantly alludes to shared white trauma while at the same time courting a kind of desirable ideological neutrality—somehow a cross between *Southern Living* and a Greek Revival Levittown. Throughout the twentieth century, the university steadfastly maintained an attachment to a modified Jeffersonian vision, that is, a grand and planned academic village that made physically central and partially performative the campus's destruction. The university required at strategic moments in its twentieth-century development both the influx of outsiders—both faculty and student resources—and sustained markers of the Lost Cause, all staged within purposeful management of the social system of segregation.

Our goal is to promote reflection on the resources that exist in our most immediate physical surroundings not as a forgetting or dismissal of the teaching of conventional historical narrative but as partial acknowledgment of the significant filters and anxieties our students carry with them. The minutest number imaginable of our students are neosecessionist ideologues, despite the uncritical embrace many make of antebellum dress-up games and so-called southern heritage parties. Most students have more likely been introduced to the key twentieth-century episode in our racial history through an encounter with Forrest Gump than through guided systematic reflection.

So our instinct is that we have an opportunity to do work that is both disruptive yet nonthreatening in the short term by directing attention to aspects of the mundane spaces that students travel each day. We suspect too, in evaluating the collective work that this shared project represents, that the question of the evolution of the physical space of our campus (related to but not wholly overlapping with work in recent years at Vanderbilt and elsewhere in examining naming practices) may be our distinct contribution. There is a distinct and unusual relationship between commemorated slave graves on our campus, the smoldering ashes of a destroyed university in 1865, and the proverbial schoolhouse door of 1963. That relationship points not only to so-called structures of feeling but also—in the most particular and revealing ways—to crucial institutional decision-making practices that reveal the mechanisms that sustained segregation and, most present of all, the difficulties we face in the contemporary United States to shape satisfying practices of racial reconciliation.

First, we provide a very quick inventory of the pedagogical resources available to us as represented by the space in which we do our work, and then we conclude with a slightly more detailed meditation on two of those resources. They include

- commemorated slave graves near the center of our campus;
- commemoration of key figures of the slaveocracy on most every building around our campus quadrangle;
- historical markers that designate heroism in the great conflict or highlight federal troops' destruction of the campus;
- our presidential mansion, protected by southern womanhood and surrounded by slave quarters; and
- Foster Auditorium and the new Malone-Hood Plaza with the Autherine Lucy Clock Tower.

The slave quarters adjoining the president's mansion, prior to renovation, from Hill Ferguson's scrapbook. Courtesy of the W. S. Hoole Special Collections Library, University of Alabama.

The slave quarters, 2011. Photo by Tawny Fowler. Courtesy of Tawny Fowler.

Malone-Hood Plaza, dedicated to Vivian Malone and James Hood, the two African American students who desegregated the University of Alabama in 1963, with the Autherine Lucy Clock Tower, honoring the first black student to enroll in 1956. Photo by Tawny Fowler. Courtesy of Tawny Fowler.

Two additional sites on our campus are particularly suggestive of both the possibilities and the challenges of this pedagogical approach. The Ferguson Center, the campus student union, was named for alumnus William Hill Ferguson (class of 1896) in 1969, just a half dozen years after the arrival of James Hood and Vivian Malone Jones. (The board of trustees agreed to name the building in honor of Ferguson in 1969; it was dedicated in 1973.) William Hill Ferguson was a remarkable presence for close to seventy years at the Tuscaloosa campus. He was the son of Frederick Summerfield Ferguson, a self-designated Confederate "captain" who actually spent most of the Civil War as a prisoner of war in New York and Boston. "Captain" Ferguson sent his son Hill to the University of Alabama, where he became a member of one of the last cohorts of Alabama Cadets, gray-suited students who were committed to military values and discipline but who had no formal relationship to the U.S. military. He thrived as a student and athlete and earned Phi Beta Kappa membership. In the first decade of the twentieth century, following a stint as secretary to President John William Abercrombie, who served from 1902 to 1911, and, admittedly, following a period of wandering and no sense of vocation, Ferguson found purpose in his new role as president of the nascent alumni association and became the driving force in the Greater University Campaign. The campaign sought funds for the first major building boom in the post-Reconstruction period and further established the first campus master plan. An active shaping presence in the development of the plan, Ferguson insisted, as had university leaders twenty years earlier, on the preservation of the Mound as a permanent presence on the landscape. Ferguson also took a leading role in the campaign during the late 1940s to preserve the old campus core with state and federal historic designation and was relentless in his efforts to ensure that the campus core and the narrative of heroic Confederate resistance were sacralized. By this time in his life and career, he was a venerable member of the University of Alabama board of trustees, and he had served for many years as the vice president of Jemison Real Estate Corporation in Birmingham, Alabama, the company that played a large role in the permanent shaping of that city's segregated housing patterns and the eventual emergence of exclusive "over the mountain" communities. He was the key strategist on the board of trustees in developing active resistance measures to the emerging desegregation mandate in the 1950s and the only trustee to vote against the admission of Autherine Lucy.[23]

Ferguson was a classic New South apologist; within his person were entangled civic boosterism, relentless faith in and drive for modernization of the South, and unshakeable commitment to an imagined traditional set of social values with rigid segregation at its core, all rooted in a deep and personal sense of grievance and mourning. Ironically—or perhaps inevitably—he was also an amateur historian and archivist, compiling some of the most valuable collections of materials related to University of Alabama and Birmingham heritage. When the process of desegregation was complete and he had moved into retirement, Ferguson wrote a regressive and, by 1963, anachronistic screed to then president Frank Rose, bemoaning the inevitability of "mongrelization" and diminishment of southern values that he imagined were marked by the arrival of two black students. The student center building memorialized Ferguson, then, precisely at a time when university officials were moving away from Ferguson's segregationist views. (President Rose replied politely to Ferguson's diatribe and quietly filed his letter away in a folder labeled "Crank Letters.")

One further example reveals how the histories of slavery, Reconstruction, modernization, and desegregation are permanently entangled in the landscape by official and unofficial patterns of recognition and usage and, similarly, official and unofficial patterns of forgetting. Another striking attempt to memorialize the fading past is embodied in what is arguably the most remarkable work of art to be displayed in a university building. In 1925 the United Daughters of the Confederacy (UDC) commissioned a Tiffany window honoring the Knight of the Confederacy and had it installed in the university library. The dedication ceremony was attended by members of the Tuscaloosa community, by university community members, and, most notably, by seven surviving Confederate veterans, part of the corps of cadets who had defended the university sixty years earlier. This striking window was relocated to the new Gorgas Main Library in 1939 and remained in prominent public display until 1993, when the UDC paid to have it moved again, this time to the W. S. Hoole Special Collections Library. The window highlights the view from inside the Hoole second-floor lobby, but in some ways the more striking and significant views are to be seen from the outside. Mary Harmon Bryant Hall was designed to serve as a collections site not only for the university library but also for the Alabama State Geological Survey and the Alabama Natural History Museum. It is one of a very small number of buildings not shaped in Greek Revival style and is really a fairly brutal piece of modern architecture, appropriate for its function but not attracting attention. Indeed, the Knight of the Confederacy—now guarding Alabama's natural and historical heritage—is nearly the only window in a big brick box. But standing as it does forty feet above street level in a building few undergraduates will enter over the course of their careers, the transient knight now largely stands unnoticed.[24]

In a course called Southern Narrative before Civil Rights, students are taken to see the Tiffany window as part of a larger exercise that considers the way in which the campus landscape embodies stories about the meaning of the South and was consciously shaped by generations of institution builders. We work and walk our way backward from the recently unveiled Foster Plaza, an elegant acknowledgment of the significant heroism of young African American trailblazers, if historiographically complex and fraught with silences, across the campus quad to the Mound, the formal and informal site of initiation into leadership. From the Mound we make our way to the markers acknowledging the burial of university-owned and -hired slaves and then farther down

The Knight of the Confederacy, depicted in the Tiffany window commissioned in 1925 by the United Daughters of the Confederacy. Photo by Zachary Riggins. Courtesy of the University of Alabama.

Hackberry Lane to our last stop, which is the site of the Tiffany Knight of the Confederacy.

Most students have not been into the W. S. Hoole Special Collections Library in Mary Harmon Bryant Hall, so the trip up the elevator and the standard but unfamiliar archives rituals of dispensing with backpacks and signing in mark a distinct occasion and location. The window itself dominates the gateway to the institution's heritage. Indeed, if anything, the knight seems to function as the keeper of that past and to cast judgment on all who would plan to interpret it critically. We talk about the United Daughters of the Confederacy and their efforts to recapture an honorable and honored South, about the presence of the last surviving Confederate veterans at the window's dedication ceremony, and about the tension between New South boosterism and apologists for antebellum romanticism. The librarians themselves are torn, we can tell, between appreciating the aesthetic richness of the Tiffany glasswork in an otherwise drab environment and a slight embarrassment at its privileged position, seemingly tainting all who are associated with it in an official capacity and always demanding explanation.

The students are sophisticated-enough interpreters of the more recent southern past to recognize that the knight is, on the whole, "a bit much." It is hard to reconcile a specific accounting of the realities of slavery on the campus, especially the modest acknowledgment given the slave graves, with this generous helping of courtly myth and churchly sacralism. Female students, in particular, are able to articulate discomfort about just what message the knight's defense of their purity must have sent to generations of young women, just as a few men courageously note that maybe, just maybe, there might remain something valuable in a martial ideal. There's a relationship, they say, between the knight's readiness and the emergence of Alabama in the mid-1920s as "Dixie's Football Pride." If Alabama and the South are doomed to the economic, educational, and cultural bottom for at least another half century, why not embrace a radical ideal attainable through character, grit, and "toughness"?

As the class of fifteen crams itself back into the notoriously bumpy and slow elevator, small talk is nervous but authentic. It is like having watched a politically incorrect YouTube video and laughed. For a "mixed" group of longtime and part-time southerners, it is hard work looking behind the screen. The visit's pedagogical value always feels immediate even when it does not translate into a neat new thesis about race, education, and history. The work of making people move self-consciously through their own work landscape rewards not by any fixed articulation of the meaning of racial justice but by making movement through that landscape always fraught with the possibility of new discovery.

NOTES

1. See E. Culpepper Clark, *The Schoolhouse Door: Segregation's Last Stand at the University of Alabama* (New York: Oxford University Press, 1993).

2. Josiah Clark Nott, *Two Lectures on the Natural History of the Caucasian and Negro Races* (Mobile, Ala.: Dade and Thompson, 1844), 1–53.

3. Leslie M. Harris and Jody Usher describe a model program in this field in "Difficult Dialogues: From Disenchantment to Dialogue and Action: The 'Transforming Community' Project at Emory University," *Change*, March/April 2008, 18–23. Others have linked

research and dialogue, such as the visits to Oxford College that have played an important role in the research-based fact-finding project called "Gathering the Tools," developed also by the Transforming Community Project at Emory.

4. Alfred L. Brophy, "The University and the Slaves: Apology and Its Meaning," in *The Age of Apology: Facing Up to the Past*, ed. Mark Gibney (Philadelphia: University of Pennsylvania Press, 2008); Max Clarke and Gary Alan Fine, "'A' for Apology: Slavery and the Discourse of Remonstrance in Two American Universities," *History & Memory* 22, no. 1 (Spring/Summer 2010): 81–112.

5. Jim Vertuno, "Klansman's Name Stripped from Dormitory," *Atlanta Journal Constitution*, July 16, 2010, A8.

6. Henri Lefebvre, *The Production of Space* (Cambridge, Mass.: Blackwell, 1991); David Harvey, *Justice, Nature and the Geography of Difference* (Malden, Mass.: Blackwell Publishers, 1996); Doreen B. Massey, *Space, Place, and Gender* (Minneapolis: University of Minnesota Press, 1994); Edward W. Soja, *Postmodern Geographies: The Reassertion of Space in Critical Social Theory* (London: Verso, 1989).

7. David A. Gruenewald, "The Best of Both Worlds: A Critical Pedagogy of Place," *Educational Researcher* 32, no. 4 (May 2003): 3–12, 9. For more on critical and place-based pedagogies, see, for example, Peter McLaren, *Life in Schools: An Introduction to Critical Pedagogy in the Foundations of Education*, 3rd ed. (New York: Longman, 1998); and Paul Theobald, *Teaching the Commons: Place, Pride, and the Renewal of Community* (Boulder, Colo.: Westview Press, 1997).

8. Ian Frederick Finseth, *Shades of Green: Visions of Nature in the Literature of American Slavery, 1770–1860* (Athens: University of Georgia Press, 2009), 2.

9. Ibid.

10. Ellen Griffith Spears, "'Renovated Hopes': A Reinvigorated Conception of Environmental Justice in a Changing Racial Landscape," paper presented at the Publishing the Long Civil Rights Movement Conference, University of North Carolina, Chapel Hill, April 4, 2009, 4–5.

11. Addenda to Report, President's Report, box 001, folder 1, President's Reports, 1841–97, University Archives, W. S. Hoole Special Collections, University of Alabama. The report is unsigned and undated, but it was later marked "1887–1888" and gives enrollment figures that suggest it was written in 1887–88, when Henry Clayton was president. See also Addenda to Report, President's Report, "The Campus," 5.

12. Sidney Bland Gorchov, "The Mound," centennial magazine, *Crimson White*, 1931, 44, range 48, shelf 009, box 115, Hoole Collections.

13. Addenda to Report, President's Reports, 4.

14. James B. Sellers, *History of the University of Alabama, Vol. 1, 1818–1902* (Tuscaloosa: University of Alabama Press, 1953), 38.

15. After repeated pleas to compensate the university for the destruction by fire of the

campus by Union troops near the close of the Civil War, in 1884 the U.S. Congress increased the endowment of the University of Alabama by transferring more than forty-six thousand acres of public land for "restoration of the library . . . and scientific apparatus which had been destroyed by fire." James B. Sellers, *History of the University of Alabama, 1818–1902* (Birmingham: University of Alabama Press, 1953), 345–46. This distinct language is also used on a plaque outside Clark Hall acknowledging the building's origins: "in reparation for the 1865 destruction of the campus by Federal troops."

16. Personal communication with Jerry Oldshue, January 5, 2011.

17. Gorchov, "The Mound," 43.

18. Larry Isaac, "Movement of Movements: Culture Moves in the Long Civil Rights Struggle," *Social Forces* 87, no. 1 (September 2008): 33–63, at 50.

19. Ibid., 56, citing Jacqueline Dowd Hall, "The Long Civil Rights Movement and the Political Uses of the Past," *Journal of American History* 91, no. 4 (March 2005): 1233–63.

20. Ibid., 50.

21. The history of slavery at the University of Alabama has only begun to be studied. The University Special Collections and University Archives have rich resources that speak to the character and quality of intellectual, cultural, and literary life in and at the University of Alabama, Tuscaloosa, and surrounding counties. Al Brophy has done an outstanding job at establishing the base presence of slaves at the institution and the relationship of some aspects of faculty life, university operations, and the business of teaching and learning with slavery. There remain rich opportunities to evaluate and establish the relationship between the economic life of the university more generally and the evolution of the situation of black labor into the postbellum period. Furthermore, we have only scratched the surface here in suggesting the ways in which the memorialization of a particular version of the southern past is deeply inscribed in the physical landscape; other researchers might engage student life and rituals, the folk history of local black communities, and informal patterns of meaning making through individual acts of memorialization. See Brophy, "The University and the Slaves," 109–19, 111.

22. As invoked often in his superb comic novel, *Love in the Ruins* (New York: Farrar, Straus and Giroux, 1971).

23. On Hill Ferguson, see Carl Martin Hames, *Hill Ferguson: His Life and Works* (Tuscaloosa: University of Alabama Press, 1978). Ferguson's careful documentation of the Greater University Campaign is to be found in scrapbook 3, box 107, Hill Ferguson Papers, Hoole Collections. His long account of desegregation efforts at UA is to be found in box 006-19803921-006, folder "Integration, Crank Letters 1963," Frank A. Rose Papers, Hoole Collections.

24. See Robert Mellown, "A Stained-Glass Tiffany Knight," *Alabama Heritage* 27 (Winter 1993).

CHAPTER SIXTEEN

Forgetting Slavery at Yale and Transylvania

R. Owen Williams

There are names from America's past that inevitably make us think of slavery. Two such names stand out—John C. Calhoun and Jefferson Davis. Both men were slaveholders and prominent southern political figures who stridently defended the right to own slaves. Both men also had important academic facilities named in their memory at Yale University in New Haven, Connecticut, and at Transylvania University in Lexington, Kentucky. The surprising part is that these buildings were dedicated generations after the demise of slavery.

Early in my days as a graduate student of history at Yale in 2001, I initiated a quixotic campaign to change the name of Calhoun College, one of Yale's dozen residential colleges. Established in 1933, the college was named for John C. Calhoun, a member of Yale's class of 1804 and later a U.S. senator from South Carolina who earned political notoriety for his insistence that slavery was a "positive good."

A decade later I found myself president at Transylvania University, the third Yale alum to serve as president since the university's founding in 1780.[1] Things had come full circle: the Transylvania faculty presented me with a resolution to change the name of Davis Hall, a dormitory built in 1963 (at the height of the civil rights movement) to honor Jefferson Davis, president of the Confederacy. Davis attended Transylvania for three years in the 1820s before accepting an appointment to West Point—an appointment he received from his mentor, John C. Calhoun.[2]

This essay will briefly introduce Calhoun and Davis before examining the circumstances that led Yale and Transylvania to honor them. Though the essay is focused on nineteenth-century political figures and the twentieth-century institutional honors paid to them, its object is to illuminate a twenty-first-century question: Should Yale and Transylvania change the names of Calhoun College and Davis Hall? Yale has recently answered that question in the affirmative. Transylvania has sidestepped the question. But my own answer to that very thorny question has changed since my graduate school days—indeed, it has changed more than once. I have become convinced that name changing is bad history. Such actions unjustly erase historical blemishes and unwisely forfeit educational opportunities.

Nineteenth-Century Defenders of Slavery

John Caldwell Calhoun symbolizes antebellum South Carolina, the first state to secede from the Union prior to the Civil War. An accomplished statesman, he strenuously supported the "national" mission when young, only to metamorphose into a philosophical stalwart of state's rights when old. As America's most prominent proslavery theorist and politician, he probably did more than any other single person to propel the South toward secession. Even more to the point, he was a proud slaveholder who tirelessly defended the institution of slavery.

A dedicated autodidact, Calhoun earned acceptance to Yale University in 1802 as a third-year upperclassman. The six-foot, two-inch farm boy lived a largely solitary existence at Yale. Despite his penchant for solitude, Calhoun took full advantage of the tutelage offered by both Benjamin Silliman and college president Timothy Dwight. Graduating with high honors among the sixty-six members of his class, Calhoun was selected to present the commencement address, which he entitled "The Qualifications Necessary for a Statesman."[3]

A life-threatening illness prevented Calhoun from delivering the address, but nothing could keep him from becoming a statesman himself. Apart from his reserved nature, perhaps the defining aspect of Calhoun's character was aggressive ambition, which earned him all but his most coveted political office. In a career that spanned the Twelfth to the Thirty-First Congress, Calhoun served in the House of Representatives, as secretary of war (1817–25), and as vice president under John Quincy Adams and Andrew Jackson. Aside from his brief stint as secretary of state (1844–45), Calhoun spent the last two decades of his life in the U.S. Senate. The presidency, for which he incessantly (though not always openly) campaigned, proved beyond his grasp. So focused was he on that office that Calhoun went to his grave convinced he was a failure for not attaining it.

Senator Calhoun was probably the most notable proslavery theorist and politician in the United States, as well as one of the intellectual fathers of secession. The events of the early 1830s—Nat Turner's Rebellion, increased abolitionist activism and antislavery petitions in Congress, the British abolition of slavery in the West Indies, and the increased might of manufacturers—all generated enormous anxiety among southerners. Calhoun rose to the challenge to articulate a proslavery interpretation of the Constitution and a proslavery political theory that supported a militant southern identity.[4]

Slavery fixed Calhoun's attention. On February 19, 1847, Calhoun addressed the Wilmot Proviso from the floor of the Senate: "I am a planter—a cotton planter. I am a Southern man and a slaveholder—a kind and a merciful one, I trust—and none the worse for being a slaveholder."[5] Calhoun consistently spoke in such terms. A decade earlier, also from the Senate floor, Calhoun insisted that slavery was "a good—a great good."[6] His perception of slavery was predicated upon the inferiority of blacks. In arguing against allowing free blacks to serve in the navy, for example, he maintained, "It was wrong to bring those who have to sustain the honor and glory of the country down to the footing of the negro race—to be degraded by being mingled and mixed up with that inferior race."[7] Calhoun believed slavery worked to the benefit of all involved. Adamant in his position, he declared, "Come what will, should it cost every drop of blood, and every cent of property, we must defend ourselves."[8] Calhoun was never shy in making his point, and the point he cared most to make was that the South should concede nothing regarding "the peculiar institution" of slavery.[9]

Like Calhoun, Jefferson Davis championed slavery most of his life. More famous in his day than Calhoun, Davis was the first and only president of the Confederate States of America. A committed white supremacist, he owned slaves and defended slavery as a moral and social good. He did not believe the Declaration of Independence or the U.S. Constitution applied to black people, nor did he believe that the Constitution permitted any federal interference with slaveholding, whether in states or in territories.

While historians have evinced a grudging respect for Calhoun's intellect and political tenacity, they have not treated Davis kindly. David Potter, for example, bluntly claimed that, had Lincoln and Davis changed offices, the Confederacy would have won the Civil War.[10] Nevertheless, Davis is still lionized by many whites in the South. In the Kentucky Capitol Rotunda, there is a statue of Davis with the inscription, "Hero, Patriot, Statesman."

Jefferson Davis was born in Christian County, Kentucky, on June 3, 1808, the tenth and final child of Samuel and Jane Davis. He was named for his father's hero, Thomas Jefferson. Shortly after his birth the family moved to Mississippi. While none of the first nine children was educated, Samuel insisted that Jefferson return to Kentucky for a proper education, first at a Dominican Catholic school and later at Transylvania University. Transylvania, Latin for "across the woods," was the name given to the nation's sixteenth college, the first west of the Appalachian Mountains. When Davis entered Transylvania, it enrolled four hundred students, roughly the same number as Princeton and Harvard. According to Davis's most recent biographer, Transylvania was "a thriving and sophisticated university that offered its students a first-class education.... [It was] as much a university as any other place in the United States."[11]

Like Calhoun, Davis held many positions of military and political responsibility. After attending Transylvania University and West Point, he emerged with a military commission and fought as a colonel in the Mexican-American War. He served briefly in the House of Representatives, twice as U.S. senator from Mississippi, then as secretary of war under President Franklin Pierce before becoming president of the Confederacy. Near the end of the Civil War, Davis eluded Union forces, but he was eventually captured and charged with treason. Though never tried for his crime, Davis (along with all other Confederate leaders) was prohibited (by the Fourteenth Amendment to the Constitution) from holding public office, a stigma finally erased by special legislation from Congress in 1978.[12] That Davis's rights of citizenship were restored, the legislation noted, "officially completes the long process of reconciliation that has reunited our people following the tragic conflict between the States."[13]

Twentieth-Century Naming

In 1933—exactly one hundred years after Calhoun stepped down as vice president to lead the secession movement from the U.S. Senate during the Nullification Crisis—it seems many Americans had either forgotten or ceased to care about John C. Calhoun's proslavery politics. Indeed, it is likely that they had forgotten him altogether, dispatching the South Carolinian to the same oblivion reserved for other ex–vice presidents. Jefferson Davis, however, was still widely remembered and much revered by white southerners and Civil War enthusiasts in general. In 1933 at Yale and 1963 at Transylvania, these two venerable universities chose to name facilities honoring these stalwarts of slavery. What were the circumstances under which these decisions took place?

Through the extraordinary generosity of a single benefactor, Edward S. Harkness, Yale University was able to construct seven dormitory clusters in the early 1930s, modeled after the colleges at Oxford and Cambridge.[14] A special Committee on Nomenclature, composed of senior administrators, including university president James Angell, deliberated for more than a year as to who should be honored in the naming of these colleges. From 230 years of graduates, Yale selected two men: Jonathan Edwards and John C. Calhoun. As university secretary Carl A. Lohmann explained, the two were "chosen to represent Yale's most eminent graduate in the Church and Yale's most eminent graduate in the field of Civil State."[15]

The new housing facilities were much needed, for Yale was growing rapidly. The entering class of 310 students in 1900 had swelled to a class of 849 in 1930 and to more than 1,300 by 1940.[16] Housing all the students had become the university's single most pressing problem. The residential plan proposed by President Angell called for the construction of several dormitory quadrangles.

Although the Education Policy Committee oversaw all issues associated with the project, Angell immediately appointed several subcommittees to address such matters as personnel, student employment, and housing allocation of students. Of these various committees, President Angell was especially concerned about the Committee on Names and Terminology, chaired by the university secretary. That committee was created to consider such issues as what to call the new buildings (quads, houses, colleges, or halls), titles for senior administrators (head, dean, master, provost, principal, president, or warden), and, most importantly, the actual names for the structures. In fact, the last concern was so great that yet another subcommittee, including the secretary and the dean, was assigned solely to address it.[17] President Angell wanted to name some of the new colleges after esteemed graduates, but he admitted a fear of an "acute controversial atmosphere" in dealing with "contemporary affairs." He suggested that controversy could be avoided through the use of historical figures, the farther back in time, the better. So in April 1933 the Yale Corporation resolved, "The quadrangle which will be built at the corner of Elm and College... shall be named Calhoun College to honor John Caldwell Calhoun, B.A. 1804, L.L.D. 1822, statesman."[18]

If avoiding controversy was a priority, why select Calhoun? Was the current memory of William Howard Taft, a Yale alumnus from the class of 1878 and the only American to become both president of the United States and chief justice of the Supreme Court, more apt to generate controversy than the memory of a man whose political career was dedicated to militant defenses of nullification, sectionalism, and slavery?[19] Yale offered no justification whatsoever for honoring Calhoun.[20] Evidently, no justification was needed. While it may strike contemporary readers as odd, the naming of Calhoun College aroused very little controversy on or off campus. The *New York Herald Tribune* reported the naming on October 15, 1931, in an article entitled "Three New Colleges Named in Yale Residential Plan," noting one named "in honor of Senator John C. Calhoun, of South Carolina, who was graduated from Yale in 1804." The next day, the *New York Times* also carried the story "New Colleges Named at Yale," which mentioned "Calhoun College in honor of John C. Calhoun, the statesman, Yale 1804." Neither paper had another word to say about the man himself. A month later, the *New York Times Magazine*, writing about the designs of the respective colleges, offered the following: "The one college that [architect James Gamble] Rogers did not build is curiously (for Connecticut and New Haven) named after John C. Calhoun, a Yale man, though the great South Carolina nullifier." Beyond that, the article offered no further commentary.[21]

Of the various Yale publications, the *Alumni Weekly* reported nothing relating to Calhoun College specifically, focusing instead on the larger college plan. The *Harkness Hoot*, a campus literary magazine, contained an editorial entitled "Colleges for Sale," which offered the following rather curious observation: "No, away with University ideals.... [T]hey have been sold for a cathedral city of movieland magnificence and *negroid taste* to the wealthiest purchaser of a memorial or two."[22] The *Whole Houn Catalogue*, an annual brochure introducing Calhoun College to arriving students, was one of the few publications to address the memory of Calhoun directly. Calhoun, authors of the inaugural catalog wrote, had "influenced the political history of the United States more deeply than any other graduate during Yale's first two centuries." The catalog did not then, and still does not, specify what that influence had been.[23]

In the *Yale Daily News*, a rather strange reference can be found. The paper reported that Calhoun College had originally been intended for a location closer to Sterling Library on the site of what is now Trumbull College. But plans were changed "when the University authorities realized that J. W. Sterling, the donor of the present Trumbull, was a Yankee who had fought in the

Civil War, against the principles for which John C. Calhoun had stood so strongly, and that it would be tactless to name his college in honor of a secessionist."[24] The article suggests that at least some at the time were aware of the symbolism of naming a college after Calhoun, but the emphasis seems more on reconciliation than repudiation.

Student reaction to the use of Calhoun's memory was muted. In interviews conducted with the current class secretary of each of the first classes to live in the new residences (class of 1933 as dorms; classes of 1934, 1935, and 1936 as colleges), none remembered any controversy whatsoever about the name Calhoun. "For most of us," according to Yale alumnus Edwin Clapp, "the moral elements of American history were simply not ingrained, slipped right by us." Indeed, Clapp recalls that his senior thesis "advisor was startled" by his conclusion that "John Brown had been on the right side."[25]

There was, however, at least one objection to Calhoun. During a formal dinner to celebrate the opening of Calhoun College on October 31, 1933, Yale professor of rhetoric and oratory Leonard Bacon read a poem he had composed for the occasion:

> I suppose that I ought
> To have bayed at the moon
> Singing the praises
> of *John C. Calhoun*.
> But I cannot, although
> He was virtuous and brave,
> And besides my great-grandfather
> Would turn in his grave,
> If he dreamed of a monument
> Raised to renown
> *Calhoun* in this rank
> Abolitionist town.

If only we could know how this poem was received. It seems unlikely that the author intended to offend the other guests, but did he generate stirrings of discomfort? Or had Calhoun's paternalistic perception of slavery as a "great good" somehow become palatable? At the same time, had pride in the abolitionist tradition completely vanished?

It is odd that Yale honored Calhoun while also naming a college for his university tutor, Benjamin Silliman, who vehemently criticized the senator from South Carolina. Soon after Calhoun's death, Silliman noted in his diary:

> John C. Calhoun died at Washington last Sabbath. . . . I have known him from his youth up. . . . If the views of Mr. Calhoun, and of those who think with him, are to prevail, slavery is to be sustained on this great continent forever. . . . While I mourn for Mr. Calhoun as a friend, I regard the political course of his later years as disastrous to his country and not honorable to his memory, although I believe he had persuaded himself that it was right, and that he acted from patriotic motives.[26]

But that voice was nowhere to be heard in 1933 when Calhoun College was named.

A similar story unfolded thirty years later at yet another university. In 1963, exactly a century after emancipation and just months before Congress passed the Civil Rights Act, Transylvania University, through what appears to have been a mixture of obliviousness and defiance, enshrined the memory of Jefferson Davis. The college named a new dormitory in his honor during a time of renewed neo-Confederate fervor.

Although Transylvania housed the same number of students as Harvard and Princeton in the 1820s, its subsequent growth was much slower. By the 1960s Transylvania had only doubled in size, to about eight hundred students, the bulk of the increase having been quite recent. The university responded by constructing two new dormitories, which were connected by a common room. At the opening ceremony, on November 16, 1963, Ben P. Eubank of Lexington, general contractor for the building, presented the keys to J. Douglas Gay, president of Transylvania's board of curators (or trustees), who in turn presented them to university president Irvin E. Lunger. According to the *Transylvania College Bulletin*, "The dormitories have been named in honor of two distinguished Americans who had a close association with Transylvania." Those two Americans, pictured on the cover of the dedication ceremony program, were former U.S. senator from Kentucky Henry Clay and Jefferson Davis.[27]

What induced Transylvania to honor Jefferson Davis, president of the Confederacy, one hundred years after the Civil War? The answer might be found in the board of curators' executive committee minutes from February 28, 1963, which contained the following entry: "Dr. Lunger reported an anonymous gift of $25,000 toward the new dormitory and recommended, in keeping with the request of the donor, that the new dormitory be named Jefferson Davis Hall since Jefferson Davis was a student at Transylvania . . . and since Transylvania is the repository of the Jefferson Davis letters. Dr. Lunger was instructed to express gratitude of the college to the donor." In fact, Transylvania is among several repositories of Davis's letters, and Davis never graduated from the university, having completed his studies at West Point. But those are minor details when compared to the larger issue: Who was that anonymous donor?[28]

At the same time the dormitory was named in honor of Davis, the college newspaper carried an article announcing that the United Daughters of the Confederacy (UDC) had "voted unanimously to give a portrait of Jefferson Davis to Transylvania to be placed in the new Jefferson Davis Hall for men." The article went on to observe, "The portrait, worthy of the great soldier and statesman and worthy of Transylvania, will be done by a well known portraitist and will be completed by the time the new Jefferson Davis Hall is ready for occupancy."[29] Is it possible the UDC also donated the money necessary to secure Davis's name on the hall?[30]

Assuming the donor at Transylvania University was the UDC, the facts that they gave anonymously, that their gift represented less than 10 percent of construction costs, and that there was nothing like a contract formalizing their gift all make the situation at Transylvania barely comparable to the Calhoun naming at Yale. Yet there are two similarities between the naming at either institution that deserve our attention.

To begin with, Transylvania, like Yale, exhibited complete racial insensitivity. It is essential, of course, to understand the spirit of the times. First, in 1963, Transylvania College, like most small colleges at the time, struggled to attract students. It was common for these colleges to celebrate the names of famous graduates. Transylvania staff and alumni often boasted about the many historic figures who had attended (or worked at) the college; these included Henry Clay and Jefferson Davis, among many others. Actually, Transylvania bragged about Jefferson Davis until the very end of the twentieth century. The college's primary publicity brochure, as late as 1999, opened with the observation, "Throughout its history, the University has educated leaders such as Stephen Austin, a founder of Texas; Cassius M. Clay, the fiery abolitionist; Jefferson Davis, the president of the Confederacy . . . " Readers might easily have concluded that, according to Transylvania at least, Cassius Clay was something of a troublemaker, while Davis was a dignitary. Although the task was to attract applicants, it is not hard to see that southern sensibilities die hard.

The second thing to bear in mind about the era is that some people on campus were eager to move forward with the times, to support civil rights. Many students, in particular, questioned the racial insensitivity of the era, especially as demonstrated by the Kappa Alpha fraternity. One of four fraternities on campus, Kappa Alpha held the annual Southern Ball, in full Confederate regalia, which glorified the "Old South." The fraternity is devoted, even in the present, to the manners and memory of Robert E. Lee.[31]

In the 1963 *Crimson*, Transylvania's annual, there is a photo of Kappa Alpha "guarding the flag on Robert E. Lee's birthday." The flag in question is the Confederate flag, flying atop a large flagpole on campus. But then as now, that group did not represent the whole. Then president of Transylvania, Irvin Lunger, spoke to the board of curators about the "racially exclusive character" of the college, insisting, "Transylvania has an obligation to be as tolerant in the area of race as in the field of religion."[32] By most accounts, there was a budding awareness on campus, especially among students, of racism in America. Actually, in 1963 Transylvania matriculated its first African American student, Lula Bee Morton. In a report to the board of trustees, President Lunger stated, "The policy of racial exclusiveness troubles the conscience of many of our best students and most valued faculty members. Let whatever policy we may finally endorse reflect our finest thought, our highest values and our trust in democracy."[33] Just six years later, students elected a black student, James Hurley, to be Mr. Pioneer, the college's highest social honor for men.[34]

Third, in several interviews I conducted with Transylvania staff and alumni who were on campus when Jefferson Davis Hall was named and constructed, interviewees voiced a common sentiment: most people were so conditioned by their past that they just did not think clearly about "southern traditions." One of the more articulate alumna of that era, an award-winning history major later known for her social justice work, reported: "Most of us at Transylvania were raised in the southern tradition, proud of our southern gentility and the reputations of our ancestors. Racism, often unconscious, was prevalent, even among the Transylvania students from the North. Many of us had great-grandfathers who fought with [the still revered rebel leader] John Hunt Morgan in the Confederate army." When asked whether the Transylvania community stood in defiance to the civil rights movement, she added, "We were not so much defiantly defensive of the southern attitudes as thoughtlessly oblivious to the tides of time, to the injustices of racism, segregation, and blind to our own white privilege. Some among us were defiant, perhaps, like the Daughters of the Confederacy or the brothers of Kappa Alpha fraternity, but the majority of us were just thoughtless."[35]

Finally, there is something else that gets lost when talking about southern ancestry. The same alumna also reported a discussion that took place among a number of Transylvania students during their graduate school years about the cultural racism in which they had been raised. A PhD candidate among them noted that the South was missing a generation, given how many died during the Civil War. Whereas most northerners at that time were four or more generations removed from the war, many in the South were only three (sometimes only two) generations removed from the death of family. Memories were closer, and the wounds remained deeper. "None of this is to condone racism, not even slightly," said the alumna, "but it does provide context and help explain southern intransigence."[36]

That both institutions were evidently oblivious to their racism might explain yet another similarity that exists between the naming of Calhoun College and Davis Hall, which is that these names caused almost no resistance at either university. The Transylvania University newspaper certainly evidences no resistance to the Davis name. Indeed, there appears to have been no controversy anywhere in Kentucky regarding the naming of Davis Hall at Transylvania University.

Actually, to the extent there ever was any contention over the name of Davis Hall, it came many years later due to an ugly racial incident on the Transylvania campus. In 1999 a racial slur written on the door of an African American student's dorm room at Transylvania touched off a prolonged furor. In response, university officials decided to remove a floor-to-ceiling portrait of Jeff Davis that hung in the foyer of Davis Hall, the very same portrait donated by the United Daughters of the Confederacy.[37] The removal so agitated some from the community that they issued threats against college officials, threats that were so upsetting to the parties involved that all correspondence related to this matter was destroyed, and the recipients would not speak to me of the matter when I became president twelve years later.[38]

On April 9, 2001, university president Charles Shearer submitted an article to the local newspaper, stating, "We embrace our history and those alumni who played prominent roles in our country's past. At the same time, we want every Transylvania student to feel embraced by a campus environment that emphasized respect and civility." A columnist for the *Lexington Herald Leader* suggested various solutions to the problem, including these words: "The Confederacy is a vital part of Lexington's heritage. Jefferson Davis was a great leader, but he was misguided. We realize this now, because we have the benefit of historical perspective, which makes most failures seem inevitable. We cannot toss history aside simply because we now know better." Indeed. Even more to the point, as Transylvania student Chris McClellan wrote in the college newspaper, "The ideas I found most challenging and uncomfortable were the ones that led me to learning the most."[39] That is clearly the spirit toward which any good university must strive.

Yet, sadly, that spirit did not inform events at Yale occurring precisely when Transylvania struggled with the memory of Jefferson Davis. Three graduate students at Yale wrote a research report, entitled "Yale, Slavery, and Abolition," published by the Amistad Committee on August 13, 2001.[40] The report claimed that Yale University relied upon slave-trading money for fellowships, professorships, and the library endowment. The university contested much of the report. At a conference in 2002, cosponsored by Yale Law School and the Gilder Lehrman Center for the Study of Slavery, Resistance and Abolition, most of the accusations proffered by the report went largely ignored. Curiously, very few of the claims within the report were even mentioned, the bulk of the conference having been devoted to a general examination of slavery rather than Yale's ties to slavery.[41]

That report, when combined with Yale's tepid response, motivated my campaign to change the name of Calhoun College, mentioned at the outset of this chapter. The idea I proposed was that Yale amend the name of Calhoun College to Calhoun/Bouchet College, thus adding the name of Edward Alexander Bouchet, the first African American to receive a doctorate, which he did at Yale in 1876.[42] Alas, at the time I was unable to even convince my friend Jonathan Holloway, an African American historian and master of Calhoun College from 2005 through 2014. He has, however, publicly acknowledged that Calhoun College "is named for someone who I find repugnant."[43]

It would appear that the naming of Calhoun College at Yale in 1933 and Davis Hall at Transylvania in 1963, as well as the controversy concerning both in 2001, are all of a piece with the American story, a story significantly shaped by racism. For over a century following emancipation, the South set the tone of American memory regarding slavery. As a nation, we have regularly tried to forget slavery, even as we fondly remember those who defended it. The myth of the Lost Cause, or what Robert Penn Warren termed the Great Alibi, romanticized the reasons for war and transformed the "rebel yell" into an underdog's heroic cry. Organizations such as the United Daughters of the Confederacy simultaneously glorified antebellum southern gentility, vilified the era of Reconstruction, and minimized the brutality of slavery. As David Blight so effectively demonstrated in *Race and Reunion*, America was everywhere "forging unifying myths and making remembering safe." Safe was defined in a way that "Southern victory over Reconstruction replaced Union victory in the war and Jim Crow laws replaced the Fourteenth Amendment in their places of honor in national memory."[44] The same pattern of compromise that enabled Americans to live with slavery also allowed them to forget it. As observed by W. E. B. Du Bois in a chapter from *Black Reconstruction in America* (1935) entitled "The Propaganda of History," Americans "fell under the leadership of those who would *compromise with truth* in the past in order to make peace in the present and guide policy in the future."[45]

By 1933, when Calhoun College was named, race relations in America were arguably as bad as they had ever been. Beginning early in the twentieth century, insensitivity and hatred toward blacks became America's lingua franca. Stamped as inferior, black people were expected to comply with a perverse "step-and-fetch-it" etiquette. A distorted image of blacks based on a song-and-dance routine, "Jumpin' Jim Crow," became synonymous with a codified system intended to segregate the races.[46] Worse, not only did popular literature, minstrel acts, and vaudeville shows represent blacks as buffoons, but films like *The Birth of a Nation* (1915) incited whites to vigilantism. Membership in the Ku Klux Klan soared.[47] The anti-immigration movement (exemplified by books such as Lothrop Stoddard's *The Rising Tide of Color Against White World-Supremacy* [1926]) licensed lynching. Between 1880 and 1930, thousands of blacks were exterminated. As historian Leon Litwack has pointed out, "Not even a liberal president, Franklin Delano Roosevelt, was willing to endanger his southern white support by endorsing [antilynching] legislation," which was scuttled by filibustering in the U.S. Senate precisely when Yale contemplated the name of Calhoun.[48] It is thus no surprise that when Margaret Mitchell's 1936 novel *Gone with the Wind* lamented the loss of southern culture, that wind carried away with it the reality of slavery.

Such strained race relations cleared the way for rehabilitation of the Confederate image. Interest in the antebellum South was everywhere apparent. The Thomas Jefferson Memorial Foundation began restoration of what was to become perhaps the most famous residence in America. As Stephen Knott suggested, "Monticello was, in a larger sense, emblematic of the twentieth-century airbrushing of history by Jeffersonian politicians and scholars." The *American Mercury* reported on a Confederate reunion and pondered whether a better era had long since passed: "Maybe, after all, they should have won the War. . . . It would have given us a technique of leisure, a calmer estimate of life's values."[49]

Yale was significantly responsible for this rewriting of history. Among the faculty at Yale—at the very time the university chose names for its new colleges—was the famous American historian U. B. Phillips, who wrote positively about the plantation culture of the Old South in *American Negro Slavery* (1918). According to Phillips's account, slavery was a benign, if inefficient, labor system that lifted blacks from the barbarism of Africa. That view proved easy to accept, encouraging Americans increasingly to forgot the grim realities of slavery. Calhoun could be less remembered for his defense of slavery and more for his central role in national politics.

Yale University needed names for its new colleges, and the selection of those names provided an opportunity to emphasize Yale's intellectual heritage and hierarchical stature. Over time, it became increasingly convenient—and easy—to forget Calhoun's "peculiar institution." During the 1930s students at Yale developed a local culture around the new colleges, giving each a nickname. Pierson College's white-painted courtyard, "reminiscent of slave quarters on a Carolina plantation, suggested 'Slaves.'" A nickname of Slaves presented little threat for young men of privilege. As the Depression dragged on, only the wealthy went to college at all, let alone to an elite private college.[50] White supremacy solidified its position in America as the nation developed an intense amnesia regarding the injustices of slavery.

By 1963, when Transylvania University named Davis Hall, the racism of previous decades had turned into defiance in some parts of the country. On June 11 of that year, Governor George Wallace stood in a doorway at the University of Alabama and symbolically denied admission to two black students. In Lexington, Kentucky, where Transylvania is located, the University of Kentucky's staunchly segregationist basketball coach, Adolph Rupp, refused to recruit black players, much to the evident approval of Confederate flag–waving fans.[51] All of this is anecdotal, but it confirms southern belligerence. Whether the board and administration of Transylvania were themselves openly defiant or just casually complicit may never be known.

Twenty-First-Century Renaming

In my capacity as the new president of Transylvania University in 2011, I received the following petition from the faculty:

> Resolved: Whereas Jefferson Davis has historical relevance as the political leader of the Confederate States of America, he also directed [as CSA commander in chief] the military effort to defend a society characterized and sustained by race-based slavery. Because Jefferson Davis is associated with the painful legacy of slavery, we find it inappropriate for Transylvania University to continue to honor him by maintaining his name on a campus residence hall. Therefore, the faculty of Transylvania University requests that the administration develop a plan to change the name of Davis Residence Hall by May 2012.

This is strikingly similar to claims I made about Calhoun College while a graduate student at Yale. It sickened me then that Yale honored Calhoun, seventy-five years after the Civil War, just as it sickens me now that Transylvania paid homage to Davis at the height of the civil rights movement. Nevertheless, by the time I received this petition, I had come to believe that it would be a mistake for Yale to drop the name Calhoun from its residential college because, like the Transylvania resolution, it would invite "bad" or incomplete history.

The Transylvania resolution is clearly correct, of course, that "Jefferson Davis is associated with the painful legacy of slavery," perhaps more than any other person. Where the resolution is incorrect, I believe, is in suggesting that we "continue to honor [Davis] by maintaining his name on a campus residence hall." At this point, what we must honor is the truth, and the painful truth is that racism existed throughout the twentieth century and continues in substantial measure to exist today. Most of us hate the thought of living with names like Calhoun and Davis, just as we detest the racism that made it acceptable to honor them. But until we have truly extirpated racism from our culture and society, we need these reminders. Slavery, the Confederacy, and postemancipation racism are all embarrassingly real elements of our nation's past; it is essential that we not forget any of it. Keeping Calhoun's and Davis's names around makes it harder to forget the injustices of our past.

Were Transylvania to indeed change the name of Davis Hall, I would suggest something similar to what I ultimately proposed when at Yale. Let us not erase either the Calhoun or the Davis name; rather, let us hold on to them as reminders of nineteenth-century slavery and twentieth-century racism. Let us use these names as springboards for education. Complicate the names by adding to them, perhaps, but do not whitewash or eliminate them altogether.

In response to the faculty petition, I recommended a combined name, but without suggesting a particular person. I also suggested that Transylvania celebrate its fiftieth year of integration with a mixture of academic panels and ceremonies starting in the fall of 2012. As part of those proceedings, we invited our first African American student, now Dr. Lula Morton Drewes and a teacher in Germany, to deliver the 2012 convocation speech; we also granted her an honorary doctorate in what became a very inspiring and emotional commencement in 2013.

It is worth briefly mentioning that there is a name of relevance to both Yale and Transylvania that could have been added to either Calhoun College or Davis Hall: Cassius Marcellus Clay.[52] Clay attended Transylvania and Yale from 1828 to 1832. Unlike his slightly older cousin Henry, "the Great Compromiser," who taught at Transylvania's law school, served on the board of trustees for most of his adult life, and also had a building named for him on the campus, Cassius was unwilling to compromise with slaveholders or slave states. He was an exceptional southern aristocrat who risked life and wealth for antislavery. When his emancipationist views cost him his seat in the Kentucky House of Representatives, he started an antislavery newspaper entitled the *True American*. His is a name that, when coupled with Calhoun or Davis, would invite a more reflective discourse about slavery and racism on our campuses. It might make even better sense to add the name of one of the enslaved men and women that Jefferson Davis once owned.

Neither Yale nor Transylvania followed my suggestions. In 2014 I stepped down as president of Transylvania. In 2015 Transylvania demolished Jefferson Davis and Henry Clay Halls, replacing them with Bassett Hall and Pioneer Hall. Bassett Hall is named for James E. "Ted" Bassett III, a longtime member of the board of trustees who provided the project's initial leadership gift. Pioneer is a reference to the school's mascot. No public acknowledgment was made of the earlier controversy about Jefferson Davis.[53] In 2017, following the removal of Confederate flags and monuments around the country in the wake of the June 2015 white supremacist shootings in Charleston, South Carolina, and extensive student protests that fall and into 2016, Yale University renamed Calhoun Hall for Grace Murray Hopper. Hopper, a Yale graduate, was a leader in developing the earliest computer languages. She served in the navy during World War II as a naval reservist and then on active duty again at age sixty until her retirement as rear admiral at age seventy-nine, the oldest serving officer of the U.S. Armed Forces at the time. In addition, Yale named a newly built college for Anna Pauline, or Pauli, Murray, an African American civil rights activist and the first black woman to be ordained a priest in the Episcopalian Church.[54] It is hard to imagine that these names will ever invoke the same enmity as Davis and Calhoun.

But honoring and remembering are not the same. Not so long ago, the leaders of Yale and Transylvania honored John C. Calhoun and Jefferson Davis. Today, we are embarrassed by the memory of them both, but that does not give us license to forget. Insofar as their names on our campuses make us squirm, they also invite us to confront the legacy of racial injustice that we inherit from them. We not only have to contend with the fact that men like Calhoun and Davis defended slavery; we also have to explain how their successors comfortably accepted, decades after emancipation, buildings whose names evoked that repulsive institution. In changing the names, do we evade that challenge?

The very soul of a nation is rooted in memory. But memory, like history, is a complicated and fallible narrative, vulnerable to error and manipulation. As a monument describes a subject from the past it also defines the values of the present. Stated another way, memorials speak *of* the past but *to* the present and future. There is no limit to the myriad forces—government officials, academics, corporate chieftains, journalists, historical societies, to name but a few—vying for control of a nation's collective image.

The natural impulse for any group or organization is to marginalize, reconfigure, mock, or simply dismiss any reflection that undermines its legitimacy. Ernest Renan highlighted what is perhaps the defining element in this process. "Forgetting," he suggested, "is an essential factor in the creation of a nation, and that is why progress in historical research is often a threat to nationality."[55] Americans purchased their nationality at a great cost. By honoring Calhoun and Davis when they did, Yale and Transylvania dishonored themselves and committed a true disservice to the nation. By forgetting the inhumanity of slavery, both universities perpetuated racism and postponed racial justice. In erasing the evidence of these twentieth-century acts, do we leave ourselves open to twenty-first-century forgetting?

NOTES

1. The rather short path from graduate school to the president's office can be partly explained by the fact that I started graduate school at the age of forty-eight after a twenty-four-year career in investment banking. Transylvania University is located in Lexington, Kentucky. During the Civil War, Kentucky was a Border State with intensely divided loyalties. As in America at large, families fought within and among themselves over whether to side with the Union or the Confederacy. Historians often jest that Kentucky joined the Confederacy only after the Confederacy lost the war.

2. Secretary of War John C. Calhoun appointed Jefferson Davis to the United States Military Academy in 1824. The two men's relationship remained close throughout their lives. Indeed, Davis sponsored Calhoun for president in 1844.

3. For biographies of John C. Calhoun, see especially Charles M. Wiltse, *John C. Calhoun: Nationalist, 1782–1828* (New York: Bobbs-Merrill, 1944); Wiltse, *John C. Calhoun: Nullifier, 1829–1839* (New York: Bobbs-Merrill, 1949); Wiltse, *John C. Calhoun: Sectionalist, 1840–1850* (New York: Bobbs-Merrill, 1951); Margaret L. Coit, *John C. Calhoun: American Portrait* (Boston: Houghton Mifflin, 1950); and John Niven, *John C. Calhoun and the Price of Union* (Baton Rouge: Louisiana State University Press, 1988). The disease that kept Calhoun from the graduation ceremony was most likely yellow fever (Wiltse, *Nationalist, 1782–1828,* 34). According to Niven, "Calhoun was obsessed with the issue of slavery" (*John C. Calhoun,* 3). Calhoun's father owned thirty-one slaves in 1790, when John was eight years old (ibid., 11).

4. As Charles Wiltse observed, "Calhoun had become by 1840 a man with one fixed idea about which all else revolved. He would save the Union if he could, but first he would save the South" (*Sectionalist, 1840–1850,* 22). For a more complete understanding of Calhoun's political philosophy, see Merrill Peterson, *The Jefferson Image in the American Mind* (New York: Oxford University Press, 1960), chap. 1; Louis Hartz, *The Liberal Tradition in America* (New York: Harcourt Brace, 1955), 132–81; Richard Hofstadter, *The American Political Tradition and the Men Who Made It* (1943; New York: Knopf, 1996), 67–91; William Freehling, *Prelude to Civil War: The Nullification Controversy in South Carolina, 1816–1836* (New York: Oxford University Press, 1965); August O. Spain, *The Political Theory of John C. Calhoun* (New York: Bookman, 1951).

5. Richard K. Crallé, ed., *The Works of John C. Calhoun,* 6 vols. (New York: D. Appleton, 1864–74), 4:348.

6. Reg. Deb., 24th Cong., 2nd sess., 718–19.

7. Cong. Globe, 27th Cong., 1st sess., 806.

8. Calhoun argued against the evil of slavery with Senator Rives from Virginia on February 6, 1837 (*Papers,* 13:390). On another occasion, he argued with Senator King from Georgia regarding the threat of abolitionist petitions (*Papers,* 13:73). For quotes on slavery, see *Papers,* 13:390, 63, 108, 24:252–53.

9. It has become common to link the expression "peculiar institution" with Kenneth Stampp's 1956 book of the same name, but it was Calhoun himself, in several speeches of the 1830s, who coined the term.

10. David Potter, "Jefferson Davis and the Political Factors in Confederate Defeat," in *Why the North Won the Civil War,* ed. David Donald (Baton Rouge: Louisiana State University Press, 1960), 91–114.

11. William J. Cooper Jr., *Jefferson Davis, American* (New York: Alfred A. Knopf, 2000), 24.

12. Restoration of Citizenship Rights to Jefferson Davis, S. J. Res. 16, October 17, 1978.

13. Restoration of Citizenship Rights to Jefferson F. Davis Statement on Signing S. J. Res. 16 into Law, Pub. L. No. 95-466.

14. Edward S. Harkness was the son of Stephen V. Harkness, original investor with John D. Rockefeller in the Standard Oil Company. Edward donated $20 million to his alma mater, Yale.

15. Of the seven colleges opened in 1933, only two were named after graduates of Yale College. There are a total of twelve residential colleges at Yale, two of which opened in 1935 and one in 1940. The final two (Morse and Stiles) were constructed in the 1960s. Some colleges were named to honor important figures from the early years in the New Haven colony (Trumbull) or because they helped give rise to Yale (Berkeley and Davenport); some were named for faculty or administrators (Silliman, Pierson, and Dwight—two Timothy Dwights graduated from Yale, the first in the class of 1769 and then his grandson in the class of 1849, and both went on to become presidents of the university); while other colleges were named to honor significant places in Yale's history (Branford and Saybrook). Of the total twelve colleges, six are named for graduates of the college. Secretary Lohmann's quote is taken from Minutes of the Education Policy Committee, RU 24, box 70, file 716, Minutes of Meeting February 6, 1931, Manuscripts and Archives, Sterling Library, Yale University. (Hereafter only the file and not the archive will be noted.)

16. The class of 1933 enrolled 849; class of 1934, 846; class of 1935, 882; and the class of 1936, 838. These were the first classes to occupy the residential colleges.

17. This committee was also referred to as simply the Committee on Names or the Committee on Nomenclature. For terminology, see February 8, 1930, letter to Harkness and February 25 Seymour letter to Malcolm Aldrich, Provost Files, RU 38, box 5, file 72. For establishment of committees, see Minutes of Education Policy Committee, April 10, 1931, RU 24, box 70, file 716.

18. Minutes of Yale Corporation, April 11, 1931, and May 9, 1931 (microfiche), Yale Manuscripts and Archives. It is curious that the Education Policy Committee had voted to provide the corporation with five, not just four, names, including a name that was ultimately selected, Jonathan Edwards, but was not among those reported to the corporation. See Minutes of Education Policy Committee, RU 24, box 70, file 716. It is also important

to note that the subcommittee on names did not keep records or minutes, so the specifics of their deliberations are unknown. According to George Wilson Pierson, *Yale: The University College, 1921–1937* (New Haven, Conn.: Yale University Press, 1955), 406, the committee "kept no minutes as they found themselves in ready agreement and the thing carried itself along." Given the total lack of notes, Pierson is obviously speculating about the presence or lack of consensus.

19. William Howard Taft was the twenty-seventh president of the United States, from 1909 to 1913, and the tenth chief justice of the Supreme Court, from 1921 until his death in 1930, just months before the naming of Calhoun College. Not only was Taft the first Yale grad to reach either office, he had a long record of service to the university that went well beyond the two years Calhoun spent in New Haven as a student. Taft was a member of the Yale Corporation, or board of trustees, from 1906 to 1913 and again from 1922 to 1925. Though Taft was the most obvious civil servant Yale might have honored instead of Calhoun, there were others: Oliver Wolcott, secretary of the treasury; John Middleton Clayton, secretary of state; and Samuel Jones Tilden, governor of New York and Democratic candidate for president in 1876.

20. The record is quiet as to the actual deliberations over names. We do not know which names (other than those selected) were considered nor which were rejected. Given that it was the New Deal era, it is certainly conceivable that some members of the naming committee wanted to celebrate Calhoun's repudiation of federal authority, but there is no evidence available to make that case.

21. *New York Times Magazine*, November 19, 1933, 5.

22. *Harkness Hoot*, October 7, 1931, italics mine. To characterize bad taste as *"negroid"* obviously speaks volumes about the times, as will be considered below.

23. The brochure pertaining to Calhoun College could be found in the master's office at the college, which is where I found it in 2006. For various reasons (building renovations, changing of the college name, and turnover in the master's office), it seems the document no longer exists.

24. While archivists at Yale believe this article is indeed from the *Yale Daily News*, there is no evidence of either date or authorship, nor are there official files at Yale that corroborate the story. Yet the original article can be found within a scrapbook collection housed in the Calhoun master's office.

25. These observations come from a telephone interview I did with Edwin Clapp, class of 1936, in 2006. Like many of his classmates, Clapp had been previously educated at a boarding school; in his case at Andover.

26. Silliman's diary, April 7, 1850, as taken from George Fisher, *Life of Benjamin Silliman* (New York: Scribner, 1866), 97–99, italics mine.

27. For part of its 232-year history, from 1915 to 1965, Transylvania University went by the name Transylvania College. For the opening ceremony program and *Transylvania College Bulletin* 36, no. 6 (October 1963), see Special Collections, Transylvania Library.

28. John D. Wright Jr., author of *Transylvania: Tutor to the West* (1975; Lexington: University of Kentucky Press, 2006) and the college historian of note, told me in an interview on February 20, 2012, that he has no knowledge of the donor's identity. He did attend the naming ceremony for Davis Hall and confirms that there was no resistance to the name of the hall from anyone, including the many northern members of the faculty at Transylvania.

29. *Rambler*, April 15, 1963, Special Collections, Transylvania Library.

30. While we cannot know for sure, it seems more than possible that the UDC orchestrated the naming of Davis Hall. They had certainly funded construction of dormitories at other colleges. In 1933, for example, during the Great Depression and at the same time Yale was honoring John C. Calhoun, the UDC provided $50,000 (one-third of the construction costs) to build Confederate Memorial Hall at Peabody College in Nashville, Tennessee, to benefit female descendants of Confederate veterans. It is worth briefly noting that, after acquiring Peabody College in 1979, Vanderbilt University conducted a $2.5 million renovation of Confederate Memorial Hall and considered dropping "Confederate" from its name. But no change took place until, in 2002, newly installed President Gordon Gee dropped "Confederate" from Confederate Memorial Hall, thus generating a lawsuit that forced Vanderbilt to reinstate and preserve the full name. For the full story of Confederate Memorial Hall and the resulting lawsuit, see Alfred L. Brophy, "The Law and Morality of Building Renaming," *South Texas Law Review* 52, no. 37 (2010): 46–51. While instructive for Transylvania, this case is sufficiently unusual as to not apply as relevant precedent.

31. *The Varlet: Kappa Alpha Order*, 12th ed. (Lexington: Kappa Alpha Order National Administrative Office, 2010). From the very first page comes this: "Kappa Alpha Order seeks to create a lifetime experience which centers on reverence to God, duty, honor, character and gentlemanly conduct as inspired by Robert E. Lee, our spiritual leader."

32. Report of the President to the Board of Curators, December 10, 1960, Transylvania Archives.

33. Quote taken from the Transylvania *Rambler*, "Transy Integrates in '63," February 15, 1996, a copy of which is in the "Jefferson Davis" file in Special Collections.

34. John Wright, *Tutor to the West* (Lexington: University of Kentucky Press, 1980), 416–17.

35. Conversations and emails exchanged with alums on January 26, 2013. Not wanting to bring attention to themselves or fearful they might alienate others in the community, these people asked not to be named.

36. This alumna asked not to be named. Fear is still a constant for many people on this issue.

37. In my communications with former president Charles Shearer, he requested that mention be made of the rehanging of the portrait in Mitchells Fine Arts Center, elsewhere on campus, so as to make clear that "we did not take it down and store it." Letter of February 6, 2013, now in Jefferson Davis File, Special Collections.

38. Only a few of those communications—either the letters and/or anonymous communications written on scraps of paper—can be found in files on the incident housed at Special Collections, Transylvania University. One such note, addressed on the envelope to "President of Jefferson Davis Hating Transylvania University," depicts a hand-drawn Confederate flag with the words "Honor it, or Resign. Honor Jefferson Davis. Shame on you." A letter from a commander of the Kentucky division of the Sons of Confederate Veterans dated April 13, 2001, boldly insists that removal of the portrait "has greatly distressed and offended Southerners."

39. These articles are on file in Special Collections at the Transylvania Library. Charles Shearer, *Herald Leader*, April 9, 2001; Cheryl Truman, April 7, 2001; Chris McClellan, *Rambler*.

40. Antony Dugdale, J. J. Feuser, and J. Celso de Castro Alves, "Yale, Slavery and Abolition," Amistad Committee, New Haven, Connecticut, 2001. For more on the report, see "Slave Traders in Yale's Past Fuel Debate on Restitution," *New York Times*, August 13, 2001.

41. I attended every session of that conference and, like many other present, was shocked by the extent to which the university obfuscated.

42. Edward Alexander Bouchet was the sixth American to receive a PhD in physics and the first African American nominated to Phi Beta Kappa.

43. "Naming a New Yale," *Yale Herald*, October 12, 2012.

44. David Blight, *Race and Reunion: The Civil War in American Memory* (Cambridge, Mass.: Belknap Press of Harvard University Press, 2001), 9, 361. Gaines Foster suggested that the Lost Cause, what he called the "Confederate celebration," "allowed southerners to distance themselves from the issues of the war without repudiating the veterans." *Ghosts of the Confederacy: Defeat, the Lost Cause, and the Emergence of the New South, 1865–1913* (New York: Oxford University Press, 1987), 196. Robert Penn Warren, *The Legacy of the Civil War* (1961; Lincoln: University of Nebraska Press, 1998), 53–55.

45. W. E. B. Du Bois, *Black Reconstruction in America, 1860–1880* (1935; New York: Free Press, 1998), 721, 722, 727, italics mine. There is an African proverb that seems appropriate here: "As long as the lion does not have his own historian, tales of the hunt will always glorify the hunter."

46. The song "Jumpin' Jim Crow" was created a century earlier by a white minstrel named Thomas "Daddy" Rice. Leon Litwack, *Trouble in Mind* (New York: Vintage Books, 1999), xiv.

47. Membership in the Klan grew from five thousand in 1911 to five million in 1925. The Ku Klux Klan most likely takes its name from the Greek word *kuklos*, meaning "the circle." It is more popularly believed to come from an onomatopoeic representation of the three separate sounds made when loading a breech-loading rifle.

48. Lothrop Stoddard, *The Rising Tide of Color Against White World-Supremacy* (New York: Scribner's, 1920). Postwar movements like "the Red scare," which thanks to people like Stoddard had a large following in the early 1920s, contributed significantly to the

growth of the Ku Klux Klan. Leon Litwack, *Trouble in Mind* (New York: Vintage Books, 1999), chap. 6; this chapter can also be found in *Without Sanctuary* (Santa Fe: Twin Palm Publishers, 2000), 33. Stephen Knott pointed out that "Franklin Roosevelt's desire to secure the support of the South for a transitory political coalition" prompted him to champion celebrations of Thomas Jefferson. Stephen Knott, *Alexander Hamilton and the Persistence of Myth* (Lawrence: University Press of Kansas, 2002), 213.

49. Knott, *Persistence of Myth*, 211; *American Mercury* 18 (March 1929): 358.

50. Pierson, *Yale*, 430. Slightly more than 75 percent of all Yale students during those years had gone to (northern) private preparatory schools, 50 percent from just eleven institutions. Furthermore, more than one in four Yale students had fathers or grandfathers who had also attended Yale. Department of Personnel Study, December 15, 1932, RU 38, box 3, file 38.

51. I am told by former sports writer Billy Reed that Rupp, who saw that times were changing and was tired of losing to teams that included black players, recruited a black player from Louisville, Westley Unseld, in 1964. According to Reed, that did not stop the local paper, the *Herald Leader*, and its editor, Fred Wachs, from relegating "black news" to one column buried in the paper. Reed, who worked at the paper at the time, states that Wachs "told his editors to either not run or play down stories about the civil rights movement, and the riots in the cities, because he figured that if Lexington's blacks didn't read them, they wouldn't be inclined to follow suit. It apparently never dawned on him that blacks owned TV and radio sets" (email from Reed, February 2, 2013).

52. Yale University grants Cassius Marcellus Clay Fellowships, one of which I was fortunate enough to hold, but the profile of that program pales in significance to the prominence of Calhoun College.

53. "New Transylvania Residence Hall to Be Named after Former Keeneland President," News@Transy, April 13, 2015, http://www.transy.edu/news/new-transylvania-residence-hall-be-named-after-former-keeneland-president.

54. Andy Newman and Vivian Wang, "Calhoun Who? Yale Drops Name of Slavery Advocate for Computer Pioneer," *New York Times*, September 3, 2017, https://www.nytimes.com/2017/09/03/nyregion/yale-calhoun-college-grace-hopper.html. In an opinion piece in the *Yale Daily News*, Jonathan Holloway, dean of Yale College, stated, "After so many years of taking the increasingly uncomfortable position that the name of the college should not be changed, I am certain that the Corporation made the right decision" ("Looking Back on Calhoun," *Yale Daily News*, February 13, 2017, https://yaledailynews.com/blog/2017/02/13/holloway-looking-back-on-calhoun/).

55. Ernest Renan, *Qu'est-ce qu'une nation?* (Paris: Ancienne Maison Michel Levy, 1882), chap. 1, penultimate paragraph: «L'oubli et je dirai même l'erreur historique, sont un facteur essential de la formation d'une nation, et c'est ainsi que le progrès des études historiques est souvent pour la nationalité un danger» (my translation).

AFTERWORD

Evelyn Brooks Higginbotham

In teaching about slavery, I often ask my students to imagine themselves as college professors during different decades—the 1920s, the 1950s, the 1970s, the 1990s, and today. I query them as to the required reading they would assign and have them explain their choice of the representative authoritative text in each decade. This exercise of identifying historiographic trends in slavery scholarship reveals dramatic shifts in findings, assumptions, sources, and methodologies over time. Reflecting upon my own education, I witnessed firsthand the magnitude of two such shifts. As an undergraduate in the late 1960s, I read Kenneth Stampp's *The Peculiar Institution* (1956), which by then had thoroughly toppled the nearly four-decades-long canonical text *American Negro Slavery* (1918) by Ulrich B. Phillips. Like the intervening years between the two publications, slavery studies were "a-changin," to borrow from the title of the 1964 song by Bob Dylan. According to Phillips's interpretation, mostly docile, happy slaves worked under benevolent masters in a plantation system that he analogized to a training school for civilization. This interpretation was discredited in the 1950s as the civil rights movement and the federal government were simultaneously dismantling the legal doctrine of "separate but equal." Kenneth Stampp, Stanley Elkins, and other historians of that era overturned the "happy slave" image by portraying instead overwhelming victimization of human chattel who were bereft of positive self-consciousness, cultural traditions, and family heritage.

I was a graduate student in the 1970s and early 1980s when Black Power and racial pride on the part of African Americans made possible a wholly new intellectual vision—one attentive to the voices of slaves themselves. While not oblivious to oppression, slavery historians in the last quarter of the twentieth century emphasized slaves' overt and everyday forms of resistance, resilience, cultural resources such as religion and song, kinship bonds, gender relations, and sense of community. Despite the scholarly differences and disagreements in perspective and emphasis among this cohort of historians, their overall impact served to challenge the dominant narrative and ultimately refuted the imagery of Sambo-like victims. Through new sources and analytical frameworks, they set the foundation for twenty-first-century historians to delve ever more deeply into such topics as gender and family, the domestic slave trade and capitalism, health, the role of the law, and slavery's distinctiveness over time and place.

When thinking about the tremendous amount of scholarship published on the subject of slavery for over a century, I find it astounding that slavery continues to be an exceptionally verdant field of study. This is especially true of the history of slavery in regard to universities, as evidenced by the emergence of related conferences, monographs, courses, memorialization projects, and social activism. Certainly, the essays in this volume, which grew out of a conference at Emory University in February 2011, present new ways to think and write about slavery. Together, their historiographical intervention signals a new scholarly direction and can even be said to constitute a new field of slavery studies for the twenty-first century. I make this claim of a new field for several reasons.

First, the focus on slavery and the university affirms the presence of slaves on university campuses in the South and North. Slaves were owned by institutions of higher learning. The plight of institutional slaves, as in the case of slaves owned by Washington College (now Washington and Lee University) and the College of William and Mary, along with the implications of their treatment, purchase, and sale, has only recently come to light. Research into the slave presence on campuses also makes visible the black men, women, and children who were recognized as the personal property of university presidents, faculty, and wealthy students who brought their slaves along to serve them. In some instances, the university setting exposed a slave to multiple voices of command and thus to the controlling desires of many masters. Nor was the presence of slaves in the university confined to a specific geographic region. Harvard University in New England, Georgetown in the nation's capital, William and Mary in the upper South, and the University of Alabama in the lower South all had slaves.

The efforts to acknowledge and recover the slave presence at institutions of learning have disclosed new sources in many unexplored places: the archives of business, medical, and law schools; the correspondence and records of school presidents, boards of trustees, faculty, and students; and petitions by slaves. Equally important, the empirical findings provide extraordinary windows onto the black lives formerly hidden from history. In April 2016 President Drew Faust of Harvard unveiled a plaque, engraved with the names of four slaves, who lived and worked for two of the school's presidents in the eighteenth century. Faust referred to the discovery of the identities of the slaves later in an interview in the *Harvard Gazette* on February 28, 2017, and in anticipation of Harvard's own upcoming March 2017 conference on slavery and universities. She stated: "One of the things happening now is that archivists, who have never looked for these findings, are finding them in odd places. Titus, one of the enslaved persons from Wadsworth House, didn't leave extensive personal papers . . . but if you dig around you can find property records, you can find baptismal records."

Second, the unique focus on slavery's legacy in academia contributes richly to the history of higher education in the United States and abroad. Scholars now investigate the financial returns from slavery and the slave trade in connection to the rise of endowments for colleges and universities such as Brown and Harvard. Ideas about racial slavery figured significantly in the role of the university in the production of knowledge, curriculum development, faculty research and scholarship, and students' coursework and extracurricular activities. The new field of slavery and universities thus calls for greater analysis of the ripple effect of ideas and information taught in American colleges, universities, and seminaries. Ethnologist Samuel G. Morton at the University of Pennsylvania and the naturalist Louis Agassiz at Harvard, for example, published works on polygenesis—the theory of racially different human origins—to a wide readership. Morton's lectures and books influenced the thinking of Agassiz; both scholars described people of African descent as anatomically and mentally inferior to whites. Morton's *Crania Americana* (1839) and *Crania Aegyptiaca* (1844) lent academic validity to racial slavery. In the South, the College of William and Mary proved to be a virtual proslavery think tank. Thomas R. Dew, chair of political law at William and Mary in 1827 and the school's president from 1836 until his death in 1846, mixed religious justification with political economy. "We cannot get rid of slavery," Dew proclaimed, "without producing a greater injury to both the masters and slaves, there is no rule of conscience or revealed law of God which *can* condemn us."[1] Such pronouncements were integral to the knowledge imparted through higher education, and they were quoted extensively by influential southern and northern judges, physicians, ministers, literary figures, and statesmen. Studied in the context of the curriculum of universities and students' lecture notes, slavery's more complex, often obscure involvement in American institutional life and memory becomes increasingly apparent. The academy profoundly influenced the American legal system. Judicial opinions involving slavery or race relations often incorporated such language as "ordained by God and Nature." Judges also incorporated scientific findings and other academic expertise into their rulings. The lectures and writings of social scientists, natural scientists, economists, philosophers, and theologians gave legitimacy to slavery as an institution and to prohibitions against racial mixture.

The field of slavery and the university also provides deeper insight into students' thinking and their activities as members of literary societies and debate teams. In the years leading up to the Civil War, topics related to slavery and states' rights served to hone Emory students' debating skills. Perhaps the earliest recorded debate between college students, however, occurred at Harvard University's commencement in 1773, when two graduating seniors took opposite sides on the question of the legality of enslaving Africans. The antislavery proponent, Eliphalet Pearson, observed: "I confess, it is a matter of painful astonishment, that in this enlightened age and land, where the principles of natural and civil Liberty, and consequently the natural rights of mankind are so generally understood, the case of these unhappy Africans should gain no more attention; that those who are so readily disposed to urge the principles of natural equality in defense of their own Liberties, should, with so little reluctance, continue to exert a power, by the operation of which they are so flagrantly contradicted." The proslavery advocate, Theodore Parsons, presented the rebuttal, asserting that it was more important to respect the happiness of the larger community, which had established and benefited from the slavery laws: "Such is the nature of society, that it requires various degrees of authority and subordination; and while the universal rule of right, the happiness of the whole, allows greater degrees of Liberty to some, the same immutable law suffers it to be enjoyed only in less degrees by others."[2]

Finally, this emerging new field of slavery studies offers innovative pedagogies for encouraging discussion of difficult subject matter. As campus protests and news articles attest, the long shadow of slavery in the history of American educational institutions has become more evident, causing those very institutions to become targets for transformative redress. Scholarly collaboration, activity-based learning, and community-oriented networks inside and outside the academy have brought together persons from across disciplines (history, law, business, medicine, literature, art, and architecture), from across private and public universities, and from sites of academic and public history (including library archives, burial grounds, museums, historic homes, and slave quarters, e.g., the still extant Royall House and its connection to the Harvard Law School). This effort joins a growing body of scholarship that transcends the traditional focus on the South and gives the study of slavery a national, even international, relevance. Rigorous research, constructive dialogue, innovative teaching, and memorialization by means of plaques, artwork, conferences, and publications have afforded a way to validate and consolidate a variety of perspectives that help us to discern what is both valuable and at stake for contemporary scholarship, coursework, and even politics. And for those who thought that nothing new could be written, slavery's haunting legacy in the academy has yet more stories to tell.

NOTES

1. For the quoted passage and an analysis of Thomas R. Dew's views on slavery, see Albert L. Brophy, "Considering William and Mary's History with Slavery: The Case of Thomas Roderick Dew," *William & Mary Bill of Rights Journal* 16, no. 4 (2008): 1130n258.

2. *A Forensic Dispute on the Legality of Enslaving the Africans, Held at the Public Commencement in Cambridge, New England, July 21st, 1773. By Two Candidates for the Bachelor's Degree* (Boston: Printed by John Boyle for Thomas Leveret, 1773), 4–5, 7, http://name.umdl.umich.edu/N10168.0001.001.

CONTRIBUTORS

MARK AUSLANDER is associate professor of anthropology and history at Michigan State University, where he is also director of the MSU Museum. He is the author of *The Accidental Slaveowner: Revisiting a Myth of Race and Finding an American Family* (University of Georgia Press, 2011).

KABRIA BAUMGARTNER is assistant professor of American studies at the University of New Hampshire. She has held research fellowships from the Library Company of Philadelphia and the Spencer Foundation, and her work has appeared in the *Journal of the Early Republic* and the *Journal of Social History*. Her forthcoming book, which is under contract with NYU Press, examines African American women's education and social activism in pre–Civil War America.

SVEN BECKERT is Laird Bell Professor of History at Harvard University. He is the author most recently of *Empire of Cotton: A Global History* (2015). He led the Harvard and Slavery Project and worked with a group of students to research the connections between Harvard and slavery. His essay in this volume is drawn from the report "Harvard and Slavery: Seeking a Forgotten History" (2011, http://www.harvardandslavery.com/wp-content/uploads/2011/11/Harvard-Slavery-Book-111110.pdf).

ALFRED L. BROPHY, editor and essayist, holds the D. Paul Jones Chair in Law at the University of Alabama. His books include *Reconstructing the Dreamland: The Tulsa Riot of 1921—Race, Reparations, Reconciliation* (Oxford University Press, 2002), *Reparations Pro and Con* (Oxford University Press, 2006), and *University, Court and Slave: Proslavery Thought in the Southern Academy and Courts and the Coming of Civil War* (Oxford University Press, 2016).

JAMES T. CAMPBELL, editor, is Edgar E. Robinson Professor in U.S. History at Stanford University. He is the author of *Songs of Zion: The African Methodist Episcopal Church in the United States and South Africa* (Oxford University Press, 1995) and *Middle Passages: African American Journeys to Africa, 1787–2005* (Penguin, 2006). Campbell served as chair of the Brown University Steering Committee on Slavery and Justice.

YWONE D. EDWARDS-INGRAM is an assistant professor in the Department of Focused Inquiry at the Virginia Commonwealth University. She completed an MA in anthropology and a PhD in American studies at the College of William and Mary, where she taught a variety of courses, mainly as an adjunct lecturer in anthropology. She worked in archaeology and public history at Colonial Williamsburg for more than two decades and is the author of *The Art and Soul of African American Interpretation* (Colonial Williamsburg Foundation, 2016), as well as a number of articles in African American history, archaeology, and slavery.

A. JAMES FULLER is professor of history at the University of Indianapolis. Among his many publications are *Chaplain to the Confederacy: Basil Manly and Baptist Life in the Old South* (2000), *The Election of 1860 Reconsidered* (2012), and *Oliver P. Morton and the Politics of the Civil War and Reconstruction* (2017).

BALRAJ GILL is a graduate student in the American Studies Program at Harvard University. Her research is at the intersection of North American indigenous history and carceral studies. Her dissertation investigates why and how indigenous peoples in the northern Great Plains and Great Lakes region of the United States and Canada are being incarcerated at staggering rates and how this relates to longer histories of indigenous confinement.

JAMES C. HALL is executive director of the School of Individualized Study at Rochester Institute of Technology. From 2002 to 2014 he was associate professor and director of New College at the University of Alabama. He is the author of *Mercy, Mercy Me: African American Culture and the American Sixties* (Oxford University Press, 2001).

LESLIE M. HARRIS, editor, is professor of history and African American studies at Northwestern University. She is the author of *In the Shadow of Slavery: African Americans in New York City, 1626–1863* (University of Chicago Press, 2003) and coeditor of *Slavery in New York* (with Ira Berlin; the New Press, 2005) and *Slavery and Freedom in Savannah* (with Daina Ramey Berry; University of Georgia Press, 2014). From 2004 to 2011, while on faculty at Emory University, Harris cofounded the Transforming Community Project at Emory University, which used history and historical research to inform dialogue and action around racial and other forms of human diversity.

WILLIAM B. HART, an associate professor of history at Middlebury College, holds a PhD from the Department of American Civilization at Brown University. He has published a number of essays on the intersection of race, religion, and identity in seventeenth-, eighteenth-, and nineteenth-century Indian Country. His essay on Martin Freeman and colonization is drawn from his current book project, "'I Am a Man': Martin Freeman and the Cant of Colonization."

JIM HENLE holds a BA in history from the University of Michigan. A staff person at Harvard, he is a member of the Harvard and Slavery Project.

EVELYN BROOKS HIGGINBOTHAM is Victor S. Thomas Professor of History and African and African American Studies at Harvard University, where she is chair of the Department of History (2018–19) and former chair of the Department of African and African American Studies (2006–13). She is also the national president of the Association for the Study of African American Life and History. Higginbotham is the author of *Righteous Discontent: The Women's Movement in the Black Baptist Church, 1880–1920* (Harvard

University Press, 1994); coeditor with Henry Louis Gates Jr. of the *African American National Biography* (2nd ed., Oxford University Press, 2014); and coauthor with the late John Hope Franklin of the classic African American history text *From Slavery to Freedom* (9th ed., McGraw Hill, 2010).

CRAIG B. HOLLANDER completed his doctoral degree at the Johns Hopkins University. From 2013 to 2015 he held the Behrman Postdoctoral Fellowship at Princeton University and worked with Martha A. Sandweiss on the Princeton and Slavery Project. He is currently assistant professor of history at the College of New Jersey and is at work on a book manuscript entitled "Against a Sea of Troubles: Slave Trade Suppressionism during the Early Republic."

PATRICK C. JAMIESON completed his undergraduate degree at Emory University and his law degree at Duke University, where he also received a master's degree in history. His essay is drawn from his 2011 Emory honors thesis, "'The Delicacy of the Subject': Creating a Proslavery Argument at Antebellum Emory," for which he earned highest honors. He is currently an associate at Hunton Andrews Kurth LLP in New York.

J. BRENT MORRIS is associate professor of history and humanities department chair at the University of South Carolina, Beaufort. He completed his doctoral degree at Cornell University. His first book, *Oberlin, Hotbed of Abolitionism: College, Community, and the Fight for Freedom and Equality in Antebellum America,* was published by the University of North Carolina Press in 2014. He is also the author of *Yes Lord I Know the Road: A History of African Americans and South Carolina, 1526–2008* (University of South Carolina Press, 2017).

JENNIFER BRIDGES OAST is associate professor of history at Bloomsburg University. She is the author of *Institutional Slavery: Slaveholding Churches, Schools, Colleges and Businesses in Virginia, 1680–1860* (Cambridge University Press, 2016).

MARTHA A. SANDWEISS is professor of history at Princeton University. She is the author most recently of *Print the Legend: Photography and the American West* (Yale University Press, 2002) and *Passing Strange: A Gilded Age Tale of Love and Deception across the Color Line* (Penguin Press, 2009). She founded and directed the Princeton and Slavery Project, a research effort begun in 2013 that had its public launch in 2017.

DIANE WINDHAM SHAW directs the Special Collections & College Archives at Skillman Library, Lafayette College. In 2016 she was cocurator of an exhibition at the Grolier Club in New York City on the marquis de Lafayette and the antislavery movement; she was also coeditor and essayist for the accompanying catalog, *"A True Friend of the Cause": Lafayette and the Antislavery Movement.* In 2012 the French Ministry of Culture and Communication named her a Chevalier of the Order of Arts and Letters.

RUTH J. SIMMONS was the eighteenth president of Brown University, from 2001 to 2012. She also served as president of Smith College from 1995 to 2001. In 2003 she established the Brown University Steering Committee on Slavery and Justice, which for many exemplified the possibilities for the investigation of slavery at institutions of higher education. She currently serves as president of Prairie View A&M University.

ELLEN GRIFFITH SPEARS is associate professor in New College and the Department of American Studies at the University of Alabama. She is the author of *Baptized in PCBs: Race, Pollution, and Justice in an All-American Town* (University of North Carolina Press, 2014), which won the Southern Historical Association's Francis B. Simkins Award and the Arthur J. Viseltear Award from the Medical Care Section of the American Public Health Association. She coordinates the university-community partnership with the Scottsboro Boys Museum and Cultural Center in Scottsboro, Alabama.

KATHERINE MAY STEVENS earned her PhD from the American Studies Program at Harvard University in 2014. She coordinated the Harvard and Slavery Research Project with Sven Beckert and was coauthor of "Harvard and Slavery: Seeking a Forgotten History." She is currently an assistant professor of history at Oglethorpe University. She studies the history of Native, settler, and enslaved people in the southern United States.

CRAIG STEVEN WILDER is Barton L. Weller Professor of History at MIT. He is the author of *A Covenant with Color: Race and Social Power in Brooklyn* (Columbia University Press, 2000), *In the Company of Black Men: The African Influence on African American Culture in New York City* (NYU Press, 2001), and *Ebony & Ivy: Race, Slavery, and the Troubled History of America's Universities* (Bloomsbury, 2013).

R. OWEN WILLIAMS is president of the Associated Colleges of the South. From 2010 to 2014 Williams served as president of Transylvania University. Williams earned his doctoral degree in history and a master's degree in law from Yale University after working for over twenty years as an investment banker. While at Yale, he led a group that called for a fuller accounting of the university's ties to slavery.

INDEX

Page numbers in italics refer to images.

1860 presidential election, 78–80

abolition, 67, 183–84, 197–210, 237–38, 300; backlash to, 55, 160–61, 233–36, 247n40; black activists for, 148–73, 181, 184–86, 192, 207, 248n54; colonization and, 51–52, 158–62, 184; immediate, 159; perceived dangers of, 50, 51, 55, 68–69, 75–76, 78–80; property rights argument against, 50, 51, 67, 80; racist abolitionists and, 183–84
Abruzzo, Margaret, 49
Adams, John, 229
African Americans: burial of, 142, 172, 278–80, 286–90, 293, 310; citizenship denied to, 75; civil rights of, 151–52; in college towns, 54, 55, 61n11, 138–39, 203–5; education of, 148–73, 179–96, 203–5, 207, 211n51; employment of, 61n11, 93–94, 168, 279–85; enslavement of, 152, 174n11; in the North, 179–96, *183*, 203–5, 207, 211n51; Revolutionary War service of, 29, 41n19, 181; "scientific" racism and, 75–76; slaves owned by, 61n11; social roles of, 138–44; violence against, 55, 190–91; in Virginia, 93–94. *See also* enslaved persons
African American students, 131–47, 255, 308, 324; in antebellum New England, 148–73, 179–96; exclusion of, 187, 188–89, 284, 298–99
Agassiz, Louis, 239–40, 241, 249n67, 249n74
Age of Apology, 118
Age of Improvement, 181–82, 186

Alison, Francis, 24
amalgamation, 160, 190–91
American Antislavery Society, 206, 212n68
American Colonization Society (ACS), 51–52, 133, 135, 139, 143; criticism of, 53, 153; Martin Freeman and, 148–49, 151–55, 164, 169–70; state auxiliaries to, 148, 159, 175n33, 183
American Revolution: black soldiers in, 29, 41n19, 181; colleges during, 21–31, 230; colleges in postwar years, 31–37
Ames, Oakes, 242
Andersen, Eric, 243
Andrew, James Osgood, 283, 287–88, 291–92, 293
apologizing for slavery, 2–3, 118, 267, 289, 299
Ashmun, Jehudi, 159
Atwater, Jeremiah, 156
Avery College, 155, 168, 170, 173n1

Baker, Daniel, 53
Baptists, 31–32
Barber, Francis, 26, 30
Beck, Charles, 236, 248n50
Beecher, Henry Ward, 56
Bible, slavery defended using, 54, 101
Birney, William, 51, 60n11
"Black Laws," 186, 189
Black Manifesto (1969), 10
Blackmon, Douglas, 219
black newspapers, 185
black schools, destruction of, 179–96
Bledsoe, Albert Taylor, 70–71, 72, 78
Blight, David, 327

347

Boardman, George, 176n44
Bogin, Ruth, 204
Bowditch family, 234, 247n38
Boyd, Catherine (Miss Kitty), 286–93, 294, 295, 297n8
Boyd, Nathan, 289
Brophy, Alfred L., 118, 304–5, 314n21
Brown, Antoinette, 201–2
Brown, Billy, 93–94
Brown, John, 34, 218
Brown University, 2, 6, 12–13, 36, 215–23; Civil War memorial at, 57; Steering Committee on Slavery and Justice, 13, 215, 217–18, 220–23
Burchard, Jedidiah, 157–58
Burke, Edmund, 69
Burns, Anthony, 237
Burr, Aaron, Sr., 59n3

Caldwell sisters, 289, 293, 295
Calhoun, John C., 73, 82n25, 315–17, 318, 319–22, 328, 329, 331, 332n2, 332n4, 333n9, 334n20, 337n54
Calhoun College, 315, 319–22, 325–27, 329–30, 334n19, 334n23, 337n52
campuses: the Revolution and, 25–26, 27–28, 31–32;, slave labor building, 243, 257–58, 294. *See also under individual college names*
Candler-Branham reunion, 285–86, 295
capitalism, 105, 231
Carnahan, James, 60n3
Carr, Julian Shakespeare, 2
Carroll, John, 24, 31, 33, 35
Catholicism, 24, 27, 31, 33
Child, Lydia Maria, 186
Christianity: denominational rivalries in, 23–24; honor culture and, 89, 114–28; North-South splits in, 283, 287, 291–92, 297n8; slavery and, 22, 101, 103–4; slavery challenged by, 78, 127–28; slavery spreading, 69, 105–6, 125–27
Civil Liberties Act (1988), 9
Civil War monuments: nineteenth century, 57, 301–3, *303*; twentieth century, 1, 14, 57, 310–12, *311*, 315–37
Clay, Cassius Marcellus, 323, 330, 337n52
Clayton, Henry, 301–2
clergy: slave ownership by, 31, 33, 49, 120, 294; church schisms caused by, 100–101, 283, 287
Clinton, Henry, 41n19
Cobb, Thomas R. R., 72–73, 75–77, 78–79, 80, 83n31
Codrington College, 23
coeducation, 199–201
College of Charleston, 70, 78
College of New Jersey, 23–26, 30, 32, 34, 49–50; funding of, 25, 43n33; Nassau Hall and, 25, 46, 57. *See also* Princeton University
College of Philadelphia, 23, 26, 43n33
College of Rhode Island, 23, 25, 27, 31–32, 34, 36. *See also* Brown University
College of William and Mary, 3, 251–76, *254*; in the colonial era, 23, 26–27, 257; slavery defended at, 67–69, 256–57, 340; slaves at, 84, 88–93, 258–60, *261*, 339
Colonial Williamsburg, 251–53, 255–57, 258–59, 265, 267–70
colonization, 132–34, 138–40, 148–78, 183–85; abolition and, 51–52, 158–62, 184; American leaders supporting, 62n26; as ethnic cleansing, 153–54, 155; failure of, 53, 68; free blacks supporting, 148–52, 153, 169–71; as mission work, 152–53
Confederate monuments. *See* Civil War monuments; memorials
Constitution, secession and the, 78–80
Conyers, John, 10
Cornish, Samuel, 185, 192
Craft, Henry, 53, 55
Crandall, Prudence, 187–89
Cruger, Henry, Jr., 21, 34–35, 37n1
Cruger family, 21, 23, 26, 29
Crummell, Alexander, 153, 170
curricula, 102–7, 109–10, 116–17, 194n21, 198–99

Daggett, Naphtali, 28, 30
Dana, Daniel, 148
Daniel, Peter V., 75
Dartmouth College, 23, 25, 28–30, 32, 162
Davies, Samuel, 59n3
Davis, Henry Winter, 87
Davis, Jefferson, 315, 317–18, 322–26, 328–31, 332n2
Delany, Martin R., 151, 155
Dew, Thomas Roderick, 67–69, 72–73, 77, 78, 256, 340
Dickinson, Jonathan, 59n3
dishonor, slavery as, 85
double consciousness, 277–78, 290–93, 295–96
Douglass, Frederick, 151, 152, 160
Douglass, Rosetta, 203
Dred Scott decision, 75, 79, 151
Du Bois, W. E. B., 277–78, 292, 296, 327
Dunmore, Lord, 41n19, 98n22
Durnford, Thomas McDonogh, 138

Eady, Virgil, Sr., 282
Easton, James, 179, 186
economy: integrated economies of slavery and, 24–25, 226–29, 231–32, 246n20; slavery in the South and, 65, 67–68, 72–73, 104–5, 257, 304–5; slavery's role in northern, 5, 37, 107, 180, 231–33, 235; workers' treatment in northern, 107
Edwards, Jonathan, Jr., 49
Edwards, Jonathan, Sr., 49, 59n3
Edwards, Melvin, 144, *144*
Eichstedt, Jennifer L., 253
Elizabethtown Academy, 26
Emerson, Ralph Waldo, 66–67, 236
Emory, Eugene, 294
Emory University, 2–3, 99–113, 277–97
Enlightenment, rejection of, 76
enslaved persons: British offering freedom to, 41n19, 98n22; burial of, 286–90, 293, 295, 298, 306; cadavers used in medical training, 6; as childlike, 73, 99, 120–21; colleges owning, 2–4, 84–98, 114–16, 258–60, *261*, 298; court cases involving, 75, 79–80, 115, 151, 230, 341; crimes committed by, 228–29; education of, 86, 94–95, 266, 267; freedom purchased by, 133; "happiness" of, 68, 69, 75–76, 83n31; health of, 260; memorials to, 2, 3, 227, 339–40; messages sent between, 263–64, 268; population of, 5, 28; punishment of, 84–92, 114–18, 121–22, 124; rape of, 124–25, 202, 204–5; religious education of, 95, 124–25, 126–27; renting labor of, 61n11; treatment by students, 84–93, 95–96, 118; violence against, 84, 86–87, 114–18; welfare of, 92–93
equality, 69–76, 143, 152, 172, 181, 186, 189–90
Erasmus Hall Academy, 33, 34–35, 36

Fairchild, James, 199
fanaticism, abolitionism as, 78–79
Faust, Drew, 112n34, 227, 339–40
Ferguson, William Hill, 308–9
Finley, Robert, 51–52, 154
Finley, Samuel, 46, 59n3
Finseth, Ian, 300
First Emancipation, 49
First Great Awakening, 23
Fisk, Wilbur, 186–87
Fitzhugh, George, 99, 110n2
Fletcher, Robert, 210n44
Follen, Charles, 233, 236, 248n50
forgetting slavery, 217, 296, 301, 304, 310, 326–31
Fox-Genovese, Elizabeth, 103
Freeman, Martin Henry, 148–78, *149*
free speech, 222–23
Friend, Craig, 93
Fugitive Slave Act, 80, 151, 236–38
fugitive slaves, 66–67, 236, 248n54

Garland, Hugh A., 75
Garrison, William Lloyd, 185, 186, 188, 190, 233, 234
Genovese, Eugene, 103, 127

350 INDEX

Georgetown University, 4, 6, 31, 33, 35, 339
Girardeau, John L., 78
Gliddon, George, 73–75
Glover, Lorri, 89–90, 93
Godfrey, John P., Jr. (J. P.), 285–86, 288–89, 294
Gorchov, Sidney Bland, 302
gradual emancipation, 5, 47, 52, 67, 72, 104, 135, 181. *See also* colonization
Gray, Asa, 241
Great Britain, 21, 37n1, 98n22, 181
Green, Ashbel, 48–49, 60n3
Gruenewald, David, 299–300

Haiti, 35, 68, 71, 152, 231
Hammond, Bob, 282, 295
Hammond, James Henry, 69–70
Hampden-Sydney College, 85, 88–89, 90, 93–94
Hardenbergh, Jacob, 32–33
Harris, Sarah Ann, 187–88
Hartford Courant, 11
Harvard and Slavery Research Project, 225–41
Harvard University, 6, 22–23, 28, 224–50, 339–40, 342; abolitionists connected to, 6, 234–36, 237–38, 241; Civil War memorial at, 57, 225, 243, 250n81; southern students at, 60n4, 237, 238–39, 243–44, 249n65
Hayden, Lewis, 237, 248n54
headstones, 278–81, 286–90
Helms, Jesse, 9
Hibben, John Grier, 57, 58
hidden transcripts, 301
Higginson, Thomas Wentworth, 241, 247n38
"higher law," 56, 63n52
historical research by students, 15n5, 225–44
Holcombe, James, 72, 76–77, 79–80
Holley, Sallie, 203, 208
Holton, Curlee Raven, 143–44
honor culture, 84–98, 114–30; Christianity and, 89, 114–28; psychological need to dominate and, 85; violence against slaves and, 84, 86–87, 114–18
Hood James, 298, 308, 309
Horowitz, David, 12, 215–16
Hough, John, 182–84

immediatism, 159
Inquiry into the Law of Negro Slavery in the United States, An (Cobb), 72–73, 75
insolence, 86–87, 88, 114–17
interracial marriage, 50–51
Irvine, Russell, 155
Isaac, Larry, 303, 304
"Is Slavery Consistent with Natural Law?" (Holcombe), 72

Jackson, Fanny, 205
Japanese Americans, internment of, 8–9, 10
Jefferson, Thomas, 32, 90, 102, 251, 253, 269, 318; colonization supported by, 62n26; southern turn away from, 70–71, 72
Jesuits, 6, 24, 31, 33, 36–37
Jim Crow, 219, 241, 280, 281, 284, 295, 327
John (enslaved boy), 48–49, 60n3
Johnson, Samuel, 25
Jones, Charles C., Jr., 54
Jones, Hugh, 23, 258
Jones, Samuel, 44n33
J. P. Morgan Bank, 18n22
judicial opinions on slavery, 75, 79–80, 115, 151, 230, 341
Judson, Andrew, 188–89
Junkin, George, 131–32, 135

Kaufman, David, 55
Kermes, Stephanie, 181
Key, Francis Scott, 159
Keys, Harriet, 204
King, Willis Jefferson, 291–92, 295
King's College, 21, 23, 25, 29–30, 35, 39n9
Knott, Stephen, 328, 337n48
Ku Klux Klan, 4, 327, 336n47, 336n48

Labaree, Benjamin, 159, 162–63, 165, 166–68, 176nn44–45
Lafayette College, 131–47, *144*
Lasser, Carol, 205
Lee, Robert E., memorials to, 4, 58, 324, 335n31
Lemon Project, 3, 266–67
Liberia, 132, 139–40, 143, 184; founding of, 52, 159; Martin Freeman and, 148–51, 153–56, 166, 169–72
Liberia College, *150*, 150–51, 170–72, 177n66
liberty: American value of, 69, 256, 262; as a human right, 70, 230; slavery and, 46–48, 68, 69
Lincoln, Abraham, 78, 79, 151, 152
Lindsley, Philip, 60n3
literary societies, 108–9
Litwack, Leon, 327
Lohmann, Carl A., 318
Longstreet, Augustus Baldwin, 100–102
Loring, Edward G., 237–38
Lost Cause, 1, 2, 288, 301–4, 326–27, 336n44
lotteries, 35–36, 43n33
Lowrie, Walter, 135–36, 138, 139
Lunger, Irvin, 322–23, 324
lynching, 55, 234, 327

Maclean, John, Jr., 52–57, 58n1, 63n42
Malone, Vivian, 298, 308, 309
Manly, Basil, 116–30, *121*, 305
Mann, Robert, 241–42
Manning, James, 27, 31–32, 34, 218–19, 220
manual labor, 3, 48–49
manual labor educational model, 131–32, 179, 180, 186–87
manumission, 49–51, 133, 181
Marshall-Linnemeier, Lynn, 290–93, 295
May, Hilary, 239, 243–44
May, Samuel J., 188, 191
Mayr, Ernst, 249n74
McClellan, Chris, 326
McCord, H. Y., 288, 297n8

McDonogh, David, 131, 132–39, 140–44, 146n28, 147n48, 147n51
McDonogh, John, 131, 133–34, 135–36, 139–41
McDonogh, Washington, 131, 132–40, 143–44
Melish, Joanne Pope, 180
memorials, 1–7; to black employees, 281–85; to black students, *308*; to enslaved persons, 1–2, 3, 227, 267, 339–40; to slaveholders, 3, 4, 330. *See also* Civil War monuments
memory quilt (Marshall-Linnemeier), 290–93, 295
memory work, 277–96, 298–314, 331
Mercer, Charles Fenton, 51–52
Merrill, Edward, 161–62
Merrill, Thomas, 158, 161
Methodist Church, 106, 287–88, 297n8; schism in, 2–3, 100–101, 283–84, 287, 291–93
Meyers, Terry, 95
Middlebury College, 148–49, 153, 155, 156–68, *157*, 182–83
Milledoler, Philip, 36, 44n34
Minor, Warner W., 86–87
Miss Kitty (Catherine Boyd), 286–93, 294, 295, 297n8
Mitchell, Henry "Billy," 282–85
Morgan, John, 202
Morgan, Philip D., 92
Morison, Samuel Eliot, 225, 229, 245n6
Moss, Hilary, 187
Murrin, John, 49
Muse, Henry Kirk White, 56

natural law, 72–76
Newark Academy, 24, 25, 35–36
New England: reliance of economy on slavery, 5, 37, 231–33, 235; slavery and the slave trade in, 22, 24, 180–81, 225–31, 339–40; white supremacy in, 188–89
New York City, 5, 29
Nivison, Kenneth, 182

Noll, Mark, 50
North, the: economy of, 5, 37, 107, 231–33, 235; free blacks in, 179–96, *183*, 203–5, 207, 211n51; slavery enriching, 5, 37, 231–33, 235; slavery in, 180–81, 227–30, 246n26
Northrup, Solomon, 174n11
Nott, Josiah, 73–75, 300, 305
Noyes Academy, 189–92

Oberlin College, 6, 197–212; activist societies at, 202–3, 206–7, 210n44; founding of, 6, 198–99
Oldshue, Jerry, 302
Osborne, Peter, 185

Paley, William, 103–4
paternalism, 102, 105–7, 120–21, 124–27, 134
Patterson, Orlando, 85
Perkins, Stella, 277, 278–81, 295–96
Phillips, Wendell, 234–35, 237, 247n38
Phoebe (enslaved woman), 48–49, 60n3
place-based studies, 298–314
Poe, Edgar Allen, 87
"politics of recognition," 8
preparatory schools, 24, 26, 33
Presbyterianism, 47, 131–33, 135, 137–38
Preston, Margaret Junkin, 136–37
Price, Clement Alexander, 144
primates, Africans compared to, 74, 75
Princeton and Slavery Project, 3, 60n6
Princeton University, 3, 6, 21, 46–64; antebellum division at, 56–57; antislavery leaders trained at, 49–53; slaveholding among presidents of, 46–47, 48–49, 59n3; slaves working at, 48, 60n11; students from Southern states, 47, 53–54, 60n6, 64n56
professors, violence against, 87–88
property rights, 50, 51, 67, 80

Queen's College, 23, 30, 32–33, 36, 44n34
Quincy, Josiah III, 231, 233–34, 242

race relations, 3, 327, 340–41
racial difference. *See* "scientific" racism
Rankin, J. E., 165, 176n51
rape, 124–25, 202, 204–5
Ray, Charles B., 185, 186–87
Reconstruction, 1, 10, 225, 327
reparations, 8, 9–13, 215–16, 244, 294; Civil War, 313n15; disclosure and, 11, 13, 18n22; litigation and, 10, 11, 13, 216
Review of the Debate in the Virginia Legislature (Dew), 67–69
Rivers, R. H., 105–6
Rudolph, Frederick, 23
Rupp, Adolph, 328, 337n51
Russwurm, John, 182, 185, 203
Rutgers University, 23, 36. *See also* Queen's College

Sanderson, Alice, 290
Sasnett, William, 99–100, 106
"scientific" racism, 50, 73–75, 298, 300, 340–41; Agassiz promoting, 224–25, 239–41, 244, 249n74, 340
Scott, Dred, 75, 79
Scudder, Peter, 61n11
secession, 6–7, 48, 65, 77–80, 102, 107, 133, 256, 316, 318
Second Great Awakening, 119, 157–58
segregation, 278–81
Seward, William H., 63n52
Shaler, Nathaniel, 240–41
Shearer, Charles, 325–26
Shipherd, John, 199
Silent Sam, 1, 14
Silliman, Benjamin, 322
Simmons, Ruth, 2, 12–13, 215–23
Sims family, 280, 285, 296n3
Slade, William, 163
slavery: apologizing for, 2–3, 118, 267, 289, 299; banks complicit in, 10, 18n22; defended using Bible, 54, 101; "fitness" of some people for, 70–71, 75–76; forgetting, 217, 296, 301, 304, 310, 326–31; history of, 4–6, 72–73, 338–42;

integrated economies of, 24–25, 226, 227–28, 229, 231–32, 246n20; "necessity" of, 6; in the North, 180–81, 227–30, 246n26; property rights and, 50, 51, 67, 80; racial justifications of, 50, 69–76, 224–25, 239–41, 300, 340–41; religious justifications of, 54, 101; southern schools defending, 65–83, 99–113, 256, 305

Slavery and the Making of the University (exhibition), 1–2

slaves. *See* enslaved persons

Small, Stephen, 253

Smith, Francis Henney, 65

Smith, Samuel Stanhope, 50–51, 59n3

social memory, 303–4

South, the: antislavery thought in, 66, 262–63; economy of, 65, 67–68, 72–73, 104–5, 257, 304–5; proslavery political thought in, 65–83

South Carolina College, 107

Southern Baptists, 116, 118–20, 122–24

Staudt, Gary, 243

Stebbins, Giles, 153

Stewart, Maria W., 184

Stewart, Philo, 199

St. Louis University, 36–37

St. Mary's College, 35

Stockton, Betsey, 49, 60n3

Stone, Lucy, 197, 201–2, 203, 207

Story, Joseph, 235

Stowe, Harriet Beecher, 76, 237

Sumner, Charles, 7, 235, 236

Sumner, Margaret, 184

Supreme Court, 79, 80, 151

Taylor, Charles, 8

Taylor, Joseph, 77

Terry, Kaitlin, 243

Tolley, Kim, 190

Toombs, Robert, 71

Torpey, John, 8

Transylvania University, 42n22, 315, 318, 322–26, 328, 329–31, 332n1, 335n28, 335n30, 336n38

trauma, 8

Trent, Cezar, 61n11

Triennial Catalogue (Princeton University publication), 61n16

truth commissions, 8, 217

Tucker, John Randolph, 70

Tucker, Nathaniel Beverley, 69, 251–57, *252*, 259, 260–66

Tucker, St. George, 251–57, *252*, 260–64, 266, 274n28

Turner, Nat, 66, 67

Turner, Victor, 278

Tyler-McGraw, Marie, 154

Types of Mankind (Nott and Gliddon), 73–75, *74*

Uncle Tom's Cabin (Stowe), 76

University of Alabama, 6, 102–3, 112n38, 114–30, 298–314; apology of, 2; defense of slavery by, 77; images of, *115*, *116*, *307–8*

University of Delaware, 24

University of North Carolina, 1–2, 14, 109

University of Pennsylvania, 23

University of Virginia, 3, 4, 7, 86, 90; slaves at, 85, 86–87, 95, 97n11; student violence at, 86–88

Unravelling Miss Kitty's Cloak (Marshall-Linnemeier), 290–93, 295

Van Quickenborne, Charles, 36

Van Rensselaer, Stephen, 36, 44n34

Vassall, Henry, 246n20

victims' rights, 8

Walker, David, 68, 184

Washington College, 6, 30, 66, *66*

Waters, Brandi, 243

Wayland, Francis, 104–5, 117, 120

Weinberg, Zoe, 244

westward expansion, 36–37

Wheelock, Eleazar, 25, 28–29

white supremacy, 69–76, 114, 126, 188–89, 328

Whitman, Walt, 237

Wilder, Craig Steven, 154–55
Williams, Avis, 284–85, 293
Williams, Emogene, 284–85
Williamson, Alice, 289–90
Witherspoon, John, 21, 25, 30, 32, 34, 49–50, 59n3
women: femininity of, 197–99, 201–2, 205–7; at Oberlin, 197–212; rape suffered by, 124–25, 202, 204–5; "purity" of white, 312
Woods, John Witherspoon, 55
Wyatt-Brown, Bertram, 89

Yale, Elihu, 22
"Yale, Slavery, and Abolition" (online report), 11–12, 326
Yale University, 2, 11–12, 187, 333n15, 333n18, 337n50; abolitionism at, 56; during the American Revolution, 28; Calhoun and, 315–16, 318–22, 326, 328–31, 334n20, 337n54; Civil War memorial at, 57; in the colonial era, 22, 38n3; students from Southern states, 60n4
Yee, Shirley, 204
Yellin, Jean Fagan, 204

www.ingramcontent.com/pod-product-compliance
Lightning Source LLC
Chambersburg PA
CBHW011720220426
43664CB00023B/2894